James Tunstead Burtchaell, CSC is Professor of Theology at the University of Notre Dame and a Visiting Fellow in the Department of Religion at Princeton University. A former President of the American Academy of Religion, he is the author of numerous articles and books. The latter include *Catholic theories of Biblical inspiration since 1810, Philemon's problem, Rachel weeping* and – most recently – *The giving and taking of life*.

This important work engages with a long historical debate: were the earliest Christians under the direction of ordained ministers, or under the influence of inspired laypeople? Who was in charge: bishops, elders and deacons, or apostles, prophets and teachers? Rather than trace church offices backwards (they were already clearly established by the second century), Burtchaell examines the contemporary Jewish communities and finds evidence that Christians simply continued the offices of the synagogue. Thus, he asserts that from the very first they were presided over by officers. The author then advances the provocative view that in the first century it was not the officers who spoke with most authority. They presided, but did not lead, and deferred to more charismatic laypeople. Burtchaell sees the evidence in favour of the Catholic/Orthodox/Anglican view that bishops have always presided in the Christian church. At the same time he argues alongside the Protestants that in its formative era the church deferred most to the judgment of those who were inspired, yet never ordained.

FROM SYNAGOGUE TO CHURCH

FROM SYNAGOGUE TO CHURCH

Public services and offices in the earliest Christian communities

JAMES TUNSTEAD BURTCHAELL

CAMBRIDGE
UNIVERSITY PRESS

Published by the Press Syndicate of the University of Cambridge
The Pitt Building, Trumpington Street, Cambridge CB2 1RP
40 West 20th Street, New York, NY 10011-4211, USA
10 Stamford Road, Oakleigh, Victoria 3166, Australia

First published 1992

Printed in Great Britain at the University Press, Cambridge

A catalogue record for this book is available from the British Library

Library of Congress cataloguing in publication data
Burtchaell, James Tunstead.
From synagogue to church: public services and offices in the
earliest Christian communities / James Tunstead Burtchaell.
p.   cm.
Includes index.
ISBN 0 521 41892 5
1. Church polity – History – Early church, ca. 30–600. 2. Pastoral
theology – History. 3. Synagogues – Organization and administration –
History. 4. Pastoral theology (Judaism) – History. I. Title.
BV648.B83   1992
262'.1'09015 – DC29   91–36390   CIP

ISBN 0 521 41892 5 hardback

UP

To Joyce and Jerry Hank
who in diverse ways and sundry manners
both tangible and intangible
have urged forward the inquiry set forth here
a grateful author
dedicates this work

Contents

Preface

This is a study of the community organization of the Christian communities as it developed through the first century of their experience. In particular I have inquired into the public service roles with which those communities were provided: what those services and those offices were and what was expected of their incumbents.

I began with two convictions and one supposition. One conviction has to do with the value of looking into the past. I approached this project with an inveterate interest in the Christian church and its ministries. In our present time some of the more stimulating questions arise from attempts to reconstrue what public office ought rightly be. But I did not undertake the study in order to justify any proposal or theory I already had. I did it because of my belief that one can rarely investigate a tradition in the distant past – and the Christian tradition is one I am most familiar with – without jostling one's perspectives enough to make the inquiry worthwhile.

When friends and colleagues learned that I hoped to write a history of office in the earliest church, they typically would ask if I were going to argue for the ordination of women. I had personally been on record in favor of that for nearly two decades. And there are other issues, such as whether church officers ought be stipendiary, or whether ministry ought be a profession for which young people study as for a career; these questions may ultimately carry more significance. But none of that is to the point. There is no ancient precedent which by itself legitimates any contemporary policy. However, one who delves cleanly and curiously into the way people did things long ago and, if possible, why they did so, is invariably helped to address contemporary issues and decisions from an advantaged perspective. History is suggestive – compellingly so. But it is not compelling.

That was the first conviction. The second moved from purpose to method. When approaching a historical topic it is best to study all primary sources before allowing oneself to look at the secondary materials. I was aware, from the normal traffic of interest and reading, that this was a subject over which scholars had been quarreling for some centuries, and I had an undefined recollection of all that debate. But I took it as a duty to read again through every document that might provide direct evidence of Christian life during the first hundred years, before beginning to study what latter-day academics had made of those primary sources. By following such a method one sacrifices the initial advantage of knowing the "state-of-the-art" discussion. On the other hand, one gains the ability to be exposed to the original texts more freely than if one's mental agenda were already furnished by what others had determined to be most significant.

My assumption was a simple one. When I was a young man I was given much training in scripture and liturgy. I learned that these were treasures which the early church came by through inheritance. They were old when they were new. And it was natural to assume that the pattern of community organization in those earliest churches may also have been an heirloom from the Jewish past. So before reading the Christian sources it was important to read all that was available from Judaism during the first centuries BC and AD. My surmise was that since the first Christians were Jews who took a long while to reflect and admit to themselves reluctantly how their faith might be leading them away from their fellow Jews, they would instinctively create commmunities in the way familiar to them: following the patterns of the hellenistic Jewish synagogue. The first step, then, was to learn how synagogues functioned in the late Second Temple period, even before examining the Christian documents.

Only after turning to the secondary literature did I discover that my assumption had not been shared by the scholars whose work was most respected. The hypothesis which my inquiry had reinforced, not subverted, differed in significant respects from the received wisdom. For instance, the so-called monarchical episcopate which had been deplored by Ritschl, Baur, Lightfoot, Harnack, Lietzmann, von Campenhausen, Schweizer and others, cannot be considered as merely a clerical take-over of a church that had throughout the first century been spirited and spontaneous. I found it instead to have been a reassertion of a community organization that was in formal continuity with the Jewish past. My finding, as it developed, was that the emergence of various categories of officer in the early second century was not simply the stifling of a vigorous lay age in Christian history. It was the reinvigoration of a community organization that had been customary in Israel and had served as a foundational structure for the new Christian groups since before they were very conscious of it.

Eventually it became clear that since the nineteenth century there has been a consensus among most historical scholars that has coached the thinking of most theologians who have derived their understanding of the early church from the historians. According to that consensus a vitally new kind of community arose among the disciples of Jesus. It enjoyed two or perhaps three generations in which the Spirit was given free play, without formal structures or an official establishment. It was a subsequent threat of division within the community, and of perverse teaching, that persuaded the faithful to consolidate under the protection of a clerical regime with a hierarchy of officers. Christian life, so this story goes, has never been as animated since then.

Scholars and churchfolk who are made wistful by this consensus study the album of sketchy and fading memories we have of that era in our church's youth, and take it as our norm for possible reforms today. My concern in this book is to look quite carefully at the same album where I claim to see that, whatever you wish to make of it, there were the same offices in the church of the first century that we can see there in the second century. Their incumbents, however, were behaving quite differently in those two periods.

The order of exposition is often the reverse of the order of discovery. My route of inquiry led me first through the ancient literary and archeological evidence, and then to the modern theories that have interpreted that evidence. Having attempted to assess and reassess each corpus in light of the other, I now set them forth in the opposite order: first reviewing the dynamics and the validity of the modern arguments, and then reconstructing the community organization of the early Christians as seems best justified by the evidence.

The present time is an unsettled one for anybody to attempt a synthetic historical study of either the Jewish synagogues or the Christian churches during the first century AD. In the fields of Jewish and Christian historical scholarship some of the most energetic and aggressive research is aiming to discredit an old conviction: that there was such a thing as a standard synagogue or a normative church during that period. Professor Jacob Neusner has been insisting among historians of Judaism that there was a sharp diversity among homeland and Diaspora Jewry. The hope to descry a uniform community of observance is, in any case, rendered implausible by the paucity of reliable evidence and its low historical yield when examined critically. This view has been given added momentum by the publication of the Qumran and other sectarian literature, and by recent archeological finds as interpreted, for instance, by Professor A. Thomas Kraabel. A parallel but distinct revisionism among Christian historians was initiated by Walter Bauer of Göttingen, who insisted that for centuries there were several versions of Christianity existing independently of one another, with equal claims to authenticity. The discovery of the Nag Hammadi library, and the concurrence of scholars like Professor Robert M. Grant, combined to make Bauer's challenge the more credible.[1]

In parallel fashion, each revisionist school is suggesting that it was the press of events and the community's reactions, rather than any intrinsic character or imperative, which caused rabbinic Judaism and Catholic Christianity, respectively, to emerge as dominant.

My ambition here is not to assert that there was a uniform local model for either synagogue or church at the time when some Jews were first hailing Jesus as Messiah. The paucity and ambiguity of the evidence would seem, however, to restrain us equally from concluding that there was no shared pattern within either community. What Robert Wilken has written of early Christian sources seems as valid of their Jewish contemporaries:

[W]e miss the character of the early Christian movement if we see it primarily as a history of diverging traditions, each with its own logic and

---

[1] It is difficult to select appropriate citations to the work of Jacob Neusner, whose abundant publications make him a Scheherezade among scholars. See his *The Rabbinic Traditions about the Pharisees before 70* (Leiden: Brill, 1971), 3 vols.; *From Politics to Piety: The Emergence of Pharisaic Judaism* (New York: Ktav, 1979); "The Formation of Rabbinic Judaism: Yavneh (Jamnia) from A.D. 70 to 100," in *Aufstieg und Niedergang der römischen Welt* (hereafter ANRW), II, 19.2 (1979), 3–42. A[lf] T[homas] Kraabel, "The Diaspora Synagogue: Archeological and Epigraphic Evidence since Sukenik," *ANRW*, II, 19.1 (1979), 477–510; "Six Diaspora Synagogues," in *Ancient Synagogues: The State of Research*, ed. Joseph Gutman (Chico, CA: Scholars Press, 1981), 79–91; "The Roman Diaspora: Six Questionable Assumptions," *Journal of Jewish Studies*, 33, 1–2 (1982), 445–464; "Paganism and Judaism: The Sardis Evidence," in *Paganisme, Judaïsme, Christianisme: Influences et affrontements dans le monde antique*, ed. A[ndré] Benoit et al. (Paris: Boccard, 1979), 13–33. Walter Bauer, *Orthodoxy and Heresy in Earliest Christianity*, trans. Philadelphia Seminar on Christian Origins, ed. Robert A. Kraft and Gerhard Krodel (Philadelphia: Fortress, 1971); this translates and augments the second edition of *Rechtglaübigkeit und Ketzerei* (Tübingen: Mohr, 1964 [1st edn. 1934]). Robert M. Grant, *Second Century Christianity: A Collection of Fragments* (London: SPCK, 1964).

internal coherence, existing alongside of one another. A "center" was being shaped and formed during this period, and it is historically important to understand how and why this sense of communal identity emerged. I have suggested that this "center" cannot be defined solely in doctrinal terms, i.e. solely in terms of religious life, for it included, among other things, behavior and way of life, liturgical practice, even a sense of "belonging," of church if you will, and this sense of communal identity was present long before there were definable standards by which to measure it.[2]

What one can claim to see is a type, a format that is recurrent enough to be traditional and – give or take any of its elements – identifiable as a customary pattern of community. I argue as well that among the elements of community organization, some are more regular and others more marginal.

If we inspect those elements which appear to be most regular, we shall find that they include the offices of elder, community chief and assistant. Despite the fact that their appearance is so scattered geographically and temporally – indeed, for the very reason that they do appear so randomly yet widely – I am persuaded that they were typical in late Second Temple Jewish synagogues, and subsequently in the early Christian synagogues, or churches.

The tasks and the political style of each office appear to have been in flux within both communities. There also seems to have been a fluidity of titles, which eventually yielded to distinct nomenclatures. Out of a miscellany of generic and descriptive synonyms, each tradition eventually selected its own, which then were converted into specific titles. In all three features – diversity changing to standardization, generic synonyms retiring before a specific title, and intentional differentiation of titles from rival traditions – the Jews and Christians were continuing what Jewish sectaries had done throughout the first centuries BC and AD.

This inquiry began for me in Princeton, during the latter months of a leave of absence from teaching duties at Notre Dame in 1980–81. The work was pursued during the intervening summers, and acquired momentum during another study leave at Cambridge in 1985–86. Final revisions were possible during another visiting fellowship at Princeton in 1990–91. Along the way I have incurred debts for which both honesty and gratitude require acknowledgement. I am beholden to the Department of Religion at Princeton University, and especially

[2] Robert L. Wilken, "Diversity and Unity in Early Christianity," *The Second Century*, 1 (1981), 109–110.

to John Wilson, John Gager and Albert Raboteau who as chairmen welcomed me for two years and several summers as a visiting fellow there. I am likewise appreciative of the welcome given by the Faculty of Divinity in the University of Cambridge, to which I was able to return as a visiting scholar twenty years since going down from there after happy years as a research student. St Edmund's College elected me into a visiting fellowship, and Gonville and Caius College, then and during a subsequent summer, offered me the membership of their senior combination room, thus restoring me to the two households that had offered welcome when I first went up to pursue my training as a theological historian. And my own University and Department of Theology are owed thanks for giving me freedom from my other duties to complete this task.

Notre Dame must also be thanked for several grants from the Albert Zahm Travel Fund that tided me over two summers. Even more am I grateful for being allowed to reside at the home of Jacques Maritain in Princeton, his benefaction to us which Notre Dame once put at the disposal of its faculty members who needed a haven for study. I must express appreciation to the Council for International Exchange of Scholars in this country and the Fulbright Commission in the United Kingdom for a grant-in-aid as a Senior Fulbright Scholar; to the Fund for Theological Scholarship and Research of the Association of Theological Schools in the United States and Canada for a research grant; and to the American Philosophical Society for a research grant.

I have derived profound scholarly benefit from the Firestone Library of Princeton University, the Speer Library of Princeton Theological Seminary, the University Library of Cambridge University, the Krauth Memorial Library of the Lutheran Theological Seminary at Philadelphia, the Historical Society of Pennsylvania and the Hesburgh Library at Notre Dame. Special gratitude is offered to Edinburgh Professor John O'Neill, who has given the entire manuscript two meticulous readings, and offered numerous sagacious emendations. In my investigation of the hellenistic synagogue I was very much helped by correspondence and conversation with Shimon Applebaum, professor emeritus at the Hebrew University in Tel Aviv, whose critical comments on an early draft led to its improvement, though there are interpretations still present with which he will continue to disagree. My colleague Joseph Blenkinsopp has also given that material a critical reading with many helpful marginal glosses. An editorial eye and a common interest in this early era persuaded Professor Walter Murphy of Princeton to offer other helpful emendations. I am also grateful for early encouragement in the project from Henry Chadwick, then Regius Professor of Divinity at Cambridge, Professor John Gager at Princeton, the late Professor George MacRae, S.J., from Harvard University (a dear and respected friend since our student days together), and Professor Raymond Brown, S.S., of Union Theological Seminary. Professor Peter Erb of Wilfred Laurier University generously directed me to appropriate documentation of the Pietists. I want to thank my students who have studied this material in seminars with me and whose work on those early texts has been remembered with profit: Thomas Myott, Marjorie Proctor-Smith, Sheryl Chen, Lee Klosinski, Pamela Cunningham and Paul Holland, S.J. Two student assistants have labored unstintingly over the accuracy of the footnotes: Daniel Beck and Lawrence Njoroge. My colleague, Kern Trembath, has generously read the manuscript with his usual meticulous eye, to its benefit.

Translations, if not attributed to published sources, are the work and responsibility of the author. Excerpts from *The New Jerusalem Bible*, copyright © 1985 by Darton, Longman & Todd, Ltd. and Doubleday, a division of Bantam Doubleday Dell Publishing Group, Inc., are reprinted by permission. Excerpts from ancient classical, Jewish and Christian writers in the Loeb Classical Library are reprinted by permission of the Harvard University Press. These Include Philo, *Works*, trans. Francis Henry Colson, George Herbert Whitaker and Ralph Marcus (New York: Putnam, 1929–1962); Josephus, *Works*, trans. Henry St. John Thackeray, Ralph Marcus, Allen Wikgren and Louis H. Feldman (Cambridge: Harvard University Press, 1962–1965); *The Apostolic Fathers*, trans. Kirsopp Lake (Cambridge: Harvard University Press, 1959). Excerpts from *Luther's Works*, trans. Jaroslav Pelikan and Helmut T. Lehmann (Philadelphia: Fortress, 1955 –), are reprinted by permission of Augsburg Fortress Publishers.

Leitourgia is a Greek word the early Christians used to designate that public charge expected of every Christian as a community service. To be of much public help one needed a divine empowerment, and they believed that a blessed variety of spiritual enablements prompted different members of their communities to provide for its many needs, whether bringing the sick back to their strength, or making sense of the scriptures, or housing travelers, or looking in a life-giving way into others' consciences. Presiding over the community and guiding and administering its decisions were some of those *leitourgiai*. They thought it took a special knack: one that was not in their gift but one which they needed to recruit when choosing their officers. This book is about those offices and that knack.

Notre Dame, Indiana
Feast of Saints Peter and Paul, 1991

CHAPTER I

The Reformation: challenge to an old consensus

For the last century and a half historians and theologians have strenuously invested themselves in dispute regarding the polity and order of the earliest Christian communities. The controversy has flared up at intervals. In the middle of the nineteenth century the subject was addressed mostly by German scholars, like Baur and Ritschl. The closing years of that century witnessed a very contentious surge of conflicting theories, with Englishmen Sanday, Hatch, Gore and Hort voicing over against more Germans: Harnack, Sohm and von Weizsäcker. Sabatier entered a French membership into the discussion. Another wave of interest and debate marked the years after the Great War, and again the main participants bore German and English names: Holtzmann, Lietzmann and Holl; Armitage Robinson, Streeter and Dix. Lastly, a new generation of scholars has returned to the subject in the past three decades, among whom Schweizer from Switzerland, von Campenhausen from Germany, Schillebeeckx from the Netherlands and Schüssler Fiorenza from the United States are prominent contributors. The debate was joined from many quarters.

There have however been a consistency of method, a communion of assumptions and a similarity of speculation which justify one in viewing this long and open debate as having pursued a single pathway. Thus has been crafted by many hands what one must acknowledge as the dominant consensus on office and order in the earliest church.

Others who have surveyed this literature would tend to accept the observation of B. H. Streeter:

For four hundred years the theologians of rival churches have armed themselves to battle on the question of the Primitive Church. However great their reverence for scientific truth and historic fact, they have at least *hoped* that the result of their investigations would be to vindicate Apostolic authority for the type of Church Order to which they were themselves attached. The Episcopalian has sought to find episcopacy, the Presbyterian Presbyterianism, and the Independent a system of independency, to be the form of Church Order in New Testament times.[1]

It is surely true that most sponsorship for the consensus has been Protestant, with Lutherans in the vanguard and the congregational churches among the most interested audience. Virtually all resistance to the consensus has come from two sources. Catholic scholars, until recently, have defended an essentially continuous polity from apostolic times in unbroken sequence through to the present. Anglicans, especially those of a high church allegiance, have stood for a hierarchy and a succession of orders all along. While joining Catholics to sustain the aboriginal authority of the bishop, they have crossed over to the Protestant team to deny higher authority to the bishop of Rome.

It is my estimate that this has not been a symmetrical debate. Opponents of the consensus have always been in retreat. The agenda, the newly discovered evidences, the scholarly momentum: all have been to the advantage of the partisans of the consensus. Even when an earlier version was discredited or a previously load-bearing argument gave way, there was little embarrassment and no dropping back. The consensus has moved forward with sure and confident step. This is why, though we shall take note here of some of the nay-sayers, the central interest of our study will be fastened upon those creative and persisting scholars of the dominant theory who swept nearly all before them.

THE REFORMERS

To examine the consensus in its beginnings we must page back to the reformers of the fourteenth, sixteenth, seventeenth and eighteenth centuries. As spokesmen of a movement that washed over the Western world in successive flood tides, they argued from scripture that all Christians are radically called to service in the church; that

---

[1] Burnett Hillman Streeter, *The Primitive Church: Studied with Special Reference to the Origins of Christian Ministry*, Hewlett Lectures for 1928 (London: Macmillan, 1929), viii. Streeter offers his own way around this obstacle: "But while each party to the dispute has been able to make out a case for his own view, he has never succeeded in demolishing the case of his opponent. The explanation of this deadlock, I have come to believe, is quite simple. It is the uncriticised assumption, made by all parties to the controversy, that in the first century there existed a single type of Church Order," p. ix. His theory is that in different provinces of the empire there existed, in the first century AD, quite different systems of church polity.

it is empowerment by God, not ordination by a bishop, which gives the special graces of ministry; and that only the congregation had and has the authority to designate the church's ministers.

As overture to that inquiry we must first study a much earlier and haphazard venture. The principal initiators of the Reformation and of its earlier intimations in the late Middle Ages were learned men. John Wyclif had been master of an Oxford college. Martin Luther was a doctor of theology and a university-level lecturer in the scriptures. John Calvin, though not an academic, was an extra-ordinarily learned preacher. Most of their contemporaries who called for, designed or actually implemented reform in the church were proceeding on popular notions of what a church shriven and cleansed should be. Not these men. What blocked reform, as they saw it, was venality, superstition and corruption behind the rampart of clerical authority. As scholars, these men could not ignore those authoritarian claims. They meant as scholars to discredit them. No flanking attacks, but a frontal assault. They were constrained to justify another authority of higher appeal.

No reform of worship or piety or theology could have much promise of endurance unless the claim of the ordained clergy to unique office and authority were discredited. And that, in a church which validated all institutions by derivation from Jesus and his first disciples, had to be a task of historical scholarship.

John Wyclif of England, Martin Luther of Germany, John Calvin of Switzerland, the cohort of Pietists after them, and the retinue of learned divines they inspired: all undercut the theology of episcopal and papal authority by appealing to an earlier, foundational polity from which they claimed the church had quickly deviated into priestcraft and greed. This authentic church order, founded by Jesus upon the apostles, they reconstructed from the New Testament. Wyclif thought the fall from apostolic innocence had come with Constantine's acknowledgement and endowment of the bishops. Luther pursued the matter further, and found the fatal swerve already in the infant years of the second century, as witnessed in Ignatius of Antioch. The new wave of populist, spiritual reformers in the late seventeenth and early eighteenth centuries tended to identify the corruptive era as that of Constantine.

The most accomplished authors of the Magisterial Reformation were beneficiaries of the New Learning. Many of the humanists, like Erasmus of Rotterdam, were led by their sophistication to be critical and cynical about worldly rascals who held office, high or low, in Christendom. Luther and his like took their scholarship to more radical conclusions, and delegitimated and disavowed not only the incumbents but the offices as well. Thus they convulsed the church by their academic findings about the ancient past, and their forthright conclusions about how to restore it for a wholesome future.

Their revolt was creative and intellectually impressive. It was not, however, to last long enough – as a school of academic inquiry, that is – to gain the solidity that any movement can acquire from several generations of reflection on the founding masters' insights. What foreshortened the theological development of the reformers' re-construction of ancient church order was the inevitable effect of their having actually established church orders of their own. In a short time new orthodoxies and polities bristled – understandably – with defensiveness. It required scarcely one generation for the free-spirited speculations of Luther, for example – tentative enough to be recon-sidered and even modified as he examined the evidence further, yet firm enough for him to design his ideal church and redesign it over and over again – it required, I say, no more than a generation for that theorizing to age into a defensive apologetic for the actual Lutheran establishment. And the defenders of the various Protestant forms of office and organization were to prove not much more productive in their research into the primitive church than were their adversaries, the Catholic apologists.

The reformers had correctly seen that a determination to vindicate later church practices had made better scholars of the Catholics. It was the more striking that they themselves soon began to exhibit a similar defensiveness. The brilliant findings of these men deserved and required a better sequel. Their line of study was reactivated again by the Pietists and Quakers a century later, in an equally fervent yet less scholarly or creative mode. It then had to lie dormant for two hundred years, to be taken up yet again in Germany.

Thus it is essential to be familiar with the findings of the most learned reformers, before going on to study and evaluate the extended work of the intellectual continuity which I call the dominant, contemporary consensus among later scholars on the polity and order of the earliest church.

JOHN WYCLIF

"Considering the life and the task which God has specified for the priest, all that is required for a person to be a priest is for God to give him the grace to live that life and to fulfill that task."[2] In 1383 this was strong talk. It came from Doctor John Wyclif, who by then had but a short course of life left to continue troubling Oxford's theological schools.

He had first come under investigation six years earlier, when his views on church officers were not quite so strident, save for occasionally calling the pope a devil and the Antichrist. The issue on which his views were suspect was more canonical than theological. As a career theologian he had previously taken his share in the classical puzzlers regarding the technicalities of legal ordination. How could one be absolutely sure that a traveling priest was validly ordained? How could a cleric be assured that the bishop who ordained him was actually in valid possession of unbroken apostolic succession down through the centuries? Did a priest who had been ordained successively to four minor and three major orders belong to seven orders or only to one?

As Wyclif grew older, however, he had lost his taste for that sort of inquiry. Why fuss over some cleric's testimonial documents, to verify whether they be free of misspellings or a fudged seal, he wrote in 1377, when we lack all sure knowledge of how and when the apostles themselves were ordained in the first place?[3] It was not any written credential that showed the apostles to be priests, but their comportment. "The life of a priest, it seems to me, is the greatest natural evidence for assuring us of his really being a priest."[4]

In the primitive church Christ had made his apostles priests, and they in turn established the deacons. These two orders were all that seem to have been needed. God only knows, grumbled Wyclif, what good it had done the church to go and create all the other orders, which have only a ritual purpose and no other practical benefit. "We are more fascinated with the proliferation of orders which the church has created than with the inner substance of the outward sacrament which God has given. Surely the distorted way we are drawn more by

---

[2] John Wyclif, *De Quattuor Sectis Novellis*, ch. 5; in *John Wyclif's Polemical Works in Latin*, ed. Rudolf Buddensieg (London: Wyclif Society, 1883), 258.

[3] Wyclif, *Tractatus de Ecclesia*, ch. 19; ed. Iohann Loserth (London: Wyclif Society, 1886), 454–455.

[4] Ibid. 456–457.

the foliage than by the fruit has cheapened our sacraments in God's eyes."[5]

The deeper issue should not be one's legal or sacramental status but one's moral standing. Some people are Catholics in name only. They are hypocrites bound for destruction. Others possess the reality of Catholic allegiance though they lack official membership. Never mind that the church's satraps hold them in contempt; they are predestined to glory.[6] Moral reality is more determinative than ecclesial status.

A similar disparity between reality and outward appearances was to be seen in the clergy. Some of them, according to Wyclif, are set apart by little more than the cut of their clothes and the trim of their tonsures. Their tailors and barbers seem to have had more of a hand in making priests of them than their bishops did. Other clerics may have purchased their ordinations with an eye towards lucrative benefices. "'How, then,'" he quotes a decretal, "'if they are themselves anathema and unholy, can they sanctify others? If they are not within the body of Christ, how can they offer or receive the body of Christ? How can someone bless if he is under a curse?'"[7] What counts most is not the outward rite but the inward empowerment. "For God who gives the power to minister also gives the grace to accomplish the task, unless the ordained person's disposition rejects that grace."[8] In most radical fashion he then goes on to assert that "there is no solemnity or human tradition which makes a person the head or a member of Holy Mother Church, or a vicar of Christ. What that requires is a special grace of Christ and conformity to Christ in one's behavior."[9]

In defense of clerical rank, Wyclif's opponents would claim that ordination (like baptism and confirmation, the two other unrepeatable sacraments) impressed on the soul an "indelible character," or identity, which set one above the laity. But this, he replied, was another avoidance of what was essential, even though it appeared at first to be an inquiry inwards. Sacramental character, Wyclif replied, was surely not a substantive, internal "thing." It was a commission to perform specified duties, and it was a submission of oneself to those tasks, rather like the way in which kings and soldiers take on their respective duties.[10] Every cleric has been charged with ministry

[5] Ibid. ch. 21, 514–515.   [6] Ibid. ch. 4, 89.   [7] Ibid. ch. 19, 455.
[8] Ibid. ch. 21, 511.   [9] Ibid. ch. 19, 459.   [10] Ibid. ch. 21, 508.

corresponding to his rank; but by the same token so has every lay member of the church been given appropriate responsibilities. Better, in his opinion, to construe clerical identity as a duty that can be accepted and later accomplished or even laid aside, than as a permanent and magisterial ennoblement.[11]

If this view of things were to prevail, Wyclif foresaw that candidates would be investigated more searchingly. Their preferments would be awarded more gradually so as to ascertain whether their performance justified further responsibilities, and unworthy recruits would be sifted out from those who were authentically prepared to serve the church. From that process would emerge priests ready to pursue the true clerical calling – to follow Christ and his apostles in a life deprived of benefice or property – the life of a poor preacher of God's Word.[12]

Three years later in 1380 John Wyclif returned to this theme in his *Treatise on Pastoral Duty*. Now he ventured a step further, to call for the assignment of parish clergy by choice of the congregation. Once the position of curate could be disentangled from its corrupting involvements of being beholden to the nobility for the glebe and other temporalities, "then there could be a free election by the parishioners and the acceptance of a curate exclusively on grounds of his aptitude for the task." It was absurd, he argued, for remote prelates to be making such assignments. "What pope has come by an inspiration to tell him which curate should be approved for such-and-such a parish, on nomination by the patron? Quite a few would see the pope motivated more by his appetite for the fees attached to the appointment than by his concern for the benefit of the souls concerned … Take away the fee structure, and all that might be changed."[13]

The prelates pretend that their parochial assignments are as sagacious as if God himself had signed and sealed them, but the bishops have too much of a financial interest for them to be believed. "Let the devout people, who have most stake in the salvation of their own souls, choose a fit and competent priest, and in this way they will avoid unpleasant surprises later on if he turns out to be more a burden than a benefit. And if the congregation falls to quarrelling, or swerves from the true course, then let the secular lords put them back on the path of righteousness."[14]

[11] Ibid. 513.   [12] Ibid. 516–517.
[13] *Johannis de Wiclif Tractatus de Officio Pastorali*, ed. Gotthardus Victor Lechler (Leipzig: A. Edelmann, 1863), ch. 7, 39–40.   [14] Ibid. ch. 9, 43; see also ch. 7, 40.

By 1383 the hot breath of censure was scorching his neck. Wyclif in his turn was writing more angrily against the prelates of the church. The superiority of bishops, he observed, was exemplified in the rule that certain actions were reserved to them alone, such as confirmation and ordination. They alone had the prerogative of consecrating churches. But consecration was the result, not of rituals, but of holy people. Job had brought sanctification to his dung-pile, and Jesus to his stable, just as Lot had maintained his sanctity in Sodom. When a greedy bishop is brought in to consecrate a church building some people would say, Wyclif noted (he was himself usually the "some people"), that the place would probably be hallowed more by pitching out the bishop than by letting him proceed with his rites. Some prelates, when asked to expound the text of holy scripture, are tongue-tied by their ignorance. What good could men like that accomplish by all their consecrations and blessings and other contrived signs? Some of them are more meticulous about the Rite of Sarum than they are about the gospel. Wyclif concluded by saying he could see no reason why any ritual should require a celebrant that outranked a simple pastor.[15]

The pope also came in for Oxford invective. If papacy meant avaricious men like Urban IV, or a deadlock between two contending claimants,[16] then the church would be better off with no pope at all. "Christ with his law is capable of ruling the church militant by himself... A church that keeps trust with Christ is not headless, for it has Christ as its head, and that is as sufficient now as it was just after Pentecost."[17]

Much of the sacramental posturing by church prelates of every rank was simply a deception for the laity. "Better for a believer to identify the duties of any rank, which were assigned to it by God, and then to verify whether those duties are in fact being carried out."[18] That applied to the pope as well. "The pope ought to be treated with respect, but only insofar as he treads in the footsteps of St. Peter. When he deviates, then turn your back on him."[19]

Naturally Wyclif was confronted by those who disagreed. On what grounds was he so bold as to sit in judgment himself on the entire establishment of divine authority in the church? His adversaries, he

---

[15] Wyclif, *De Quattuor Sectis Novellis*, ch. 6, 260–262.
[16] The Western Schism had recently begun, with Clement VII as Urban's rival, and all Europe divided in its allegiances.   [17] Wyclif, *De Quattuor Sectis Novellis*, ch. 5, 257.
[18] Ibid. 259.   [19] Ibid. 260.

answered, were relying in large part on human institutions, not on divine authorization. He appealed higher: to reliance on the scriptures, "and to lively reasoning."[20] It was in this context that he made the assertion which we saw at the outset: that divine, not ecclesiastical, ordination empowered the true officers of the church. That was in 1383. A year later he was dead.[21]

Wyclif's appeal over the church's head to the New Testament had little by way of familiar precedent. He must not be unduly pressed for a consistency of program which his brief and rushing career could scarcely have allowed. His procedural principle was clear enough: that conventional church practice must be judged by scripture and theological conclusions grounded on scripture, and not vice versa. On scriptural grounds he argued that authentic membership in the body of Christ was a gift of divine grace, which need not (and often did not) conform to one's outward sacramental status or rank. Indeed, the non-congruence of inner relationship to God and outer relationship to the church was a principal theme of his preaching. That being so, the church's ministers had as their paramount task the preaching of the word (thus addressing the faithful directly in the order of the spirit), and only secondarily the performance of external rituals. The odious system of benefices, he grieved, had drawn into the clergy men whose false motivation became the more manifest the closer they approached the pulpit. The custom of allowing bishops to appoint candidates to livings (on predominantly materialistic grounds) had produced a hireling pastorate, and should be abolished in favor of appraisal and popular election by the local congregation. Wyclif naturally saw this proposal as likely to be resisted by the lords spiritual (yet so very temporal), and thus he appealed to the secular nobility as possessed of the authority requisite to reform the church.

---

[20] At the same time, Wyclif alleged his submission to church superiors. "Hic profiteor et protestor, quod volo ex integro sentenciare fidem catholicam, et si quidquid dixero contra illam, committo me correccioni superioris ecclesie et cuiuscunque militantis persone, que me in hoc docuerit erravisse. Sed subduco quascunque tradiciones hominum citra fidem scripture, et sic non accepto in ista materia nisi fidem scripture, vel racionem vivacem, sed adducentem aliud de perfidia et ignorancia habeo plus suspectum." Ibid. 256.

[21] In the intellectual storm of his last years Wyclif had had neither the time nor the temper to discipline his doctrine into any consistency. For instance, one of his most persistently advocated measures of reform, the unleashing of unaffiliated, unbeneficed priests to preach at large across the English countryside, was seriously compromised by the fact that Wyclif himself was living off the prosperous benefice of Lutterworth (where, contrary to his own explicit teaching, the actual pastoral work was being done by a vicar whom he paid poorly), and he was enjoying the favors of the powerful court of John of Gaunt, the Duke of Lancaster. See *Tractatus de Officio Pastorali*, ch. 8, 40–42.

It was, of course, a bold and reckless hope that would look to the princes and peers for a spiritual reform, but Wyclif had little time to appreciate the eventual price of such expediency. He was an understandably impatient man. What he did set in motion was the abiding suspicion that the order of God's doings was not identical with the order of the church's doings.

Wyclif was a pathfinder; he expounded convictions and assertions that were too new to allow him the time or the reflection to give them inner coherence or consistency. What began as an appeal to reform abuses in the church grew almost unintentionally into a much more radical theology of church order.

The Lollards were to pursue this program that Wyclif had formulated during the last years of his life. But it never did secure a substantial following in late medieval England. It was nevertheless an early expression of a bold critique that would be visited upon the church more rigorously and more vigorously by the reformers of the sixteenth century. They did not draw their inspiration or their agenda from John Wyclif, whom they largely ignored. But he was their intellectual ancestor all the same. In his venturesome way he was a first drafter of the primitive lineaments of a doctrine of church office which would not achieve full elaboration for another five or six hundred years.

Martin Luther

Nearly a century and a half later, after irresolute interim attempts at reform, the stresses in the Christian church which had angered John Wyclif now roused a member of one of the groups of mendicant friars that Wyclif had so despised: Augustinian Martin Luther. Quite like his English precursor, the German friar appealed to an inward Christianity of the spirit.

Christianity is a spiritual assembly of souls in one faith ... the natural, real, true, and essential Christendom exists in the Spirit and not in any external thing ... Beyond that, there is a second way of speaking about Christendom. According to this, Christendom is called an assembly in a house, or in a parish, a bishopric, an archbishopric, or a papacy. To this assembly belong external forms such as singing, reading, and the vestments of the mass. Here, above all, bishops, priests, and members of religious orders are called the "spiritual estate" ... Although the little words "spiritual" or "church" are violated here when they are applied to such externals, since they refer only to the faith which makes true priests and Christians in the soul, this manner of speech has spread everywhere – to the not unimportant seduction and error of many souls who think such external glitter is the spiritual and true estate of Christendom or of the Church.[22]

The essential church, being unworldly, naturally had for Luther no necessary correspondence to the visible organization of the ecclesiastical hierarchy.

[T]he first Christendom, which alone is the true church, may not and cannot have an earthly head. It may be ruled by no one on earth, neither bishop nor pope. Here only Christ in heaven is the head and he rules alone … Neither pope nor bishop can cause faith or whatever else a Christian must have to spring up in a human heart … The head must instill life.[23]

Trained as a master of scripture and theology, Luther gave exegetical evidence for his claim that the texts conventionally used to sustain the superiority of Rome could be construed to show that Rome was at best an equal of the other churches, and at worst a degenerate among them.

Christ says to St. Peter in Matthew 16 [:18–19], "You are Peter and on this *petra* (that is, on this rock) I will build my church. I will give you the keys of the kingdom of heaven, and whatever you bind on earth shall be bound in heaven, and whatever you loose on earth shall be loosed also in heaven."
On the basis of these words they have attributed the keys to St. Peter alone. But the same St. Matthew, in Matthew 18 [:18], has barred such an erroneous interpretation, for Christ says to all of them in general, "Truly, I

---

[22] Martin Luther, *Von dem Bapstum zu Rom: Widder den hochberumpten Romanisten zu Leiptzck* (1520), in *D. Martin Luthers Werke. Kritische Gesamtausgabe* (Weimar: Herman Böhlau, 1883 –), 6:296 (this Weimar edition hereafter cited as *WA*). English translation, *On the Papacy in Rome against the Most Celebrated Romanist in Leipzig*, in *Luther's Works*, ed. Jaroslav Pelikan and Helmut T. Lehmann (Philadelphia: Fortress, 1955–), 39:69–70 (hereafter cited as *LW*).

[23] He continues:

But if you ask, "If the prelates are neither heads nor regents over this spiritual church, what are they then?" let laymen give you the answer. They say, "St. Peter is one of the 'twelve messengers', and other apostles are also members of the twelve". Why is the pope ashamed to be a messenger, if Peter is no more than that? … If you should say, "Well, one messenger may indeed be above the others," I say, "One may be better and more skilled than the other, just as St. Paul was, when compared with Peter, but since they all deliver the same message, none of them, for the sake of the office, can be above the others." Why then is St. Peter not one of the twelve messengers but lord over the eleven messengers and a special one? What is the advantage of one over the others, since they all have one and the same message and vocation from the one Lord? Therefore, since according to divine order all bishops are equal and occupy the place of the apostles, I can certainly confess that according to human order one is above the other in the external church. For here the pope instills what he has in his mind, for example, his canon law and human work, so that Christendom is ruled with external pomp. But, as was said, this does not make Christians.

Ibid. *WA* 6:297–301; *LW* 39:71–75.

The year before, in the Leipzig Disputation against John Eck, Luther had asserted that while the church militant is a monarchy, "its head is not a man but Christ himself." *Great Debates of the Reformation*, ed. Donald J. Ziegler (New York: Random House, 1969), 6–8.

say to you, whatever you bind on earth shall be bound in heaven, and whatever you loose on earth shall be loosed in heaven." Here it is clear that Christ is interpreting himself, explaining chapter 16 in this chapter 18, that the keys are given to St. Peter in place of the entire community, and not to his person alone. Thus also John, in the last chapter [John 20:22–23]: "He breathed on them, and said to them, 'Receive the Holy Spirit. If you forgive the sins of any, they are forgiven; but if you retain the sins of any, they are retained'."... Therefore it is as clear as day here that all the apostles are equal in power to Peter...

You, of course, boast that Christ's word, "Tend my sheep," is a commandment and word of Christ. We ask you, where are those who keep it? You say that even knaves and scoundrels keep it. Christ says that no one keeps it unless he loves and is godly... Therefore, the pope who neither loves nor is godly does not tend or keep Christ's word. Consequently, he is no pope either.[24]

Luther, like Wyclif before him, was angered at the profound abandonment by contemporary churchmen of their duties to follow Christ in holiness and self-sacrifice. The higher their rank, the more deplorable their dereliction. Their response to accusation and rebuke, as he saw it, was a refusal to reform. They defended themselves instead by claiming to possess radical and efficacious powers through ordination to office, powers that could operate undiminished by any moral defects of their possessors. That defense, and its theological assumptions, only guided Luther's aim.

His doctrine, which began as a condemnation of clerical immorality, proceeded eventually to assert that there was nothing more to office in the church than moral rectitude. Since outward status could be so starkly at variance with its only purpose – inward holiness – he concluded that the two had virtually no essential connection. True office, then, must derive from inward endowment, not outward designation.

Scripture was equally his warrant for going on to argue that while there is a distinct Christian ministry, its traditional levels and ranks all conflate into one. Bishops, priests and deacons are fundamentally identical, for the New Testament uses these titles interchangeably.

"You are a royal priesthood and a priestly kingdom" [1 Peter 2:9]. With this saying I proved that all Christians are priests, for Peter said it to all Christians...

[24] Ibid. *WA* 6:309–312, 318; *LW* 39:86–87, 97.

Scripture makes all of us equal priests, as has been said, but the churchly priesthood which we now separate from laymen in the whole world, and which we alone call priesthood, is called "ministry" [*ministerium*], "servitude" [*servitus*], "dispensation" [*dispensatio*], "episcopate" [*episcopatus*], and "presbytery" [*presbyterium*] in Scripture. Nowhere is it called "priesthood" [*sacerdocium*] or "spiritual" [*spiritualis*]... Scripture, I say, calls the spiritual and priestly estate a service, caretaking, an office, an elder, an attendant, a guardian, a preaching office, and a shepherd ...

Now the little word "priest" stems from the Greek language in which *presbyteros* means *senior* in Latin and "the elder" [*eldist*] in German. That is why in former times the spiritual rule was always held by elders, just as the councilors of a city, *senatus* in Latin, derive their name from their age. Young people have never been very good rulers. Thus "priest" indicates age, not status; nor does it make one a cleric or a spiritual man...

"Bishop" too stems from the Greek language. For he whom they call *episcopus* is called *speculator* in Latin and "a guardian or watchman on the tower" [*warttman odder wechter auff der Wart*] in German. This is exactly what one calls someone who lives in a tower to watch and to look out over the town so that fire or foe do not harm it. Therefore, every minister or spiritual regent should be a bishop, that is, an overseer or watchman, so that in his town and among his people the gospel and faith in Christ are built up and win out over foe, devil, and heresy. Thus St. Luke, in Acts 20 [:17–18, 28] says, "Paul called to him the priests of the church," that is, the elders of the Christians in Ephesus, "and said to them, 'See to yourselves and to all the flock of Christ, over which the Holy Spirit has set you as bishops, to feed the church of God, which he has acquired with his own blood'." Here it is clear that the elders are called bishops, that is, overseers of God's church – of the Christians who are God's people.

Thus Emser [Luther's adversary] too certainly knows from St. Jerome [*Comm. in Titum* 1:7] that priest and bishop are one and the same thing in Scripture. For St. Paul says in Titus 1 [:5], "You should appoint a priest in every town" (that is, an elder over them); and soon afterward he says about the same priest, "But this same bishop must be a blameless man" [Titus 1:7]. He clearly calls the same man priest, bishop, elder, and watchman. But no one should be surprised that bishop, pastor, priest, chaplain, cathedral dean, monk, and many similar names have different meanings now, since no word of Scripture has retained its true meaning...

That is why I have called this same priesthood churchly, since it stems from the order of the church and is not founded on Scripture. For in previous times this matter was handled as follows, and this is the way it should still be done: since in every Christian town they were all equally spiritual priests, one of them – the oldest or rather the most learned and most godly – was elected to be their servant, official, caretaker, and guardian in regard to the gospel and the sacraments, just as a mayor in a city is elected from among the common mass of all citizens ... Thus consecration does not make a cleric, but it does make servants out of clerics; tonsure, chasuble, mass, and sermon are not the signs of a priest but rather of a servant and official of the common priesthood. All of us in the whole mass of people are priests without the consecration of the bishop. But through consecration we become the stewards, servants, and administrators of the other priests who may be deposed and changed.[25]

One of the reasons for propounding a ministry without essential ranks was Luther's belief that all ministry was primarily one of preaching, and only secondarily sacramental. Whereas it had been traditional to identify the various orders or offices by the sacramental prerogatives attached to each, if the essential duty of every office was to preach the word, it was difficult to verify any essential differences in rank.

The public ministry of the Word, I hold, by which the mysteries of God are made known, ought to be established by holy ordination as the highest and greatest of the functions of the church, on which the whole power of the church depends, since the church is nothing without the Word and everything in it exists by virtue of the Word alone. But my papists do not even dream of this in their ordinations ... This is especially true of the bishops who do the ordaining. How then is it possible for them to provide ministers of the Word by their ordinations? In place of ministers of the Word they only ordain priestly functionaries who offer up masses and hear confessions ...

Mostly the functions of a priest are these: to teach, to preach and proclaim the Word of God, to baptize, to consecrate or administer the eucharist, to bind and loose sins, to pray for others, to sacrifice, and to judge of all doctrine and spirits. Certainly these are splendid and royal duties. But the first and foremost of all on which everything else depends, is the teaching of the Word of God. For we teach with the Word, we consecrate with the Word, we bind and absolve sins with the Word, we baptize with the Word, we sacrifice with the Word, we judge all things by the Word. Therefore when we grant the Word to anyone, we cannot deny anything to him pertaining to the exercise of his priesthood.[26]

---

[25] *Auff das ubirchristlich, ubirgeystlich und ubirkunstlich buch Bocks Emszers zu Leypczick Antwortt D. M. L. Darynn auch Murnarrs seynsz geselln gedacht wirt* (1521), *Answer to the Hyperchristian, Hyperspiritual, and Hyperlearned book by Goat Emser in Leipzig – Including Some Thoughts Regarding His Companion, the Fool Murner, WA* 7:628–633; *LW* 39:152–157. See also *Wider den falsch genannten geystlichen stand des Babst und der bischoffen* (1522), *Against the Spiritual Estate of Pope and the Bishops Falsely So Called, WA* 10/2:142–145; *LW* 39:281–284.

[26] He continues: "A Christian, thus, is born to the ministry of the Word in baptism, and if papal bishops are unwilling to bestow the ministry of the Word except on such as destroy the Word of God and ruin the church, then it but remains either to let the church perish without the Word or to let those who come together cast their ballots and elect one or as many as are

In a single rush of commentary the Wittenberg scholar had propounded many telling ideas. All believers are priests, and some among them are elected to a single office of ministry. He presents this as a program to restore the church to its primitive simplicity.

This was an insight which would stay with Luther throughout his life. In one of his last published works he would claim that even the office of apostle is merely one instance of the single, generic ministry that all clerics share.[27]

His theory is not without ambiguity. If all are equally spiritual, and equally priests as a result, yet some are elected to be ministers to the church, what designates those chosen few for their office? Luther says that consecration does not make a cleric. But as yet he is unwilling to admit that God, either before or through an ordination, confers any appropriate grace to the candidate for the distinct tasks he must perform. There seems to be no appeal to any inward, spiritual differentiation; order in the church appears to be a matter of merely human designation and arrangement.[28]

But he goes further still. Since the principal act of ministry is to preach the Word of God, which is something to which baptism

needed of those who are capable. By prayer and the laying on of hands let them commend and certify these to the whole assembly, and recognize and honor them as lawful bishops and ministers of the Word, believing beyond a shadow of doubt that this has been done and accomplished by God." *De Instituendis Ministris Ecclesiae* (1523), *Concerning the Ministry, WA* 12:172–173, 179–191; *LW* 40:11–12, 21–37.

[27] "Hear St. Peter himself... who writes in his epistles to his bishops in Pontus, Galatia, Cappadocia, Asia, Bithynia, 1 Pet 5 [:1–2], 'I exhort the elders among you, as a fellow elder and a witness of the sufferings of Christ as well as a partaker in the glory that is to be revealed. Tend the flock of God that is in your charge,' etc. Look at that – Peter calls himself a fellow elder, that is, equal with pastor or preacher; he does not want to rule over them, but to be equal with them, although he knows that he is an apostle. The office of preacher or bishop is the highest office, which was held by God's Son himself, as well as by all the apostles, prophets and patriarchs. God's word and faith is above everything, above all gifts and personal worth. The word 'elder', in Greek 'presbyter', is in one case a word for old age, as one says, 'an old man'; but here it is a name for an office because one took old and experienced people for the office. Now we call it pastor or preacher or minister." *Wider das Papsthum zu Rom, vom Teufel gestiftet* (1545), *Against the Roman Papacy, an Institution of the Devil, WA* 54:284–285; *LW* 41:358–359.

[28] "[T]he Holy Spirit teaches us that ointments, consecrations, tonsures, chasubles, albs, chalices, masses, sermons, etc., do not make priests or give power. Rather, priesthood and power have to be there first, brought from baptism and common to all Christians through the faith which builds them upon Christ the true high priest ... But to exercise such power and to put it to work is not every man's business. Only he who is called by the common assembly, or the man representing the assembly's order and will, does this work in the stead of and as the representative of the common assembly and power." *Eyn widderspruch D. Luthersz seynis yrthumsz erczwungen durch den aller hochgelertisten priester gottis Herrn Hieronymu Emser, Vicarien tzu Meyssen* (1521), *Dr. Luther's Retraction of the Error Forced upon Him by the Most Highly Learned Priest of God, Sir Jerome Emser, Vicar in Meissen, WA* 8:253; *LW* 39:236–237.

deputes every Christian, there are situations when even the election
by the congregation is not needed for a believer to take up the work
of ministry.

For no one can deny that every Christian possesses the word of God and is
taught and anointed by God to be priest... it is their duty to confess, to
teach, and to spread [his word]...

If [a Christian] is at a place where there are no Christians he needs no
other call than to be a Christian, called and anointed by God from within.
Here it is his duty to preach and to teach the gospel to erring heathen or non-
Christians, because of the duty of brotherly love, even though no man calls
him to do so. This is what Stephen did, Acts 6–7, even though he had not
been ordered into any office by the apostles... Again, Apollos did so too,
Acts 18 [:25]...

Second, if he is at a place where there are Christians who have the same
power and right as he, he should not draw attention to himself. Instead, he
should let himself be called and chosen to preach and to teach in the place
of and by the command of the others. Indeed, a Christian has so much power
that he may and even should make an appearance and teach among
Christians – without a call from men – when he becomes aware that there is
a lack of teachers, provided he does it in a decent and becoming manner.
This was clearly described by St. Paul in 1 Corinthians 14 [:30], when he
says, "If something is revealed to someone else sitting by, let the first be
silent... "

[H]ow much more right does a whole congregation have to call someone
into this office when there is a need, as there always is, especially now! For
in the same passage St. Paul gives every Christian the power to teach among
Christians if there is a need, saying, "You can all prophesy one by one, so
that all may learn and all be admonished" [1 Corinthians 14:31].[29]

---

[29] He continues:

But if you say, "Did not St. Paul command Timothy and Titus to institute priests [1 Ti 4:13; Tit 1:5],
and do we not read, Acts 14 [:23], that Paul and Barnabas instituted priests among the congregations?"
... I answer that if our bishops, abbots, etc., did represent the apostles, as they boast, one opinion would
certainly be to let them do what Titus, Timothy, Paul and Barnabas did when they instituted priests, etc.
But since they represent the devil and are wolves who neither want to teach the gospel nor suffer it to be
taught, they are as little concerned with instituting the office of preaching or pastoral care among
Christians as the Turks or the Jews are. They should drive asses and lead dogs.

Moreover, if they were really decent bishops who wanted to have the gospel and wanted to institute
decent preachers, they still could not and should not do so without the will, the election, and the call of
the congregation – except in those cases where need made it necessary so that souls would not perish for
lack of the divine word... Rather, [the bishop] should confirm the one whom the congregation chose and
called; if he does not do it, he [the elected man] is confirmed anyway by virtue of the congregation's call.
Neither Titus nor Timothy nor Paul ever instituted a priest without the congregation's election and call.
This is clearly proven by the sayings in Titus 1 [:7] and 1 Timothy 3 [:10], "A bishop or priest should
be blameless," and "Let the deacon be tested first." Now Titus could not have known which ones were
blameless; such a report must come from the congregation, which must name the man.

Again, we even read in Acts 4 [6:1–6] regarding an even lesser office, that the apostles were not
permitted to institute persons as deacons without the knowledge and consent of the congregation. Rather,
the congregation elected and called the seven deacons, and the apostles confirmed them.

Luther had been a convincing master. In a short while a massive popular uprising occurred in Germany. The egalitarian claims of Luther and his first comrades had an appeal for the impoverished poor of the countryside, who inferred that if they should be free of servitude within the church, they should also have the domination of their secular rulers lightened. Luther sided with the nobles against the Peasants' Revolt, and henceforth made it clear that this democratic ideal from the New Testament was intended exclusively for ecclesiastical application.[30] Even within the church, Luther's tone after the revolt is a little more managerial when setting forth the necessity for directive leadership.

[T]he church is recognized externally by the fact that it consecrates or calls ministers, or has offices that it is to administer. There must be bishops, pastors, or preachers, who publicly and privately give, administer and use the ... holy possessions in behalf and in the name of the church, or rather by reason of their institution by Christ, as St. Paul states in Ephesians 4 [:8], "He received gifts among men ... " – his gifts were that some should be apostles, some prophets, some evangelists, some teachers and governors, etc. The people as a whole cannot do these things, but must entrust or have them entrusted to one person. Otherwise, what would happen if everyone wanted to speak or administer, and no one wanted to give way to the other? It must be entrusted to one person, and he alone should administer the sacraments. The others should be content with this arrangement and agree to it.[31]

Despite the original theory that all ordained ministers would be on the same level, the church's needs almost immediately required some

Das eyn Christliche versamlung odder gemeyne recht und macht habe, alle lere tzu urteylen und lerer zu beruffen, eyn und abzusetzen, Grund und Ursach aus der schrifft (1523), That a Christian Assembly or Congregation Has the Right and Power to Judge All Teaching and to Call, Appoint, and Dismiss Teachers, Established and Proven by Scripture, *WA* 11:411–414; *LW* 39:309–312.

[30] The first of The Twelve Articles of the Peasants in March, 1525, was: "First, it is our humble petition and desire, as also our will and resolution, that in the future we should have power and authority so that each community should choose and appoint a pastor, and that we should have the right to depose him should he conduct himself improperly. The pastor thus chosen should teach us the Gospel pure and simple, without any addition, doctrine, or ordinance of man. For to teach us continually the true faith will lead us to pray God that through his grace this faith may increase within us and become a part of us ... Hence such a guide and pastor is necessary, and in this fashion grounded upon the Scriptures." *Documents Illustrative of the Continental Reformation*, ed. B. J. Kidd (Oxford: Clarendon, 1911), 175.

[31] *Von den Consiliis und Kirchen (1539)*, On the Councils and the Church, *WA* 50:632–633; *LW* 41:154. He went on to say: "It is, however, true that the Holy Spirit has excepted women, children, and incompetent people from this function, but chooses (except in emergencies) only competent males to fill this office."

level of supervisory authority. Already in 1528, when Luther
accepted the request of the Elector of Saxony to draw up church
regulations to be imposed by visitors sent round to all parishes under
the Elector's authority, there was the need to create a surrogate for
the bishop. Recurring to the Greek root of "bishop," *episkopos*, he
called the new official a superintendent = *Pfarherr* = *superintendens*.
But the instructions try to make clear that just as the pastor is
exercising powers that every Christian possesses, so the superintendent is exercising powers possessed by all the pastors over whom
he presides.[32]

Superintendents coexisted alongside the traditional bishops for a
while, but as the sees became vacant the secular rulers confiscated
their patrimony. The superintendents emerged as sole middle-level
supervisors under the princes, and consistories of pastors and nobles
and gentry replaced the old cathedral chapters. They were however
given a measure of authority over policy which chapters never had,
in a way that made them resemble standing synods. This was
completed within only a few decades.

There was naturally some ambiguity about the nature of the new
supervisory positions. One view held that they were a fresh start,
made from the model of the New Testament. But there is also
evidence that for a while they were regarded as a take-over group
moving into the role of the bishops: new officers but in old offices. In
Scandinavia, for instance, where Luther's disciples had rapidly

---

[32] This is his text:

The Office of Superintendent

This pastor (*Pfarherr*) shall be superintendent of all the other priests who have their parish or benefice in
the region, whether they live in monasteries or foundations of nobles or of others. He shall make sure that
in these parishes there is correct Christian teaching, that the Word of God and the holy gospel are truly
and purely proclaimed, and that the holy sacraments according to the institution of Christ are provided
to the blessing of the people ...

If one or more of the pastors or preachers is guilty of error in this or that respect, the superintendent
shall call to himself those concerned and have them abstain from it, but also carefully instruct them
wherein they are guilty and have erred either in commission or omission, either in doctrine or in life.

But if such a one will not then leave off or desist, especially if it leads to false teaching and sedition, then
the superintendent shall report this immediately to the proper official who will then bring it to the
knowledge of our gracious Lord, the Elector. His Electoral grace will then be able in good time to give
this proper attention.

We have also considered it wise to ordain that in the future when a pastor or preacher either by death
or otherwise leaves his benefice and some one is accepted in his place by the patron, such a one shall be
presented to the superintendent before he is given the benefice or received as a preacher. The
superintendent shall question and examine him as to his life and teaching and whether he will
satisfactorily serve the people, so that by God's help we may carefully prevent any ignorant or
incompetent person from being accepted and unlearned folk being misled.

*Unterricht der Visitatorn an die Pfarhern ym Kurfurstenthum zu Sachssen (1528), Instructions for the Visitors of Parish
Pastors in Electoral Saxony, WA* 26:235; *LW* 40:313–314.

introduced the new ways with a firm welcome from the national sovereigns, the ordination ceremonies for superintendents mingle references and formularies redolent of the episcopate with descriptions of an itinerant preaching office among local pastors who are peers.[33]

Luther, like Wyclif, was blurting out a theology of church office that had no known precedent, except the New Testament as it had not been interpreted within memory. Also, he was a man with a rapid and responsive following, so that his theoretical formulations quickly begot experiments in local churches. These in turn soon exercised an influence of their own back upon his continuing speculation. Beginning as a critic, he soon had to become an apologist for his own new establishment. There is thus a lack of consistency in his writings, and continuing disagreement among scholars who interpret them.[34]

But this is not a crucial issue, for Luther was a founder, not only a scholar. The movement he began swiftly gathered force and momentum. His original ideas, though disorganized and sometimes inconsistent, were given new directions and momentum in the keeping of his allies and Lutheran successors.

PHILIP MELANCHTHON

One of the closest of these was Philip Schwarzerd, known best by his adopted Greek name, Melanchthon. Great-nephew of the distinguished humanist John Reuchlin, he was one of Luther's most capable and respected lieutenants. In 1531 it was he who drafted the compromise document for the Diet of Augsburg that was signed by the Protestant princes of Germany. On the subject of office the *Augsburg Confession* is terse: "Regarding church order they teach that no one ought to teach publicly in the church or administer sacraments, unless duly called, just as Paul instructed Titus to establish presbyters in the cities."[35]

Catholic critics replied that they too held the same doctrine,

---

[33] See Kidd, *Documents*, 322–335.

[34] See Erwin Iserloh, Joseph Glazik and Hubert Jedin, *Reformation and Counter Reformation*, in *History of the Church*, ed. Jedin and John Dolan, 5 (London: Burns & Oates, 1980), 222, n. 14.

[35] *Confessio Augustana*, in *Corpus Reformatorum* (hereafter *CR*), ed. Carolus Gottlieb Bretschneider, Henricus Ernestus Bindser et al. (Halle, Braunschweig, Berlin, Leipzig, etc.: Schwetske & Sohn, 1834–), 26:360. This is the so-called *Confessio Variata*, revised in 1535–1540 from the original, slightly briefer version of 1531; see col. 280.

provided that being "duly called" conformed to lawful and traditional practice.[36]

Near the end of the *Confession* Melanchthon takes up the vexed issue: do the bishops have authentic authority? The Catholics "feel that the power of the keys, or the power of the bishops to preach the gospel, to forgive or to retain sins, and to administer the sacraments, conforms to the gospel, that it is God's own power or command."[37] The signers of the *Confession*, he says, are willing to acknowledge this spiritual power as God's gift and benefit, just as they would the coercive power of the civil government.

Their grievance is not so much with the claim as with the way it has been exercised. Bishops have confused the true power of the keys with the power of the sword, and have involved themselves in political struggles that have nothing to do with the gospel: deposing kings, excommunicating temporal rivals, and the like. Their authentic duty "is to evaluate doctrine, to reject it when it deviates from the gospel, and to withhold communion from those known to be godless – but by word, not by force."[38] Bishops have overstepped by burdening the consciences of the people, multiplying obligatory observances and rituals. This offends the gospel doubly. People are being told they can earn forgiveness and salvation if they comply, and that they are damned if they fail. Melanchthon comments quite carefully that his fellowship does not wish to deny the rights of the clergy, but only wishes to have those rights correctly understood and limited.

The classic argument of the Catholic critics had been that when the church replaced the sabbath with Sunday observance, the bishops had claimed an authority so great as to cancel a divine commandment. Could there be any limit to such an authority? Melanchthon responded:

Let bishops and pastors make arrangements for good order in the church. But let no one ... imagine that by those arrangements we earn the forgiveness

---

[36] After the Augsburg Confession appeared it was confronted by the *Confutatio Confessionis Augustanae* quickly drafted by Jacques Lefevre d'Etaple, John Eck and John Cochlaeus. On this point they wrote: "Quando autem articulo quarto decimo confitentur, neminem debere in ecclesia verbum Dei et sacramenta administrare, nisi rite vocatum; intelligi debet, eum rite vocatum, qui secundum formam iuris, iuxta ecclesiasticas sanctiones, atque decreta, ubique in orbe christiano hactenus observata, vocatur, non secundum Ierobiticam vocationem, seu plebis tumultum, ac quamlibet aliam inordinatam intrusionem, non vocatus sicut Aaron. In hac itaque sententia confessio acceptatur; admonendi tamen sunt, ut in ea perseverent, ut neminem, neque Pastorem, neque concionatorem, nisi rite vocatum, in ditionibus suis admittant." *CR* 27:114–115.   [37] *Confessio Augustana, CR* 26:405.
[38] Ibid. 406.

of our sins, or make amends for them, or that they bind our consciences so that people imagine them to be obligatory and think they are sinning if they violate them but harm no one. It is like Paul's ruling that women wear veils in the assembly.[39]

Melanchthon has usually been understood to have acknowledged only a single ministerial office in the gospel. His correspondence at this time, however, carries repeated assertions that for the sake of unity the episcopacy had been given authority over the lower order of pastors, so that deviant teaching could be repudiated.[40] Such a compromising position naturally evoked hostile comment from both sides.

He then wrote a follow-up known as the *Apology*, much lengthier than the original *Confession*. "We have greatly desired," he insisted, "to stand by church polity, for we reckon that the peace of the church would thus best be served. And so we would not accept ministers without the authorization of the bishops, if they were only a little more flexible. But they ordain no one, they admit no one to the ministry, except under the harshest conditions: priests must not preach the gospel and they must not marry." If they would impose no more than the scriptures authorize, Melanchthon assures the Catholics that his party would with pleasure return to obedience. But never to tyranny.[41] This was written in an apparently conciliatory tone. When he expanded his defense a while later his tone had more of a bite to it. Now he spoke of the savagery of the bishops towards the reformed clergy: with "unprecedented cruelty they struck down our poor, innocent priests."[42] Still, his argument was one of policy, not one of principle. Canonical ordination was being rejected, not because it was inauthentic, but because unacceptable conditions were being attached to it.

As for the order of bishop, he continued to accept its separate existence but resisted its manner of usage by the Catholics. How, his adversaries were arguing, could a bishop rightly rule and discipline his flock without the authority to frame and impose rules that would lead them to salvation? That, he agreed, was fine, but no bishop had the power to command what the gospel forbade, or to fancy that his ruling could make any action either saving or sinful.[43]

---

[39] Ibid. 409.
[40] Erwin Iserloh, "Das Bischofsamt nach der *Confessio Augustana*," in *Episcopale Munus*, ed. Philippe Dalhaye and Léon Elder, S.V.D. (Assen: Van Gorcum, 1982), 312–328.
[41] Melanchthon, *Apologia Confessionis Augustanae, CR* 27:288–289.   [42] Ibid. 572–573.
[43] Ibid. 640–644.

This was a teaching that could have led in several directions. The momentum which Luther had initiated in the Reform, however, was not in favor of restoring a hierarchy to power. That had been back in the 1530s. Two decades later the Lutheran position had shifted and the ambiguity had faded.

The *persecutors* of the gospel are *not bishops*, and should be regarded as exiled [cf. Galatians 1:6–24]. The ceremony of the consecration, as customarily practiced by bishops, is wrong and full of error, in the same way as Masses for the dead and the consecration and transsubstantiation of the bread...

Consecration is this, and nothing more than, a confirmation of the one chosen after a judicial examination of his doctrine. It is done by several persons of the Church laying their hands on his head, entrusting him with the office according to divine order, and praying that God may give him the Holy Spirit, rule him, and that God through this preaching and administration of the sacraments will be strong, as it stands written, "The gospel is the power of God to salvation to all those who believe" [Romans 1:16].

And the command of St. Paul that Titus should arrange for priests applies not only to those with the title "bishop," but to *all* Christian shepherds of souls.[44]

Melanchthon then appealed to a string of early authorities (Cyprian, Augustine, Ambrose, Athanasius, Theodoret, and Nicaea itself) to prove that the prevailing custom of requiring confirmation by Rome before a nominee could be consecrated to a local bishopric was not the primitive practice of the church, and hence it could and should be discontinued. Like Luther he cites Matthew 18: "Where two or three are gathered in my name, there am I in the midst of them. What they bind on earth shall be bound in heaven, what they loose on earth, shall also in heaven be loosed." The local community is thus empowered to commit proper men to office, so that ministry can be provided. If the obstructive bishops will not ordain the qualified men so designated, then the locals have the right to ordain them themselves.

At this point it is clear that ordination is not seen as a transforming event. It is "a public witness and proclamation of the call to the office of preaching." In opposition to Catholic fixation on the canonical rite itself, Melanchthon systematically speaks of two phases: the examination of candidates to verify their qualifications, and public

---

[44] Melanchthon, *Loci Communes Theologici* (1555 edn.), in *Melanchthon on Christian Doctrine*, trans. and ed. Clyde L. Manschreck (New York: Oxford University Press, 1965), 262–263.

testimony to their calling by God. Now he explicitly speaks of God proffering the calling, which the church then acknowledges. The minister is to possess an inward endowment which is beyond that of the ordinary believer, but it is conferred before ordination, not through it.[45]

JOHN CALVIN

The basic Lutheran doctrine on church order was soon to find an alternative in the Reformed movement initiated by John Calvin. Nevertheless, both Luther's own critique of the Catholic tradition and of its historical justification, and his reconstruction of primitive church practice put forward as normative for the future, blazed the trail down which all Protestant theory, except that in the Church of England, was to stride.

The earliest major variant from the Saxon establishment was to arise about two decades later in Switzerland. John Calvin was proposing to restore the church in Geneva according to the New Testament. As source and model for church affairs he identified Paul's lists of inspired service-charisms. One of these lists, in Ephesians 4, enumerates apostles, prophets, evangelists, shepherds and teachers. The first three of these functions, he taught, were provided at the beginning for the inauguration of the kingdom. They do not endure as part of the permanent ministry, though God could reactivate them in an era of exceptional need. Indeed, it was Calvin's belief that the reformers who were freeing the church from the Roman Antichrist were evangelists – and possibly apostles – in that classic pauline sense.

This leaves shepherds and teachers, which the church can never do without. I see them differentiated in this way: teachers preside over neither discipline nor administration of the sacraments nor correction or exhortation. They only interpret the scriptures, so that a sound and sincere teaching can survive among the faithful. The pastoral office, however, comprises all of those duties.[46]

The traditional clerical titles, by contrast, were not authentically primitive:

[45] Ibid. 204–205.
[46] John Calvin, *Christianae Religionis Institutio* (1536) 4, 3, 4; *CR* 30:31.

I have spoken of bishops (*episcopi*) and elders (*presbyteri*) and shepherds (*pastores*) and servants (*ministri*) indiscriminately to refer to those who rule the churches. This squares with scripture, where those titles are inter-changeable: whoever practices the ministry of the Word is called bishop.[47]

Other pauline rosters of gifts (Romans 12 and 1 Corinthians 12) add powers of healing, governance, provision for the poor, speaking in tongues, and so forth. Most of those charisms were also provisional, he notes, because they were conferred upon only the first generation. Two however are permanent functions: governance and care for the poor. Calvin identifies the former office with the elders elected from the people. Alongside the bishops they regulated public behavior and imposed discipline. The latter charism was entrusted to the deacons.[48]

From Acts 6 Calvin inferred that these ministers ought not be chosen by those already in office, or by the elders. They should be elected by popular consensus. Pastors should preside at the elections, but not control them. The New Testament also gives us evidence of the apostolic custom of investing candidates with ministries by the laying-on of hands. Though it comes to us as a practice rather than as a commandment it should, Calvin thought, be continued. It was unclear from scripture whether the entire congregation had imposed hands, or only the pastors (Acts 6:6; 12:3; 2 Timothy 1:6); the latter would surely be more appropriate.[49]

The Reformed polity began, then, with four categories of office or ministry: pastors, teachers, rulers, deacons. All were to be popularly elected. Two things might be noted here. First, Calvin reaches into the New Testament for a simplified model of offices, and he disallows those offices which did not survive into the later tradition. Thus his method is not purely an appeal to scripture, but takes account also of tradition beyond the earliest generation. In this it was on all fours with the method of his Catholic opponents. Second, Calvin's theory was going to be frustrated by the ruling councils of the city, who had no desire to yield such authority to popular suffrage.

Five years after his *Institutions* Calvin was bidden by the city fathers to draft a local charter for the governance of the Geneva church. Knowing that it must pass muster with the municipal authorities, he felt constrained to compromise his earlier proposals.

As for the office of pastor, the lineaments were the same as before. Like their New Testament precursors who were called "elders" or

---

[47] Ibid. par. 8.   [48] Ibid. parr. 8–9.   [49] Ibid. parr. 15–16.

"servants," they were to proclaim the Word of God by indoctrination, admonition, exhortation and public and private correction. They were also to administer the sacraments and fraternal
correction, assisted in this by the elders and by deputies.

Candidates were to be given a rigorous examination on their
competence to construe scripture, their grasp of approved doctrine,
and their probity of personal behavior.

On the process of selection and installation, Calvin yielded.
Ministers, not congregations, were to elect their new colleagues. And
nominees first had to secure the approval of the city councils. Only if
approved were they presented for popular acceptance, which would
then be a formality.[50]

Calvin yielded to strong pressure and abolished the anciently
attested imposition of hands. "In the past there has been much
superstition, to the point of scandal, regarding this rite. In these
circumstances and unaccepting times, we shall discontinue it."[51]

Pastors, he added, should confer about doctrine once a week to
assure uniformity of preaching in the church. Thus was born the
consistory, a purely ecclesiastical collegiate body which in time
would succeed in reclaiming much of what were then the doctrinal
prerogatives of the civil powers.

Teachers were an intellectual resource meant to counterbalance
the pastors. They should hold academic degrees in scripture,
following a classical liberal education fit equally for the ministry or
for civil statecraft. The teachers were then to provide instruction that
would form obligatory schooling for all youngsters in the church.[52]

The elders, whose task of monitoring and enforcing proper
behavior in the community might seem to be enfolded within the
larger responsibilities of the pastors, were in fact the agents of the civil
arm. They were to be elected by the various councils of city

---

[50] "S'ensuit a qui il appartient d'instituer les pasteurs. Il sera bon en cest endroict de suyvre
l'ordre de l'Esglise ancienne, veu que ce n'est que practique de ce qui nous est monstré par
l'Escripture. C'est que les ministres eslisent premièrement celluy qu'on doibvra mettre en
l'office [the city council here amended the text: "l'ayant fayct à scavoir à la Seigneurie"].
Après qu'on le présente au Conseil. Et s'il est trouvé digne, que le Conseil le recoive et
accepte, luy donnant tesmonage pour le produyre finablement au peuple en la prédication,
affin qu'il soit receu par consentement commun de la compagnye des fidelles. S'il estoit
trouvé indigne de demonstré tel par probations légitimes, il fauldroit lors procéder a
nouvelle élection pour en prendre un aultre." Calvin, *Projet d'ordonnances ecclésiastiques*
(1541), i, [2]; *CR* 38:15. Appropriate excerpts from Calvin's original *Projet*, matched with
the municipality's modifications, can be seen in Kidd, *Documents*, 589–597.
[51] Ibid. [3].   [52] Ibid. ii.

government; the pastors were only to be informed of their choices, not consulted, and the congregation had no say in their selection.[53]

Deacons in the early church, Calvin asserted, were of two kinds: those responsible for the eleemosynary funds of the community and those who actually looked after the sick, the aged, the widows, the orphans and the poor. Similarly he created a double diaconate of stewards and providers (*procureurs* and *hospitalliers*).[54]

Calvin's draft was taken in hand by the ruling bourgeoisie of Geneva, modified to enhance their control of church officers, and published in 1541 as *Les ordonnances ecclésiastiques de l'église de Genève*. Beyond the structural fact that the church was in thrall to the city fathers, Calvin's regime directed the services of all church officers to the paramount goal of assured virtue, which he called *la bonne police*. The purposes of church and state became difficult to distinguish from each other. While rejecting Catholic practices as opposed to New Testament community organization, he had, however, constructed an ecclesiastical polity that was acquiescent to secular concerns to a degree that could find little precedent in the memoirs of the earliest Christians.

The Catholics naturally accused the Calvinists of having terminated legitimate continuity and authority through their discontinuance of the laying-on of hands. Since Calvin himself had acknowledged that rite to be scriptural and of apostolic origin, the point was difficult to deny.

OTHER CHURCHES OF THE CALVINIST REFORM

Calvin's lieutenant and eventual successor, Theodore Beza, was called on to reply at the Poissy Colloquy convened before the Queen Mother of France, Catherine de Medici, in 1561. His coreligionists did not, he agreed, have the laying-on of hands, which was claimed to be a substantial component of official ordination. But the Catholic bishops who were lodging this protest lacked two other essential components: election by the elders of their church, and inquiry into their morals and doctrine. They were further compromised by having put gold into the hands that came down upon their heads.

---

[53] They were to be "gens de bonne vie et honeste, sans reproche et hors de toutte suspicion, sur tout craignans Dieu et ayans bonne prudence spirituelle. Et les fauldra tellement eslire qu'il y en ait en chascun quartier de la ville, affin d'avoir l'oeil partout," ibid. iii.
[54] Ibid. iv.

The stand-off between the reformers and the papists was, as he saw it, reminiscent of the feud between the Old Testament prophets and priests: one group was claiming fidelity; the other, legitimacy.

Beza's opponent, theologian Claude D'Espense of the Sorbonne, confronted him: "Yes, but show me one single example in the last fifteen hundred years that is similar to yours." Beza replied: "All that has happened is not recorded by historians. But even if there were no similar example, nonetheless it is not unfitting that God should act in these days as he has not done in the past."

Yet Beza was not all that content either to claim an unprecedented divine warrant with no authorization from the past, or to rely upon the classical reformers' vindication which appealed beyond intervening tradition to the primitive paradigms of scripture. He returned again to meet his opponent on the opponent's ground, and to counterclaim that the Catholics too rested their authority on usages that lack testimony in the earliest documents. By arguing this way he was affirming, rather than repudiating, the continuity of the New Testament with later documents for purposes of authentic tradition.

Now, if the traditions and ceremonies that our opponents advance today were apostolic, the church would have used them from the beginning. But since we can establish their authors by the historical accounts, it cannot be said that they have come from the apostles ... We must therefore fall back on the apostles whom Jesus Christ sent to instruct and teach us.[55]

By now Beza and his colleagues were the authors of a new set of traditions which had indeed been inspired by their reading of the primitive records of the New Testament. But as those traditions soon began to be weathered by their exposure to political compromise, to a dominating secular power and to revision by later generations, the New Testament was inevitably read so as to justify the authenticity of the ongoing church practices. And so Calvin and the other founder-reformers and their disciples were unwittingly reliving the experience of the postapostolic church whose authority they had disdained. And they placed themselves in a situation quite comparable to that of their Catholic adversaries, citing the authorities of the past but with operative loyalties to the customs of the present.

The Calvinist church order itself was meanwhile undergoing change beyond the confines of its Genevan birthplace. In 1559 the French Huguenots held their First National Synod and adopted their

---

[55] Ziegler, *Great Debates*, 234–239.

own equivalent of the *Ordonnances*. They ratified two documents: the *Confession of Faith* (*Confession de foi*, known also as the *Confessio Gallicana*) and the *Church Discipline* (*Ordre de la discipline ecclésiastique*).[56]

The national, rather than municipal, scope of this church showed forth in its hierarchical levels of authority. The senate of the congregation, the local consistory, the provincial synod and the national synod represented successive echelons of discretion and appeal.

Huguenot discipline specified, however, that such a hierarchy of collegial bodies not be reflected in individual ministers or individual churches. "We believe that all true pastors, wherever they may be, have the same authority and equal power under a single head, single sovereign and single universal Bishop Jesus Christ. Thus no church should claim any domination or lordship over another."[57]

The regime did have elected superintendents, however, and they were empowered to issue regulations individually within their own churches and collegially for the church at large. Thus despite its egalitarian intention the Synod was creating a position of great potential authority.

The local Huguenot church had three offices, not four: the teachers of Geneva have disappeared. The pastor both presides and teaches. The elders, also *surveillans*, govern behavior, reprove laxity and purge scandal. The deacons provide for the poor, the sick and the imprisoned, and they teach catechism privately. Certain of them who were qualified could be chosen to offer public religious instruction. Thus they had occupied some of the ground vacated by the departed teachers.

Since the Huguenots were hardly enjoying the patronage of either local or royal government, they had no secular overlords in the way that their cousins in Geneva had. They were accordingly free to elect all officers themselves in an ecclesiastical context. It was not, however, a democratic proceeding. Pastors, or ministers, were elected by the consistory, a body composed of church officers somewhat out-numbered by prominent laymen. Popular assent was secured after the election, and was generally a foregone conclusion. The election was followed by prayer and imposition of hands by the ministers involved, "but without any superstition." This and the omission of

---

[56] See especially the *Confession*, arts. 29–32; the *Discipline*, arts. 9–28; *CR* 37:731ff. See also Kidd, *Documents*, 670–677. Both texts had been drafted by Calvin's pupil, Antoine de la Roche Chandieu.   [57] *Confession*, art. 30.

Calvin's fourth office, of teacher, demonstrate the considerable independence exercised within the various branches of the Calvinist movement. The ministry, though transferable to other congregations, and in some circumstances allowing of deactivation through retirement, was explicitly understood to be lifelong.

Elders and deacons were elected by the local senate, a congregational body composed of all the elders and deacons with the pastor presiding. Their office was not perpetual, and they did not receive the laying-on of hands.

The 1559 Synod expressed the same conviction as Calvin, that although the church must now secure its reform by establishing an orderly regime, the new beginning itself derived from a certain extraordinary yet necessary rupture with the degenerate order of the past. The revolutionaries, however, hastened to deny legitimacy to any who might be disposed to revolt afresh.

We believe that no one ought to act on his own authority to assume governance over the church. That ought to occur only by election, as far as may be possible and as God allows. We note that an exception to this is possible, for it has several times occurred, even in our day (when the state of the church was interrupted), that God has raised up individuals in an extraordinary manner, to rebuild the church which was in ruins and desolation. Be that as it may, we believe that this rule must always be observed: that all pastors, elders and deacons require credentials before being called to their office.[58]

At precisely the time when the Geneva church and the French Huguenots were devising their church orders, a third branch of the Calvinist reform was doing the same thing in Scotland, under the influence of John Knox. The Scottish Parliament in 1560 adopted the *Confession of Faith* and the *First Book of Discipline*. Even though they were denied the royal assent by Queen Mary, these served the kirk as normative documents until first the kirk and then the Scottish Parliament adopted the *Form of Church Government* and a *Directory for Public Worship* (1643) and the *Confession of Faith* (1647) drawn up by the Westminster Assembly of Divines, which had been aided in its deliberations by Scots Commissioners.

Like their continental confederates, the Scots reformers knew that they faced a twofold task. They must justify a radical breach with the church of the past, yet secure for their own establishment unchallengeable and enduring divine credentials. As innovators

---

[58] Ibid. art. 31.

themselves, they could not claim too absolute an authority for any church order; yet as founders of a disciplined and even coercive regime they had to claim strong warrants for its future. "We speak of the ordinarie vocation in Kirks reformed; and not of that which is extraordinary, when God by himselfe and by his onely power, raiseth up the Ministerie such as best pleaseth his Wisedome."[59]

As in some other Calvinist patterns, authority was vested in assemblies: general (national), regional, local and congregational. The ministerial membership of those assemblies was in every way overshadowed by the lay estates: the nobles and the commissioners of the town councils. Even the General Assembly could not be sovereign while the parliament exercised ultimate jurisdiction over the church.

The four offices of the Geneva format were here: pastor, teacher, elder and deacon. All four were to exercise virtually the same duties as their Reformed counterparts in Switzerland.

It was theoretically a point of principle that pastors be elected by their own congregations. In practice it did not work out that way. Lay patronage had been declared at an end. Nevertheless, when the patrons continued to exercise their ancient right of presenting nominees for local benefices (patronage and benefices were not suppressed for quite some time), the churchmen insisted that at least the right of examination and admission should then be reserved to the ministers.[60] With or without this compromise, popular selection of ministers was a hope, not a reality.

The laying-on of hands was distasteful to them as an ordination rite, and was considered unnecessary. "Other ceremony than the public approbation of the people, and declaration of the chief minister, that the person there presented is appointed to serve that Kirk, we cannot approve; for albeit the Apostles used the imposition of hands, yet seeing the miracle is ceased, the using of the ceremony we judge is not necessary."[61]

---

[59] *First Book of Discipline*, 9, 16, 3; see Kidd, *Documents*, 707–708.

[60] *A Source Book of Scottish History*, 2, 2nd edn. (1424–1567), ed. William Croft Dickinson, Gordon Donaldson and Isabel A. Milne (London: Nelson, 1958), 172, 209–211; 3, 2nd edn. (1567–1707), ed. Dickinson and Donaldson (1961), 8–11.

[61] *First Book of Discipline*, in *Source Book*, 2:172–173. The same document had asserted that "it is neither the clipping of their crownes, the greasing of their fingers, nor the blowing of the dumb dogges called the Bishops, neither the laying on of their hands that maketh true Ministers of Christ Jesus: but the Spirit of God inwardly first moving the heart to seeke to enter in the holy calling for Christ's glory and the profite of his Kirk, and thereafter the nomination of the people, the examination of the learned, and publick admission as before is said, make men lawfull Ministers of the Word and Sacraments." Kidd, *Documents*, 707.

Pastors had a two-tiered corps of understudies. The reader, who might serve a small, rural congregation for which no pastor was available, or might assist the pastor of a sizeable church, was trained to read the scriptures and to lead the people in the prayerbook services and to help catechize the laity. Signs of proficiency might be rewarded by promotion to the rank of exhorter, which allowed a man to preach as well, and to aspire to the possible future honor of elevation to the ministry itself, which would authorize him to administer the sacraments.[62]

There was the insistence – by now conventional – that all pastors were of equal rank and authority. That notwithstanding, the position of superintendent was undeniably exalted beyond that of ordinary pastors. The superintendent was to evangelize and found new churches. He was to superintend all congregations in his territory. He was to examine, approve and admit new ministers. He was to supervise and discipline all pastors. He was remunerated more generously.[63] The office bore numerous features of the old Catholic episcopacy.

The Scottish situation was peculiar in that the reform was so slow and gradual in superseding the old church. There were some bishops who continued in place as Catholics. Others came over to the Reform, kept their titles and benefices, yet functioned under the authority of the assemblies as superintendents. And some of the superintendents were viewed as successors of the *ancien régime*.

There were several ways of accounting for the relationship. Some texts stress the differences between the old bishops and the new superintendents: the latter have no benefices, do not live idly at a distance but ride circuit constantly through their churches, and are active preachers.[64] When however the two offices are presented as in continuity, it is in order to verify the legitimacy of the newer one. The lack of differentiation is presented as similar to the interchangeability of titles in the New Testament.

Scottish policy on this shifted in the early years, for the imposition of hands was shortly afterwards reintroduced; see *Source Book*, 2:208, n. 2.   [62] Ibid. 173.
[63] Ibid. 174, 212. The *Second Book of Discipline*, approved by the General Assembly in 1578, deplored the old pattern, but in so doing gave evidence that it had continued despite the Reform: "As to bishops, if the name *episkopos* be properly takin, they ar all ane with the ministers, as befoir was declairit. For it is not a name of superioritie or lordschip, bot of office and watching ... Trew bischops sould addict themselves to ane particular flock, quhilk sindry of them refuses; neither sould they usurpe lordship over their brethren and over the inheritance of Christ, as these men doe. It agries not with the Word of God that bischops sould be pastors of pastors, pastors of monie flocks." Ibid. 3:27–28.   [64] Ibid. 2:174.

Pastors, bischops or ministers ar they wha ar appointit to particular
congregationes, quhilk they rewll be the Word of God and over the quhilk
they watch. In respect whairof sumetymes they ar callit pastors, becaus they
feid their congregation; sumetymes *episcopi*, or bischops, because they watch
over their flock; sumetymes ministers, be reason of their service and office;
and sumetymes also presbyteri, or seniors, for the gravity in manners quhilk
they aucht to have in taking cure of the spirituall government, quhilk aucht
to be most deir unto them.[65]

Lord Chancellor Glamis, writing to explain the particular needs of
the Scottish reform, tells Theodore Beza that the people have proven
to be too little in awe of the new superintendents, and that the kirk
has therefore had to restore some of the old episcopal authority in
order to elicit their obedience. Also, if the leading churchmen wanted
to have clout in the councils of state they had to come there in the
recognized role of the older bishops. He explicitly admits that "the
power of all ministers in the church of Christ seems to be equal and
identical," but he pleads some sobering realities as their reason for
maintaining a two-level ministry.[66]

The *Second Book of Discipline*, adopted by the General Assembly in
1578, even offered a theological explanation for this, by explaining
that the line of authority from Christ runs from him through the
ministers to the conregation, rather than from the people to the
ministry. This was in clear contrast with the more populist theology
brought from Geneva only two decades earlier. The 1578 doctrine
states:

This power ecclesiasticall is an authoritie granted be God the Father, throw
the Mediator Jesus Christ, unto his kirk gatherit, and having the ground in
the Word of God; to be put in execution be them, unto quhom the spirituall
government of the kirk be lawfull calling is comittit.

The policie of the kirk flowing from this power is an order or forme of
spirituall government, quhilk is exercisit be the members appoyntit thereto
be the Word of God; and therefore is gevin immediatly to the office-beararis,
be whom it is exercisit to the weile of the haill bodie.[67]

The Scots church, then, in its earliest years, encountered stress
when the formulae of Geneva were exposed to the test of local
practice. Some sobering and conservative resistance brought its
leaders to model the church order, not only upon the paradigms
Calvin had discerned in the scriptures, but also upon the developing
needs of the faithful. Though they were evidently unaware of it, this

[65] Ibid 3:24.   [66] Ibid. 24.   [67] Ibid. 22.

was drawing them to reconsider and modify their church order in much the same ways as the early Christian communities had done.

It was precisely their pastoral responsiveness and pragmatism that exposed their main theory to question. For their claim was to do nothing but what was mandated by the Word of God. Yet from the start they were adapting their structures to perceived and timely needs of their own people. This anomaly was pointed out to them by Ninian Winzet, a Catholic priest and academic who had been dismissed from his post for resistance to the new religion.

Gif ye will admitt in your kirk na ceremonie except expreslie commandit in scriptuir, quhy will ye nocht baptize the barne except the father thairof hald it in his airmis afoir your pulpet? ... Quhy mak ye your communioun afoir dennar, sen our Salviour institutit his haly sacrament efter suppare? Quhy use ye at your communioun now four, now thre coupis, and mony breidis, nothir keipand the ceremonie expressit in the Evangel nor confessing the treuth of the mysterie with us? ... And quhy will ye nocht solemnize your band of matrimonie, except thai be proclamit thre bannis afoir? Quhy caus ye at mariage the persones that mariit to tak uthiris be the hand, and in sum places a ring to be gevin? Thir thingis we speir nocht that we repreve thame all, bot to knaw quhou ye establiss your doctrine, to the quhilk ye will that we astrict our selfis, sen ye teche na thing to be useit at the sacramentis or in religioun except thai be expreslie commandit in scripturis.[68]

THE ARGUMENT OF THE MAGISTERIAL REFORMERS

Martin Luther was a master of the scriptures. John Calvin was a theologian and an active pastor. These differences project themselves through the church orders that descended from their original insights. Luther is much more explicitly anxious to expound the biblical texts as justification for his experiments. Calvin added little to the scriptural lessons Luther had published, but was more attentive to the organizational imperatives of the social and political limits his communities encountered. The Calvinist concerns were less doctrinal, more moral. The Lutheran tradition had more of a flair for persuasive and even passionate preaching, while the Reformed literature was more insistent upon assuring a disciplined response. In this regard, precisely because it supposed itself to be totally derivative from the model of the New Testament church, the Calvinist tradition was more and more likely to assume, without being at such pains to

[68] Ninian Winzet, *Certane Tractatis for Reformation of Doctrine and Maneris in Scotland* (1562), 78; *Source Book*, 2:214.

verify it, that its church order did reproduce that of the apostolic communities.

No direct line of theological development runs from Wyclif through Luther to Calvin. Presumably the independence of each gave increase to the next movement's free-mindedness. And certain themes of faith found emphasis in all of their programs. Where they do coincide they witness, not to an intellectual succession, but to a growing dissent from the received doctrine of the church: a dissenting reconstruction from scripture that was being assembled by many hands in many lands. What, we should inquire, were the shared lineaments of this reconstruction?

Both Lutheran and Calvinist doctrine began with Wyclif's conviction that one might judge and reform the church on biblical evidence, rather than accepting the church's self-serving exposition of scripture. They held, likewise, that the true order of God's grace was not under the control of either the authority or the sacraments of the church: indeed, church order was often at cross purposes with God's. Therefore the only authentic Christians are those possessed of inward holiness. Their sacramental or even creedal status may be technically correct, but unsanctifying and thus valueless. The magisterial reformers also saw preaching as the prime function of ministry, they deplored benefices in the gift of lay powers with their secular interests, they called for free-will offerings to support the clergy and they favored discernment by local congregations in the selection of ministers on their merits.

The reforming principle that divine empowerment is God's uncontrollable gift led to a variety of conclusions. The mildest, which the Reformers shared with their Catholic opponents, was that insincere sacraments were a sham. Some moved beyond that to claim that since outward sign and inward grace were so separable, the sacraments could at best only point to, but not effect, any divine empowerment. On reconsideration, some of the Reformers drew back from such a drastic dogma. They acknowledged only two sacraments, baptism and the Lord's Supper, and were willing to recognize in these what they denied in other rituals: an inherent power to transact God's grace.

All believers are priests in virtue of their baptism. Even if clerical status exists within the universal priesthood, it – like baptism – is verified not by ritual admission to office but by moral excellence. Ordination, then, is not a sacramental empowerment for ministry, for that comes with faith and baptism. It is a human arrangement to assign certain Christians to posts in the humanly created organization: necessary for the church but not of divine institution.

Paul had reported a wide variety of inspired functions within the community. Many such functions, like those of prophecy and healing, were appropriate to the unique circumstances of the founding of the church. They may occasionally be awarded by God's un-anticipable gift, but they form no part of the permanent Christian endowment. The ministry of New Testament times which would continue was designated by several names: *presbyteri, episcopi, diaconi, ministri*. The fact that those titles were interchangeable implies that there was a single, unranked ministry. There were no bishops, priests and deacons at three successive levels of subsidiarity: only coequals doing various functions.[69]

The polity of the primitive church was essentially egalitarian. Though ministers might preside, they had no headship or hierarchy of rank. The power of the keys, to bind and to loose, was given to the community, not to its officers. Thus the rights of governance did not belong to the clergy. The polity was also congregational. No church authority was superior to another. Ultimate authority was vested, not in a primatial see, but in a representative synod.

The ancient rite of laying-on of hands was of apostolic origin and hence desirable. Since however it had been an essential component of the corrupt claims of Catholics to ritually transmitted legal status and authority, it might be discontinued, and thus it need not be considered essential.

This, in brief, is the emergent account by the reformers of normative church order in apostolic times. It relied upon a newly available sophistication in biblical and historical scholarship. And as a scholarly theory it posed a formidable challenge to the traditional and defensive theory of the Catholic establishment. It had taken Wyclif's sense of the church as the gathering of the truly sanctified, and discredited the sacraments and offices intended as the resources of grace but corrupted by the Catholics into grace's surrogates. Luther and Calvin and their successors then went on to a much more extensive concern for church polity than Wyclif had ever had.

[69] As might be expected, this position sustained sharp criticism. See Dionysius Petavius (Denys Petau), S.J. (1583–1682), *Dissertationum Ecclesiasticarum Libri Duo, In quibus de Episcoporum Dignitate, ac Potestate, deque Aliis Ecclesiasticis Dogmatibus Disputatur* (Paris: Sebastien Cramoisy, 1641); Louis Thomassin, C. Orat., *Ancienne et nouvelle discipline de l'église touchant les bénéfices et les bénéficiers* (Paris: François Muguet, 1679–1681).

But it was not, as has been observed, a mere theory. It became the argument devised to justify a new church order – in fact, several new church orders. And these establishments quickly gathered mass and movement sufficient to exert powerful gravitational pulls on the theories of church polity which gave them legitimacy.

The promotion of graced, inward excellence over legalized ritual lost much of its momentum when virtuous behavior was severely and coercively monitored by church authority: this was legalism resurgent. The ideal scheme of congregational sovereignty and of a single, unranked ministry did not long endure. Supervisory needs prompted the creation of various hierarchies which, however differently from traditional episcopacy they were explained, in form and function resembled nothing so much as a reformed order of bishops. Congregational say-so often subsided to a perfunctory endorsement of the judgments of the clerical professionals. The aspiration to be free of prelates who acted like lay lords was not furthered when the new movement had recourse to the lay lords themselves as patrons, and when these patrons established themselves as dominant in the synods and consistories, and occasionally as the recognized authorities of last resort over the churches. To sidestep the Catholic claim of legally transmitted dominical and apostolic authority in the papacy and episcopacy (which they saw as a license for the incumbents to excuse their all-too-human willfulness), the reformers claimed the Lord's own authority through the New Testament. In time this would in comparable ways be used to justify rather than to judge some questionable fancies and pursuits. The more trenchantly the reformers sustained their own break with previous tradition, the more difficult it became to insist that their followers and successors be bound by the innovative church order they themselves had so recently designed.

The reformed churches were on the way to experiencing exactly the problems and ventures of the primitive churches. And in so doing they converged more than could have been anticipated with the Catholic establishment that with peevish and lumbering slowness was meanwhile recapturing some of its own youth.

INDEPENDENCY

Before the Reformation was much more than a century old it would be overtaken – as an establishment, more than as a teaching – by an impatient revolt from within, and rebuked for having so forgetfully regressed back into the very corruptions it had aspired to uproot. The Protestant churches had become submissive to the princes; clerics in echelons of hierarchical office had been re-established; theological disputes had provoked a scholastic orthodoxy that muffled the inspired Word; and fussy and formalized worship had once again subsided into an *ex opere operato* magical routine. The gospel church had risen from the dead, only to succumb again to corruption and the grave.

That the ecclesiastical tumult of the early sixteenth century had, in retrospect, introduced a change of forms more than a change of spirit provoked frustration and prompted dissent in England. The Acts of Uniformity and Supremacy enacted in 1559, less than a year after the accession of Elizabeth I, and the legislation of the Elizabethan Settlement in 1570, whereby Parliament established and imposed the Church of England's constitutional prayer and polity, drew out into the open the resistance of many whose agenda for renewal had not been realized. They were first known as Puritans, but soon the dissidents themselves split (as dissidents often do) into two parties. Those who continued as Puritans struggled and hoped for further transformation from within the established church, by clerical and parliamentary authority; they were, in the phrase then much used, prepared "to tarry for the magistrate" who was slow to enact thoroughgoing reform. Those who saw this as the time to reject the Settlement were the Brownists, succeeded by the Separatists, forerunners of the Independency, who would later come to be known as Congregationalists.[70]

[70] The Independents disavowed identification with the older Brownists, and some scholars trace them back to the conforming Puritans, rather than to their nonconformist contemporaries; Champlin Burrage, *The Early English Dissenters in the Light of Recent Research (1550–1641)*, 1 (Cambridge: Cambridge University Press, 1912), 281–311. To the contrary, the Brownists and their Separatist allies are rightly acknowledged as the pioneers of Independency and indeed the progenitors of both Congregationalists and Baptists; Horton Davies, *The English Free Churches*, 2nd edn. (Westport, CT: Greenwood, 1985), 31–33, 49–53. To appreciate the continuity, see "The Savoy Declaration of the Institution of Churches, and the Order Appointed in them by Jesus Christ" in *The Savoy Declaration of Faith and Order 1658*, ed. A. G. Matthews (London: Independent Press, 1959), 121–127. This normative confessional statement, which Matthews styles "a high-tide mark on the sands of time" for Congregationalism, p. 39, would have suited the early Separatists handsomely.

Their antipathy for the old Catholic ways was only slightly sharper than their disgust with Anglicanism. And they were challenged by the new churches as the Reformers and Anglicans and Presbyterians had been by the Catholics: how could they ascribe to Christ a form of Christianity that had no intervening history? In reply, they appealed not only to a normative pre-existence in the New Testament or subapostolic age, but to a continuous yet quasi-underground existence of independency in the church. Harbingers included Clement of Rome and Ignatius of Antioch and Polycarp of Smyrna, Cyprian, Jerome, Augustine, Chrysostom, and of course the more modern pre-reformers: Robert Grosseteste, Wyclif and the Lollards, Erasmus and More, and the Marian martyrs Hugh Latimer and Nicholas Ridley.[71]

Despite various reports of lawmen bursting in on illegal worship gatherings in the 1560s and 1570s, the movement was first openly formulated by a young cleric from Cambridge, Robert Browne (1550? – 1633). Under the articulate influence of Thomas Cartwright, the Lady Margaret's Reader in Divinity, Cambridge was already a Puritan center, but Browne began to preach a more radical form of dissent when he insisted that preachers should be free to expound the Word without authorization from a bishop – and when he began to act upon that along with an early colleague, Robert Harrison of Norwich (d. 1585?). After several imprisonments he crossed over to Holland to join a Puritan community there, and in a burst of publication quickly made the case for autonomous local congregations faithful to the apostolic model.

The principal corruption of the Protestant churches, whether Lutheran, Reformed or Anglican, was their governance by civil authorities (Constantine, as might be expected, is the much-deplored founder of this perversion). The way Browne put his point was to berate churchmen for allowing – or even inviting – their princes to exercise sovereignty over them in matters spiritual.

Yea they have given up these keyes [of the Kingdome] to the Magistrates or to the Spirituall Courtes, and therefore have no right to call them selves the

---

[71] John Waddington devotes one large volume to this claim of continuity: *Congregational History 1200–1567*, 1 (London: John Snow, 1869). See also Henry Martyn Dexter, *The Congregationalism of the Last Three Hundred Years* (New York: Harper, 1880); Joseph Fletcher, *The History of the Revival and Progress of Independency in England, with an Introduction, Containing an Account of the Development of the Principles of Independency in the Age of Christ and His Apostles, and of the Gradual Departure of the Church into Anti-Christian Error, until the Time of the Reformation*, 1 (London: John Snow, 1847), 101–260. See also note 87 below.

Church of God, or lawfull Pastors thereof. Christ is at the right hande of God, gone up into heaven saieth Peter [1 Pet 3:22], to whom the Angels and powers and might are subiecte, howe then shoulde his kingdome tarie for the Magistrate, except they thinke that they are better able to upholde it then he. Yes we must presse unto his kingdome not tarying for anie, as it is written ...

Yet under him in his spirituall kingdome are first Apostles, secondlie prophetes, thirdlie, teachers &c. Also helpers and spirituall guides: But they put the Magistrates first, which in a common wealth in deede are first, and above the Preachers, yet have they no ecclesiasticall authoritie at all, but onely as anie other Christians, if so they be Christians ...

Therefore if Ieremie was set over the Nations and over the Kingdomes, to plucke up and to roote out, and to destroye and throwe down, to builde and to plante, Then have we also an authoritie against which if the Kings and Nations doo sett themselves, we maye not be afraide of their faces, nor leave our calling for them. Howe long therefore will these men take the inheritance from the right heire, and give it to the servant? ... Therefore the Magistrates commaundement, must not be a rule unto me of this and that duetie, but as I see it agree with the worde of God. So then it is an abuse of my guifte and calling, if I cease preaching for the Magistrate, when it is my calling to preach.[72]

The principle invoked was the obligatory unity of doctrine and discipline: the two gifts and services of teaching and governing must be joined in the same persons, and thus authority could reside only in those who also administered the Word of God to the congregation. This obviously denied to civil rulers any exercise of authority within the church.[73]

Browne went on to disallow the legitimacy of bishops, having reflected that

thei shoulde be chiefest, which partake unto us the chiefest graces, and use of their callinges. And that doeth Christ, as it is written, and of his fullnes have we receaved, and grace for grace [J 1:16]. And to him hath god made all thinges subiect saieth Paul [Eph 1:22] even under his feet, and hath appointed him over all thinges, to be head of the church, which is his bodie, even the fullnes of him, which filleth all in all thinges. Nowe next under Christ, is not the bishop of the dioces, by whome so manie mischiefes are

---

[72] Robert Browne, *A Treatise of Reformation without Tarying for Anie, and of the Wickednesse of those Preachers Which Will Not Reforme till the Magistrate Commaunde or Compell Them* (Middelburg [Holland], 1582); in *The Writings of Robert Harrison and Robert Browne*, ed. Albert Peel and Leland H. Carlson, Elizabethan Nonconformist Texts 2 (London: George Allen & Unwin, 1953), 155, 157, 158–159.

[73] Browne, *A True and Short Declaration, Both of the Gathering and Ioyning Together of Certaine Persons: And Also of the Lamentable Breach and Division Which Fell Amongst Them* [Middelburg, 1583], in *The Writings of Robert Harrison and Robert Browne*, 419.

wrought, nether anie one which hath but single authoritie, but first thei that have their authoritie together, as first the church ... and the voice of the Whole people, guided bie the elders and forwardest, is saied to be the voice of God ... Therefore the meetinges together of manie churches, also of everie Whole church, & of the elders therein, is above the Apostle, above the Prophet, the Evanglist, the Pastor, the Teacher, & everie particular Elder.[74]

In Browne's proposed polity the congregation would, as a "gathered" (entirely voluntary) assembly, stand above any individuals. The three corporate entities which exercise the office of teaching and guiding corporately are synods, meetings for prophecy (i.e., for extemporaneous prayer) and the meetings of the "eldershippe." Individual graces and offices are those with authority over many churches (the offices of apostle, prophet and evangelist, proper to the founding age and now extinct) and those with authority over a single local church: the pastor (whose principal gift is exhortation), the teacher, and the elder (for overseeing and counselling). The further offices of reliever (or deacon) and widow are for cherishing and relieving affliction.[75] Brown made clear, however, that the authority of these officers derived, not only from dominical founding, but from a free covenant between the ministers and their congregation.

The nomenclature of Browne's offices is not unlike that of the various Calvinist configurations. His sense of office is, however, decidedly more informal than in any of the church polities yet to emerge from the Reformation.

Wherefore for the offices of Pastor & elders etc. I say that everie Church of Christ hath them in effect, though not in name, & that no church of Christ can be or is without them. Yet againe I say that such offices of Pastorship, eldership & doctorship etc as they [the Catholics] seeke for, is in no church of Christ nor can be ... That the Church of Christ can not be without a pastorship or eldership is evident, because the Church it self is that most grave & ancient elder whereof Christ is the Elder & pastor being called the ancient of Daies & the cheif shepherd & pastor of the flocke ...

Further seeing an elder is nothing els in the scripture but anie person of special wisdome & honestie, lawfully allowed & called in the church to counsel, teach & geive advise without anie forcing, it is [*sic*] must needs follow that there are manie such elders in our churches or at least wise may be without anie such titles or popish usurping as they seek for. Wherefore if

[74] Browne, 399.
[75] Browne, *A Booke Which Sheweth the Life and Manners of All True Christians, and Howe Unlike They Are unto Turks and Papistes and Heathen Folke* (Middelburg: Richarde Painter, 1582), in *The Writings of Robert Harrison and Robert Browne*, 268–275.

in anie Church neighbours can wisely & godlie take up matters end controversies & redresse disorders without anie iniurie to other officers, & if some have special direction by authoritie to deal in such manner, they are no doubt lawfull elders before God & man & yet have no name of presbiters & elders.[76]

One imperative gift of the minister must be the capacity to lead the congregation in sincere, informal prayer. Worship within the Independency movement had fostered extemporaneous prayer and despised the Catholic readiness to rely entirely upon the reading of set liturgical formularies, which the Separatists called "stinted prayers." "Nowe then iff it be the office off the pastor and preacher, and part of his calling, toe pray, then must he be able off himselfe to do it: Whie then should a service, or reading off praiers be stinted unto him? For iff his lippes keep not knowledge [Mal 2:7], iff he can not minister the word With praier [Ac 6:4] he is not fit to be a pastor or watchman over the people."[77]

The authenticity of a renewed clergy would require, as well, that a pastor not be thrust upon a congregation by any outside authority, and that the clergy be supported by free-will offerings, not enforced tithing.[78] In a word, the seat of religious sovereignty was to be the autonomous congregation, within which the individual also retained significant liberties.

Browne's sometime partner Harrison took up the same theme, but with a pen dipped in a starker ink. The ministry in the established churches was rank with greed, sloth and ignorance.[79] This was due to

---

[76] Browne, "An Aunswer to Mr. Flowers Letter" (1588/1589), in *The Writings of Robert Harrison and Robert Browne*, 518–522. Browne is sure that the nomenclature is much less important than the spirit of the office. "In England also I have founde much more wronge done me by the preachers of discipline, then by anie the Byshops and more Lordly usurping by them, then by the other, so that as in Scotland, the preachers having no names of byshops did imprison me more wrongfully then anie Bishop," 519.

[77] *A True and Short Declaration*, in *The Writings of Robert Harrison and Robert Browne*, 415–416. Browne's Dutch venture in new community foundered on a dispute between himself and Harrison, who prevailed. Browne was excommunicated by them and returned to England, where he conformed eventually to the established church but through the course of his life continued uneasily before the law due to his persistence in congregational convictions. Those of like mind were for awhile called Brownists. [78] Ibid. 419.

[79] Robert Harrison, *A Little Treatise uppon the Firste Verse of the 122. Psalm. Stirring Up unto Carefull Desiring & Dutifull Labouring for True Church Governement* ([Middelburg,] 1583), in *The Writings of Robert Harrison and Robert Browne*, 119–120, 83; *A Treatise of the Church and the Kingdome of Christ* (unpublished, 1580/1581), ibid. 36. A typical appraisal by Harrison: "In Sion, which is the lordes Church The priests are clothed with salvation, but in these Churches the mynisters are clothed with destruction, for most of them are blinde guides, & dumbe dogges, destroiers and murtherers of soules, the rest which seem to have knowledge, are malitious." Ibid. 35.

clergy being imposed on local congregations by the government and
by bishops.

Often have I heard that kings and princes should waite what the L[ord]
should say unto them by the mouth or prophets & priestes, but never the
contrarie, that the prophets or any mynisters, should waite what god should
say to them by the mouth of magistrates.
   For none can preach the word of message but those that ar sent from the
mouth of the lord onlye and alone but they that com not only & alone from
the mouth of the lord but taketh ther warrant by antichristian autorytye
from the byshope ... [80]

How would the choice of the Lord be verified? Harrison answers
this in two ways. Every congregation has the right to provide for its
own needs, including those of preaching and ministry. And every
person who senses a call from the Lord has the right to enter the
ministry and invite others to authenticate that ministry, not by an
official warrant from those in higher authority, but by the intrinsic
worth of the minister's service. What, then, if a church should have
no access to officially called and ordained ministers?

Shall that church fer ever be deprived, after they have once wanted a
minister, for default of authoritie to call and ordain an other? By this reason,
every church should not be perfect in it selfe, nor have in it selfe meanes and
power to continue by that measure of lines which the Lord have measured
out unto it. And is it not a dishonour to Christ Iesus the head of every
congregation, which is his bodie: to say that his body together with the
heade, is not able to be sustained and preserved in it selfe?
   Moreover I demaund what calling the dispersed disciples of the churche
at Ierusalem had, that they did preache and teach the Gospell as they went?
Were they all ordained ministers, by whose meanes it is said that manie did
believe, and that the Lord was with them [Ac 11:21]?[81]
   I lay no more [burthen] upon them, but that they havinge the approval
and consent of their flocke, doo the works of a Minister, namely, that they
feede their flocke whereof the holy ghost have made them overseers ... their
worke shall commende them, and testifie their calling, and shall be in stead
of an Epistle or rather a licence written in their owne harts: undestood [*sic*]
also and redd of all men. Our Saviour Christ being demaunded whither he
were sent Saviour, or they shoulde look for an other: did not answer that he
was sent a Saviour, but saide: Tell Ihon what you have herde and sene: The
blinde see, the lame walke, the lepers are clensed, the deafe heare, the dead
are raised up, and the poor receyve the Gospell.[82]

[80] *A Treatise of the Church*, in *The Writings of Robert Harrison and Robert Browne*, 56, 40.
[81] *A Little Treatise*, ibid. 100.   [82] Ibid. 99.

The rhetorical warmth of the Independency advocates was heated up considerably by another Cambridge man, Welshman John Penry (1563–1593), who gave the movement a spunky turn in a series of satirical tracts which he is thought to have published clandestinely at the end of the 1580s, in the already hypersensitive atmosphere of the Armada and all that. His ardor was of no small account in giving early congregationalism a swell of sympathy in Wales.[83] Under the pseudonym of Martin Marprelate, he addresses his first tract impudently "To the right puissant and terrible priests, my clergy masters of the Confocation-house, whether Fickers-General, worshipful Paltripolitans, or any other of the Holy League of Subscription…

"Marprelate" spoke of "this false and bastardly government of archbishops and bishops,"[84] and referred to the episcopal regimen as "a superfluous honor, and a lewd libertie," its incumbents as "false prophets," "none of the Lord's anointing, but servants of the Beast," "ministers of antichrist."[85] The New Testament knows four offices only, he asserts, and they were instituted and retained by Christ because the church would always have need of them: "As, of pastors to feed with the word of wisdom; of the doctors to feed with the word of knowledge; and both to build up the body in the unity of faith; of elders to watch and oversee men's manners; of deacons to look unto the poor, and church treasury."[86] Abrogating some of these offices and accepting episcopal ones instead is a "maiming of the bodie of Christ," a violation that "hath been gainsaid and withstood by the visible church of God successively, and without intermission, for these almost 500 years last past."[87] Episcopacy deforms the church by its

[83] On Penry and the evidence for his authorship, see Donald J. McGinn, *John Penry and the Marprelate Controversy* (New Brunswick, NJ: Rutgers University Press, 1966). Erik Routley says of Marprelate's tracts: "It is the first appearance in England of the 'Publish and be Damned' technique: a burning social and religious conscience finding expression in unscrupulously personal and particularized language handled by a born columnist," *English Religious Dissent* (Cambridge: Cambridge University Press, 1960), 63.
[84] Martin the Metropolitan (Marprelate) [John Penry], *Hay Any Worke for Cooper: Or a Briefe Pistle Directed by Waye of an Hublication to the Reverende Byshopps…* [Coventry, 1589], in *The Marprelate Tracts 1588, 1589*, ed. William Pierce (London: James Clarke, 1911), 237.
[85] "Martin Marprelate" [John Penry], *Theses Martinianae: That is, Certaine Demonstrative Conclusions, Sette Down and Collected (As It Should Seeme) by that Famous and Renowned Clarke, the Reverend Martin Marprelate the Great: Serving as a Manifest and Sufficient Confutation of Al That Ever the Collodge of Catercaps with Their Whole Band of Clergie-Priests, Have or Can Bring for the Defence of Their Ambitious and Antichristian Prelacie* [Wolston, Warwickshire, 1589], in *The Marprelate Tracts*, 315–316.
[86] *Hay Any Worke for Cooper*, in *The Marprelate Tracts*, 236.　　　[87] Ibid. 312.

claim to a lordly superiority over other ministers ("Our Saviour Christ hath forbidden all ministers to be lords [Luke 22:25]");[88] by its merger with the peerage of the realm, the civil magistracy, giving lay lords rule over the spiritual realm and allowing churchmen to meddle in matters civil ("for a lord bishop to be of the Privy Council in a kingdom, according to the doctrine of the Church of England, is as profitable unto the realm as the wolf is to the lambs");[89] and by its entitlements to temporal revenues and assured affluence.[90]

The only act of jurisdiction he would wish the government to exercise would be the eradication of the illegitimate offices it had imposed:

I desire therein no more offices to be thrust out of the church at one time but archbishops and bishops. As for deans, archdeacons and chancellors, I hope they will be so kind unto my Lord's Grace as not to stay, if his Worship and the rest of the noble clergy-lords were turned out to grass.[91]

That the Independency movement had quickly caught the popular imagination is evidenced by the cascade of responses that each of Penry's successive tracts summoned into print, and by the fact that when he was arrested on other charges in 1593 and was strongly suspected to be the elusive Marprelate, he was quickly sent to the gallows.[92]

---

[88] Ibid. 221, 226.   [89] *Theses Martinianae*, in *The Marprelate Tracts*, 316.

[90] *Hay Any Worke for Cooper*, in *The Marprelate Tracts*, 220. For Penry's views, see further ibid. 229–237; *An Epitome of the First Booke of That Right Worshipfuill Volume Written against the Puritans in the Defence of the Noble Cleargie by as Worshipfull a Prieste John Bridges, Presbyter, Priest or Elder, Doctor of Divillity and Deane of Sarum* [Northamptonshire, 1588], in *The Marprelate Tracts*, 127–128.   [91] *Hay Any Worke for Cooper*, in *The Marprelate Tracts*, 230.

[92] Concurrent and congruent testimony to the founding beliefs of the English Separatists may be found in the works of two of their earliest martyrs, John Greenwood and Henry Barrow (also Cambridge men) who were arrested, imprisoned and executed at Tyburn in 1595 for seditious publications. *The Writings of John Greenwood 1587–1590, Together with the Joint Writings of Henry Barrow and John Greenwood 1587–1590*, ed. Leland H. Carlson, Elizabethan Nonconformist Texts 4 (London: George Allen & Unwin, 1962), 126–127, 160–166, 188–196, 200–213, 228–230, 242–259, 292–304; Henry Barrow, *A Brief Discoverie of the False Church* (1590), in *The Writings of Henry Barrow (1591–1593)*, ed. Leland H. Carlson, Elizabethan Nonconformist Texts 3 (London: George Allen & Unwin, 1962), 259–673. It ought be noted, as well, that the Separatists' depiction of the church, not as the nominally baptized membership carried indiscriminately on the parish rolls, but as the spiritual assembly of purposeful believers, drew down upon them frequent accusations of Donatism. See Harrison, *A Little Treatise*, 215; George Gifford, *A Plaine Declaration that Our Brownists be Full Donatists ...* (1590); Gifford, *A Short Treatise against the Donatists of Englands, Whome We Call Brownists* (1590); Greenwood, *An Answere to George Gifford's Pretended Defence of Read Praiers and Devised Liturgies* (Dort, 1590), in *The Writings of John Greenwood (1587–1590)*, 30–92. Barrow is remembered most for his insistence on spontaneous worship, but his views on church polity are quite coherent with those set forth above.

Swift and savage repression by an understandably threatened government drove the Separatists into exile in the Netherlands, into the company of a previously "tarrying" band of Puritans with whom they made common cause under the ardent leadership of John Robinson, into lasting memory as the source of the *Mayflower* Pilgrims, into eventual respite under the Cromwells' Protectorate, and then more systematic repression under the Clarendon Code of 1662. But for the purposes of this study, it ought be noted that their sojourn in the Netherlands helped to draw their doctrines to the later attention of the first continental Pietists, whose views on authentic Christian polity were beholden to their doughty British predecessors of a century earlier.[93]

THE PIETISTS

The Pietist movement, as it came (derisively at first) to be called, was an outburst of spiritual renewal, a third attempt at reform, that had broader and more enduring effects than could have been anticipated then or than have been adequately remembered now. Arising simultaneously amid Lutherans and Calvinists, it created lively schools in Halle, Württemberg, Saxony, Denmark and the Netherlands. Its influence flowed into Wesleyan Methodism, the Anglo-American evangelical Awakenings, the Moravians, the Mennonites and the various Brethren. And, as its founders were conscious of predecessors such as Tauler, Ruysbroeck, Suso and Kempis, they had like-minded, reforming Catholic contemporaries such as Teresa of Avila and John of the Cross, Francis de Sales, the Jansenists, the Quietists and the devotees of the Sacred Heart.

As regards our concern with ancient church services and offices, the Pietists would have had little to say, since they were little inclined to historical curiosity. But several very basic theological claims, with historical implications about early Christian polity, were made at the outset by the man often honored as Pietism's founder, Philipp Jakob Spener (1635–1705), an Alsatian Lutheran pastor. It all began with his brief manifesto, *Pia Desideria*, first published in 1675 and reissued

[93] Hans Leube, *Die Reformideen in der deutschen lutherischen Kirche zur Zeit der Orthodoxie* (Leipzig: Dörffling & Franke, 1924), 162–180; Leube, *Orthodoxie und Pietismus* (Bielefeld: Luther, 1975); Erich Beyreuther, "Der Ursprung des Pietismus und die Frage nach der Zeugenkraft der Kirche," *Evangelische Theologie*, 11 (1951/1952), 137–144; Friedrich Wilhelm Kantzenbach, *Orthodoxie und Pietismus* (Gütersloh: Gütersloher Verlag, 1966), 130–132; Martin Schmidt, *Pietismus* (Stuttgart: Kohlhammer, 1972), 24–28; Schmidt, *Der Pietismus als theologische Erscheinung* (Göttingen: Vandenhoeck & Ruprecht, 1984).

many times as a popular (though bitterly controverted) pamphlet.[94]
In it he evoked what he called Luther's doctrine of the spiritual
priesthood:

[N]ot only ministers but all Christians are made priests by their Savior, are
anointed by the Holy Spirit, and are dedicated to perform spiritual-priestly
acts. Peter was not addressing preachers alone when he wrote, "You are a
chosen race, a royal priesthood, a holy nation, God's own people, that you
may declare the wonderful deeds of him who called you out of darkness into
his marvelous light" . . . all spiritual functions are open to all Christians
without exception. Although the regular and public performance of them is
entrusted to ministers appointed for this purpose, the functions may be
performed by others in case of emergency. Especially should those things
which are unrelated to public acts be done continually by all at home and
in everyday life.
    Indeed, it was by a special trick of the cursed devil that things were
brought to such a pass in the papacy that all these spiritual functions were
assigned solely to the clergy ... and the rest of the Christians were excluded
from them, as if it were not proper for laymen diligently to study the Word
of the Lord, much less to instruct, admonish, chastise, and comfort their
neighbors, or to do privately what pertains to the ministry publicly,
inasmuch as all these things were supposed to belong openly to the office of
the minister.[95]

As he returned to this theme Spener augmented it with several
points of a disciplinary nature, which he did not, however, sustain
with much historical evidence. The assignment of public ministry to
preachers and private ministry to ordinary Christians (including, he
noted explicitly, women) could be modified insofar as any believer
might confer the sacrament of baptism when it was urgently needed
and no preacher was available. But since the eucharist could not

---

[94] "The existence of over five hundred controversial pamphlets dating from the last decade of
     the seventeenth century testifies to the extent of the strife. The charge of the theological
     faculty of the University of Wittenberg that pietists were guilty of at least 284 heresies
     suggests something of its bitterness. Radical excesses were ascribed to the conservative
     Spener, who was called a Quaker, a Rosicrucian, a chiliast, a fanatic." Theodore G.
     Tappert, ed. and trans., in Spener's *Pia Desideria* (Philadelphia: Fortress, 1964),
     Introduction, 23.
[95] Spener, *Pia Desideria*, 93–94. This translates *Pia Desideria: oder, hertzliches Verlangen nach
     Gottgefälliger Besserung der wahren Evangelischen Kirchen* (Frankfurt: J. D. Zunner, 1680 [1st
     edn. 1675]) 104–106; reproduced in Philipp Jakob Spener, *Schriften*, ed. Erich Beyreuther,
     I (Hildesheim and New York: Georg Olms, 1979), 250–252. Five strident years later Spener
     restated this doctrine, sustaining it with numerous references to the New Testament: *Das
     Geistliche Priesterthum auss Göttlichem Wort Kürtzlich beschrieben und mit einstimmenden Zeugnüssen
     Gottseliger Lehrer bekräfftiget* (Frankfurt: J. D. Zunner, 1677), qq. 11, 26, 31, 40, 44, 54–61, 70,
     reproduced in *Schriften*, I (1982), 569ff; translated by Peter C. Erb in *Pietists: Selected
     Writings* (New York: Paulist, 1983), 50–64.

entail such urgent necessity, it might not be initiated by non-preachers.[96] Some years later, however, he allowed that a dearth of preachers might in particular instances work such a hardship on believers that it would not be wrong for them to celebrate the Lord's Supper by themselves. Since any believer has the right and power to preach publicly when preachers are not available, and since sacraments only put the seal on God's Word, then believers ought also be enabled to enact both sacraments rather than go without them for want of a preacher.[97]

The relationship between preachers and listeners he described in ambivalent terms. On the one hand, Christians were to listen critically and to judge the authenticity of their preachers.[98] On the other, they were to look to their preachers as moral exemplars,[99] follow and obey their instruction,[100] and submit to their governance for they are God's envoys.[101] Yet even when they preside the preachers are not to function like a landed aristocracy. They are not to lord it over one another, for preachers, whatever their titles, are all of the same rank.[102] Nor are they to lord it over their fellow Christians, for though they are called directly by God they are also called through the church and accountable to the appraisal of their fellow believers.[103] In one context an egalitarian Spener portrays the preacher as "oldest brother"; in another, he speaks of the preacher as "father."[104] In some passages he stresses that preachers are chosen for fidelity, not intellectual prowess;[105] on the other hand, he says that they require education in order to offer reliable instruction and shrewd counsel.[106]

Spener's reconstruction of the early church is largely controlled by his own reforming determination to activate ordinary believers. His

---

[96] *Geistliche Priesterthum*, q. 66. On the public role of preachers, qq. 59; also *Einfältige Erklärung der christlichen Lehr nach der Ordnung dess kleinen Catechismi dess theuren Manns Gottes Lutheri* (Frankfurt: J. D. Zunner, 1677), reproduced in *Schriften*, 2, 1 (1982), qq. 236, 1215; on women as equals, *Geistliche Priesterthum*, qq. 60–61.

[97] *Kurtze Catechismuspredigten* (Frankfurt: J. D. Zunner, 1689), 451–452, reproduced in *Schriften*, 2, 2 (1989).   [98] *Geistliche Priesterthum*, q. 70.

[99] *Einfältige Erklärung*, qq. 1219, 1223.   [100] Ibid. q. 1227.

[101] *Geistliche Priesterthum*, q. 68; *Einfältige Erklärung*, qq. 1227, 1228, 1230.

[102] *Einfältige Erklärung*, qq. 1213ff, 1219; *Kurtze Catechismuspredigten*, 691.

[103] *Einfältige Erklärung*, q. 608; *Kurtze Catechismuspredigten*, 691. See also Spener's *Consilia et Judicia Theologica Latina: Opus Posthumum* (Frankfurt: J. D. Zunner & J. A. Jungius, 1709), 1, 2, 2, pp. 304–324; *Schriften*, 16 (1989); German version: *Letzte Theologische Bedencken und andere Brieffliche Antworten* (Halle: Wäysenhaus, 1711), 351–420; Schriften, 15 (1987).

[104] *Pia Desideria*, 109 (*Schriften*, 1:255); *Einfältige Erklärung*, q. 1230.

[105] *Geistliche Priesterthum*, qq. 31, 37.7; *Einfältige Erklärung*, q. 1220.

[106] *Geistliche Priesterthum*, q. 65; *Einfältige Erklärung*, q. 1185.

program was to form them into small *collegia pietatis*, or scriptural reflection groups, which would elicit mutual support for a more intentional life of faith. These *ecclesiolae in ecclesia*, which proved more centrifugal than he anticipated, seemed to his opponents to fragment the church exactly to the degree they succeeded in summoning the laity (a designation Spener deplored) to active and autonomous responsibility for each other. As a historical reconstruction it was not very systematic or scholarly, but Spener was to be followed by a gifted and more radical Pietist who is often thought of as Protestantism's first church historian and who may have had the longest impact upon Protestant thinking of any first-generation Pietist.[107]

Gottfried Arnold (1666–1714) began his scholarly career with several monographs on figures of the early patristic period.[108] Then he produced, in rapid succession, two immense works which served as the authoritative reconstructions of early Christianity for Protestant readers throughout the eighteenth century: his *Erste Liebe* in 1696 and his *Kirchen- und Ketzer-Historie* in 1699–1700.[109]

The earliest Christians are described by Arnold as all that Spener could have hoped for. Filled with the Spirit, they performed miracles and even their children were given the understanding of mysteries.

---

[107] Erich Seeberg, *Gottfried Arnold, in Auswahl herausgegeben* (Munich: A. Langen & G. Miller, 1934), 535ff.

[108] Gottfried Arnold: *Zwei Send-Schreiben aus der ersten Apostolischen Kirchen: Deren das eine ist des heiligen Jüngers und Paulinischen Gefehrten Barnabae, das andere des heiligen Märtyrers und Aufsehers zu Rom Clementis*, together with *Erstes Martyrthum oder merckwürdigste Geschichte der ersten Märtyrer* (J. G. Lipper, 1695); *Fratrum Sororumque Appellatio inter Christianos maxime & alios quondam Usitata, tum & Cognatio Christianorum Spiritualis, ex Antiquitate Monumentis Commentatione Illustrata. Accessit Christanorum ad Metalla Damnatorum Historia* (Frankfurt: J. C. König, 1696); *Des heiligen Macarii Homilien, oder Geistliche Reden um das Jahr Christi CCCXL gehalten* (Gosslar: J. C. König, 1696); *Ein Denckmahl des alten Christenthums bestehend in des Heil. Macarii und anderer hocherleuchteter Männer ... Schriften* (Gosslar: J. C. König, 1699); *Auserlesene Sendschreiben derer Alten zum gemeinen Zug gesammlet und verteutscht* (Frankfurt and Leipzig: T. P. Calvisius, 1700); *Des heiligen Clementis von Rom Recognitiones oder Historie von denen Reisen und Reden des Apostels Petri* (Berlin: J. M. Rüdiger, 1702); *Güldene Send-Schreiben derer alten Christen mit Sonderbaren Fleisz gesammlet und ins Teutsche gebracht* (Büdingen: J. F. Regelein, 1723).

[109] *Die erste Liebe der Gemeinen Jesu Christi. Das ist: Wahre Abbildung der ersten Christen nach ihren lebendigen Glauben und heiligen Leben, Aus der ältesten und bewährtesten Kirchen-Scribenten eigenen Zeugnissen, Exempeln und Reden, nach der Wahrheit der ersten einigen Christlichen Religion, allen Liebhabern der historischen Wahrheit, und sonderlich der Antiqvität, als in einer nützlichen Kirchen-Historie, treulich und unparteyisch entworffen* (Frankfurt: G. Friedeburg, 1696), cited herein from the 1712 (Frankfurt: Bensch) edition; and *Unparteyische Kirchen- und Ketzer-Historie, vom Anfang des Neuen Testaments bisz auf das Jahr Christi 1688* (Frankfurt: T. Fritsch, 1699–1700), cited herein from the 1740 Schaffhausen (E. & B. Hurter) edition. The latter simply melds into the original text a series of glosses that had previously been published as *Supplementa, Illustrationes, und Emendationes Zur Verbesserung der Kirchen-Historie* (Frankfurt: T. Fritsch, 1703).

Layfolk preached, and preachers were judged by their audience. No Christian sought or was granted command over another, and even the officers deferred to the common mind of the congregation.[110]

When the community called forth some members to office, they chose persons of high and low social status: some were manual laborers who retained their crafts. No premium was put on erudition, because teachers were chosen for their devout lives, since their most salient teaching would be their exemplary integrity. Far from being a salaried sinecure (indeed, during persecution it was most exposed to risk), public office was often accepted only after repeated refusals. The call to serve was ascribed to the Spirit and to the whole community. Though a variety of titles emerge from the literature (teacher, community chief, president, etc.) incumbents usually preferred the simple designation of "fellow workers." They were honored for their humility, for they acted as servants, not masters.[111]

Apostolic missionaries, in Arnold's reconstruction, first roved the world as itinerant teachers. When local communities were formed with their own resident leadership, they sometimes had lay teachers like Origen to instruct them. There were no high walls at first between these local churches. The communities were independent of any authority higher than their own, yet when their bishops acted beyond the boundaries of their local church (for example, Polycarp in Rome, Epiphanius in Jerusalem, Paulinus in Barcelona), it was by virtue of their unbounded zeal, not any hierarchical jurisdiction. In this universal spirit Clement, Ignatius and Polycarp sent letters to other churches, and Cyprian, Ambrose, Augustine and Basil sent out circular letters. Visiting preachers were offered the local pulpit freely.[112]

After several centuries of this fraternal zeal, the primitive community was victimized by a new style of clerical official, and deformed into a style patronized by the Roman papacy. The local bishop, who had previously been a peer of the college of elders (the titles of *episkopos*, *presbyter* and *diakonos* had originally been interchangeable), became a tyrant in the Roman style. Dioceses were fragmented into parishes and the bishop claimed monarchical authority on the strength of spurious "apostolic" regulations. The rigorous ancient prohibition against the transfer of bishops (usually from smaller to wealthier sees) testifies to a noticeable and growing greed in their

---

[110] *Erste Liebe*, 2, 5.   [111] Ibid. 2, 8–10.   [112] Ibid. 2, 11, 1–5.

ranks. Scholars, observes Arnold, were generally in agreement that
the single, authoritative bishop was an innovation (probably during
the second century). If the texts of Clement, Ignatius and Polycarp
could be restored to authenticity, it would become evident that in
their time a great shift had occurred, marked by a change in their
attitude from pastoral care to a craving for power. Paul's ideal of an
alert watchman, Ignatius' and Augustine's ideal of an attentive
servant: these vanish before a new notion of bishop identified with
rank and honor.

The ancient Hebrew notion that one people, or one tribe, was
God's inheritance (*kleros*) had been superseded by the Christian
doctrine that the entire priestly people of Christ were God's
inheritance. The officers then took that title to themselves. They
alone would be the clerics, and even within their own ranks an
echeloned structure of command destroyed the primitive order of
deference to virtue. (This stratification of bishops, likening them to a
civil government, dates from the time of Cyprian, according to
Arnold's reading of scholarly opinion.) An early sign of this
perversion was the audacity of bishops to forbid presbyters to preach
in the presence of bishops, and to prevent laity from preaching
altogether. The so-called laity had been stripped of their native
dignity by a clergy that had usurped their original powers.[113]

At first sight Arnold seems unclear about when the degeneration of
the early church occurred. In some passages he sees it in the second
century, yet it is clear that for him Ignatius is a paragon, not the
villain he had been to the Protestant reformers and would be to later,
especially Lutheran, scholars. Cyprian's age is identified in other
passages as the evil season, yet Cyprian is often cited as an exemplar
of the servant-bishop. It is in the concluding book of his great work
that Arnold focuses his attention on the cataclysmic event for
authentic Christianity: the settlement of Constantine.[114]

In several respects Arnold brings to the issue of office in the church
a sophistication well beyond that of either the Magisterial Reformers
or their systematizing successors. He commands a library of texts far
richer than any of them could have used, and he is the beneficiary of
a growing scholarship about textual authenticity and integrity.[115]
Also, in a brief period of untypical ecumenicity that Pietism was

---

[113] Ibid. 2, 11, 6–20. *Kirchen- und Ketzer-Historie*, 1, 2, 2.   [114] Ibid. 8, esp. chs. 7–19.
[115] In his *Auserlesene Sendschreiben*, for instance, he capably discusses textual problems in
    Clement and Ignatius, 4v – 5v.

encouraging, he had sympathetic access to works by the Catholics and the Calvinists, thus providing him with some new perspective on his own Lutheran doctrine. But his use of this apparatus was handicapped by an undisciplined use of texts without much orderly sense of their chronological and geographic identity. Thus he is likely to substantiate a particular point about early second-century practice by a jumble of quotations from 1 Peter, Gregory of Nazianzen, Jerome, Osiander, Tertullian and Chrysostom.

Also, as we have seen in some of his antecedents, there is rarely a protest that is not also a program. His presentation of evidence was ordered, not simply by the scholarly array of ancient evidence, but by the thriving religious community whose ideals and reform he was at pains to justify. Arnold was a polemicist who was ransacking history to give a scholarly rationale for a spiritual renewal in the church. In many respects his intellectual agenda was dictated by the earlier classical historians of the Reformation he wished to refute: the Centuriators of Magdeburg. As Eduard Fueter has said, his work figures more in the history of ecclesiastical polemic than within church history itself.[116] His determination to verify a specific church order put his scholarship under strict obedience to the Pietist ideal.[117] Also, just after publishing his two great historical works he took up pastoral ministry himself, and his own changing perspective then added a new commitment to which his later handling of the evidence deferred.[118] What marks his work as interesting was his designation of Constantine in the fourth century, not Ignatius in the second century, as the force that compromised the charismatically free leadership of the apostolic era by the establishment of ordained officers in the early church.

[116] Eduard Fueter, *Geschichte der Neueren Historiographie* (Munich and Berlin: R. Oldenbourg, 1911), 267–269.
[117] This has been noticed by F. Ernest Stoeffler, *German Pietism during the Eighteenth Century*, Studies in the History of Religions 24 (Leiden: Brill, 1973), 178, 181; also Martin Schmidt, *Der Pietismus als theologische Erscheinung*, Gesammelte Studien zur Geschichte des Pietismus 2 (Göttingen: Vandenhoeck & Ruprecht, 1984), 122, 131–132.
[118] Jürgen Büchsel, *Gottfried Arnold: Sein Verständnis von Kirche und Wiedergeburt*, Arbeiten zur Geschichte des Pietismus 8 (Witten: Luther, 1970), 11. Shortly after taking up ministry Arnold published a parson's handbook, *Die Geistliche Gestalt Eines Evangelischen Lehrers, Nach dem Sinn und Exempel der Alten Ans Licht gestellet … mit … Anhang Eines Antwortschreibens An einen Prediger, über mancherley Angelegenheiten In deszen Amt und Beruff* (Halle: Wäysenhaus, 1704), cited here from the 1723 edition (Frankfurt and Leipzig: J. G. Böhmen). In this book Arnold comes to amplify his sense of the minister's task (which he had previously restricted essentially to preaching) and to be much less suspicious of ministry as the primary obstacle to a church of born-again, spontaneous Christians. See Büchsel, 184; also Seeberg, *Gottfried Arnold*, 150.

THE QUAKERS

In 1656 Richard Hodden, governor of Kinsale, wrote to Oliver Cromwell's son Henry in command of the English army then ravaging Ireland, to appeal against an order that the Quakers in the area should be rounded up as a threat to the peace. "My Lord, I beseech you consider that Reformation is began not finished, and the foundation and principal part thereof spiritual, without which all outward forms are but deceit ... "[119] By the middle of the seventeenth century in England religious dissent had spawned such a bewilderment of antagonized sects that they threatened to capsize the established religion. All of these movements regarded the Reformation as "began not finished." To begin with, the establishment itself was given a split personality when the Solemn Covenant of 1643 secured Scottish support for Cromwell's parliamentary army by pledging not only to establish Presbyterianism in Scotland but also to reform the Churches of England and Ireland in the Calvinist mode. Hobbled by such an inward schism, the establishment was then surrounded by a swirl of dissent: Puritans and Brownists, Baptists and Congregationalists, Ranters and Levellers, Muggletonians and Seekers and Watchers. Standing out among them all for the radicalism of their articulated views on early church order were the Friends, who soon accepted the epithet of "Quakers."

Their founder, the intrepid George Fox, was nearly as hostile towards the Protestants as towards the Papists. It was his contention that authentic Christian religion could consist only in sincere inner devotion, of which external institutions were not the embodiment or the incarnation, but the inevitable counterfeit.

The true ministers of Jesus Christ have always been, and are still, such as come not by the will of man, but by the will of God, neither are they fitted for the work by anything of man, but by God alone: for the true ministry is the gift of Jesus Christ, and needs no addition of human help and learning; but as the work is spiritual, and of the Lord, so they are spiritually fitted only by the Lord, and therefore he chose herdsmen, fishermen, and plowmen, and such like ... And as they "received" the gift freely, so they were to "give freely" ...

But the ministers of the world receive their learning at Oxford and Cambridge, and are taught of men, and speak a divination of their own brain, which is conjuring: and bewitch the people with those things that are

[119] William C. Braithwaite and Henry J. Cadbury, *The Beginnings of Quakerism*, 2nd edn. (Cambridge: Cambridge University Press, 1955), 216.

carnal: [such] as to sprinkle infants, and tell them of a sacrament which there is no scripture for; and saying they are the ministers of Christ, [while they] act those things which he forbids, [such] as to "have the chiefest place in the assemblies."[120]

Fox's ministers, of whom the prototypes were called Publishers of Truth, were in the pure prophetic model. They presented themselves as divinely gifted to preach, they required authentication from no person or assembly, and they required neither education nor ordination.

> For the Lord had sent me with his everlasting gospel to preach, and his word of life to bring them off all those temples, tithes, priests and rudiments of the world, that had gotten up since the apostles' days, and had been set up by such who had erred from the spirit and power the apostles were in; so that they might all come to know Christ their teacher, their counsellor, their shepherd to feed them, and their bishop to oversee them and their prophet to open to them, and to know their bodies to be the temples of God and Christ for them to dwell in.[121]

Fox was a vehement reformer, and his convictions about ministry and office stemmed from several antipathies to which he made repeated reference. He despised, for instance, the term "church" to denominate a building (he preferred "steeplehouse") because it derogated from the first sense of "church" as a community of believers. Similarly, he deplored tithing as an involuntary tax upon the faithful for their ministers, and benefices as a corrupting incentive for the ministry. He rejected the notion of ministry as a learned profession because it displaced the notion of ministry as a divine call and a sincere response. And, like the Pietists, he rejected all notion of rank that would divide laity from clergy or exalt some clergy over others.

Like most exuberant founders Fox was followed by a systematic, second-generation disciple who would articulate his insights more coherently. Robert Barclay was that disciple. Converted after an early training in a Jesuit college under his uncle as headmaster, he was able to give an account of Quaker polity which he published first in Latin, and only then in English. The church, he explained, is the

---

[120] George Fox (with James Nayler), *Saul's Errand to Damascus* (1653), quoted in *Early Quaker Writings, 1650–1700*, ed. Hugh Barbour and Arthur O. Roberts (Grand Rapids: Eerdmans, 1973), 259, 256–257.
[121] *The Journal of George Fox*, ed. John L. Nickalls (Philadelphia: Religious Society of Friends, 1985), 109.

mystical body of Christ, provided by divine gift with a diversity of specially endowed members: apostles, pastors, evangelists, etc. This "Catholic Church" is called, or gathered, by God, and comprises "those who profess Christ and Christianity in words, and have the benefit of the scriptures, as become obedient to the holy light and testimony of God in their hearts, so as to become sanctified by it, and cleansed from the evil of their ways." It is a church, therefore, that has always existed, and which comprises many (even unwitting) members among all Christian sects, and Turks and Jews as well, for it is an invisible fellowship.[122]

Those who publicly profess belief in Jesus Christ in a particular "gathered" church are in a visible fellowship, by contrast. As a visible fellowship, it was summoned into being by Jesus but fell into great apostasy almost immediately after the age of the apostles:

For after that the princes of the earth came to take upon them that profession, and it ceased to be a reproach to be a Christian, but rather became a means to preferment; men became such by birth and education, and not by conversion and renovation of spirit; then there was none so vile, none so wicked, none so profane, who became not a member of the church. And the teachers and pastors thereof becoming the companions of princes, and so being enriched by their benevolence, and getting vast treasures and estates, became puffed up, and as it were drunken with the vain pomp and glory of this world: and so marshalled themselves in manifold orders and degrees; not without innumerable contests and altercations who should have the precedency. So the virtue, life, substance, and kernel of the Christian religion came to be lost, and nothing remained but a carcass of Christianity.[123]

Every good Christian – man and woman alike – is a preacher, Barclay taught, but God calls some to ministry. The call is not transmissible through ordination or succession, for the gift becomes extinguished in a lifeless church and can never be passed on by one who is ungodly. Ministers are called directly by God. Other humans cannot ordain them, but other human beings can detect the Spirit at work:

Christ ... doth also, for the preserving them in a lively, fresh, and powerful condition, raise up and move among them by the inward immediate operation of his own Spirit, ministers and teachers, to instruct and teach,

---

[122] Robert Barclay, *An Apology for the True Christian Divinity, Being an Explanation and Vindication of the Principles and Doctrines of the People Called Quakers* (Philadelphia: Friends' Bookstore, [1918?]), Proposition 10, par. 2, p. 258. This book was first published in Latin in 1676, and in English in 1678.   [123] Ibid. 10, 5, pp. 261–262 .

and watch over them, who thus being called, are manifest in the hearts of their brethren, and their call is thus verified in them, who by the feeling of that life and power that passeth through them, being inwardly builded up by them daily in the most holy faith, become the seals of their apostleship.[124]

Ministry then has three prerequisites: the call of the Spirit, mental talents and professional training. But the first of these is the only essential one, "because the Spirit and grace of God can make up this want in the most rustic and ignorant; but this knowledge can no ways make up the want of the Spirit in the most learned and eloquent... A man of a good upright heart may learn more in half an hour, and be more certain of it, by waiting upon God, than by reading a thousand of their volumes [of scholastic theology]; which by filling his head with many needless imaginations, may well stagger his faith, but never confirm it."[125]

Quakers repudiate all hierarchical authorities: the pope and bishops of the Papists, the primates of the national episcopal churches; the consistory and synod of the presbyterian churches. The Spirit of God is the only order, ruler and governor in the church, and the diverse gifts for apostles, prophets, pastors, teachers, etc. are different operations of one Spirit, not separate offices. Indeed, "speaking from the Spirit of truth is not only peculiar to pastors and teachers, who ought so to prophesy; but even a common privilege to the saints. For though to instruct, teach and exhort, be proper to such as are more particularly called to the work of ministry; yet it is not so proper to them, as not to be, when the saints are met together, as any of them are moved by the Spirit, common to others."[126]

Like the Pietists, the Quakers meant by "ministry" only the call and empowerment to preach. But already in Fox's time another office had been admitted: elders. These were always non-ministers, whose task was described as encouraging and supporting those who went forth to preach. They quickly moved in, however, to discipline ministers in whom a spirit breathed with too harsh or foul a breath.[127]

---

[124] Ibid. 10, 14, p. 281.
[125] Ibid. 10, 19, p. 291; 10, 21, p. 295. For further exposition of the antipathy between the academics and the Quakers, see Braithwaite and Cadbury, *Beginnings of Quakerism*, 294–299. [126] Barclay, *Apology*, 10, 26, p. 302.
[127] Another writer, Robert Barclay of the nineteenth century (a descendant of Robert Barclay the [seventeenth century] Apologist), noted the steady move of the elders into positions of supervision over the ministers as a severe compromise in authentic Quaker piety and polity. *The Inner Life of the Religious Societies of the Commonwealth* (London: Hodder & Stoughton,

Elders, "though they be not moved to a frequent testimony by way of declaration in words, yet as such are grown up in the experience of the blessed work of truth in their hearts ... watch over and privately admonish the young, take care of the widows, the poor, the fatherless, and look that nothing be wanting, but that peace, love, unity, concord, and soundness be preserved in the church of Christ; and this answers to the deacons mentioned [in] Acts 6."[128]

THE SPIRITUALIST REVOLT

The Magisterial Reformation of the sixteenth century created churches that proved disappointing to their most ardent disciples. The Lutheran, Reformed/Presbyterian and Anglican establishments were thus faced with local insurrections, led by charismatic figures, that in their turn would beget another wave of reform that (often contrary to the intentions of their founders) yielded a new generation of churches of protest, all of them concerned with church polity, as expressed in the classical writers we have reviewed.

All three movements concurred in the elements of their polity. The church, they agreed, is a "gathered" assembly of those who as adults draw apart from a sinful world, and are actively called by the Spirit to minister to their fellows. Thus there is no fundamental division into "clergy" and "laity." Though the church may retain from its founding era a differentiation of titles and functions among its public ministers, there is no hierarchy of honor or authority among them.

The warrant to minister publicly in the church is a calling from God. It is not conferred by ecclesial ordination. It may be recognized by the church: by mutual covenant with the local congregation (Independents), by election within the church and incorporation by the ministers (Pietists), or by simple acknowledgement (Quakers).

The populist/democratic spirit of the church requires that there be no social stratification separating ministers from one another

1879 [1st edn. 1876]), ch. 22, pp. 522–540. He sees the encroachment of ruling elders as a Presbyterian influence. Braithwaite and Cadbury see them as a Baptist-inspired measure to curb disorderly conduct by ministers, and they likewise consider the empowerment of this office as regressive: *Beginnings of Quakerism*, 140–142, 310ff, 332–333; *The Second Period of Quakerism*, 2nd edn. (Cambridge: Cambridge University Press, 1961), 541ff.

[128] Barclay, *Apology*, 10, 26, p. 305. This exposition of church and ministry is more briefly set forth in another work of Barclay which was one of the most influential of all early Quaker publications, his *Catechism and Confession of Faith* (1673), ch. 9, reprinted in *Early Quaker Writings*, 314–337.

(Pietists), ministry from laity (Independents), or believers among themselves (Quakers). Thus class, affluence and gender are de-emphasized among believers.

Ministers were to be moral paragons for the faithful; they need not be learned academically, but must be capable of initiating articulate worship and offering incisive preaching. To remain faithful, the ministers must not be supported by tithing or any other non-voluntary taxation.

To remain faithful, the church must not be subject to princes or civil governors.

In a sense, this moves along the trajectory laid out by Calvin, but does so with a dogged consistency that pursues Calvin's early thoughts more stubbornly. It differs most in emphasis, which purposely forfeits detail in order to highlight the primacy of spiritual proficiency, and of congregational and individual liberty.

Independency, Pietism and Quakerism were all reactive to a Reformation that had seemed to go back on its original promises. They differed in their manner of argument. As they were all spiritual correctives to deadening formalities supported by a theological orthodoxy, they were not likely to be primarily intellectual move-ments. Yet there was variance among them. George Fox took an approach so explicitly anti-intellectual that it did not even aspire to present a learned argument. The Quaker claim to resume the apostolic ministry is grounded on no references to any ancient documents except the scriptures, and these are for the most part treated only homiletically. Gottfried Arnold, on the other extreme, was pleading his case with abundant documentation from the early church.

There is another difference. The Separatists and the Pietists were at great pains to protect their appeal for a devout ministry from accusations of Donatism. The Quakers, by contrast, though perhaps unaware of the heresy that had torn the Western church apart in the counter-establishment protest of the fourth and fifth centuries, qualify as vigorous, wholehearted Donatists. Despite the fundamental Quaker teaching that through an inspired ministry Jesus is now directly and immediately leading his people, the moral virtue of the preachers was considered the essential conduit of divine grace:

It is the life of Christianity, taking place in the heart, that makes a Christian ... therefore when this life ceaseth in one, then that one ceaseth to be a Christian; and all power, virtue, and authority, which he had as a Christian, ceaseth with it; so that if he had been a minister or teacher, he ceaseth to be so any more; and though he retain the form, and hold to the authority in words, yet that signifies no more, nor is it of any more real virtue and authority, than the mere image of a dead man.[129]

This created serious ambiguity for the classical Quaker understanding of divine influence. On the one hand, God was asserted to act without human intermediaries when he confers ministry on a person. Yet the divine endowment is given precisely so that this person can and will then affect others ... as a human intermediary. And this enablement is a fragile endowment, one that will be destroyed by serious sinfulness in its bearer. The church thus begins with a strong sense of the mediation of divine grace through humans, equivocally joined to a strong repudiation of the stability or even the admissibility of humans as mediators of grace at all.

Another anomaly is the early Quaker understanding of the autonomy of preachers. The originating theology portrays every inspired minister as a divinely empowered individual accountable to no one. Almost immediately, however, an office with equally valid New Testament warrants (named after the elders but modelled on the deacons as well) is acknowledged and reinforced as having governance over the charismatic, prophetic ministers. Contrary to the radical Quaker principle that human appointment cannot carry divine authority, the elders are appointed by the meetings to bring the inspired preachers to heel, thus effectively subordinating divine messengers to human appointees.

Through the course of reform movements in the fourteenth, the sixteenth, and the seventeenth and eighteenth centuries, there was a repetition of several themes regarding the polity of the church.

The primitive church of the apostolic period, as known by the testimony of the New Testament, was to serve as the norm for the restoration of the church in their day. As response to the Catholic claim that there was an invariable tradition of ministries and offices from which they had estranged themselves, the reformers distinguished two classes of ministry in the New Testament: those which were needed for the foundational period (apostles, prophets, evangelists) and those which were to be ongoing (*episkopoi, presbyteroi* and *diakonoi*). Rather than agree with the Catholics that the succession of bishops had retained the presence of the apostolic office in the church, they claimed that the extraordinary charismatic ministries

---

[129] Barclay, *Apology*, 10, 10, p. 270.

had been revived for the renewal of the church in their time, a moment in the life of the church as momentous as its founding. Rather than agree with the Catholics that the three permanent official titles represented an ordered and differentiated hierarchy, they claimed these were originally synonyms for one unranked ministry. Thus they could construe their controversy with the Papists as a reiteration of the ancient dispute between legitimacy and fidelity: the Catholics may have retained some formal continuities with the past, but those traditions were corrupt and had to be overthrown to renew the spirit of the church. Fidelity to the gospel required a new legitimacy.

The purpose and source of all ministry being a holiness that God alone confers, the reformers denied any sacramental character in ordination. The clergy could not confer it; their role was to examine candidates in their character and capacity to preach the word; to ask the popular membership of the churches to select the candidates they wished in ministry; and to ratify that congregational or synodal choice.

Since the intrusion of the secular authorities and the creation of taxation for the support of the clergy had been two innovations that corrupted the ministry, the reformers urged that the authorities of the state have no say in the church, that there be no coercive civil laws that sent people unwillingly to church; and that the ministry be supported by freewill offerings.

As we have seen, however, these contentions of the first generation in each wave of reform were difficult to sustain. The threat of new rogue political forces in the Reform induced the princes and nobility and statesmen to put the churches on a tight leash; financial needs and legacies soon gave the new churches a financial establishment; the need for supervision brought back an ordered hierarchy; professionalization of the ministry eventually put effective power of selection and admission back in the hands of the clergy; resistance to further breakaway movements led the new establishments to appeal to their own traditions as normative for Christian legitimacy. Already in each movement's second generation (Melanchthon, Beza, Barclay, etc.) there was the realization that authentic reform was a matter of spiritual renewal, and that the old formalities could have been acceptable if redeemed by a purified personnel.

The conviction that ministry in the apostolic age was normative for all time, that it was exercised by men inspired by the Lord and chosen by the faithful, that it was egalitarian, not hierarchical, that it was empowered to gather the people and preach the word but not to interfere with each believer's direct transactions in grace from God, and that it was meant to be unbound from the civil power and financial endowments – this was a conviction that endured in the consciences of the reformed churches even when it was compromised in practice.

The Protestants and their spiritual predecessors and successors started out to reform what they perceived to be a perverse and corrupt establishment. Resistance to their demands enlivened not only their determination but also their speculation. Almost to their own surprise they were carried, not only to reform the church, but to redesign it. Their theological method was to appeal to the earliest Christian community as norm and model. Their reconstruction of that model – whatever the stresses put upon it by the vagaries of church life and politics that ensued – deserves to be remembered as perhaps three successive reformations. They were ventures of repristination in the church (or, as it turned out, churches) that proved to be the early ancestors of a great and sustained theological effort to which we must now turn our attention.

CHAPTER 2

The nineteenth century: a new consensus is formulated

The discussion – or wrangle – over community organization in the early church revived in the nineteenth century, and with the availability of new sources and refined critical methods it became more complex, developed and lively.

The beginnings of biblical criticism had made it possible – though not in sophisticated enough fashion to justify the confident reliance scholars would put upon it – to discern earlier from later New Testament publications, and hence to reconstruct a chronology of events and of theological development in the first (and, as many thought, early second) century. In addition, textual criticism of the patristic literature now enabled scholars to date texts and to verify their authenticity better than before. This led the partisans of the consensus to hypothesize that in the most primitive period there were no officers or church organization, but that they had become solidly established in the course of the second century. This raised the question: what had caused a change which (in the view of these scholars) represented such a retrograde step?

To track this new phase of the consensus one must begin in Germany, and with three early protagonists: Richard Rothe of Heidelberg, Ferdinand Christian Baur of Tübingen and Albrecht Ritschl of Bonn.

RICHARD ROTHE

Throughout the apostolic age, as reconstructed by Rothe, there was no Christian church; there were only isolated Christian communities. The obvious need for them to communicate and treat with one another was fulfilled by the apostles, who dealt individually with their own foundations and collegially with matters that affected general policy. Their delegates, for instance Timothy and Titus, were field agents of this coordinating ministry. It was however nothing they did in any official capacity, for there was no conferred office of coordination. It was simply a voluntary service of personal zeal.

As that era drew to a close, though, and those apostolic linkages with the Lord and with other communities were about to disappear, a crisis of unity was bound to threaten the scattered churches.[1] Partisan groups were already at odds with each other: the petrine judaizers and the pauline universalists, for instance. Gnostic dissidents were preaching a dissonant gospel. But a central authority, no matter how timely and necessary, would have faced resistance as something alien to their tradition. A convulsive emergency would be required to justify so deep a break with tradition. The catastrophe of 70 provided that crisis. The last vestiges of the nation of Israel were swept away, along with its international center of worship. Eliminated as well was the erstwhile headquarters of the apostles. In Christian eyes, this would serve to justify the provision of some successor establishment to them. The old resistance of the Peter-and-James party must have relented and allowed the pauline group to take the lead in structuring that new unity.

How that was actually accomplished it is difficult to know, confessed Rothe, since the period 70–100 AD has yielded virtually no written evidence. Yet something drastic obviously transpired, for in the early second century Ignatius of Antioch describes for us an organized network, a "Catholic Church" already functioning. The petrine and pauline parties have made their peace. And the change must have occurred rather early in the period, for the pattern reflected in Clement of Rome's letter to the Corinthians, in Ignatius of Antioch's letters and in that of Polycarp to the Philippians seems already settled in place awhile.

Surely apostolic authority would have been required to legitimate so profound a change. There must, Rothe conjectured, have been a meeting after the fall of Jerusalem at which the apostles left behind a supplementary set of ordinances and instructions about how they themselves were to be replaced. The instrumentality the remaining apostles chose for ruling and coordinating those thitherto isolated churches – an institution that had not existed before – was the episcopate. John, surviving in Ephesus, would then have put it into

---

[1] Richard Rothe, *Die Anfänge der Christlichen Kirche und ihre Verfassung* (Wittenberg: Zimmermann, 1837).

effect, beginning in Asia where he had founded a theological school and where we encounter the first reports of a strong episcopate.

FERDINAND CHRISTIAN BAUR

Rothe's rather singular thesis provoked an extensive, critical review by F. C. Baur, who was in process of forming the Protestant theological school in Tübingen. Baur went on to formulate his own account of early church order.[2]

Christianity has been rent, he stated, by a fundamental conflict between two great perspectives: the Catholic Idea and the Protestant Idea. They are typified as a juridical society whose doctrines, rites and morality are sacred sources of salvation; or as a personal encounter with the saving God, leading one towards the free assembly of the saved. These two ideas had their ancestor traditions in the primitive church in its Jewish and gentile branches. And in their reaction to Gnosticism and Montanism it was the Judeo-Christian party which, typically, resorted to an authoritarian hierarchy of officers.

The belief that the traditional offices – *episkopos* and *diakonos* – go back to the Lord himself (an idea expressed in the first century by Clement) is implausible, says Baur, for Paul's authentic epistles do not reflect such a church order. There, for example, *diakonia* is a service, not an office. Election, not appointment, seems to have been the original manner of choosing officers. Teaching was open to all, as one would infer from Paul's effort to block women from it. Baptism could be exercised by the laity in urgent need.[3] He also concludes that

---

[2] Baur's first publication on the topic in 1838 was prompted by Rothe's theory: Ferdinand Christian Baur, "Über den Ursprung des Episkopats in der christlichen Kirche," *Tübinger Zeitschrift für Theologie*, 11, 3 (1838), 1–185. Fifteen years later he dealt with the subject again, in the course of his large work on early church history. His thesis, however, was a critical reaction, this time, to the recent publication by Albrecht Ritschl (see below): Baur, *The Church History of the First Three Centuries*, ed. Allan Menzies, 2 vols. (London and Edinburgh: Williams & Norgate, 1878–1879), 2:11–61. This translates *Das Christenthum und die christliche Kirche der drei ersten Jahrhunderte* (Tübingen: L. F. Fues, 1853). Though Baur was senior to Ritschl and the latter was a critic of his former mentor and of the Tübingen School, there is a sense in which Baur, reacting to Ritschl, comes later in this public argument.

[3] On the eucharist, Baur equivocates: "So with the Lord's Supper; it was the custom of Christendom that only the president dispensed it, as, according to Justin, it is the *proestòs* who blesses the bread and wine; but, asks Tertullian, are not the laity also priests? Where only three are gathered together, though they be all laymen, there is the church. Thus all that the clergy afterwards claimed especially to be, all that they regarded as their peculiar attribute,

the first communities had not been given a hierarchical governance. *Episkopoi* and *presbyteroi* were synonyms. It was only when the collegial prerogatives of the elders began to be transferred to one overseer that the relatively informal self-rule began to give way to a new autocracy. And that did not happen overnight. The pastoral epistles already know of a single *episkopos* and plural *presbyteroi* and *diakonoi*. But later, even after Clement of Rome and Ignatius of Antioch had insisted that all, including elders, must defer to the one overseer, Irenaeus and Clement of Alexandria are still speaking of him as one of the elders.

Baur sees the tendency to exalt the *episkopos* in both Jewish and gentile wings of the church. But whereas the gentile Christians legitimated the overseer as a successor of the apostles (a link with their normative beginnings), their Jewish coreligionists did the same by seeing the *episkopos* as a vicar of Christ (who is embodied and thus becomes vitally present). And just as a single overseer could be a guarantor of unity within each church by presiding there, the college of overseers of all the churches required a unifying center, which the Roman *episkopos* claimed to be, legitimated by the story of Peter's residence, bishopric and martyrdom in that city. Thus the endowments of the church – the power of the keys and the Spirit – came to be concentrated in the order of overseers.

What hoisted the *episkopos* to power, and subordinated the *presbyteroi*, the *diakonoi* and the *laos* = people, was a pair of deviations: Gnosticism and Montanism. The Gnostics were a vexing threat to the church, for the conventional appeal to the scriptures was useless against their teaching. They challenged the authoritative list of sacred books, and also the traditional interpretation, by claiming a private tradition of secret revelation and interpretation. Against them Irenaeus and Tertullian had to construct a new set of standards to resolve controversy. The norm was the teaching of the apostles, to be found not only in the apostolic writings received by all the churches, but also preserved trustworthily by the traditional teaching in the sees founded by the apostles. The authentic pedigree linking those present churches to their founders was the verifiable line of *episkopoi*. These were listed as single incumbents back to the founding apostles. And the overseer soon came to be respected, not simply as a

was claimed by Tertullian for the laity as a universal right of Christian priesthood." *Church History*, 2:21–22. Tertullian had indeed advanced the principle, but had not drawn that sweeping a conclusion.

guarantor of the tradition but also as its authentic repository and interpreter. Thus the doctrinal conflict of the second century provoked a procedural conflict that touched on the very nature and organization of the church.

It was in the contest with Gnosticism that tradition was first placed in that relation to Scripture which it has ever since maintained in the doctrinal system of the Catholic Church. At a time when the canon of the writings held to be apostolic was still extremely unsettled, the whole fabric of Christianity rested on tradition. But what tradition was in its notion and principle, this was not learned till opponents of a particular kind had to be dealt with, – opponents who could not be rebutted without founding upon something that was nearer the source than Scripture, and stood above the authority of Scripture.[4]

At almost the same time the Montanists were stirring up a disciplinary conflict. They were reacting against what they regarded as laxity and worldly compromise in a church grown soft. They upheld a rigorous morality, and disclaimed ecclesiastical forgiveness because only God could forgive. Their opponents, the order of *episkopoi*, held that no sin was incapable of absolution. The overseer of Rome gave the verdict that proved decisive: that those guilty of deadly sin could find forgiveness once after baptism. The overseers also deplored the freakish ecstasy of the Montanist prophets, and insisted that God's will and guidance was to be sought rather in their own, more sober, deliberations and teaching. Thus the officers emerged as patrons and possessors of an authority that was compassionate, practical and predictable.

[T]he great offence felt by the Catholic party arose from the vague, arbitrary, fortuitous nature of Montanist prophecy, from its tendency to introduce novelty, to set up a new principle of faith in the separate individuals whom it made its organs ... If they believed themselves to be the first who received the Paraclete promised by Christ, they thereby denied the possession of the Paraclete to the apostles ...
    [T]he working of the Holy Spirit, who in the Montanist Paraclete moved in the free scope of the subjectivity of separate individuals endowed with the gift of prophecy, was now fixed and regulated in accordance with Catholic ideas. As the keys of the power to bind and to loose, claimed by the Montanist prophets for themselves, came into the hands of the bishops

---

[4] Ibid. 11.

exclusively, so the bishops were now the sole acknowledged organs of the Holy Spirit. The principle of individuality, on which Montanist prophecy rested, was now opposed by the maxim that the Holy Spirit, as the governing principle in the Church, spoke only in the collective number of the Church's representatives, and that the latter might the more surely believe themselves to be inspired by him, the firmer and clearer was their consciousness that they represented the Church.[5]

ALBRECHT RITSCHL

Younger German Protestants, however, were beginning to revert to the earlier individualism of which Idealism had been a suppressant. They would not share Rothe's or Baur's account of anything as Catholic as a coordinating authority. Albrecht Ritschl, son of a Protestant bishop superintending all the churches in Pomerania, was a spokesman for that contrary school of thought. As a more recondite scholar, Ritschl was unprepared to accept Rothe's massive conjecture that the second-century consolidation was the handiwork of the remnant of the apostolic college. But his objection ran more broadly than that. It was not only the fact but also the alleged character of these new church offices that he found to be discontinuous with the church of the New Testament.[6]

Some early documents recall that the apostles had established officers in churches they founded.[7] That would seem to be an obvious and necessary provision for any effective community. But there is also evidence of an alternative arrangement. Stephanas and his household are said to have put themselves at the service of the church at Corinth.[8] Also, Paul in several passages describes the tasks of community service, not as offices, but as endowments of the Spirit: *didaskaleia* = teaching, *kybernêsis* = direction, *antilêmpsis* = administration. Ritschl maintained that this did not invalidate church office as such. But it made clear that the ultimate claim of Christian office to obedience was the God-given competence of its incumbent. The charism of leadership, given by God and then recognized by the

---

[5] Ibid. 53.

[6] Albrecht Ritschl, *Die Entstehung der altkatholischen Kirche* (Bonn: Adolph Marcus, 1855), 365–475, 577–603. After Baur published his history of the early church in 1853 Ritschl published an expanded, second edition; see pp. 347–449. Both Baur and Ritschl claimed to have revised their earlier views in their latter publications, but as regards the scope of our inquiry their accounts of early church polity remained substantially stable.

[7] Ac 14:23; 1 Th 5:12–15; Tit 1:5; Clement of Rome, *Letter to the Corinthians* (hereafter *1 Cl*), 42.   [8] 1 Cor 16:15–16.

community, becomes office. The origin of the office is divine; the recognition and installation of its incumbent is human. And since it is immaterial which human authority testifies to God's preemptive empowerment, it did not require apostolic action, but devolved upon the community itself (through election). Paul thus acknowledged Stephanas' leadership after he had been in office. Hence Ritschl sees no warrant to ground episcopal authority in apostolic succession.

The apostles may have established the community offices, but they did not pass on to the officers their own gifts, tasks and authority. Preaching and teaching were the apostles' proper function, yet the basic capacity to preach was a given to all Christians. Even if official permission was required for laity to preach, the *episkopos* = overseer was the one to give it because of his disciplinary responsibility to maintain order at worship, not because he had any inherited empowerment to share.

This principle worked in all directions. Officers, Ritschl notes, were elected by the community. But the community was not the source of their powers (nor, he adds, were the apostles). The Spirit was their true source, for electors recognize and defer to a charism but they cannot confer it. The officers preside, then, but they are not the mediators of salvation. They order worship but they do not own it, for it belongs to the church that cries "Amen." The president represents the community, he does not generate it.

In his earlier study of the episcopate,[9] Baur had relied much on his sharp differentiation between Paul and the older apostles. It was Judeo-Christianity, descended from the latter, that gave rise to the authoritative episcopate, which was so alien to Paul's more charismatic vision. Ritschl, however, ascribes the change to the ancient Catholic church (it was Ritschl who coined the term *altkatholische Kirche* to identify the stage of the church when it first existed under officers).

This tradition, which deviated from both Judeo-Christianity and pauline Christianity, was the eventual work of second-century figures such as Ignatius, Pseudo-Clement, Irenaeus and Tertullian, who laid down the principles from which later, more unfortunate conclusions were to be drawn. Baptism, on Tertullian's account, was reserved to the *presbyteros*, except in an emergency. But that very exception shows

---

[9] Ferdinand Christian Baur, "Über den Ursprung des Episkopats in der christlichen Kirche," *Tübinger Zeitschrift für Theologie* (1838), 1–185. This was written as a reply to Rothe.

that it was community order, not inherent liturgical power, which dictated the reservation in the first place, and which explains all distinction between an officer and a layperson.

It was the same, Ritschl went on, with the ministry of forgiveness. Catholic teaching sees Christ as having entrusted the power to forgive to the apostles, after which it passed to the *episkopoi*. Ritschl will have none of that. All believers are enjoined to admonish sinners and to pray for their forgiveness. No believer, layman or officer, can do more than pray for someone's forgiveness, because only God can forgive. Ritschl explained baptism, forgiveness and ordination all in the same way: the rite aroused the gifts of the Spirit, and through prayer it made the beneficiary more receptive, and confirmed that grace had indeed (and already) been imparted. But no human was an effective agent of God's power.

That was the authentic and ancient Christian theology. A later, depraved (Catholic) belief imagined *episkopoi* dispensing the Spirit by the laying-on of their hands, and recognized in them a liturgical, or priestly, character.

Christianity's vitality derived from the certainty of having been born again to grace, of salvation through faith alone. That surety of rebirth through faith was later replaced by the sure power of sacramental performance. God was no longer its cause, and the Christian people were no longer the intermediaries. Replacing them both, the clergy was empowered to mediate salvation, and to effectuate it. The claim of apostolic origin for this office was, of course, a ploy to bolster such a bold new claim to plenipotentiary authority. It had exalted clerical status to a far remove from the original concept of office as a human arrangement for the sake of community order.

In Ritschl's account of it, the single, presiding bishop did not even appear in the documents until the early second century, and did not become the established norm until perhaps the end of that century.

The New Testament, he noted, uses *episkopos* and *presbyteros* interchangeably, and both typically appear in the plural. Clement of Rome displays the same usage, and adds another synonym: *hêgoumenos* = ruler. Wherever the titles appear the same duties are performed, such as handling the offerings at worship. Polycarp, early in the next century, mentions a single *episkopos* distinct from the *presbyteroi* in Smyrna, but he reports the older regime in Philippi. That must mean that a process of change was underway: complete in one locale but not in the other. There is evidence of this change in the literature ascribed to Ignatius. His authentic writings show the emergent solo *episkopos* as essential to the good order of the community; the later, spurious additions make the *episkopos* into a surrogate for God.[10] Ritschl concludes that the single, or "monarchical" episcopate, as it came to be called, was a second-century institution, locally developed (without apostolic influence) as a pragmatic provision for the direction of community worship.

The practice of the Jerusalem church, however, had been different from the beginning. Acts reports that that church had a single presiding figure: James, the brother of Jesus, who was not an apostle. Hegesippus reports that he was succeeded after apostolic deliberation by Simeon, a cousin to James and Jesus, who presided there until the time of Trajan in the early second century. He was chief of the church in Jerusalem, and that church was chief of all the churches in Palestine. This was an entirely distinctive church order, and Ritschl identifies it as typical of Judeo-Christian communities. They virtually all disappeared during the punitive invasion by Hadrian's army in the middle of the 130s, except for some deviant and insignificant prolongation among the Nazareans and the heretical Ebionites.[11] No aboriginal pattern of a single presiding officer, therefore, connected the first century with what eventually emerged as the universal norm.

It was the gentile-Christian church order that eventually prevailed, and in that order the *episkopos* was a *presbyteros* who had been chosen to preside. Irenaeus of Lyons, for instance, is still calling himself a *presbyteros*. The college of elders is still charged with *episkopê* = superintendence of the community. Any of the *episkopos'* prerogatives, such as the exclusive right to ordain, are human arrangements, not divine or apostolic endowments. As a community officer, the *episkopos* was at first ordained by his fellow *presbyteroi*, and only later was that reserved to his fellow *episkopoi*.

---

[10] There was in the mid-nineteenth century a general suspicion about the authenticity of the Greek corpus of Ignatian letters. One version, the longest, included thirteen documents. Another included only seven of the letters, and omitted much amplifying material in them. Shortly before Ritschl wrote, a still shorter version of only three letters was translated from the Syriac and published by Cureton. Scholars have subsequently settled upon the seven-letter edition as authentic, recognizing the amplifications as interpolated during the fourth century. Ritschl, however, accepted only the Curetonian version, and consequently much of what he rejected as spurious was in fact authentically Ignatian. In order to sustain his reconstruction, Ritschl also had to disallow other possible evidence of a single *episkopos* in 3 J, Rv, 1 Cl, Hegesippus, Tertullian and others.

[11] Ray A. Pritz, *Nazarene Jewish Christianity* (Leiden and Jerusalem: Brill & Magnes, 1988).

The church in Alexandria, with its predominantly Jewish origins, had the exceptional custom of electing its *episkopos* by and from the twelve principal *presbyteroi*, who alone then ordained him. This continuation of the old Judeo-Christian organization lasted there until the mid-third century, then gave way to the prevailing gentile-Christian episcopate. Another Jewish holdover in Egypt was the fact that there, as in Palestine, the president of the capital city was the only *episkopos* in the country. All local churches, as far as we know, were presided over by *presbyteroi*. Local communities were dependencies, whereas in the gentile tradition they were component churches in their own right. Ritschl obviously saw that prevailing church order as more faithful to Paul's inspiration, and healthier (just as he reckoned Protestantism was healthier).

This opposition between Jewish and gentile Christianity is central to Ritschl's theory. For the latter, "church" has two senses: the local congregation and the entire fellowship of believers. Jewish Christianity did not experience this distinction, for Jerusalem ruled all and the local community had much less sense of its own integrity. It all came to a clash when Jerusalem attempted to govern the Antioch church by delegate, for it collided with Paul's area of influence where churches were independent. Paul exercised over them a personal authority that was charismatic, but not official. It was not a logical structure or subordination that bound Paul's churches into unity, but a common faith, similar charismatic gifts, mutual hospitality and subsidy. Another instrumentality of unity was the correspondence between churches and their leaders, much of which is still extant.[12]

Authoritarians like Irenaeus and Tertullian argued on behalf of apostolic succession through the episcopate, and subordination of churches to the apostolic sees. They claimed that this was what preserved the orthodox belief in the churches. Even at the latter end of the second century, Clement of Alexandria was teaching otherwise. The apostles, according to Clement, transmitted the faith because of their charismatic excellence, not because of any office. As *episkopos* of the great see of Alexandria he laid claim to no apostolic succession. The guarantors of right teaching, he insisted, were not church officers at all but what he called "true Gnostics": those inspired to meditate

[12] Clement of Rome to Corinth; Ignatius of Antioch to Polycarp, Ephesus, Rome, [Magnesia, Tralles, Philadelphia and Smyrna]; Polycarp of Smyrna to Philippi; Dionysius of Corinth to Soter of Rome and to many churches; Polycrates of Ephesus to Victor and Rome; the Gallic martyrs of Lyons and Vienne to Asia and Phrygia and to Eleutherus of Rome; Smyrna to Philomelium and the Catholic Church.

upon and grasp the delivered faith. Clement, for Ritschl, is a timely disproof of the Catholic theory of office.

Ritschl's cleavage between the two sectors of Christianity, Jewish and gentile, so elaborately evidenced that it is difficult to sustain, is stressed so as to ignore the question of how the daughter church could have inherited so remarkably little of its community format from its parent. Also, in favor of his hypothesis he is obliged to disregard much contrary evidence that will not easily remain silent.

Here were three scholars, all known to one another as rivals and antagonists, who offered three quite distinct accounts for the formation of the classical church offices in the second century. Rothe imagines an unrecorded synod of apostles who provide for their own succession. Baur sees the new order as a defense measure against dissidents that claimed a private source, either secret or ecstatic, of authority. Ritschl sees the innovation as an inevitable concomitant of an expanded global community, and the needs of autonomous churches to make common cause.

Yet there was much on which the three concurred. They were sure that the classical echelons of office did not exist in the first century because there is no satisfactory record of them in the authentic pauline writings. When the offices did arise, it was an ominous step in a long journey that would lead eventually – and perhaps inevitably, but certainly regrettably – to the Inquisition, the Tiara and Trent.

The churches had developed from an early innocence into a seasoned toughness by providing themselves with an institutional authority. Without this development was the church as yet immature and incomplete, or was it single-hearted, with its heart set on the higher things?

These scholars wrote at a time when newer criticism made it possible to date documents better, and to separate authentic originals from spurious additions. The result was a vastly improved ability to reconstruct events in chronological order. One ought remember, however, that it was a scientific advance that was not fully refined, and which still was overshadowed by other, not-always-scholarly convictions. For example, the authentic pauline letters were being differentiated from the later documents pseudonymously attributed to Paul. One of the tools of differentiation was precisely this matter of church order. The pastoral epistles (1 & 2 Timothy, Titus) were identified as post-pauline since they reflected settled orders of *episkopoi* and *diakonoi*, because of the determined belief that these orders had to have developed later. But then, by a circular argument, the fact that the pastorals mentioned these orders was seen as evidence that these orders had to have developed later. Also, Ritschl used the same differentiator to separate the Ignatian letters, and ended up rejecting most of the authentic ones because of their strong support of the church officers. Baur went even further and declared the entire story of Ignatius' journey and martyrdom to be a fiction, fabricated to justify the church order that the Ignatian writings so strongly advocate. Thus these careful scholars were not unmoved by their own preferences, which were hostile to the emergence of official authority in the church.

J. B. LIGHTFOOT

Skepticism about Ignatius and his exaltation of episcopacy was not to become a settled view among theologians. Textual criticism would soon establish the authenticity of the fundamental Ignatian letters. Indeed, the writings of Clement, Ignatius and Polycarp, all of them strong advocates of official hierarchical authority (and for that reason assigned by many scholars to later dates when they could be less evidentiary), were in the next years to be verified as arising close to the turn of the second century.

J. B. Lightfoot of Cambridge, therefore, writing several years later, took up the matter of early church order without the more unfounded historical assumptions of Ritschl and Baur.[13] But he was also critical of Rothe. Had episcopacy really been ordered by the apostles, its spread would have been more swift and more uniform.[14]

The three classical orders, according to Lightfoot's reading of the data, each came into existence differently. Acts 6 narrates the establishment of the diaconate, an entirely new office at the time. He recognizes no evidence of deacons previously, no continuation of the Levite from the temple or of the *hazan* from the synagogue. The proper role of the new officers was the relief of the poor. The fact that Stephen and Philip forthwith distinguished themselves for preaching came by charism, not by office. The fact that all of the *diakonoi* were "Hellenists" (Judeo-Christians whose preferred language was Greek, not the Aramaic favored by their "Hebrew" fellow Christians) Lightfoot sees as proof of the "liberal and loving spirit of the

---

[13] J[oseph] B[arber] Lightfoot, *The Christian Ministry*, ed. Philip Edgcumbe Hughes (Wilton, CT: Morehouse-Barlow, 1983). Originally published as an Excursus in his *St. Paul's Epistle to the Philippians* (London: Macmillan, 1868).   [14] Ibid. 53–56.

'Hebrews'."[15] Also, he infers that the traditional seclusion of women in Jewish society must have required the existence of female deacons, whom he sees represented by Phoebe of Cenchreae and the "women" mentioned in 1 Timothy.[16] The order of deacons, then, is an early innovation of the mother church that spread quickly to all sectors of the global community.

Presbyteroi were a holdover from the synagogue organization that was shared with the gentile churches as well. Their duties as elders were to govern and to instruct. It may have been in the gentile environment that they acquired their alternative title, of Greek rather than Jewish derivation: *episkopoi*. The one title connoted venerable status; the other, inspection. It may also be that *episkopos* was commonly used to designate the directors of religious and social clubs in Greco-Roman society, and that heathens fastened it as a recognizable label on the Christian elders.

Up until Clement of Rome at the earliest, there is no evidence of a presiding *episkopos* distinct from the college of *presbyteroi*. Nor does Lightfoot see any Jewish antecedent for that office.[17] A review of all the evidence persuades him that the single *episkopos* emerges gradually. In earliest times the apostles had presided over the communities, and later they deputized their delegates to do so. This is as far as the New Testament carries us. During 70–100 (Rothe's silent interval), to stave off disorder and disunity threatened by growth and dissidence, the *presbyteroi* in various churches agreed to designate one of their number to preside.

This concentration of power in one man, to whom was now reserved the previously generic title of *episkopos*, was a practical strategy. It was however a strategy with progressive and probably unintended results. The *episkopos* who was chief of the elders evolved into an *episkopos* who was chief over the elders: no longer a president but a ruler.

[15] He quite misses the point of the text. The revolt of the Greek-speaking widows was provoked because those who controlled the Jerusalem church had long been ignoring the way in which the deacons, who all belonged to the Aramaic-speaking inner circle of the community, had been mistreating and discriminating against them as second-class members. It was precisely the want of a "liberal and loving spirit" in the first deacons and the power group behind them which embarrassed the authorities into creating a second, Hellenist cadre of deacons to look after the needs of that aggrieved sector of the community.

[16] *Christian Ministry*, 36; see Ro 16:1; 1 Ti 3:8ff. Hughes, his editor, disagrees, 21–25. Phoebe is a *diakonos* in the same way that Paul is: a servant of the church, not an officer. The "women" are wives.

[17] He specifically dissociates it from the *archisynagogos* of the synagogue. Ibid. 56, no. 104.

In a *tour d'horizon* of scholarship Lightfoot proceeds to marshal the evidence of all known Christian settlements in the early period: Jerusalem, Antioch, Syria, Asia Minor, Macedonia and Greece, Crete, Thrace, Rome, Gaul, Africa, Alexandria. It is a fact, he verifies, that the second-century writers testify regularly to the existence of presiding bishops in all of these regions.

Earlier texts remember that the *episkopos* is still one of the *presbyteroi*. But the role and rank of the overseer underwent a doctrinal change. When Clement of Rome and Ignatius preached obedience to the officers they did so because they were centers of unity and discipline. Later pseudonymous writers who published under their names – the Ebionite author of the Clementine Homilies and the Ignatian interpolator – took a stronger line and promoted the officers as essential intermediaries for access to the Lord. Irenaeus wrote of them as depositaries of the apostolic tradition, and Cyprian proclaimed them as direct vicegerents of Christ. As the presiding bishop waxed in authority, his warrant was derived, first from below, from the elders, and later from above, from the apostles or from the Lord. This increasingly exalted theological understanding was inevitably written into the historical record, through a revised recollection of the origins of the order.

As a historian Lightfoot was at pains to set the record straight. But he was also a theologian, and conceptual preoccupations had at least as strong a hold on his concern. What he regarded as most inappropriate in the exaltation of the episcopacy (a decade later he would himself be the bishop of Durham) was not the concentration of power but its investiture with a misbegotten notion of sacerdotal character. By this he meant largely what Ritschl had meant by sacramental or liturgical character.

An authentic notion of priesthood had emerged quite early. Christians, in Christ, all had priestly access to the Lord. There was no human intermediary, professional or hereditary, through whom they were obliged to go. Earliest allusions to the priesthood of Israel, such as in the Letter to the Hebrews, mentioned it as a foil for contrast with the priesthood of Jesus. There were, however, two other usages of the Old Testament priesthood which made it an analogy more of comparison than of contrast. Both Paul and the gospels wrote of the eucharist as making present the sacrificial character of Jesus in his dying. And Clement was the first of several writers who saw in the high priest, priests and Levites of the temple a foreshadowing of the triple level of Christian offices: *episkopos*, *presbyteroi* and *diakonoi*. Granted the eucharistic roles of these officers, it could be no surprise that some believers would run with the analogy, and would see in their officers the very essential intermediaries that Hebrews had announced to have been discontinued.

It was no early turn of thought, though. Clement, Ignatius, Polycarp, Justin, Irenaeus and Clement of Alexandria were all very forthright in asserting and reinforcing the authority of the officers. And none of them resorted to sacerdotal vocabulary to strengthen that argument. Later writers – Tertullian, Hippolytus, Origen – do apply sacerdotal language to officers. But since they also affirm it of all baptized believers, they must mean either that the clergy exercises sacerdotal functions belonging to the people, or that theirs is a priesthood of higher degree. Cyprian, finally, is the one who is outright in his claim for officers of proper priestly identity, and he is followed by the *Apostolic Constitutions*. It may be at that point that it ceased to become a metaphor. The process of confusion was finally complete much later, with the rise of the modern vernaculars: German, French and English all offer only a single word (*Priester*, *prêtre*, priest) to translate both elder = *presbyteros* = *senior* and levitical priest = *hiereus* = *sacerdos*.

Lightfoot is emphatic that the Christian ministry is a priesthood only in a representative sense, representing God to humans and humans to God. The analogy goes awry when the function is seen, not as representative but as vicarious. The ordained officer is then seen as an indispensable and essential mediator who replaces all direct intercourse. Christians commune with God directly, and are reconciled by him directly. In the absence of ministers, initiative in worship and prayer rightly reverts to laity. This, however, Lightfoot admits is an ideal. Being a human society, the church does need a ministry of reconciliation, "an order of men who may in some sense be designated a priesthood … the ideal conception and the actual realization are incommensurate and in a manner contradictory."[18]

It is this hesitation which puts Lightfoot in two minds about the evolution of episcopacy. The emergence of a president, standing functionally as a pivot between community and God, he accepts as a legitimate outgrowth of the church of the first disciples: legitimate whenever and by whomever it was established. When that president

[18] Ibid. 27.

became a ruler, however, it was a change of species, not of style. And the spurious theology of ordained priesthood, along with the revision of historical memory, was the stratagem devised to authenticate the coup.

Dissent had first arisen to challenge the received Catholic account of the origins and nature of church offices in the fourteenth century. Wyclif's aggravation then was the high and secular life lived by the bishops, and by some of the more comfortably placed priests. By the sixteenth century it was the papacy that was the chief irritant, but there was a residual antagonism towards the episcopacy which found voice in the new congregationalism. That was a remedy which many reformers wished to apply to the church's wasting illnesses, and it led scholars of that mind to scrutinize the history and theology of the episcopal office, and to cast doubt upon the bishop's legitimacy and authority. Much of the research that followed tended to deal relatively little with the orders of presbyter and deacon. That continued to be true in the nineteenth-century revival of the topic, especially among German Lutherans. It had also found its reflection in the Catholic literature, which defended the episcopate as essential to the church in a way the lower offices were not. And of course the papacy continued to be sustained, to the point where one imagined it had contributed more to the church than the entire membership of the order of presbyter.

EDWIN HATCH

As Anglicans with their episcopal tradition now entered the discussion in favor of the growing challenge, the discussion altered its course. A division in Protestant practice and theory now relieved the literature of the antiCatholic preoccupation which had unified it previously. Questions now began to be asked, not just about the proper role of *episkopoi*, but about the purpose and propriety of all office in the church. Others then took that question to new lengths. Rudolf Sohm, whom we must consider in his time and turn, was probably the most radical in his answer to that question, but others had already begun to open their studies out upon that larger issue: why any offices at all? Edwin Hatch of Oxford, an Anglican convert from Nonconformity, was one of the first, and one of the most free-minded.

Lightfoot's contribution had been made possible by recent

advances in the scientific study of early Christian documents from the "subapostolic" period. Hatch in his turn was greatly influenced by several decades of prodigious publication of Greek and Roman inscriptions, and impressive advances in classical philology. And his life's main work was to assert the dominant influence of Greco-Roman institutions upon the still pliable Christian establishment. Greek education, exegesis, rhetoric, philosophy and ethics had left their heavy stamp, for instance, on the Christian theology of God as creator, moral governor and supreme being. The Nicene Creed, for instance, has had a more potent intellectual influence than the Sermon on the Mount on Greek, and later Aryan, Christianity.[19]

Hatch was also persuaded that the most primitive model of church need not be the most exemplary. Too much effort, said Hatch, had gone into reconstructing (or supposing) what the Lord and the apostles had laid down, while later modifications were downgraded as secondary. Indeed, church historians seemed perversely determined to disengage from their studies a single, "right" form of church order.

They are almost clamorous in asserting that its builder and maker is God; and yet they commit the paradox of trying to limit the divine operation to that which would have been probable, if men had been not only the agents, but the authors of the plan. If Christianity had been an artificially-devised religion, there would have been, in all probability, a single life of the Founder, and a single systematic exposition of his teaching; instead of that,

[19] This was the conclusion of his last great publication, the Hibbert Lectures of 1888: *The Influence of Greek Ideas and Usages upon the Christian Church* (London: Williams & Norgate, 1890). His conclusion is a thoughtful epitaph for his career's work.

It is possible to urge, on the one hand, that Christianity ... which grew on a soil whereon metaphysics never throve – which won its first victories over the world by the simple moral force of the Sermon on the Mount, and by the sublime influence of the life and death of Jesus Christ, may throw off Hellenism and be none the loser, but rather stand out again before the world in the uncoloured majesty of the Gospels. It is possible to urge that what was absent from the early form cannot be essential, and that the Sermon on the Mount is not an outlying part of the Gospel, but its sum. It is possible to urge, on the other hand, that the tree of life, which was planted by the hand of God Himself in the soil of human society, was intended from the first to grow by assimilating to itself whatever elements it found there. It is possible to maintain that Christianity was intended to be a development, and that its successive growths are for the time at which they exist integral and essential. It is possible to hold that it is the duty of each succeeding age at once to accept the developments of the past, and to do its part in bringing on the developments of the future ...

But whether we accept the one or the other, it seems clear that much of the Greek element may be abandoned. On the former hypothesis, it is not essential; on the latter, it is an incomplete development and has no claim to permanence ... [Further study] will enable us, if on the one hand we accept the theory that the primitive should be permanent, to disentangle the primitive from the later elements, and to trace the assumptions on which these later elements are based; and if on the other hand we adopt the theory of development, it will enable us, by tracing the lines of development, to weld the new thoughts of our time with the old by that historical continuity which in human societies is the condition of permanence. *Ibid.* 351–352.

there are four different lives, written apparently for different classes of minds and from different points of view. If the Church had been an artificially-devised institution, there would probably have been a single definite code of rules, and a single prescribed form of government; instead of that, there are no authoritative rules, and there is an almost absolute elasticity of form. In the one case the diversity of record, in the other the variability of form, and in both cases the contradiction of human analogies, are indications of a deeper than human unity.[20]

All historians agreed that Christian church organization had developed gradually, and that it had adopted elements from secular society (for weal or for woe). Hatch reckoned that "not only some but *all* the elements of the organization can be traced to external sources."[21] And in his mind the entire Christian polity was borrowed from Greco-Roman institutions.

The early empire was honeycombed with associations under religious patronage (sometimes to elude the state religion). These associations had a well-documented legal status and organization. And in the imperial world the Christian communities could gain legal standing and protection by incorporating as civic associations rather than as local units of an illegal religion.[22]

Particularly significant was the associations' custom of maintaining a common fund for philanthropic purposes. One of the *presbyteroi*, or governing body, was designated as *episkopos*, or financial officer. As steward, or almoner, his was the responsibility to subvent the widows, orphans, prisoners, travelers and dispossessed, and other correlative tasks were added to his agenda in time. This, Hatch asserted, was the prototype of the Christian *episkopos*: he was the community's financial

---

[20] Edwin Hatch, *Diversity in Unity the Law of Spiritual Life*, A Sermon preached before the University of Oxford on the morning of Whitsunday, June 5, 1881 (London: Rivingtons, 1881), 12–13.

[21] Hatch, *The Organization of the Early Christian Churches*, 1880 Bampton Lectures (London: Rivingtons, 1881), 208–209. "Nothing will really be gained by showing that this or that element of Church government is more primitive than another: nothing will be really lost by the admission that this or that element in the great aggregate of historical developments is later than another. That for the preservation of which we have to contend is not so much ancient form as historical continuity," 211.

[22] This view did not go unchallenged. "Christianity was a religion, not of colleges, but of cities. As early as the first generation, wherever it is established, for instance in large cities like Antioch and Rome, it forms neither separate synagogues like those of the Jews of Rome, nor autonomous colleges, like the pagan collegia: its followers have for their meeting-place the house of such or such a Christian. All the Christians of the city, however large it may be, make up but one and the same confraternity or ekklèsia which is called after the city ... and no church in any part of the world is isolated from other churches." Pierre Batiffol, *Primitive Catholicism*, trans. Henri Brianceau (London: Longmans, Green, 1911), 33. This translates *L'église naissante et le Catholicisme*, 2nd edn. (Paris: Lecoffre, 1909).

administrator. The Seven in Acts 6 fit in perfectly as episcopal assistants, for their duties are to lend staff help to this social welfare program.

The *presbyteroi*, however, were a carry-over from Judaism. Among the Jews they functioned as a college, responsible for worship and for discipline, and so it was in the Judeo-Christian communities. It would be several centuries, however, before the presbyterate functioned this way throughout an ethnically amalgamated church.[23] Eventually, when *presbyteroi* became no longer a college of policy-makers but a corps of delegates sent by the *episkopos* to preside over suburban and then town and village congregations, their title remained but their role had become utterly transformed.[24]

How then did the *episkopos* gain supremacy? There was at the time a drift in the secular society towards creation of a presiding officer in municipal councils, private associations, provincial assemblies, boards of magistrates and even Jewish councils. In any case the church, whether under its aspect as a disciplined community or that of a worshipping society or that of an eleemosynary group, would require central direction. Hatch surmises that Ignatius' stout promotion of hierarchical leadership in the early second century reflected an organization that had been functioning for some time. But it was a primacy, not the supremacy it would later become.

Agreeing with his Germanic predecessors, Hatch says it was the need to sustain the threatened unity of tradition that induced the Christians to look to this new presiding officer as custodian of the rule of faith. "He was the depositary of doctrine, and he was the president of the courts of discipline. But the primary character of these functions of administration is shown by the fact that the name which was relative to them thrust out all the other names of his office ..."[25] And this centrality gradually hoisted the former financial manager to a high authority indeed.

Shortly thereafter the churches were rent by the quarrel over readmission of the *lapsi*, those who had defaulted under persecution

---

[23] Hatch, *Organization*, 65–66.

[24] "What powers, if any, were possessed by a single presbyter acting alone there is no evidence to show. But by one of those slow and silent revolutions which the lapse of many centuries brings about in political as well as in religious communities, the ancient conception of the office, as essentially disciplinary and collegiate, has been superseded by a conception of it in which not only is a single presbyter competent to discharge all a presbyter's functions, but in which also those functions are primarily not those of discipline, but 'the ministration of the Word and Sacraments'." Ibid. 76.   [25] Ibid. 46.

and later repented and sought reconciliation. The normal traffic of appeal from any disagreeable consensus or decision passed inevitably upwards, to the newly presiding *episkopoi*. "In this way it was that the supremacy of the bishops, which had been founded on the necessity for unity of doctrine, was consolidated by the necessity for unity of discipline."[26]

Thus it was that the *episkopos* who had originally been a steward answerable to the community elders was upgraded into an administrative presidency, and later found himself the leader of worship, the arbitrator of controversy, the ruler of the community and the definitor of orthodox, traditional belief.

And once there was this three-tiered establishment of officers in place, they proceeded to draw unto themselves, gradually but ineluctably, most of the initiatives, prerogatives and responsibilities that had been native to the *laos*, the people as whole. Laymen who had freely preached, baptized, presided at the eucharist,[27] elected and deposed their clergy,[28] were now rendered passive and impotent. "By the force of changing circumstances, and by the growth of new conceptions, the original difference of rank and order became a difference of spiritual power ..."[29]

Later, when the civil power turned benign and then intrusive, it found single bishops easier to treat with than the presbyteral councils or the Christian membership at large. It was therefore in the rulers' interest to enhance further the hegemony of the *episkopoi*. And by confederating in synods, the bishops who enjoyed the power either of special position (metropolitan sees) or of persuasion could consolidate their power still further and suppress dissent even among their own peers.

Hatch cast a sad eye over this development. What if the dominant officers or the majority were lax in discipline or unsound in faith? The answer that won the day was that of Irenaeus: true discipleship is maintained by acquiescent communion with the great church network, through submission to the bishops. Hatch is not at all sure

---

[26] Ibid. 102.

[27] Hatch relies here upon Ignatius, who said there was no valid eucharist without the *episkopos*. Ignatius, as Hatch understands him, really meant "church officer," and his tone of mild reproof implied that the issue is one of propriety, not validity. Ibid. 114.

[28] Hatch argues at some length that there was originally no rite of ordination. Ecclesiastical officers, like those in civil offices, simply assumed their elected post by functioning formally for the first time. The laying-on of hands, he is sure, cannot be essential, for there is no evidence that it was employed always and everywhere in the earliest days. Ibid. 126ff.

[29] Ibid. 125.

that this outward institution had harbored well enough the inner treasure: what he calls "that interpenetrating community of thought and character."[30] His sympathies run instead towards those early rebels, the Montanists, who asserted the primacy of spiritual gifts over office. He remembers their movement as unsuccessful but correct, "a beating of the wings of pietism against the iron bars of organization."[31]

What he proposes is not, like many historians, a return to the primitive church of the New Testament, for in that period the community order was still in an undefined state.

It has the elements of an ecclesiastical monarchy in the position which is assigned to the Apostles. It has the elements of an ecclesiastical oligarchy in the fact that the rulers of the Church are almost always spoken of in the plural. It has the elements of an ecclesiastical democracy in the fact, among others, that the appeal which St. Paul makes to the Corinthians on a question of ecclesiastical discipline is made neither to bishops nor to presbyters, but to the community at large. It offers a sanction to episcopacy in the fact that bishops are expressly mentioned and their qualifications described: it offers a sanction to presbyterianism in the fact that the mention of bishops is excluded from all but one group of Epistles. It supports the proposition that the Church should have a government in the injunctions which it gives to obey those who rule. It supports on the other hand the claim of the Montanists of early days, and the Puritans of later days, in the preeminence which it assigns to spiritual gifts.

Which of these many elements, and what fusion of them, was destined in the divine order to prevail, must be determined, not by exegesis, but by history.[32]

In another mood, though, there is one note of the early church he would restore. "In the first ages of its history, while on the one hand it was a great and living faith, so on the other hand it was a vast and organized brotherhood. And, being a brotherhood, it was a democracy..." It later degenerated into a monarchy. It must, thought Edwin Hatch, though organized, recover some form of popular, active and responsible democracy. What forms that polity ought take are dictated by need. Or, rather, "the history of the organization of Christianity has been in reality the history of successive readjustments of form to altered circumstances."[33]

---

[30] Ibid. 188.   [31] Ibid. 122.   [32] Ibid. 21.

[33] Ibid. 213. More than any figure we have seen thus far, Edwin Hatch is more prompted than governed by what he knows of the past. His historical erudition, especially as regards Greco-Roman antiquities, is vast. It is unfortunate that no comparable scholarly access to Jewish history was available to him. His argument not infrequently sweeps a few data centuries and

ADOLF VON HARNACK

Hatch's 1880 Bampton Lectures on early church organization secured widespread attention. One reader was moved to translate them into German, and quite swiftly, for they appeared only two years behind the original edition. For the translator, Adolf Harnack, professor of church history at Giessen, it was the beginning of a virtual publishing career on this one subject alone. His printed views on early church polity are notable in that they represent a progression of changing theories that result from debate with the leading scholars who were dealing with the topic: William Sanday, Pierre Batiffol, Louis Duchesne, Rudolph Sohm. He even argued with himself, and the great professor's own stated position never remained still long enough for critics to get their bearings firmly fixed upon it. He was always the readiest to rethink and then revise his own previous constructions.

Already in his germanizing of Hatch, Harnack was moved by the Oxford writer's research to take up a dissenting stance.[34] Hatch's conclusion had been traditional: that the episcopate had developed from within the presbyteral college. Harnack saw the two orders differently, as two different structures, each with its own character and history.

Elders were always collegial. They had general responsibility for discipline and nothing to do with worship or finance. Bishops (who might at the same time be serving as elders) were virtuosi, not collegial, and in their administrative area each one was sovereign. Their work of fraternal solicitude was specifically Christian, while that of the elders was legal and secular in nature. Thus Hermas could write warmly of the former and coolly of the latter.

---

continents apart into a spindly generalization, reminiscent of what one historian remarked about the work of Hilaire Belloc: "I would be happy to substantiate in one career as much as he asserts on one page." Hatch's handling of the facts, however, is less hampered by an ecclesiastical model he wishes to canonize, and his own theoretical reflections are unusually provocative and thoughtful. One weakness of his, which will show itself more frequently in the work of scholars to follow, is an over-reliance upon nomenclature studies. The borrowing by Christians of the title *episkopos*, for instance, leads him too easily to assume that it must then denote a financial officer, without checking to see whether that was in fact his primary function (it was not). For other publications on this topic by Hatch, see his articles in the *Dictionary of Christian Antiquities*: "Holy Orders," "Ordination" and "Priest." For a critical review of his work, see Norman F. Josaitis, *Edwin Hatch and Early Church Order* (Gembloux: Duculot, 1971).

[34] See "Analecten von A. Harnack," in Edwin Hatch, *Die Gesellschaftsverfassung der christlichen Kirchen im Altertum*, trans. Adolf Harnack (Giessen: J. Ricker, 1883), 229–251.

It was in the mid-third century that a silent revolution occurred. The *episkopoi* had moved to become presidents of their colleges. Harnack can date this functional change so much later than Hatch or practically anyone else because he now interprets the passionately pro-bishop language of Ignatius, in the early second century, as an exaltation of the *episkopos*, not as a ruler or a president, but only as a chief at worship. Once they were in the chair, drawn out of their religious ambit of community cult and cast into another world of power and law, the bishops rapidly changed. Harnack construed it as no fault of theirs, for the Christian populace was looking for divinely warranted despots. What befell the *episkopoi* from the third to the sixth centuries was what the community wanted.

The deacons got pushed out of their traditional position during this great rearrangement. They had been junior associates of the *episkopoi*, and in some cases possibly of presbyteral rank. Episcopal and diaconal qualifications and functions were nearly indistinguishable. After the *episkopoi* moved to power the *diakonoi* occasionally succeeded them in office. But in the rise of the *episkopoi* they somehow chose not to haul their adjutants up with them, as a class. Synods forbade deacons to preside at the eucharist, or even to sit on the presbyteral benches round the eucharistic table. Still, the fact that as late as the seventh century councils were still reminding deacons to respect the precedence of the elders indicates that their subsidence into third place was a reluctant and a slow one.

No sooner had Harnack found illumination over the Oxford sky to the west than a startling omen flashed through the eastern heavens. Metropolitan Philotheos Bryennios published, just as the Hatch–Harnack volume appeared, the text of the *Didache*, or *Instruction of the Apostles*, a Syrian document which, amid controversy, some were dating back to the late first century. This would have made it older than any non-biblical Christian writing, and older perhaps than some portions of the New Testament itself. Harnack rushed out an annotated translation the next year, and along with it his thoroughly revised account of the constitution of the early church.[35]

What was disconcerting in this new find was that it gave little prominence or even notice to the much-discussed *episkopoi*, *presbyteroi* and *diakonoi*. The main movers in the church of the *Didache* were the

---

[35] *Die Lehre der Zwölf Apostel, nebst Untersuchungen zur ältesten Geschichte der Kirchenverfassung und des Kirchenrecht* (Leipzig: Hinrich, 1886), esp. 88–170.

apostles, prophets and teachers. These were not officers at all; they were charismatic enthusiasts. Harnack set aside his earlier theory of the opposing episcopal and presbyteral traditions, to develop further the contrast the two triads. The charismatics, he said, did the teaching while the officers did the administration. The charismatics were inspired; the officers were elected. The former were extra-territorial, often wandering, at the service of the universal church, while the latter had status only in their local congregations. The charismatics, as events were to prove, had a dominant ministry but one that would endure only for a while. Their prerogatives and preeminence in teaching and in worship would eventually be vacated as their kind ceased to be reproduced, and their place was then occupied by the second group: at first by way of exception, then as a matter of course. The bureaucrats ended up replacing the inspired. A few years later Harnack was to publish his analysis of the *Apostolic Canons*, an adaptation of the Didache produced possibly in Egypt two hundred years later. By then, he confirmed, local officers had all but displaced the charismatically gifted ones. The reader = *anagnôstês*, for instance, was now only a tamed evangelist.[36]

Harnack was taken to task, not for his latest but for his first views, by William Sanday, Hatch's protégé at Oxford where he held the Lady Margaret professorship in divinity. Sanday is no less critical of Hatch's theory. He is not persuaded that the *episkopos* was borrowed intact from Greco-Roman associations.[37] Nor is he ready to accept Harnack's early theory of the *episkopos* as a spiritual provider. There is, for instance, no more evidence linking the *episkopos* to worship than there is for the *presbyteroi*. Nor is there early enough evidence to underwrite the conclusion that the *episkopos* presided over the presbyteral college.

Sanday's own view was simple.

It appears to be admitted on all hands that the diaconate was a novel institution, devised by the first Christians for a special practical purpose. The deacons seem to have been chosen, as they are chosen now, from the

---

[36] *Sources of the Apostolic Canons with a Treatise on the Origin of the Readership and Other Lower Orders*, trans. L. A. Wheatley (London: Adam & Charles Black, 1895). This translates *Die Quellen der sogennanten apostolischen Kirchenordnung, nebst einer Untersuchung über den Ursprung des Lectorats und der anderen niederen Weihen*, ed. Otto von Gebhart (Leipzig: Hinrich, 1886).

[37] His arguments are: (1) *epimelêtês*, not *episkopos*, was the more typical designation used in the associations; (2) it was apparently not a permanent post; (3) nor was it restricted to finance. W[illiam] Sanday, "The Origin of the Christian Ministry," *The Expositor*, ser. 3, 5 (1887), 1–22, 97–114.

younger men, and is it not a simple hypothesis to suppose that the *episkopoi* were elders who were afterwards appointed to exercise supervision over them?[38]

The two roles, *diakonein* = to serve and *episkopein* = to supervise, go together. The *episkopoi* replace the apostles as the supervisors of the *diakonoi*.

Sanday is more impressed by Harnack's later theory that Montanism had obliged the church of the Spirit to yield to the church of the bishops. The ministry of the free-spirited prophets and teachers, a ministry of word and sacrament, must have come into the charge of the locally grounded bishops and deacons. "Something that was good perished, or at least was driven inwards, with the fall of Montanism. It broke out again – never more, we will hope, to be extinguished – at the Reformation."[39]

Harnack bounded back with a reappraisal of the episcopacy.[40] The earliest church order, he was sure, had been presbyterian. The bishop arose, not from any Jewish antecedents,[41] but from secular ones. The character of the office, however, is necessarily to be sought from Christian sources, since the members of the new faith made it their own. From the title itself we can infer only that this position is that of

---

[38] Ibid. 100.

[39] Ibid. 110. Sanday is another student of the method of historical research by the tracing of vocabulary. "No doubt we must look not at names, but at things. Names are, however, the indications of things. And in the case of institutions, the only means we have of tracing continuity is by following the course of the name. Institutions are in this respect like persons. We are told that every particle of our bodies changes, if I am not mistaken, once in every seven years. Yet personal identity survives, and is marked by the name. In like manner the name of an institution may change its contents; these may be added to, or subtracted from, or transformed in one way or another; but the process is a historical one, and the track of its history follows the course of its name. Now it is true that Timothy and Titus are called 'bishops', but in authorities so late as to be practically worthless. And on the other hand they are represented in the Epistles addressed to them, not as being bishops themselves, but as appointing others to be bishops. It is to these other persons that we must look to see what the attributes of a bishop were; and it is by comparing the different instances in which the name occurs that we must trace their development." Ibid. 112–13. It might also have been observed that if a single title be applied over the course of time to distinct and different roles, then to trace the name with the presumption of role-continuity is to be deceived, just as it would be to imagine that wherever a title appears it denotes the same function.

[40] Adolf Harnack, "On the Origin of the Christian Ministry," *The Expositor*, ser. 3, 5 (1887), 321–343.

[41] "The primitive bishops may certainly be compared in many respects with the *Archisynagogi*; but the name Archisynagogus is not found in the Gentile Christian Churches, and the name Bishop is not found among the Jews." Ibid. 338. This is a classic example of the argument from vocabulary. The possibility of a function being continued under different titles does not seem to suggest itself to Harnack.

overseer. It is in the late first century that the first distinct Christian evidence shows itself. From Philippians we know that the *episkopoi* have a role in the collection being taken up for Christians in Judaea. In Clement they preside at worship and offer the gifts. In the *Didache* they are appointed to office to receive the community offerings. In Hermas the *episkopoi* care for travelers and widows. In sum:

> They are called overseers insomuch as they direct or superintend the assembly met for worship. Out of this function all others have been necessarily developed. There have naturally grown out of this: (1) the administration of the gifts generally; (2) the administration of the property of the congregation; (3) the charge of the poor and needy; (4) the care of the visitors and strangers; (5) the representing of the Church to those without.[42]

Harnack's career moved forward: after an appointment at Marburg he was called to the chair in Berlin, where he became Germany's leading theological scholar. And still he continued to revise his views on the constitution of the early church.[43]

His attention continued to focus upon the charismatic triad prominent in the Didache: apostles, prophets and teachers (evangelists became a replacement category when the apostles began to thin out; both were itinerant preachers). The charismatics were the church's informal missionaries to Israel. And all three categories were traditional among the Jews. A Jewish apostle = *shaliach* (*shelechim*: plural) was, after 70 AD when we first learn of the institution, a nuncio of the new Jewish *Nasi* = Patriarch, sent round to the communities of the Dispersion to collect tribute, convey circular letters, exercise surveillance and discipline and, when at home in Palestine, to join the council around the *Nasi*. Prophets who uttered divine oracles, and teachers who interpreted the sacred writings and oracles, were also held in familiar esteem among the Jews.

All three were direct counterparts, Harnack thinks, of the Christian triad. The Christian charismatics were inspired, not elected. They shared a common mission and style, and a member of one rank might be taken into another. A prophet, for instance, might be called to move to other towns, and become an apostle. The apostles were to be itinerants, while the other two were resident. All were to remain penniless. Their great decline set in during the second century, and

[42] Ibid. 338.
[43] Harnack, *The Expansion of Christianity in the First Three Centuries*, trans. James Moffatt (London: Williams & Norgate, 1904). This translates *Die Mission und Ausbreitung des Christenthums in den Drei ersten Jahrhunderte* (Leipzig: Hinrichs, 1903).

for a variety of causes. Freeloading got them an unsavory reputation. A preference arose to reserve the apostolic title for the original Twelve. The *bizarreries* of the Montanist prophets shed suspicion and discredit on that calling among Catholics as well. And the teachers slowly settled down into academics, competed with the clergy as learned interpreters of the sacred tradition, and began to save their pennies. After the second century the three charismatic categories were peopled only by strays and stragglers. In the end, it was the martyrs and the confessors (those who braved arrest and prison for the faith, but were eventually spared a martyr's execution) who proved to be the most potent missionaries.

It was the teachers who survived the longest. Their decline coincided with the assumption by the new clergy of the whole of the teaching responsibility. And at this point in his reconsideration of the evidence, Harnack speaks with a revised respect of the role played by the bishops who so newly occupied center stage:

> The extent to which the episcopate, along with the other clerical offices which it controlled, formed the backbone of the church, is shown by the fierce war waged against it by the State during the third century (Maximinus Thrax, Decius, Valerian, Diocletian, Daza, Licinius), as well as from many isolated facts. In the reign of Marcus Aurelius, Dionysius of Corinth writes to the church of Athens that while it had well-nigh fallen from the faith, after the death of its martyred bishop Publius, its new bishop Quadratus had reorganized it and filled it with fresh zeal for the faith. Cyprian tells how in the persecution bishop Trophimus had lapsed along with a large section of the church, and had offered sacrifice; but on his return and penitence, the rest followed him, "none of whom would have returned to the church, had they not had the companionship of Trophimus." When Cyprian lingered in retreat during the persecution of Decius, the whole community threatened to lapse. So that one sees clearly the significance of the bishop for the church: with him it fell, with him it stood.[44]

RUDOLPH SOHM

As Harnack was beginning to soften his estimate of the clerical *arrivistes*, though, a much more severe dissent was being thrust into the public discussion by Rudolph Sohm, a professor of law from Leipzig. Sohm's position was not a murky one. He stated it starkly in paragraph one, page one, of his great work on church law: "Church law stands in contradiction to the essence of the church ... The whole

---

[44] Ibid. 2:57–58.

nature of Catholicism consists in this: that it affirms legal regulation as necessary for the church: indeed, as necessary for spiritual reality to be available."[45]

Sohm was dissatisfied with the reach of recent historians, particularly Hatch and Harnack. Received scholarship had been identifying early church office, not as a spiritual empowerment to preach the gospel, but as governance, discipline, administration, command. They were differentiating two separate organizations – one for teaching and the other for authority – and tracking their eventual convergence into a unified and omnicompetent clergy. They had distinguished the officers, who had status only in the local church, from the charismatics, whose mission was to the universal church.

That, says Sohm, is a monumental misunderstanding of what the church is. There is no such thing as a local church. The use of *ekklêsia* as the Christians' favorite corporate title invokes the controlling image of the Greek Old Testament. The proper sense of the title is not a local congregation or the membership meeting of a hellenistic association. For the Jews the *ekklêsia* was the entire people of Israel formally convened as God's people. For Christians it is the assembly of the full fellowship of those who believe in Jesus as Lord. There never was any notion of a local church until legal organizations introduced it.

God's people, Sohm went on, must discern and follow his will. But God's Word follows no rules. Therefore there can be no decisive "rules" of operation for the church. "Is it thinkable that any legal enactment could decide whose word is God's word for the church? The essence of a legal warrant is not that it coercively achieves its purpose, but that it is of a formal nature. On the strength of certain facts of the past it establishes, without recourse or discussion, whether it has been satisfied or not."[46]

The only authority possible is a charismatic one. All believers are bearers of the Spirit, and some of them are given a heavier dose. They are the true leaders. Obedience to their authority is unstructured, free, grounded in a recognition of charism. *Liebespflicht, nicht Rechtspflicht*: it is an obligation of love, not of law. Sohm identifies these

---

[45] Rudolph Sohm, *Kirchenrecht*, 1 (Leipzig: Duncker & Humblot, 1892), 1. Volume 2 appeared posthumously, ed. E. Jacobi and O. Meyer (Munich & Leipzig, 1923). Important sections of it had already been published in *Weltliches und geistliches Recht: Festgabe für Karl Binding* (Leipzig, 1914).   [46] Ibid. 23.

charismatics with the triad of apostles, prophets and teachers. Their teaching is their mode of governance, their exercise of the power of the keys. Authoritative teaching he saw as including prophecy (a revealing utterance), instruction = *didaskaleia* (unfolding God's Word) and exhortation (applying it). The charismatics who alone have the gift to offer this teaching are charged with pastoral care and rule, as the priests and shepherds of the church. There are no others.

And how does the populace participate? Not by being the authority of last resort, he says. Sohm claims that all authority comes from God, not from the community. Therefore the church is monarchical, but only under the Lord. Still – the hands are the hands of a monarchist, but the voice is the voice of a democrat. To function publicly the charismata require prior permission and subsequent acceptance by the community. There may well be a laying-on of hands, but as in healing, confirmation, exorcism and absolution, the gesture presupposes that the grace has already been given, and it invokes God's further help to remove sinful impediments to its free operation.[47]

Sohm's critique drew Harnack into a published exchange in which the latter yielded not a little ground. But this did not satisfy, for Sohm perceived that his Berlin correspondent had still not grasped or accepted the radical nature of his challenge.[48]

The primitive church knew itself as the body of Christ, God's flock, a brotherhood. It held together by inner force without any social organization or procedural rules. It existed in no particular place, but wherever God's Word was proclaimed. "The Christian community belonging to any place is nothing as a local entity, for as a local entity it is of no account. It has its identity as an embodiment, an expression of an ecumenical community, of the religious reality of general Christendom." One spoke, not of the "church at Corinth," but of "the church of God sojourning = *paroikousa* in Corinth."[49] The hellenizing of Christianity was an instance, but not the essence,

[47] Sohm lays down his dogmatic principles, and then arrays historical evidence to which they can be applied. Though he is an erudite historical scholar, he fits scriptural texts to his doctrine pretty much the way Cinderella's stepsisters fitted their feet into the slipper. His sharp intervention elicited sharp opposition. One of his most balanced critics was Karl Ludwig Schmidt, *Die Kirche des Urchristentums: Eine lexicographische und biblisch-historische Studie* (Tübingen: Mohr [Siebeck], 1932).
[48] Sohm, *Wesen und Ursprung des Katholizismus*, Abhandlungen der Philosophisch-historischen Klasse der königlich sächsischen Gesellschaft der Wissenschaften 27 (1909), 333–390.
[49] Ibid. 359.

of what Sohm despised as Catholicism. The essence of Catholicism is the failure to make a stark and utter distinction between the church as a spiritual reality and any ecclesiastical regimen whatsoever. The Catholic Church began – instinctively, naïvely, unwittingly – when Christians first imagined their fellowship as an empirical entity, just as Israel had been a visible society.

Therefore there can be no regulatory relationship between local memberships. When the church sojourning in Rome addresses the church sojourning in Corinth (as in Clement's letter), it cannot send an order, any more than a city congregation could order a house congregation around, or Peter could address Ananias and Sapphira as a judge. All that any person or group can address to others is God's Word. No issues can be decided by right or rule.

Harnack was continuing to think, Sohm grieved, that it was simply a contrast between the larger, spiritual agenda of the great church and the narrow, pragmatic outlook of the local church. But, insisted Sohm, there was no local church! Or Harnack contrasted Jewish and hellenistic influences. Yet what Harnack identified as primitive Judeo-Christian tradition was not that at all, for the disciples had quickly broken all dependence upon Jewish institutions and hence all avenue for alien influence. They were left with pure, unconditioned Christianity. Harnack differentiated elected from charismatic leaders. But that was a meaningless distinction, for election need not exclude charism: it ratified it.

This brought Sohm to his own quite singular account of how the officers had originally been spiritual leaders and charismatic shepherds. What is astounding, Sohm exclaims, anticipating puzzlement, is not that spiritual anarchy could have produced a healthy church, but that it could have degenerated into the Catholic Church![50]

The primitive church congregated in two ways. To hear the word, there was no president, no reader, no privileged commentator, no rule of order save that two could not speak at once (this meant, not that one must defer to the speaker, but that any speaker had to sit down when another rose). "It amounted to spiritual anarchy."[51] The other gathering was eucharistic, and that would have been impossible without a format. It required someone to lead, to recite the thanksgiving prayer, to preach, to bless and pass the loaf and cup, to sit in Christ's seat as a reiteration of his supping with the disciples.

[50] Ibid. 377–380.   [51] Ibid. 384.

Behold the *episkopos/presbyteros*. Some sat while others stood. Behold the clergy and the laity. Some of those seated later assisted in distributing the elements as crowds grew larger. Behold the *diakonoi* distinguished from the *presbyteroi*. It must have been those who sat round the table who were the charismatics: the elect = *klêros* of God to serve the church.

Then near the end of the first century the two gatherings were merged into one, and the order of the eucharist unintentionally became the order of the church. Responsibility for finance and welfare was put in the hands of the elect, and power over the word as well. The president emerged as the solo shepherd-bishop. Yet it was not a legal order. Election to those tasks acknowledged God-given charisms, and gave no rights, for one might be unseated, as did occur in Corinth.

But as the eucharist gained in importance, as a source of eternal life, rank there became rank in the religious life of the church. It all fell apart after the Christians in Corinth unseated some *presbyteroi* and *diakonoi* and put the eucharist in the hands of some ascetics. Rome intervened, arguing that the offices were meant to be lifelong and could not be vacated without cause. Behold church law. Recourse was had to a rule, allegedly transmitted through the apostles. God's activity was thenceforth to be hedged in by correct form.

Clement, the villain of Sohm's piece, did not wish to eliminate the spiritual factor. His aim was to enhance and to emphasize it, but by legalizing and formalizing it. Nor did he set out to subvert the universal church, for it was a universal rule he imposed on Corinth, in military fashion. It is simply the case that the religious authenticity of the local congregation, according to the Catholic system of which Clement is the founder, would now depend on its conformity to a universal church regulation.

The man who finally stood up to restore the church from this devastating lapse was Luther. Wyclif and other reformers had held for a primary, invisible church of the predestined, but none of them had gone on to eliminate the visible, legal church. Luther, by Sohm's account, was the first to climb out of the secure bark and clasp Christ's hand in trust. The fundamental repugnance between legal bonds and Christ's fellowship, and the notion of an exclusively invisible church that was manifest only to the eyes of faith: this was the greatest and most powerful idea in the history of the church, Sohm believed.

Harnack was not so sure.[52] "In my opinion," he wrote in the words of Leibniz, "Sohm is essentially right in what he maintains, but wrong in what he rejects."

Harnack conceded that the churches were under government by charism, not by organization, until the second century. He agreed that it was a monarchical rule – of Christ – communicated through apostles, prophets and teachers. And he agreed that the eventual regimen under the officers was a step that led to disaster. He also concurred with the Leipzig jurist that the early lineaments native to the church were not adopted from either the Jewish synagogue or the heathen civil associations.

But he rejected any absolute opposition between invisible and incarnate church. That there was a tension between local church and world church, between charismatics and officers, between greater churches and their suffragans, between gospel fidelity and redemption of the culture – this he saw. But not an outright mutual repugnance.

Legislation resulted (still always invested with a divine sanction) in consequence of the development of the charismata. This led to various forms of organization, for "charisma" and "law" do not exclude one another in this connection; indeed, the charisma creates certain rights for itself. Finally the Church, when she began to become naturalized on earth and was compelled to regulate the social relations of her members, found herself unable simply to take over the public regulations already in force or to give them her adherence. Accordingly she increased the severity of the moral and social ordinances which she found already in existence and began, although comparatively late, to set up regulations of her own. These are in principle moral, but since in part they are made compulsory on the communities (marriage regulations, etc.), there arises an ecclesiastical law of a mixed character, *i.e.* a mixture of moral and legal elements and a confused compound of divine and secular law. Just for this reason the Church persistently felt and maintained that she stood above and beyond the secular legal system of the State.[53]

---

[52] Harnack had written an extended entry, "Verfassung, kirchliche usw." in Hauck's *Protestantische Real-Encyclopädie*, to which Sohm's *Wesen und Ursprung* of 1909 was a response. Immediately thereafter, Harnack brought his growing essay out in book form: *The Constitution and Law of the Church in the First Two Centuries*, trans. F. L. Pogson, ed. H. D. A. Major (London: Williams & Norgate, 1910). This translates *Entstehung und Entwickelung der Kirchenverfassung und des Kirchenrechts in den zwei ersten Jahrhunderten, nebst einer Kritik der Abhandlung R. Sohm's "Wesen und Ursprung des Katholizismus" und Untersuchungen über "Evangelium," "Wort Gottes," und das trinitarische Bekenntnis* (Leipzig: Hinrichs, 1910).

[53] Ibid. 169–170.

In support of that theory he itemized an array of authorities that had been acknowledged in the very earliest church: the Old Testament and ancient rabbinical ordinances; the sayings of Jesus; the Twelve under Peter as leader; certain individuals including Peter, John and James of Jerusalem; and the assembly of believers. The community in Jerusalem also occupied a unique position for all other communities, though they retained their own autonomy. "These were all absolute authorities, which kept within narrow limits the freedom of the individual, and also his independence and 'equality'."[54] There had never been a time when the church was without authority of an externally verifiable kind.

Eventually the system of authority was perverted, but not because it had been anti-Christian of its very nature. When, according to Harnack at this stage in his thinking, was the worm first in the wood? He thinks it was when the line of Jesus' kinsmen – James and Simeon – was given the ascendancy in the mother church in Jerusalem. James and the local elders then superseded the Twelve. This was the result of Judeo-Christianity gone wrong, and for Harnack James "is the pope of the Ebionite fantasy."[55]

The ascendancy of the monarchical episcopate was a response to a variety of perceived needs by the church of the second century. Harnack deplores its Catholic outcome in Rome, but he is unsatisfied by Sohm's starkly anti-institutional Protestant alternative.[56]

[54] Ibid. 23. In general, though, Harnack was cautious about admitting that any individual in the primitive church might have an authority that could stand up to any corporate authority. This may derive from one abiding preoccupation in his work. The work makes constant references to the typical Catholic claims: divine authority, apostolic succession in the episcopate, infallible pope, and the like. To fend off those claims he is led to generalize as a theologian and say that no individual enjoyed authority in that church, though as a historian he is repeatedly describing certain individuals who because of their positions had extraordinary prerogatives. Were he relating his material backward to Jewish antecedents instead of forward to Catholic sequelae, he might non-defensively have noted that there were individuals in Jewry to whom everyone deferred in community dealings. It is unfortunate that the consciousness of Rome has made these scholars so concerned to disallow granting precedent to Catholic claims in the primitive record, for it may also have made them unwittingly neglect how that record may enshrine continuations of Jewish institution and custom.

[55] Ibid. 35. Harnack, like many contemporaries, saw the line of Jewish influence in the church as a dead end. With it was presumably interred most of the Jewish institutional inheritance, which was regarded to be pathological, as was its host church.

[56] "The external features of ecclesiastical organization appear indeed in a great variety of forms, but in no century have the essential features of the Western Catholic constitution of the Church been simpler than in our own. A breach has been made by the Reformation, and by the Reformation only. Here, in relation to the organization, constitution, and law of the Church, the Reformation has cut more deeply into history and historical development than at any other point. It has not only destroyed in its own compass the medieval constitution

The influence of a scholar as active, accomplished and prestigious as Adolf von Harnack is not easy to reckon. For one thing, he published half-a-dozen major reconstructions of early church order, each one significantly varying from the last, yet with hardly any acknowledgement of change. Every account was sustained by plentiful detail, but rather less consideration of its main beams and joists. Thus Harnack was a difficult and moving target.

KARL VON WEIZSÄCKER

It was due in part to Harnack's work, nevertheless, that a conventional theory began to establish itself. One early carrier of the doctrine was Karl von Weizsäcker, professor of church history and chancellor of the University of Tübingen. His style is much simpler and also more synthetic than Harnack's.[57]

A first principle for Weizsäcker is that Paul's authentic letters provide our most direct evidence of the earliest Christian period, and they have the additional advantage of not being affected by the theological predilections of later editors (as exegetes were discovering had been the case with the gospels). Therefore all other data must bend to what we find, or do not find, in Paul. One pauline doctrine is given particular emphasis: that Christian faith had left Israel behind. Paul's insistence that the Torah has been repealed, and that the new faith has vacated the old ways, leads Weizsäcker and others of this mind to conclude that Christians had created a community which, in structure and in value, was pure innovation.

A second guiding principle, which followed easily, is that the first Christians could not have modelled themselves on any previous institutions, because the church was such a new creation. In particular he is swift to disallow any Jewish influences. The church was not like a rabbinical school, for the Christian disciples were not in training to be teachers themselves. One alone would remain their *didaskalos* = teacher.

of the Church, but it no longer possesses any connection with the Church of the first and second centuries. The Reformation, in so far as it is Lutheran, has fallen back on the only principle which it was admittedly able to prove from the oldest documents, and with which it goes to the root of the matter, namely, that the word of God must be proclaimed and that an office for this proclamation dare not be wanting." Ibid. 171.

[57] Karl [Heinrich] von Weizsäcker, *The Apostolic Age of the Christian Church*, trans. James Millar, 2 vols. (London and Edinburgh: Williams & Norgate, 1894–95). This translates *Das apostolische Zeitalter der christlichen Kirche* (Freiburg im Breisgau: Mohr, 1892; 2nd edn. [1st edn. 1886]).

Nor did they resemble the synagogues. He gives several grounds for this conviction. First, the Jewish synagogue was a civil community, and he is convinced that the Judeo-Christians persisted in their civil existence as Jews, and consequently as members of their old synagogues.[58] Second, the style of synagogue worship was unfitting for the Christian assemblies: "what was done in these meetings had become something wholly original, the independent creation of the faith, resting only in external features to some extent on historical precedents and foundations."[59] Third, the very fact that there were many special-interest synagogues in Jewry at that time, but that Christians chose not to use "synagogue" as their own designation (preferring *ekklêsia* = church instead), shows an explicit sense and assertion of a break with the past.[60]

The purpose in this argument is to discredit any "Catholic" assertion of an authority source that might have an independent and ultimate supremacy. Weizsäcker's patron is Paul, in his struggle against the judaizers.

He flatly denies that the apostolic church had any official structure. It was a community held together by an inspired good will, without any authority figures. Every community was self-governing, and made its decisions by democratic vote in which every member counted as much as any other. "An ecclesiastical office endowed with independent authority could not subsist along with this self-government. It could only take the form of a ministry whose warrant rested from day to day on the voluntary approval of the members, just as it began with a free offer of self, and was therefore included by Paul among the charismata."[61] The apostles were respected, not

---

[58] Ibid. 2:316.

[59] Weizsäcker "precludes all those ideas of a ritual observance which have been borrowed, either from the older religions, or from the later practice of Christian churches. In point of fact a Divine service in the stricter sense held no place in those meetings. What was done at them was not meant to influence Deity; not even worship was the chief object; the central idea was the common expression of the faith as such. Our nearest parallel to this practice is the synagogue, whose service consisted essentially in instruction in the law, and was devoted to the sacred writings. In the Church the object already was to cherish the religious possession in the spiritual life. But among believers another possession took the place of the law, namely, Christ, and this change involved a different kind of observance." Ibid. 246.

[60] "The name synagogue was avoided, and the fact that it was avoided, in spite of the ease with which by a qualifying word or phrase it could have been distinguished from that of the Jews, warrants the conclusion that their meeting even in form had nothing in common with that institution. The name *ekklêsia* applied to them the idea which belonged to the whole body of God's people, and indeed the earliest expression is *ekklêsia tou theou*, the Church of God. Believers who recognized the distinctive character of their faith could not be satisfied with forming a separate synagogue." Ibid. 1:48.   [61] Ibid. 2:314.

because they held any rank or office, but because they were so impressively filled with the Spirit. Theirs was a ministry, not an office. They gave no orders, save on the strength of some saying of the Lord. Likewise, of course, prophets and teachers.

What of the presbyters, whose presence and importance in Acts is taken by so many exegetes to be a holdover from the Jewish office? Proceeding from his doctrine that no authoritative rank is possible, he concludes that neither James nor the Jerusalem elders could have had any power to command. Much more reliable did he consider Paul's account of his churches, where all titles denote ministries that generous and endowed individuals had simply undertaken spontaneously and voluntarily.

Thus, at the end of that period *presbyteroi* are simply the (super)natural leaders from the earliest days. Their voluntary service had acquired for them the respect of the community, but no office. There were no deacons. Groups of volunteer women lent their hands to the community's material needs. And *episkopoi* were an inner circle of *presbyteroi* whose labors were the most assiduous, and who took on the most prominent burdens of service. As the original apostles died off, the elders became a sort of class in the church: the valiant veterans, tried and true. And those among them who had presided enjoyed a trust that invited them to assume a more formalized role, which stabilized later into a permanent office around Clement's time. And when, still later, teaching became reserved to that office, the monarchical episcopate had come into existence.[62]

Auguste Sabatier

The polarity of Weizsäcker's proposal is clearly derived from what he regards as the root convictions of Catholicism and Protestantism: official authority vs. congregational sovereignty. An interesting dissent from this now widely accepted theory came from Auguste Sabatier, the founder and *doyen* of the Protestant theological faculty in Paris.[63] Sabatier pressed home the doctrine that other Protestant scholars had only inconsistently applied. If religion is an inner inspiration, how can any institutional authority, even a congregational one, claim its allegiance? Beginning with an axiom like that

[62] Ibid. 334.
[63] Auguste Sabatier, *The Religions of Authority and the Religion of the Spirit* (London: Williams & Norgate, 1904). This translates *Les religions d'autorité et la religion de l'esprit* (Paris: Fischbacher, 1903).

of Sohm, he will not conclude that the Reformation had really freed the Spirit. He classifies both Catholicism and Protestantism as religions of authority: both alike are dogmatic and antagonistic to spiritual freedom.

It is the property of the method of authority to base all judgment of doctrine upon the exterior marks of its origin and the trustworthiness of those who promulgated it. In religion this method appeals to miracles, which accredit God's messengers to men, and stamp their words or writings with the divine imprint.

On the other hand, the modern experimental method puts us in immediate contact with reality, and teaches us to judge of a doctrine only according to its intrinsic value, directly manifested to the mind in the degree of its evidence. The two methods are so radically opposed that to accept the latter is at once to mark the former as insufficient and outworn.[64]

Jesus was an apocalyptic prophet who announced the imminent judgment of God. He neither willed nor foresaw a church, for the world was in its last days. His apostles were messengers, not functionaries. Their preaching invited listeners into no social relationship with Jesus or any organization. The elect cohered through sheer good will and mutual service.[65] Their unity was founded neither on government nor on rites nor on dogmas. Obviously, they had repudiated the externalized structures and mentality of Judaism.

The hardening of self-ordained service into ranked offices followed when the moral enthusiasm of the church had cooled, and when its family character had lost its spontaneity. "In proportion as Christianity grew inwardly cold, it felt the necessity of strengthening its external unity by a more closely knit organization. The discipline, authority, and unified government of the bishop must henceforth

[64] Ibid. xxi. Sabatier considers Protestant treatment of the Bible to be as authoritarian as Catholic treatment of the hierarchy.

[65] Sabatier is derivative in his scholarship. His portrayal of early church development runs along rails with no rust on them:

Above or side by side with the apostles, prophets, and teachers who held their vocation directly from God alone, and who were essentially itinerants, each community naturally drew from its own body its settled ministers, *elders, bishops, and deacons* charged with the general interests of the community, and with the maintenance of discipline and the distribution of alms. Thus came into being and grew up side by side with the free and nomad apostolate a settled ecclesiastical functionality, which was destined little by little to replace and absorb it ... The first Christian communities, composed at first of members equal among themselves and distinguished only by varieties in the gifts of the Spirit, became in time organized bodies, veritable churches, which at first developed and took on different physiognomies according to the diversities of their geographical and social surroundings. In Palestine and beyond the Jordan the Christian community was modelled upon the Jewish synagogue, and apparently bore the same Aramean name. In the Occident it appears to have reproduced the form of pagan colleges or associations, so numerous in Greek cities at that epoch. Ibid. 24–25.

make good the ever growing deficit in faith, hope, and love."[66] Ardor had frozen into order.

What Catholics did to subject their membership to officers, Protestants did to make the scriptures an ultimate authority. Sabatier calls for a third alternative, a religion with no institutions, wherein people believe only what they find persuasive.

THE EMERGENT CONSENSUS

The scholars of the nineteenth century disposed of biblical and historical competence considerably more advanced than had been available to their predecessors, the reformers of the fourteenth to eighteenth centuries. This new knowledge naturally played a leading part in their contributions to the consensus. They were not, however, indifferent to theological considerations, though that feature of their work was surely more openly known to them in the conclusions they drew than in the presuppositions with which they began their work. Thus was it ever.

Broad as was the span of their diversity, most of these writers took the earliest Christian period of Jesus' preaching and the first enthusiastic and expansive apostolic generations as a high point, and they reckoned the more maintenance-oriented church of the second century to be a disappointment. The springtime of courtship and the summer honeymoon had autumned into bickering and bureaucracy – somehow. That "somehow" was the sparsely documented bafflement presented by the evidence which they had to unpuzzle.

The earliest churches had been created, motivated and led by men and women with obvious divine endowments that held those communities in one mind and one heart. By some authors those leading figures were described as servants, workers, stewards, overseers, preachers, ambassadors, companions-at-arms, God's helpers, and the like. This flexible, informal vocabulary designated divinely imparted energies for service, not offices or official titles. Another school of thought paid more attention to the three cohorts of charismatics: the apostles, prophets and teachers. Though their titles became fixed and their manner of performance stylized, they came by their powers through no human agency, and so they could not be considered as the designees of the church. Even Paul could not appoint a prophet. Whether one drew more attention to those

[66] Ibid. 82.

zealous in service during the first generation, or to those outstanding in the Spirit's endowments during the second generation, the framers of the consensus considered the foundational period well served by them, and fully provided for by God without the need or call for officers of their own making.

There was the same measure of agreement that a century later the churches had fallen into the hands of a hierarchical network of clerical officers – *episkopoi, presbyteroi* and *diakonoi* – who came by their positions through one or another political process and who inexorably displaced the primeval leadership categories.

Though some scholarly inquiry was devoted to tracing the origins and activities of the lower orders of "elder" and "servant," the crux of the debate was the "overseer." Some followed Hatch in seeing the *episkopos* as a direct replica of the financial officer of the Greco-Roman associations. Harnack construed the *episkopos* as a generic administrator; Sohm, as the presiding figure at worship; Weizsäcker, as the most zealous of the leading activists. But they commonly agreed that a crisis of unity which threatened the churches' survival created a felt need and a role for solo leadership that had not previously existed. The Gnostic heresy and the Montanist schism combined to supply that crisis. And the *episkopos*, who had had a specific, limited role (whatever it was) was transformed into the overall president of the local church. Through swift consolidation of power and the acquiescence to pressing need by the community, the *episkopos* acquired despotic power locally. Through corporate interaction with his peers in other churches, he created a class that claimed to define doctrine and make policy for the churches of the region and of the world.

The earliest documents describe leadership of the first days as provided to the church by inward, spiritual gifts. The evidence of the next century describes officers provided by the church through an appointment or electoral process. Albrecht Ritschl, who deplored that change, nevertheless saw charism as what properly underlay office. Election could not empower any candidate, but it was meant to acknowledge the spiritually gifted, while the rite of ordination would ratify those gifts and rouse them to more fervent activity. What went wrong was that churchmen imagined they had within their personal gift powers that were really God's; it was then only natural that they would come to fancy the gifts as awarded for their own personal exaltation rather than for the sake of the community.

It was not an unnatural conclusion for this line of thought finally to reject all attempts to integrate and align charism with office. The only authentic leadership in the church must come from the unregulated Spirit, and all attempts to institutionalize the church are hostile to that Spirit. This followed eventually from the dictum that divine undertakings must transcend human initiative, rather than create it, transfigure it and invest it with a higher character.

What befell the early church, in their view of it, was therefore an unfortunate turn of historical events. But it was more than that – much more. It was a radical perversion of the liberating forces Christ had brought them. It was a regression to the worst aspects of the Jewish Law and temple priesthood. The inspired believer who came from personal conversion into the believing community to find support against a predatory world encountered instead a despotic administration, in some ways more menacing (because of its blinded pretensions) than the pagan society he or she had left behind. Thus ran the consensus as the century was closing.

CHAPTER 3

The early twentieth century: the consensus is disputed

Auguste Sabatier had appeared to march off by himself, with idiosyncratic doctrines and a sparse following. But he was fundamentally ratifying a received view of early church order: Jesus as a simple prophet/preacher, followed by a golden age of inspired, unorganized discipleship with a spontaneous allotment of tasks, followed by a crisis of unity threatening enough to induce the members to accept an authoritative regimen. That regimen, with its officers and its claims, was at best a natural response to crisis, and at worst a poisoning of the true gospel.

Stark though Sabatier's formulation was, he was substantially following the received view. By then that shared understanding had become established firmly in continental Protestant scholarship. Whatever might be the wrangling over detail which kept the discussion alive, there was a large consensus that had to await the turn into the twentieth century to encounter any major dispute.

It was the new ecumenical movement that was to put the consensus under new challenge. The legitimacy of officers, and in particular of episcopal succession from the apostles, was now to be defended not merely by Catholics who were the traditional and distant (and controlling) adversaries, but by Anglicans who, as also rooted in the sixteenth-century break from Rome, and now amicable partners with the Protestants, Lutheran and Reformed, in the convergence of the ecumenical movement, deserved a more considerate reply to their criticisms. But then they in turn became embroiled in heated debate with their British neighbors, Presbyterian and Congregationalist and Methodist, over the matter of bishops. Although scripture and the Fathers were quoted and interpreted fastidiously during the early years of this century, the conclusions one drew were very severely governed by one's theological loyalties on the matter of apostolic succession.

Heinrich Holtzmann

Only then did it appear that not everyone had been convinced. Heinrich Holtzmann, trained in Heidelberg, much influenced by Rothe, and eventually a professor in Strassburg, withstood to the teeth both the assumptions and the conclusions of the consensus which had dominated most Protestant scholarship of the previous century, and which was grounded on the earlier work of the Tübingen faculty.[1]

The preferential attention accorded to pauline material in the New Testament canon, according to Holtzmann, has obscured from sight other theological influences that shaped the infant church. Paul's emphasis on new creation and on the sharp disjunction from the Jewish past was balanced by a very different and influential school of interpretation in Alexandria, where the divine plan was explained not as a clean break with the past but as a progressive continuity. The New Testament grows out of the Old. Gospel was but a fulfilment and flowering of Law, never a repudiation of it. In fact, none of the early writers had followed Paul's assertion that the only purpose for the Hebrew Law had been "to render crimes explicit" (Galatians 3:19), to make sin more visible by criminalizing it. They wanted to use the Torah, not to void it. Residual piety from their Jewish past led them to use allegory and other interpretive devices to find divine guidance in the Law. In similar fashion they used the prophets to accredit Jesus as Messiah, and cited the wisdom books to establish the soundness of the renewed faith. Thus alongside Paul there was a strong alternative view which looked with the reverence of an heir on its Jewish legacy.[2]

It was a misreading of the early church to imagine, as so many scholars had long agreed to do, that it witnessed a struggle between gentile Christianity, championed by Paul, and a Judeo-Christianity that was authoritarian and perhaps Gnostic. It was wrong to suppose that the one party had hounded the other out of the church. Holtzmann recalls much in the Judeo-Christian tradition – in Hebrews, John, the Pastorals, Barnabas, Ignatius – that had been integrated, in healthy form, into the enduring church.

Despite the fade and eclipse of Judeo-Christianity as a distinct

---

[1] Heinrich Julius Holtzmann, *Lehrbuch der neutestamentlichen Theologie*, 2 vols., 2nd edn. (Tübingen: Mohr, 1911 [1st edn. 1897]).

[2] "Das Neue Testament und die alte katholische Kirche," ibid. 2:562–580.

wing of the great fellowship, marked especially by the devastations of Jcrusalem and Judaea by Vespasian and Titus (68–70 AD) and by Hadrian (135 AD), the global church inherited much of its permanent structure from Jewish sources: its exegesis and use of the scriptures, its principle of tradition, the shape of its worship, and its community organization, which was patterned after that of the synagogue.

Sohm had assessed the changes in Christianity as a smothering of the ideal by legalism. Holtzmann would rather see it as a tempering process whereby an only partially reflective faith had matured. The earliest period was not so much ideal as it was simple. It had no complete program save for monotheism, Jesus' high status as bearer of an absolute divine revelation, and the coming of his kingly rule. In time this proliferated into a medley of forms: Judeo-Christian, pauline, alexandrian, Gnostic, Catholic. The ideal was actually mingled with the real: the sinless character of the church combined with sinful disciples; community possession of the Spirit, combined yet conflicting with a stratification of classes and roles; no one to be a teacher, yet the community wanting to have many learners; local churches pulling against the full fabric of the church; Jesus' preaching overlaid with the emergent concerns of later churchmen; all were one in the Lord, yet factionalism was rampant.

What developed was not a triumph of one side of the tension over the other or even a compromise. It was an amalgam of both. Subjective enthusiasm got leaned on by the community. Confessional formulae were elaborated. The explicit rights of the community asserted in the pastoral epistles were combined with the diversity of offices reported in later documents. The offices modeled on Jewish tradition were revised by borrowing from Greco-Roman parallels. The church organization which resulted in the early second century did not push aside the antecedents of the first generation; it was the product of a process that was already underway in the New Testament.[3]

Holtzmann paints his challenge with a broad brush, and he did not stipple in much detail about actual office or organization in the church. One handicap facing scholars in his time was the lack of

---

[3] It was later in the second century that outside influences became unhealthy, Holtzmann believed. The cults of heathen fellowships contaminated Christian worship with notions of sacrament and priesthood. Thus the form of the Catholic Church witnessed in Irenaeus, Tertullian and Clement of Alexandria is something alien to the messianic communities of the apostolic period. Ibid. 576–580.

available sources that might familiarize them with the Jewish institutions of the hellenistic-Roman period. Emil Schürer's great *Geschichte des jüdischen Volkes* had been appearing volume by volume in the eighties and nineties, and it quickly became the text Christians quoted for Jewish institutions as they bore upon the New Testament or early Christianity. But there was hardly a Christian scholar who dealt with the primary sources directly. Therefore few footsteps widened the trail that Holtzmann had stamped through the underbrush.

HANS LIETZMANN

The Harnack theory meanwhile was being recounted and reinforced, with variations, by creative researchers. One of these was Hans Lietzmann, who was later to replace Harnack in his chair at Berlin. Lietzmann discovered two distinct church orders.[4] One order (seen in Paul and in the *Didache*) was dominated by the apostles, prophets and teachers, but had also appointed *episkopoi* and *diakonoi* in subsidiary, technical roles.

[B]ishops and deacons could be chosen from amongst the known men of the church, and what was required of them did not go beyond the capacities of an ordinary person. The charismatics, on the other hand, were supermen to whom God had granted miraculous powers ... Only the charismatics were officers of the church of God which embraced the whole world, the one church of Christ. The bishops and deacons were merely assistants in the service of the local church, i.e. of an accidental institution existing under mundane conditions, with no independent life-force in the Christian sense. These men were of lower status and lower authority.[5]

A next development was that the officers then became associated with worship, as the prophetic charism grew less frequent. This united spiritual and secular power made the officers the *de facto* energizers of the community. They quickly replaced their charismatic predecessors – and in so doing changed the nature of their own incumbency, which became permanent.[6]

---

[4] Hans Lietzmann, "Zur altchristlichen Verfassungsgeschichte," *Zeitschrift für wissenschaftlichen Theologie*, 55 (1914), 97–153.

[5] Lietzmann, *The Beginnings of the Christian Church*, trans. Bertram Lee Woolf, 2nd edn. (London: Lutterworth, 1949 [1st edn. 1937]), 146. This translates the first of four volumes of Lietzmann's great *Geschichte der alten Kirche* (Berlin: Walter de Gruyter, 1932–1944), issued in English as *History of the Early Church*, with each volume under a distinct title.

[6] "As long as they were only the business and financial officers of individual churches they could be regarded as analogous to Jewish or pagan leaders in a similar community, and a temporal limit to their office could be required and applied. By the nature of the case, a

Thus the church order of the *Didache* was not very durable. Another church order which knew little or nothing about *episkopoi* and *diakonoi* was built upon *presbyteroi*. It was of Jewish origin, as were they. They healed the sick and forgave sins, preserved the traditional teaching, and led the flock as a shepherd guides his sheep. The three tasks of apostles, prophets and teachers which the *Didache* community had set apart from one another are in these presbyteral communities found combined into the role of the college of elders.

In time, calculated Lietzmann, these two distinct constitutions merged. The terms *episkopos* and *presbyteros* at this point are not so much titles as they are interchangeable descriptions of a function that has absorbed most of the ministries of the church. The same people are styled *presbyteroi* insofar as they are senior and influential, and *episkopoi* insofar as they have supervisory reponsibility.[7]

AN ANGLICAN STATEMENT: THE SWETE SYMPOSIUM

Eventually a group of conservative English scholars rose up against this *Licht vom Osten* that so many continentals were taking to be the light of the world. In 1918 a book of essays on early church and ministry appeared, edited by H. B. Swete. Swete, the Cambridge Regius Professor of Divinity, had chosen contributors who had the wits and wherewithal to formulate theories of their own, but they proved as intent as were their countrymen under arms in pursuit of only one purpose: to vanquish Berlin.[8]

Harnack's finding that charismatics and officers were at cross-purposes was something that these Anglicans could not find in their review of the evidence. All ministries were charismatic, whether they were inspired or elected. The episcopacy had in earliest times been

charismatic could not be deposed, because he had been appointed by God through the gift of the spirit; and he could only lose office by God's intervention, and this at the same time as he lost the gift of the spirit. If now the elected *episcopos* took the place of such a prophet, the next thing was to grant that the former could no more be set aside than the latter – and it is this very point that the epistle of Clement explains to the Corinthians." Ibid. 193–194.

[7] "Zur altchristlichen Verfassungsgeschichte," 132–139. Thus Paul's *episkopoi* in Philippi become Polycarp's *presbyteroi*; Clement describes *presbyteroi* as having been established as *episkopoi* by the apostles. Lietzmann remarks that *diakonoi*, by contrast, have few other designations. By the late first century theirs is a title, a name, not a mere description. Lietzmann goes on to accept the consensus about how the monarchical episcopate emerged: *The Founding of the Church Universal* [vol. 2 of *A History of the Early Church*], trans. Bertram Lee Woolf, 2nd edn. (London: Lutterworth, 1950 [German original: 1936]), 58–68.

[8] H[enry] B[arclay] Swete, ed., *Essays on the Early History of the Church and the Ministry* (London: Macmillan, 1918). Swete had died in 1917.

supported by prophecy. Arthur Mason wrote: "We may surmise that the development of the Christian hierarchy was in great measure due, not to the intrigues of self-seeking presbyters and bishops, nor to the cravings of the natural man, but to the exhortations of Christian prophets, speaking by the word of the Lord and in the Spirit."[9] It was only when the prophets began to pull away from the *episkopoi* that the latter began to discipline them. And that occurred well before the Montanist prophets were in full cry.

It had been the Germans who minted the category "charismatics" thirty years earlier. But Paul used *charisma* of any and every manifestation of grace; it was never so specialized a term, argued J. A. Robinson, that it could apply to apostles, prophets and teachers but not to overseers, elders and deacons.[10]

Robinson also contradicted Harnack's doctrine, now so widely received, that the "charismatics" enjoyed a universally accredited teaching authority, unlike the officers who were elected by local jurisdictions to transact business. On the contrary: Paul did not single out apostles, prophets and teachers from the variegated crowd of those with different *charismata*. He acknowledged authority in apostles, but he allowed prophets to be contradicted. The *Didache*, though it enjoined general reverence for preachers ("My son, honor him who speaks the Word of God to you"), also advised cautious discrimination between devout prophets and hucksters.[11] The prophets in the *Didache*, in fact, are not the same as the prophets in Paul. For him, prophets are those many Christians who speak out. For the *Didache*, they are (as Paul feared they would become) professionals.

Robinson disagrees also with the German belief that *episkopoi* and *presbyteroi* were originally different. He agrees with his old mentor Lightfoot that they were a single office, so diversified as to merit a plurality of titles. They were not bureaucrats who competed with the inspired orders for power. They were already a cadre of leaders who shared authority, and whose continuity through changing styles of

[9] Arthur James Mason, "Conceptions of the Church in Early Times," ibid. 1–56 at 30. He refers to a number of passages which described the selection of officers on the strength of prophetic oracles. Mason, once Swete's colleague at Cambridge as the Lady Margaret's Professor of Divinity, was now a distinguished preacher at Canterbury.

[10] Joseph Armitage Robinson, "The Christian Ministry in the Apostolic and Sub-apostolic Periods," ibid. 57–92 at 72. Robinson, another Cambridge man, had been Norrisian Professor of Divinity and then dean of Westminster and, lastly, of Wells.

[11] Ibid. 70.

office makes for unity in the church: unity within a church, unity between churches, and unity down through the succession of churches.

KARL HOLL

A most extraordinary voice entered the discussion at this point: that of Karl Holl, protégé, friend and then fellow professor of Harnack in Berlin. Holl, in a much-circulated paper read before the Berlin Academy in 1921, was ostensibly taking issue with Sohm. But the view he propounded was as much at variance with Harnack as with Sohm.

The very earliest Christian community deferred, Holl insisted, to "a regulatory hierarchy, a divinely sanctioned order, a divine church order, an institutional church into which individuals are received. A *numerus clausus* of apostles – James and the Twelve (if there is any pope here it is James, not Peter) – enjoys an abiding superiority that no one else can aspire to, and is accordingly acknowledged as the rightful leadership."[12] Their testimony quickens the church; they are its "pillars."

James, Cephas and John are called "pillars" by Paul, even when he is sarcastic: pillars of the general church, not merely of that in Jerusalem. Cephas himself, in an early church gloss that became Matthew 16:18, is the rock on which the church is grounded, in defiance of Sheol's gates. The community, on this view, was God's handiwork, but built on specific persons specifically related to Jesus.

James, who was not one of the Twelve, was the chief, and first among the pillars. When his agents criticized Cephas they were not silenced as by one with higher authority, but were accounted to as deputies of a decisive superior. James also had the advantage of Paul, who admitted that James was visited by the risen Lord during the statutory and foundational appearances, whereas Paul's vision was after the basic resurrection appearances had come to an end, and when the revelation was already complete and its personal transmitters were known.

The notions of authority and of tradition are implicitly related in this scenario. The appearances have aroused the free prophetic spirit. In their aftermath a rich spiritual life flourishes: not only in the primitive

---

[12] Karl Holl, "Der Kirchenbegriff des Paulus in seinem Verhältnis zu dem der Urgemeinde," *Gesammelte Aufsätze zur Kirchengeschichte*, 2 (Tübingen: Mohr, 1928), 44–67 at 54. This appeared originally in the *Sitzungsberichte der Berliner Akademie* (1921), 920–947.

community, but in all Christian communities. The fact that the most vivid revelations – those that vouched for the resurrection in the most palpable way – came to be confined to a limited time period, is what created the notion of tradition. For only thus could the most important revelations be handed on to the era that would follow: "I handed on to you in the first place what I received." Charism and tradition, therefore, do not stand apart in meaning or in time, as if tradition were only a remnant of the original. Both notions enjoy a mutuality of growth and rationale. Tradition, in fact, will surpass charism for there is no charism potent enough to attain the level at which the visions of Christ took place.[13]

The members of the founding group do not hesitate to claim specific rights. They forgo table-serving, just as Paul would forgo baptizing. They claim a living from the gospel, and a corps of assistants.

Besides these authoritative individuals, there is an authoritative community: the church in Jerusalem, which enjoys a juridical status. It is to be the city of the *parousia*, or final appearance of the Lord, and the city from which faith in Jesus issues forth. Thus Luke moves the chief appearance stories there, and John locates most of his ministry gospel there. Paul can speak of the Jerusalem Above, and Revelation can portray the Heavenly Jerusalem. Its status bridges past and future: there the apostles are to be found and there the testimony originates. When the threat of violence disperses the Christians resident there the apostles alone remain, for that is their duty post. Peter and John are sent out on missions, but Jerusalem is their church.

Now this, insists Holl, is no late, first-century notion of an authoritative center; it was there from the first. Paul records early annoyance with his apostolic overlords, but he continues to be supervised by Jerusalem. He may say that by agreement Peter will work among the Jews and leave him free with the Gentiles. But there was no true division of turf. Peter is active later in Antioch (and perhaps in Corinth), and Jewish minorities in Paul's churches are protected by Jerusalem as faithful observers of Torah. Jerusalem remained supreme.

The collection also revealed Jerusalem's rank. Contributions were due, not simply because of the fact of great want in Judaea, but because Jerusalem had been a spiritual benefactress of all the churches, including Paul's. The beneficiaries were not only the poor,

---

[13] Ibid. 50–51.

but *hoi hagioi* = the saints. *Hoi hagioi* becomes a synonym for the mother community in Jerusalem, as well as *hoi ptôkoi* = *ha-ebionim* = the poor. Thus the collection was a duty imposed by Jerusalem on the gentile communities. Paul softened the duty with much talk of community and mutual service, but Galatians makes clear that it was not entirely a spontaneous offering: Freely you have received [the faith, not money], freely give [money, not faith]. Agabus the prophet foretells a worldwide famine, and the message is: send money to Jerusalem, to lay at the feet of the apostles.

Holl concludes that it is absurd to imagine the original Christians regarding all churches as autonomous peers, or all believers as equals. The mother church governed all, and was to be supported by all, and it maintained the faith of all. There were, as well, privileged individuals who did the same.

Paul agreed with this view, to a certain extent. He held that:

1 the church is no one-level mass; there are levels of precedence;
2 the apostles were put by God in first place;
3 honor is due to the mother church, which was Paul's own point of departure.

But he diverged in several ways:

1 beneath even the foundational apostles is the living Christ, the bedrock on which the church is founded;
2 the apostles are thus instruments, servants, heralds, ambassadors, not sovereigns;
3 as for their personal selves, God does not have favorites;
4 the individual believer is not totally a derivative of the community, for each one possesses the Spirit; and, while they are unweaned babes, they are also called to judge (*inter alia*, whether Paul's is the right gospel);
5 the true measure of each community is the Christ-given life it displayed, more than its conformity to Christ's apostles;
6 everyone in Christ is numbered among "the saints."

Paul struggled with Jerusalem, and his claim to a personal primacy was one factor that helped weaken the acceptance of a primatial church. Another factor was the killing of James and the scattering of the Jerusalem church, while the gentile churches went on growing prodigiously without the supervisory attention of the mother church.

But the essential points of Paul's argument had not been fully vindicated. In fact it was his own aloofness towards Jerusalem that helped make possible a successor church to be designated in Rome. For Rome's primacy was sustained by the claim that Peter and Paul had given their last witness there. Paul's defensive exaltation of the rank of apostle also actually had a reverse effect of enhancing the rank of those who, unlike himself, had been there from the start.

Thus Holl, Harnack's close colleague, rejects the accepted view that the first church was a network of peer communities peopled by egalitarian democrats, where there was no office or authority. There were, he insists, both communities and individuals that had authoritative status as anchors and guarantors of the tradition. They outranked charism.[14]

One implication of Holl's line of argument – though not the one he himself would draw – is that the monarchical episcopate might be neither as foreign nor as novel nor as sinister a development as many had been thinking. There had been such authority in the church from the beginning. One scholar who pursued such a dissident possibility was Karl Götz, who wrote as an exegete rather than as a church historian. His hunch was that Matthew 16:17–19 was edited with the intention of portraying Peter as the prototype for the monarchical bishop.[15]

[14] See his "Kirchenbegriff," 64–67, where he remarks that Paul's points had much merit, and found some resonance in writers like Clement of Alexandria in the East, and in Augustine in the West, but that Luther was the first to comprehend them fully. It should be borne in mind that Holl joins Harnack and even Sohm in his opposition to any attempt by Catholic scholars to support their church's claims by pointing to the primitive data. This is given color in some early correspondence between Holl and his mentor, Harnack. In 1904 Holl had been working in the Vatican Library. He wrote Harnack how he had been befriended by the scholars on the staff: Ehrle, Mercati, Le Grelle, Vatasso. The last-mentioned had been working years on a book of incipits (an index of documents by their opening lines) to the fathers. Holl thought it *eine enorme Arbeitskraft*, and considered Vatasso "a really good and brilliant man." "However, this winter he survived an appendix operation, and how did he show his gratitude? By a pilgrimage to Lourdes. One is always astonished at how successful Catholicism is at inducing a split life mentally in its faithful. Not the faintest ray of one's considerable intelligence shines through to the religious domain. As good-natured as they can be: in that domain they are, and they all remain, children." *Karl Holl (1866–1926), Briefwechsel mit Adolf von Harnack*, ed. Heinrich Karpp (Tübingen: Mohr, 1966), 34.

[15] Karl Gerold Götz, *Petrus als Gründer und Oberhaupt der Kirche und Schauer von Gesichten nach den altchristlichen Berichten und Legenden*, vol. 13 of *Untersuchungen zum Neuen Testament* (Leipzig: J. C. Hinrichs, 1927), esp. pp. 49–54.

KARL G. GÖTZ

Matthew's gospel is thought to derive from a Judeo-Christian milieu in Syria or Palestine. Following Schürer, Götz sees the office of the Jewish *archisynagôgos* = synagogue chief as taken over into Palestinian Christianity. There is evidence that even the title was used in some Christian communities. The presbyterate, the patriarchate (by which he means James' presidency in Jerusalem) and the apostolate were also borrowed from the Jews. What Christian office, then, derives from that of the synagogue chief? Götz thinks the episcopate was.

Wherever the title *episkopos* came from, the functions of the Jewish and the Christian offices are similar. The *archisynagôgos* presided over worship, over welfare programs and over synagogue staff.[16] The *episkopos* presided over order at meetings, over welfare, over correspondence, archives and treasury, and over community relations. Deacons stood at their side, like synagogue servants. The similarities Götz finds convincing.

But whence the monarchical episcopate? He speculates that the Jerusalem patriarchate of James and Simeon was a likely model, and that the struggle against heresy was the provocation. But when the Gospel according to Matthew was in process of late editing (he puts that in Trajan's time, early second century), the line of Jesus' kinsmen was lapsing in the Jerusalem church. A new model was required. Thus Peter in the gospel passage is depicted as a primate, a model for *episkopoi*. It was edited at the very time the *episkopoi* were replacing the charismatics as the effective leaders of their churches. Peter would have a special appeal for Syrian Christianity. Galatians acknowledges both Paul and Peter as having led the Antioch church. Eusebius and some of the Apocrypha say Peter was bishop there. And there Peter was honored as apostle of the circumcision, the faithful defender of monotheism.

Thus Götz sees a Jewish functional model for *episkopoi*, and Peter as paradigm for the governing bishops. This would have been put forth, not for a dead-ending and deviant Judeo-Christianity that was on its way to extinction, but for the church at large. This was another evidence that personal and official authority was not a foreign intrusion, but a developing native reality.

---

[16] Götz thinks they presided over not only the synagogue but the civil community as well. He is apparently unaware that the synagogue *was* the civil community, as well as the religious community.

B. H. STREETER

As we have now seen, much of what was written on early church order was history hammered upon the template of the writers' own loyalties and experiences. One of the first to notice it out loud was the Oxford New Testament scholar B. H. Streeter, whose remark to that effect was cited at the outset of this study. There are two reasons why he could see the discussion as having been fenced in by denomination. Though he was a lifelong Anglican and a clerk in holy orders, his personal religious interests had in later years been expanding. He had recently published a major study on Buddhism. And he was shortly to enroll himself in Frank Buchman's Oxford Group, which sat lightly to any belief or usage that was too emphatic or precise. A second change in Streeter's environment was the ecumenical movement that had made much progress in the years after the First World War. Streeter himself was a vitally interested participant, especially at the Lausanne Conference in 1927, which saw the founding of the Faith and Order movement.

On church order he had a theory which he considered an alternative to the entrenched formularies of Lightfoot and Harnack. At the outset and throughout the formative period of the early church, Streeter believed, there were widely differing systems of church government.

Consider, he says, what a diversity of doctrine there was. The great churches all had their own local roots, stresses, leaders and perspective on the rest of the churches. They had independent traditions about the date of Easter, the biblical canon, liturgical rites, the gospels, the exegesis of scripture, and theological emphasis and style. The history of the first five centuries is one of progressive standardization. Most of that had to take place in Rome, because Rome was the church to which every deviant creed unerringly migrated. Thus, for example, when the casual and informal Roman faith was challenged by Marcion with his definite roster of inspired books and an aggressively coherent theology, the Roman church was compelled to respond by standardizing its own canon and its creed.[17]

Piecing together the sherds of data, Streeter says there was a similar diversity in the church orders that originated in the major centers. In Jerusalem they followed Jewish patterns. Christians

---

[17] Burnett Hillman Streeter, *The Primitive Church: Studied with Special Reference to the Origins of Christian Ministry*, Hewlett Lectures for 1928 (London: Macmillan, 1929), 53–65.

founded synagogues and maintained three levels of office: deacons,
elders and president. No other tradition, insists Streeter, had the
tripartite office at that early date. In Syria and its capital Antioch the
prophets and teachers were in charge, with no sign of *episkopoi* or
diakonoi. Paul's churches seem to have followed no uniform constitution. Corinth gives precedence to apostles, prophets and
teachers; those with the gifts of "helping" and "governing" were of
lesser importance. *Episkopoi* and *diakonoi* led the church in Philippi. In
Ephesus the shepherds had moved ahead of the teachers, and the
New Testament letter to that church stresses office over gift, thus
reinforcing our suspicion that the order of things was undergoing
stress and change. Paul's speech in Acts, bidding farewell to the
episkopoi = presbyteroi of Ephesus, had undeniably assigned them
responsibility for the church there.

Streeter interprets Paul as shifting from an older emphasis on
personal gifts of the Spirit to a new emphasis on authoritative office.
By the end of the century that trend has taken hold and consolidated
the governance by officers in the major churches. In Asia Minor the
monarchical episcopate is in place then, as well as in the metropolitan
authority of Ephesus. Syria has been drastically converted from the
spontaneities of the prophets to the sovereignty of Ignatius. Rome is
in the hands of elders, with a presiding but not ruling central figure.
In Egypt, Alexandria's pre-eminence gives its bishop and board of
elders jurisdiction over all churches in Egypt. "In fact – to put it
paradoxically – the office of Archbishop would seem more primitive
than that of Bishop."[18]

His meticulous survey, tracking the evidence by locality and by
stages of development, persuades Streeter that the churches of his
own time, who yearned for reunion yet were depressed by the
divergent usages and constitutions that held them apart, should be
encouraged at the discovery that the principal Christian communities
in the apostolic age were no less divided.[19]

---

[18] Ibid. 260.

[19] In the epilogue to his study of church order, Streeter gives the moral to his own story: "In
a book which aims at being a contribution to historical research, a discussion of issues which
are a matter of controversy in the Church of today would be out of place. It would, however,
be futile to pretend that the historical conclusions here reached are without relevance to
practical questions keenly debated at the present time. All over the world – more especially
in India, China, and Africa – disunion among Christians is recognized as a source of
weakness amid surrounding paganism. The obstacles to be overcome are many; and they
are real. No one who has given serious study to the question will condemn out of hand those

The primitive variegation did, for diverse reasons and needs, yield to an eventual uniformity. Streeter wants to argue that such a trend towards standardization need not have been irreversible, and that the Great Church might be more haunted than inspired in its search for a single format of governance and ministry.

OLOF LINTON

By 1932 the dominant theory had had the run of the roads for some eighty years. A survey of its advancement – a survey that is astute, critical and constructive – was published that year by Olof Linton, a Swede whose work reached a wider audience because he wrote it in German.[20]

Protestants had thought that their inquiry into church origins was historical and scholarly, in contrast with the dogmatic approach of Catholics. Rather than projecting later institutions back onto those sparsely documented times, Protestants would not allow themselves to let those silences speak by conjectures according to their own preferences. Linton found, though, that the sources themselves had been honored only to the extent that they sustained the received consensus. For instance, Ignatius' vigorous advocacy of a strong presiding bishop would show the monarchical episcopate to have been in existence quite early in the second century: too early to suit many scholars, who therefore rejected his letters as inauthentic. After Lightfoot finally vindicated Ignatius' authorship, scholars launched a quiverful of challenges: the letters were dated no earlier than 150 AD; or, they described a church order that existed only in Syria and Asia Minor and was unknown in Rome; or, they expressed Ignatius'

who are apprehensive lest ill-considered attempts at premature reunion may hinder rather than advance the cause. But perhaps the greatest obstacle is the belief – entertained more or less explicitly by most bodies of Christians – that there is some one form of Church Order which alone is primitive, and which, therefore, alone possesses the sanction of Apostolic precedent. Our review of the historical evidence has shown this belief to be an illusion. In the Primitive Church no one system of Church Order prevailed. Everywhere there was readiness to experiment, and, where circumstances seemed to demand it, to change." Ibid. 261–262.

Streeter's argument is one of immense complexity. At every step he proposes definite conclusions about the authorship, provenance, date, suppositions and context of documents that are elaborate, disputable and conjectural. The book involves the most recondite scholarship, yet is a sequence of argument with so many potential breaks in it. In the end, its weakness is its intricacy.

[20] Olof Linton, *Das Problem der Urkirche in der neueren Forschung: Eine kritische Darstellung*, Uppsala Universitets Årsskrift 1932: Teologi 2 (Uppsala: Almqvist & Wirksells, 1932).

hopes for what the church might be, not a factual account of how it was. It is Linton's estimate that this resistance to Ignatius was more dogmatic than historical.

Scholars had identified Paul's authentic letters, especially those to Corinth, as the best of all sources. They reconstructed from them a self-regulating community without organization, presidency or structures, directed only by the Spirit's gifts. Linton observes that this was indeed a conjecture which supplied, according to its fancies, much that was simply not in Paul or, probably, in Corinth. What guides this kind of reconstruction is the high premium scholars put on individuality. The community, they are convinced, should not be subordinated to any higher authority, and the individual members ought not to be subject to any other members of the community.

"[I]t ought to be clear that behind that 'consensus' stands an ideology: modern Protestant, Reformed congregationalist, politically democratic, idealistically individualist."[21] The abiding assumption was that religion originates with a private relationship between God and the individual. The believer then seeks to join with others to form a supportive congregation. It was a quite alien thought to envision religion as a corporate reality wherein the individual is approached and called by the community, enfolded within it, and there finds a relationship with God. On the view that individuals are the creators only and not the beneficiaries of the community, it was inevitable that these studies would interpret church order in socio-political terms, especially terms that were congenial to post-Enlightenment Protestant social theory, favoring democratic and parliamentary models.

The consensus had been remarkably able to appeal to divergent sectors within Protestantism. Critics who saw history as fully explained by human interplay agreed with Pietists who saw the divine hand intrusively superintending daily events. What held them together, as a legacy of the Reformation but perhaps even more of the Enlightenment, was the shared axiom that God's gesture and mankind's device were not the same. They discountenanced sacred office as a generative and stabilizing life-source in the church, for that would too confusingly have combined the human and divine. God's hand was to be seen in what was unorganized and uninstitutional, and anything institutional was designated as a mere external, to be

---

[21] Ibid. 9.

analyzed by profane and political categories. The consensus, accordingly, was the result of something less openly accessible than pure historical analysis.[22]

The consensus had received its most lively and strenuous reconsideration in the 1880s. Hatch and Harnack both denied the long-accepted tenet that *episkopos* and *presbyteros* in early documents were interchangeable designations for one and the same function. Hatch described the *episkopos* as a comptroller, while *presbyteroi* presided. Harnack thought rather more kindly of the *episkopos*, for he was the soul of the community's most religious aspects: worship and the care of the helpless. The new-found *Didache* then cast both *episkopos* and *presbyteros* into the shade, in favor of the charismatics-at-large. Critics found it difficult to accept that all of these roles could have existed together peaceably in any one locale, or that there could have been a large variety of church orders in which one or the other of these many categories of personage predominated.

All continued to agree, however, that true religion was an interior reality, essentially autonomous of institutional order or office. Sohm's challenge was not to hold to a different dogma, but to apply it so indefatigably. His piety rejected any human model for church, and all language of organization. Legalism, for Sohm, does not amount to coercion, but to any presently controlling power of past facts. The consensus had rejected the sovereignty of any officer. By its own principles, however, Sohm believed that it should have rejected popular sovereignty of the assembly as well.

Since that period of turbulent debate, Linton estimated that the consensus had been restored. Subsequent scholarship had gone on to examine details while leaving the fabric intact. But not without stress. The conviction that apostles carried charismatic but not official authority had suffered because it was now noticed that the apostles had been honored by category, not by their individual personalities (the Twelve were differentiated from the Twelve-plus-James, and they from all who had been disciples from the beginning, and they in turn from all who had ever seen the Lord, and all of them from latter-day itinerant preachers). Thus apostleship did seem to have something to do with office, not just individual inspiration. Doubt was also rightly being cast on the conventional belief that *episkopoi* were chosen either by inspired choice or by democratic election; why

[22] Ibid. 3–30.

not by both? Studies of early missionary activity (which the consensus had ignored) suggested that *episkopoi* were provided by act of the founders, not the locals.

Meanwhile, there were also some new trends that reinforced the consensus, or at least its presuppositions. Albert Schweitzer and others had been portraying Jesus as an eschatological visionary who called for the kingdom but got the church instead. This reinvigorated the notion that ecclesiastical structure was all foreign to Jesus' true gift to his people. A new psychological interest in spiritual phenomena (William James et al.) understood religious events as miraculous, irrational eruptions. That only confirmed the belief that spirit and office must be polar opposites.

The history-of-religions school (founded by Gunkel and Weiss) moved powerfully to challenge that antithesis between office and spirit, order and enthusiasm. The officers had always been identified as having special roles at worship. As long as worship was seen as an expression of individual piety, rather than as a vital, communal source of spiritual empowerment, a liturgical role was bound to seem like an administrative assignment. But this school of historical research came to prize the mysterious more than what it regarded as the sterile rationalism of a religion reduced to morality. It saw the congregation not as an assemblage of autonomous, inspired individuals, but as a true collectivity, a locus and a source of the sacred. Worship, then, was a spiritual gift, no less than was prophecy.[23]

This re-evaluation of the Kingdom of God, of the spiritual, of worship, in which the History-of-Religions School was to play a leading role, also put the issues of church and organization in a new light. A challenge was now obviously being raised to the presuppositions of the consensus wherein the interior privacy of the person stood opposed to the supernatural and the eschatological, individualism to a worship community, the personality of a superpersonal Spirit to extraordinary powers, and administration to worship.[24]

Sohm's insistence that only the worldwide fellowship of believers was truly church now made no sense: it would have been an assembly that never assembled. The local, concrete congregation was for its members a vital source of grace; it did meet, and its gatherings were salvific. Therefore both general and local fellowships were truly

[23] Ibid. 119.　　　　[24] Ibid. 131.

church. A new interest now sprang up in Old Testament models of church, models that were Jewish and that were communal, like "people of God," and "true Israel." The church then might be in continuity with Israel: the same people, but in a different era. Sociological parlance began to welcome terms, not simply of association or corporation (of individuals), but of structured collectivity. "Institutional" would never work, for it was too Catholic. But Tröltsch popularized the distinction between church and sect, and there began to be learned talk about discipleship and authority.

Linton brings his review round at the end to propose some amendment to the consensus.[25] One reason scholars have been so chary of authoritative personal office is, of course, their unanimous resistance to Catholic, and especially papal, claims. But there was an additional reason. It seemed to them that such office is, by its very existence, a negation of any fellowship's being free to govern itself. This, Linton thinks, is a typical view of Westerners who are unfamiliar with Eastern tradition.

Take Harnack, for instance. As he reconstructs the Jerusalem assembly in Acts 15, the community resolved the issue of gentile membership in the church by taking a ballot on the proposal of the elders. Harnack imagines that "yea" and "nay" were the two options. That would show convincingly that the community held final authority. But what if only "yea" were imaginable? In an assembly of equals a majority rules. In an assembly of unequals a minority of select people decides. The *presbyteroi* were not a college apart from the Jerusalem church; they were the dominating group within the assembly. Our Western understanding is that democratic institutions represent the people's interests and stand against the claims of elite groups. Acts implies an oriental tradition wherein deliberative councils or assemblies bring rulers and people together, as a collectivity, to formulate and adopt a consensus. The methods for reaching the consensus may be informal, but they are well understood.

Paul judges a man. Then the community judges the man and reaches the same verdict. Is their concurrence a mere sham? No, says Linton, it is a collectivity at work, and its work is the work of Paul, and also of the church, and also of the Lord. The people are not the ultimate authority. And Paul is not just one vote.

[25] Ibid. 186ff.

That the ancient church had no juridical order such as a Greek city-state or a European Protestant would recognize, need not mean it had no regimen at all. It means that there were realities of custom and usage and informal tradition which conferred power and responsibility without always being spread upon the page of history. Custom can be a sterner format than statute.

Linton suggests that the relations between churches were also not to be understood by a Western political reference. The Great Church is not constructed out of communities; the communities come forth from the Great Church's mission. Each is fully formed, yet nonetheless fully derivative.

As between humans, filial relations are lifelong, not restricted to the immature period of childhood. The mission begot daughter churches, not autonomous communities. The apostolic founders seem not to have governed them personally *in absentia*, but to have left them possessed of chosen leadership. Thus from earliest days the communities were in a web of relational dependency, yet they had responsibility for their own internal life and activities.

Subordination and responsibility were not, as we persist in supposing, mutually exclusive. As a fragment of the general church a local church looked beyond itself for direction. As a replica of the general church it found leadership in its own midst. The church of the *Didache* emphasized the one aspect: an eschatological outlook, no sharp community boundaries, no monarchy. The community was a splinter of the church. Ignatius' church was a contrast: ordered worship, an echeloned community, and a structure of rule. The community was a replica of the church. The eventual victory of cult over eschatology, of God met here-and-now rather than only then-and-there, finally established the replica-model as dominant.

The gospel teaching that all men and women are brothers and sisters without division cued the scholars to see a modern democracy in autonomous ancient communities. Here they also betrayed an unfamiliarity with the traditional oriental ways of acceding to honor. The charismatics were honored and so at eucharist they were invited to pray. Eventually that honor faded, and the bishops emerged in more enduring honor. But when the charismatics were praying in an honored way, the church had not ceased its prayer. So also, when the officers were governing, it did not mean that the church had thereby forfeited responsibility for its own common life. Authority need not be exclusive; it might be shared.

A salient contribution of Linton's study is his criticism that the consensus always assumes that faith is God's creation but that church order is ours. With that in mind, one can evaluate the interventions of someone like Karl-Ludwig Schmidt, a typical adherent of the consensus who wrote a few years after Linton.[26] The church exists, Schmidt says, wherever anyone is in communion with Christ. Communion with other believers, creating a local church, follows on that. Similarly, further communion between that church and others is a result, not a cause, of the local church's existence. No instrumentality of the worldwide church can be required to establish the church locally. Thus Schmidt. Linton might have remarked that the theory lacks symmetry. Schmidt's principle is that wherever Christ is at work, there the church is. He is unprepared to put forward the reverse: that wherever the church is at work, there Christ is. He understands the church as a result only, and never a means or instrumental cause, of salvation. It follows then that Schmidt will recognize a ministry generative of faith and further ministry only in Christ himself, and possibly the apostles, but in no other church people. Theirs is a ministry that proceeds from Christ, but Christ does not use it as an mediating instrument for transforming others.

The writing of Otto Michel follows a path similar to that of Schmidt.[27] He cites the fact that in the early New Testament documents written before the definitive break with Judaism, after which *ekklêsia* came to mean Christians and *synagôgê* came to mean Jews, both terms were still usable for Christians, and they might apply to either a local congregation or the total fellowship. From that fact Michel infers an eschatological character in the local church. It is an assembly of the last days, wherein no one shall teach his brother for all shall be taught of the Lord. Like Schmidt and so many other advocates of the consensus, Michel sees no two-way traffic possible. He acknowledges the sublime and mystical aspects of *ekklêsia*, but ignores the down-to-earth aspects of *synagôgê*. Since the church is God's enterprise, it (unlike Israel, says Michel) cannot be studied by the methods or categories of the social sciences. This, of course, is because the church was an entirely interior reality. He says it was the fault of Clement and the Roman church that they supposed the

[26] Karl-Ludwig Schmidt, "Le ministère et les ministères dans l'église du Nouveau Testament: Les données bibliques et celles de la tradition," *Revue d'Histoire et de Philosophie Religieuses* (1937), 313–336.
[27] Otto Michel, *Das Zeugnis des Neuen Testaments von der Gemeinde* (Göttingen: Vandenhoeck & Ruprecht, 1941).

church was a human society, and they ignored the vitality and freedom of a purely charismatic community. Michel proceeds on the common assumption that social organization must thwart, rather than engender and enhance, the individual's spiritual life.

Two events of the early twentieth century served to transfer the center of the church order controversy from Germany over to Britain. The World Conference on Faith and Order in 1927 was the formal inauguration of the ecumenical movement. Though the Orthodox Churches would later become full and weighty members of the movement and of its organizations, at that point they were only hesitantly involved. The role of the Anglican communion, then, as the principal episcopal church accredited to Lausanne, was accentuated. All eyes naturally looked forward to possible reunion. It became centrally important to everyone what terms the Anglicans would consider, for most of the other churches represented were non-episcopal. If a formula acceptable to the Anglicans could be negotiated, the delegates saw that as a plausible welcome to the hesitating Orthodox and – who knew? – possibly even to the Catholics who had not accepted an invitation to come to Lausanne. The question was only broached at Lausanne, and spent years in international committees. It put the Anglican theologians on the *qui vive*, however. It also accentuated the great cleft within their communion, between the catholic and evangelical wings, which became visible in the readiness that they showed to be intransigent or conciliatory on the necessity of episcopacy and of apostolic succession.

AN ANGLICAN DEFENSE OF APOSTOLIC SUCCESSION

Charles Gore, one of the most articulate Anglo-Catholic theologians and bishops around the turn of the century, had published *The Church and the Ministry*, in which he suggested that bishops are heirs to the ministry of the apostles of the primitive church, transmitted through their deputies. The resulting bishop was a localized apostle, more than a promoted presbyter. Gore's book had secured limited attention when it appeared in 1886. But in the wake of Lausanne, the book was revised and reissued precisely in order to counteract the effect of Streeter's work, and to argue against bargaining away the episcopacy.[28]

[28] Charles Gore, *The Church and the Ministry* (London: Longmans, Green, 1886). Revised edition edited by C. H. Turner (London: SPCK, 1936). Cuthbert Hamilton Turner had contributed the chapter on apostolic succession to the Swete volume.

A second event that heightened British interest was the active proposal, under consideration by the Church of England for a decade and a half after World War II, to enter into full communion with the Church of South India, a church which had not had a tradition of episcopacy. This brought the issue home as the ecumenical movement had not done, and elicited more emphatic publications by those who wished to stress that without authentic episcopacy and its associated orders, there could be no proper Christian church. But this was a conversation that was overheard. The Anglicans had Christian neighbors who were mostly not episcopal: Presbyterians, Congregationalists, Methodists, Baptists. Every Anglican book that came out in criticism of the Church of South India was one more implicit expression of disdain for these fellow Christians. And so a strenuous exchange began, mostly between Anglicans and free churchmen.

The non-episcopals began to be heard from. In 1938 R. N. Flew, the principal of Wesley House, Cambridge, one of the leading Methodist theological colleges, brought out his study which showed the early communities to have been independent and unstructured.[29] James Vernon Bartlet, a Scottish Congregationalist who had been at Lausanne, had been a party to the Assembly of the Congregationalist Union two years later, when they responded to the Conference by insisting that the church is constituted by the gathering together of believers for worship and service, and does not require for its validity any specific ministerial structure. Congregationalists stated that they might be prepared to accept episcopacy as a benefit for the church, but only if no theory of the episcopacy, or of apostolic succession, were endorsed.[30] Flew and Bartlet were two of the early and more formidable British Protestants who resorted to the continental consensus as a defense against Anglican claims.

---

[29] R[obert] N[ewton] Flew, *Jesus and His Church: A Study of the Idea of the Ecclesia in the New Testament* (London: Epworth, 1938). Flew, who would eventually become president of the Methodist Conference, had just been at the Edinburgh Conference of 1937, the first great follow-up to Lausanne.

[30] James Vernon Bartlet, *Church-Life and Church-Order during the First Four Centuries*, The Birkbeck Lectures of 1924, ed. Cecil John Cadoux (Oxford: Blackwell, 1943). Bartlet taught at Mansfield College, the new free church theological center at Oxford, which was becoming the center of resistance to the episcopal claims of the Church of England. He was not a scholar who brought texts easily to the point of publication, and Cadoux, another firm believer in the non-episcopal system, had virtually to rewrite the lectures from an incomplete manuscript left by Bartlet when he died. Bartlet generally followed the views of Sohm. See his earlier *The Apostolic Age: Its Life, Doctrine, Worship and Polity* (New York: Scribner, 1899).

THE KENNETH KIRK SYMPOSIUM

The end of World War I saw the publication in England of the volume edited by Swete, intended as a combined Anglican critique of the German-sponsored consensus. Another Anglican collection appeared just after the close of World War II, edited by Kenneth Kirk, bishop of Oxford. It too took a conservative direction, but its concern was less the German theologians who had been persevering in the consensus, than the fellow Britons – Presbyterians, Methodists, Congregationalists, Baptists – who were taking comfort from the continent in their persistent dismissal of episcopacy and the claims of apostolic succession. The ecumenical conversations between the churches had been inviting more explicit attention to this question. Some of the most noted Anglo-Catholic savants contributed essays to the Kirk volume.[31]

Austin Farrer, whose usual license was to deal in systematic theology, writes on ministry in the New Testament. He begins with an entirely new interpretation of the story of the choosing of the Seven in Acts 6. The story is intentionally reminiscent of Moses' selection of seventy elders in Numbers 11, and Jesus' appointment of seventy-two (or seventy) disciples in Luke 10. The Seven (identified by other scholars as deacons or as *episkopoi*) Farrer thinks to be *presbyteroi* = elders. Their selection by the Twelve he also sees as creating a parallel to the arrangements in contemporary Jewish communities. A synagogue would have a corps of rabbinic elders, who were called teachers; it would also have a corps of executive officers. "There were a sort of churchwardens called 'rulers' or 'rulers of synagogue,' responsible for the synagogue building and the provision of services, and there were commissioners of charity. These officers would normally be elders but need not be rabbis."[32] According to this model, the Twelve served the Jerusalem Christians as the teaching elders, and the Seven were elders of a non-teaching order. Thus when Acts 15 reports action by the apostles and the elders in Jerusalem, it was referring to the Twelve and the Seven. This is significant because it relates the early prominence of the most ancient offices in the church.

In a later stage, the apostles have been replaced by their

---

[31] Kenneth E. Kirk, ed., *The Apostolic Ministry: Essays on the History and the Doctrine of Episcopacy* (London: Hodder & Stoughton, 1946).
[32] A[ustin] M[arsden] Farrer, "The Ministry in the New Testament," ibid. 113–182 at 142.

companions and heirs, who continue to ride circuit and continue their apostolic ministry to the churches they founded and supervised. By this time the local communities have their own boards of elders, and they are beginning to be provided with presidents, who tend to be called *episkopoi*.

[T]he apostolic word-ministry was not domiciled and the *episcopoi* presided over the presbyteries, the apostolic ministry being an occasional visitant and supervisor. By contrast with it, the episcopal power was reckoned as presbyteral: the presbytery, as assessors to the *episcopoi*, exercised *episcope* and ruled or presided. This cleavage between the visiting word-ministry and the settled *episcope* could not persist. The *episcopoi* exercised more and more teaching and pastoral functions, under the direction of the disciples of the apostles, until these latter became the bishops of the apostolic sees and adopted the local *episcopoi* as their sacred colleagues. Thus the apostolic commission, with all that we have seen it to mean, devolved upon the episcopate except for the reserved powers of the original apostles which could not devolve, but are expressed in the form of the Church, the creed, and the Scripture of the New Testament.[33]

The apostolic lieutenants – Timothy, Polycarp et al. – are thus proposed as the link of succession through whom the necessary features of the apostles' ministry was imparted to a line of successors. "If our Lord made twelve disciples with full authority to teach in His name, is it not equally essential that their companions and delegates shall succeed them as custodians of the Gospel?"[34]

These were ideas that Farrer only incompletely presents. They were carried further by the most serious contributor to the Kirk collection: Dom Gregory Dix, the liturgical historian who had been a major commentator on the recently published edition of Hippolytus' *Apostolic Tradition*. That document, a complete church order from late second-century Rome, is the centerpiece of Dix's inquiry into the doctrine of apostolic succession, of which Hippolytus was one of the early expositors.

The doctrine appears only in the last quarter of the second century, to counter the Gnostics' alleged possession of a private tradition of belief passed on secretly from the apostles. The Catholic counter-strategy was twofold: to define its list of approved apostolic writings, and to vindicate its lineage of public, traditional teaching from the

---

[33] Ibid. 180.

[34] Ibid. 132. Farrer, whose strong suit is not New Testament studies, offers unsophisticated exegesis here.

apostles. For those who would find the doctrine of apostolic succession a late and therefore inauthentic novelty, coming at such a remove from the primitive times, Dix notes that the canon of scripture is no less an innovation.

The true sense of apostolic succession in the late second century refers to a continuity of traditional teaching, not to a lineage of ordination. A bishop was seen, not as a successor to those who consecrated him, but as a successor to the previous incumbents of his teaching chair. Hippolytus' stress, like that of Irenaeus and Tertullian, was on the *episkopos* as a teacher, for they were locked in struggle against heresy. Schism, not heresy, was the prevailing problem of the third century, and the task of the bishop accordingly came to be framed in terms of discipline and pastorate. In that altered context he came, says Dix, to be seen as the successor, not to a see, but to an office. The lineage then came through his consecrators rather than his predecessors. This change was accentuated even more in the East, where the laying-on of hands constituted the bishop's inauguration, while in the West the election remained a real component of the process and was emphasized along with consecration.

The formula for ordination of elders in Hippolytus specifies that they are charged with government and teaching. Other sources inform us that they presided at the daily prayer service, shared in the ordination of other *presbyteroi* and deputized at eucharists and baptisms. Elders are cast in a role of some independence, unlike the deacons who are the bishop's explicit assistants. In Hippolytus' prayer the deacon is typified as the bringer of the offertory gifts: quite in continuity with the earlier service of tables, as were his other duties to locate and visit the sick, and to distribute communion.

The well-ordered ministry of the late second century, Dix is assured, is in continuity with earliest Christian origins. And what were those origins? "All that we know of the life of Jesus of Nazareth and of the apostles of the New Testament – not excluding the ex-pharisee Saul of Tarsus – is a guarantee that any institutions which can fairly claim to be aboriginal in the Christian religion will prove on investigation to be Jewish rather than Hellenistic in their affiliations."[35]

[35] Dom Gregory Dix, O.S.B., "The Ministry in the Early Church: c. AD 90–410," Kirk, *Apostolic Ministry*, 227. It should be noted that the theory which Farrer and Dix, and indeed the Kirk collectivity in general, elaborate and defend was mooted a half-century earlier by Charles Gore.

Dix utterly dismisses Harnack's theory of a church led by the charismatic triad of apostles, prophets and teachers. Even in the *Didache*, which is written with a distinct bias towards the prophets, one is offered little information to distinguish the other two charismatic categories, and it never presents them as a hierarchy. Other Syrian sources are diffident about the prophets altogether.[36]

Following the recent publication by J. B. Frey of Jewish funerary inscriptions, and his reconstruction of synagogue organization in the early Christian centuries, Dix describes Christian apostles, after the Jewish model, as plenipotentiaries whose actions irrevocably commit their sender. Elders, the other well-attested Christian office, formed the ruling boards of each congregation. The function of governance exercised by the *presbyteroi*, and by them alone (Dix says that even apostles do not govern: they exert influence, and receive reverence, but they do not command), is called *episkopê* = superintendence. Thus the elders were also called *episkopoi*, not as a title, but as an appropriate synonym. From Paul to Clement, the two terms are interchangeable. How then did *episkopos* become, only decades later, the title of a distinct officer?

The apostolate, Dix believes, found a second-generation continuation through appointed successors like Timothy, Titus, John (the "elder" of Ephesus), Polycarp and Clement of Rome. The functions of the apostles transferred down to them. After years of itinerant service they settled into major sees as residential figures. And eventually their apostolic functions came to be absorbed by the emergent monarchical bishops. The rearrangement in church order that is of massive significance for continuity is not the appearance of the single presiding elder as monarchical bishop. It is the domiciling of the apostolic successors and the indigenization there of their apostolic mission. The later bishop then is the offspring and continuator of one of the only two original offices we know: but it comes from the apostolate, not the presbyterate.

It is no use trying to establish the monarchical episcopate as historically authentic or inauthentic by testing how far back we can

---

[36] "Read apart from [the *Didache*] and the elaborate but questionable theories to which it has given rise, the New Testament evidence contains no indication at all that the exercise of any charisma in itself carried with it any office in the Church. On the contrary, the evidence makes it plain that the earliest Church knew only two kinds of ministerial office, both of which were traditionally Judaic, the *shaliach* or apostle appointed as such by our Lord himself, and the *zaken* or elder appointed with the laying on of hands." Ibid. 242.

trace it. If the issue were simply one of historicity, archdeacons would be as essential as bishops. In fact, many of the early *episkopoi* who are cited as the ancestors of our present episcopate are "prehistorical," for they were presiding before the apostolic office became absorbed by their order. "Thus the apparent transformation of the 'apostle + presbyter-*episkopoi* + deacons' hierarchy of the first century into the '*episkopos* + presbyters + deacons' hierarchy of the second century does not mask the creation of any new 'order' in the Church. It only records the permanent localization of the apostle and the consequent permanent transfer to him of a function in the life of the local Church in addition to his own personal commission as the *shaliach* of the Lord."[37]

Dix reiterates: what is essential is not the possession of the episcopal office, but the inheritance of the apostolic office. In episcopal churches this carries on in the bishop. Dix believes that the non-episcopal Protestants also possess *episkopê* = superintendence, whatever their constitutions; it is simply vested differently (and with sound pre-Nicene precedents). It is thus quite possible to have *episkopê* with elders and without bishops. What those churches may lack, however, is the apostolate. "The episcopate is the only means by which our Lord's own commission to stand in His Person before God and man is given afresh to each new minister of His Church (according to his own order) to the end of time."[38]

The sixteenth-century Reformers and their traditionalist opponents had operated under a great handicap when they inquired into early church order. Jewish institutions were almost entirely unknown and inaccessible to them. Christian documents were often unavailable, or interpolated, or wrongly dated, or forged: they did not possess accurate knowledge of the *Didache*, Clement, Ignatius, Irenaeus, the *Didascalia*, *Serapion*, the *Apostolic Tradition*, and the *Apostolic Constitutions*, all crucial to this question.

Besides, there was, as Streeter had said, much bias at work in their historical scholarship.[39] Dix's own thesis is the historical claim that

---

[37] Ibid. 292.   [38] Ibid. 303.

[39] "Yet Streeter's rather cynical diagnosis of the cause of this – that each has found only what he hoped to find – is by no means the whole truth; and there is no need whatever to accept his conclusion that the primitive Church had no discoverable principles of Church Order, but was indifferently episcopalian, or presbyterian, or independent in different Churches as suited the local tastes and circumstances. On the contrary, this conclusion only expresses the judgement of an enthusiastic member of the Lausanne Conference finding the primitive Church to have been Lausanne – because he hoped to do so." Ibid. 290–291.

the episcopate of the second century inherited the functions of the apostles of the first century, and that this was intended by the apostles and known to and accepted by the Church at large when it happened. This historical statement is now widely challenged on historical grounds. But the historical challenge was preceded by and is still largely inspired by a purely theological denial of the doctrine involved, a denial which began in quite different circumstances and for quite different reasons from those which originally caused the doctrine to be put forward. It must be obvious to any student of the literature that the desire to justify or at least to palliate the setting-up of non-episcopal ministries in the sixteenth century lies behind a great deal of the modern treatment of the history. It may be retorted that the opposite is also true, that the historical defence of the "Apostolic Succession" of bishops cannot nowadays be undertaken without at least a consciousness that its vindication must brand such ministries as to some extent illegitimate.[40]

Another gremlin in the works was the readiness of many historians to believe that when they traced a word   especially a title – they were tracing an institution. Dix has some cautionary observations on this:

[A]ll parties to the modern discussions have allowed themselves, when considering the ancient evidence, to be hypnotized by certain words, forgetting that words – even when used as technical terms – can and often do change their whole connotation between one generation and the next in the history of institutions without any breach whatever in institutional continuity ... We shall have to get behind words to the ideas and realities they express, before we can either understand the ancient historical evidence or solve the modern ecclesiastical problem ...

It would help considerably towards disentangling the discussion if we could all accept the fact that the ancient evidence about *episkope* and *episkopoi* is largely irrelevant to our own ecclesiastical controversies. From the ancient standpoint there is no "development of episcopacy," no "emergence of the episcopate," either at the turn of the first and second centuries or at any other point. *Episkope* is there from the beginning; it is a necessary function from the start in the corporate life of any *paroikia* [= community] or Christian local Church. In the primitive Church *episkopos* is not the title of an "order" at all. It is a description of anyone who fulfills *episkope*, applied indiscriminately to those who fulfill it, whether an individual or a college. Just so there was a time when anyone who fulfilled *diakonia* was called *diakonos*. "Order" and "function" are not necessarily the same thing in the primitive Church. "Functions" are many and various, and the equipment for handling them are the *charismata*. The primitive "orders" are two only – the "apostles" or *shelihim* and the "presbyters" or *zeqenim* (supplemented soon by the "deacons"). It was only the customary discharge of a particular "function" by a particular "order" which led in time to a criss-cross use of "functional" terminology to describe the "orders," and ultimately to the technical terms we know.[41]

One comes away with the impression that Dix's views on method are more worthwhile even than his particular findings or theory. He was a formidable patristics scholar, but perhaps not as competent working in the very earliest times as when he read the documents of the fourth or fifth centuries. Also he was unfamiliar himself with Jewish sources, and could deal with them only at second hand. But his contribution is more significant than could be measured by the opinion his particular theory has rallied behind it.[42]

T. W. MANSON

The next volley was from the free churches. One of the most forthright replies to the Kirk volume came from a prominent Presbyterian, T. W. Manson, professor of biblical criticism and exegesis at the University of Manchester. It was a reply that in some respects moved the discussion right back to where Sohm had wished to fasten it. Manson's abiding theme was that no external arrangements can have any determinative control over ministry. Countering the thesis common to the Kirk authors that episcopacy is the essential ministry and the presbyterate is a dependent one, he bid trumps. Ministry, he wrote, is not following the example of the Messiah; it is the continuation of Jesus' work by Jesus. His is the essential ministry; all of ours are dependent.

The Church can create the environment favorable to the growth of Christians: it can bring spiritual influence to bear on people inside and out: but in the last resort the decision by which an individual becomes a disciple of Christ and a child of God is a private and personal affair between Christ and himself. It has always been so ever since Jesus first said, "Follow me." The Church is prior to any particular member; but equally that member's personal decision is prior to his Church membership.[43]

Manson finds several weaknesses in the theory of a subapostolic link to the episcopate. The Jewish *shaliach* is a questionable prototype

[41] Ibid. 291–292.
[42] There is no solid evidence that Timothy, Titus or the other apostolic assistants themselves had plenipotentiary successors. It is certainly more diaphonous than the evidence which does show us the emergence of a strong presiding *episkopos* who became the successor but not the descendant of the apostles.
[43] T[homas] W[alter] Manson, *The Church's Ministry* (London: Hodder & Stoughton, 1948), 23.

for Christian apostles, for in Israel he was sent exclusively to the members of Jewry, never out on mission to the gentiles. And there is no persuasive evidence that the Jewish apostles could, or that the Christian apostles did, subdelegate or transmit their own status. For at least a century and a half there was an unpatterned ministry. When after Hippolytus various ministries of the word and sacraments occupied the attention of the *presbyteroi*, they were not being deputized by the *episkopoi*, as so many have thought, to share in the bishops' prerogatives. They were simply resuming functions that had been theirs to begin with.

As the churches were now contemplating one another, it must surely be unthinkable, pleads Manson, that either half of the worldwide family, episcopal or non-episcopal, would really desire to condemn the other as entirely inauthentic.

The final test in a living Church is not, "Did this or that exist in the age of the Apostles?" but "Is it here and now accompanied by the 'signs of the Apostle'?" We may and must go back to the records of the Ministry of our Lord in Galilee and Judaea; for there the standard and pattern of the continuing Ministry were laid down once and for all. We may go back to the achievements of the Church in the past for inspiration, guidance and encouragement. But to set up the Church of the first or any other century as the final court of appeal, while professing faith in the continuing presence of Christ in His Church and the continuing guidance of His Spirit, seems to me to savour of inconsistency ...

What difference, then, does it make whether a minister is ordained by a bishop or a presbytery or a congregation? So far as his qualification to minister is concerned, none whatever. If he has been called and equipped by Christ, all the bishops, presbyteries, and congregational meetings in the world cannot make him any more a minister than he already is.[44]

The standard of authenticity, then, is one of content, not of form; of the substance, not the procedure. "Churches are apostolic if and in so far as they have a call from the Risen Christ to carry out the business of proclaiming the Kingdom and bringing men into it. If it be asked how we are to know whether any particular Church is apostolic, the only answer is that where there is a genuine apostolic ministry, there you may expect to find the 'signs of the Apostle'. If we can accustom ourselves to look for these, and, having seen them, to keep our attention fixed on them rather than on nice points of law about pedigrees and inheritances, we shall be well on the way

[44] Ibid. 86–87, 97.

towards that full and frank recognition which is the pre-condition of mutual eligibility."[45] The underlying orientations in the controversy were becoming ever clearer.

W. D. DAVIES

Another response, from Congregationalist ranks, came from W. D. Davies, a young New Testament scholar later to become a professor at Duke.[46] Though Davies will come out on the side of the non-episcopals, he calls down a plague o'both their houses. On the one side are the Catholics and the High Church Anglicans. He dismisses Catholic scholarship for being "adamantly consistent" in seeing a full-blown church order in the most primitive communities. As for the Anglicans, he argues that when they uphold the episcopacy they talk theology, but when they reject the papacy they switch to history. "The appeal to history is as devastating to [their] view of the episcopate as it is to the Papacy. Thus when [A. M.] Ramsey writes such a sentence as: 'There is no Christian community mentioned in the New Testament which has not behind it some authority responsible to a larger whole...' we must rejoin that we simply cannot know what every community of Christians in the first century was like or how they were founded or to whom they felt or did not feel, responsibility."[47] On the other side of the controversy lay the Free Churches, and Davies admitted that it was only scholars from their tradition who seemed unable to find no early *episkopoi* in the evidence.

For him the New Testament communities are not formless, nor is

[45] Ibid. 73–74.
[46] W[illiam] D[avid] Davies, "A Normative Pattern of Church Life in the New Testament – Fact or Fancy?" *The Presbyter* (London) 7, 1 (1949), 1–13; 2 (1949), 5–14. Davies was replying directly to D[aniel] T[homas] Jenkins, *The Gift of Ministry* (London: Faber & Faber, 1947); see also Jenkins, *The Nature of Catholicity* (London: Faber & Faber, 1942). Jenkins' argument was close enough to that of Kirk that Davies was understood to be responding to it as well.
[47] Ibid. 1:9. See A[rthur] M[ichael] Ramsey, *The Gospel and the Catholic Church* (London: Longmans, 1936), 46. Ramsey, who would himself be elevated to the sees of Durham, York and Canterbury, reissued the book in 1956 as the South India controversy continued. Davies criticized Ramsey's rejection of papacy as a source of truth over and above the general mind of the church, as it would thus wield an authority that depressed the due working of the other functions of the Body. The same point, in Presbyterian polity, could be made against Anglo-Catholic bishops. Christ's is the only essential ministry (he follows Manson here), and all claims to special privilege are alike in conflict with him, whether it be the Catholic hierarchy, the "caliphate" the Booth family had held over the Salvation Army, or the selfish isolation of independent churches. Ibid. 2:11.

their form an indifferent matter. But there were many forms, and it is therefore up to the contemporary churches to choose among them. "The Apostolic Age is full of embodiments of purposes and principles of the most instructive kind: but the responsibility of choosing the means was left for ever to the Ecclesia itself, and to each Ecclesia, guided by ancient precedent on the one hand and adaptation to present and future needs on the other. The lesson book of the Ecclesia, and of every Ecclesia, is not a law but a history."[48]

Looking back at the 1880s, Davies claims to see a common thread of conviction running through the opposing theories. Lightfoot, Harnack, Hatch, Sohm: all really believed that the official organization was a social necessity, not a divine ordinance. It was an essential ministry because no human enterprise could long endure without one. Thus Davies. One would have to wonder what Sohm himself would say to this summation of his argument.

Is the church given its structure as we are given our bodies, or may we choose among structures the way we do among clothing? For Davies it is the latter case. Earlier scholars had been arguing for organizational, democratic governance on the ground that it was the one church order which had predominated in the earliest and normative period. The argument at this time was shifting. The first position had been that the unstructured sovereignty of the local congregation was what the early churches looked like, and that this should therefore be the only acceptable polity today. Now the evidence was being heard differently: there were apparently some signs of structure within and between the early local congregations. The new position is that since there were many forms, no one of them could be essential to the integrity of the church today.

One should notice, though, that what had shifted was not just the weight of the historical evidence, but something more fundamental. The point now was not simply whether historical data were determinative, but whether they could ever be. It had come to this: whereas for a century dogmatic preferences had ever been guiding the various arguments, powerfully yet covertly, now the dogmatic differences came out in the open. If the early church did not in fact impose patterns that later generations were bound to follow, then the differences in church polity could be debated on their own merits.

---

[48] Ibid. 2:14. Davies is quoting an earlier book which attracted less attention when published but now was finding much appeal with the non-episcopals: F[enton] J[ohn] A[nthony] Hort, *The Christian Ecclesia* (London: 1897), 232–233.

There was in this, though, a strong irony. It was the more evangelical, scripture-based churches, those inherently conservative about higher criticism – the churches who had most persistently done homage to apostolic teaching – who were now wanting to argue that the apostolic organization was not anything one had to imitate.[49] It was worthy of astonishment that in a matter of great importance to the fidelity of the church, evangelical churchmen would profess that one looked back to the apostolic norm, not as the final court of appeal, but for inspiration, guidance and encouragement. This was far from Luther.

J. K. S. REID

A very measured response to the Kirk group was to be published nearly a decade later by Presbyterian J. K. S. Reid, a professor then at Leeds (later at Aberdeen), who devoted most of his attention to scrutinizing the status of the apostles.[50] The Twelve, he would say, did have an office. This is shown by the need for Judas' place to be filled. But the fact that no vacancies were filled afterwards is evidence that the office could not outlast the generation of Jesus' actual disciples. The Twelve were given two commissions. On their first journey they were to announce the kingdom and to heal and to exorcize. On their second, they were to preach the resurrection and to baptize. Though their own office of word and sacrament was a

---

[49] The South India dispute had years yet to run, and other literature flowed forth into its current. See A[rthur] G[abriel] Hebert, *The Form of the Church*, 2nd edn. (London: Faber & Faber, 1944 [1st edn. 1954]); *Apostle and Bishop: A Study of the Gospel, the Ministry and the Church Community* (London: Faber & Faber, 1963). Hebert, also one of the Kirk essayists, inveighed against the stratagem proposed for the eventual reunion of the Church of England and Free Churches: a general laying-on of hands by bishops on all presbyters of all churches. It would be an equivocal procedure, he complained, for in the minds of one group it would be seen as a proper ordination, while in the eyes of the contrary group it would simply be a license to extend their previously valid ministry over a wider flock. A like procedure would be proposed again during successive reunion discussions of the Consultation on Church Union in the 1960s, and would be the rock on which they foundered. See also William Telfer, *The Office of a Bishop* (London: Darton, Longman & Todd, 1962). Telfer was master of Selwyn College, Cambridge. There were other Anglican voices to be heard, however, who criticized their Anglo-Catholic brethren for taking such a hard line. Gore's second edition was taken to task by Geoffrey W. H. Lampe, *Some Aspects of the New Testament Ministry* (London: SPCK, 1949), and A. Ehrhardt, *The Apostolic Succession in the First Two Centuries of the Church* (London: Lutterworth, 1953). Another group of divines, centered mostly in Cambridge, published *The Historical Episcopate and the Ministry*, ed. Kenneth M. Carey (Westminster: Dacre, 1954). Their point was that episcopacy was needed, not for the esse, or existence, of the church but for its plene esse, or full and intact existence.
[50] J[ohn] K[elman] S[utherland] Reid, *The Biblical Doctrine of Ministry* (Edinburgh: Oliver & Boyd, 1955).

transient one, it was obviously a ministry that was to be continued somehow in the church.

After them came the apostles, whose ministry is similar but who need not have been personal witnesses to Christ. Reid wants to suggest a third category in between the Twelve and the ordinary apostles. When Paul claims the title of apostle, he says that he came into the rank as one born out of due season. There must have been a right season, and it must have been closed. There must then have been a sense of "apostle" which is neither "one of the Twelve" nor "an evangelizing Christian." In this more select sense "apostle" was a title and an office given to few. And the rank Paul claimed obviously had a high authority.

Reid doubts that we can, however, find any ascertainable identity between the apostolate or any other offices in the New Testament, and the offices established in the later church. Some of the titles have endured, but we can infer little from them since their connotations and reference so easily change. In fact, the New Testament evidence is so ambiguous that we cannot bring the offices of *episkopos*, *presbyteros* and *diakonos* there into clear focus. Nor can we be reliably sure whether the governance functions exercised by Peter, John, Paul, Timothy and others were theirs *ex officio* or in virtue of their unique personal privileges. That there is a close analogy between apostles and *episkopoi* is clear. But evidence of actual transmission or commission is absent, or at least too scanty to sustain all the crucial importance the Anglicans have wanted to load upon it. "To credit with literally *essential* character for the being of the Church something which rests on so frail a basis is a desperate procedure; and this the present writer begs leave to think not because he read theology in Scotland, but because he read Logic in Arts. God, if He has not provided foolproof conditions for an apostolic succession, certainly seems to have provided foolproof conditions for a continual succession of theologians who fumble about in the resultant obscurity."[51]

The ministry which the Twelve and the apostles inaugurated is exercised by the church, though not restricted to any particular office. It continues when any Christian invokes the name of Jesus and speaks the Word. The specific offices of the founding generation have ceased, just as the canon of scripture has been closed. Both were to be normative for what has followed.

[51] Ibid. 37.

And what of the inveterate custom of ascribing special authority or power to officers? Reid refers back to Matthew, who with identical words ascribes the power to bind and to loose to Peter in chapter 16 but then to all disciples in chapter 18. "[T]his power resides in the Church as a whole, and when it is ascribed to the disciples, it is so, not in virtue of what distinguishes them from the rest of the Church, but precisely in what they have in common with the Church."[52]

European scholars had framed and disputed and defended the consensus on church office and order during the nineteenth century. In the first half of the twentieth century the discussion moved across the English channel to be taken up principally between Anglican and non-episcopal Protestant writers. As techniques of textual and historical criticism became more refined, the terms of the conversation became correspondingly finer. It is fair to say that scholars were still reading the ancient evidence right closely to their own confessional preferences. Except for the Anglicans (and, always in the background, the Catholics), the consensus stood firm. It had weathered well, but new and unresolved questions had been raised that guaranteed the discussion had to continue. As ecumenical relations between the churches grew warmer and closer, scholars were put under increasing obligation to offer an acceptable reading of the past that might serve to legitimate reunion in the future.

[52] Ibid. 15.

CHAPTER 4

The last fifty years: the consensus restated, rechallenged, reused

The dominant consensus regarding community organization in the early church can be construed as having developed in successive periods. The issue was first engaged by the initial ventures of late medieval and renaissance reformers – notably Wyclif, Luther and Calvin – who discerned in the New Testament evidence that the carly Christians lay under obedience to no ordained officers, but were led by the Spirit and those whom the Spirit most powerfully possessed. Reform soon visited the Reformation itself. Disillusionment exemplified in British congregationalism, continental Pietism and the Quakers, rebuked the Protestant churches for having exchanged the spiritual gifts of the Lord for counterfeit human ordinances. They had re-established a perfunctory congregation of the baptized, a hierarchical (and venal) clergy, and a craven subjection to the secular rulers. Men like Browne, Harrison and Penry, Spener and Arnold, and Fox and Barclay clamored again for an evangelical church where neither sacrament nor office nor emolument could stifle the Spirit.

Their insight was further advanced by German and English scholars in the nineteenth century. They benefited by the new biblical and historical methods to stabilize a widely respected consensus. Great scholars like Baur and Ritschl, Lightfoot and Hatch, Harnack and Sohm each reconstructed the evidence into a distinctive pattern. They concurred in this much, however: that a drastic regression in the second century had replaced a casual and charismatic community with one that awarded definitive authority to bishops. Whether those scholars deplored or merely acquiesced in that change, they portrayed it as a consolidating response to the threats from heresy and schism.

The discussion entered a third phase in the early years of the present century. Several serious challenges to the consensus were put

136

forward by continental Protestants who feared that sectarian bias had induced their colleagues to ignore or misinterpret biblical data that implied patterns and sources of official authority from earliest days. Holtzmann, Holl and Götz were among these critics. It was then that the ecumenical movement made yokefellows of the episcopal Anglican communion and the largely presbyterian and congregational churches in the World Council of Churches. This stimulated the consensus by a new surge of controversy over apostolic succession and the historical origins of episcopacy. The critics of the new consensus were now no longer Catholics at a distance, or demurring Protestants, but Anglican colleagues who shared a mutual aspiration for eventual communion. The older tones of dispute were now more muted by irenic courtesy.

A fourth and last phase now remains to be studied. The consensus has been restated with the aid of more advanced methods of critical analysis, such that the formulations of Hans Freiherr von Campenhausen and Eduard Schweizer have now become established as its last best statements. Quite recently, however, two variants have been proposed. A school of social analysis exemplified by Gerd Theissen, John Gager and Wayne Meeks has been arguing that biblical and post-biblical texts had not been sufficiently studied to distinguish what is descriptive from what is prescriptive. Paul – a case in point – must be read, not as prescribing an ideal church order, but as giving a corrective emphasis to adjust an order that was already in place. These scholars have also raised telling questions about the assumption that foundational charisms are inevitably smothered when they are institutionalized. The gift of the social analysts has been, not to deny the consensus that the earliest church lacked official authorities, but to put a more favorable interpretation on the inevitability of the officers' later emergence.

A final variation on the consensus has been introduced by Catholics such as Hans Küng, Eduard Schillebeeckx, O.P., and Elisabeth Schüssler Fiorenza, for whom the assertion of a normative first era without authoritative officers offers grounds for their appeal beyond present-day hierarchy to desired reforms in their church.

MAX WEBER

The classical debate between Sohm and Harnack – whether legal regulations and officers were an alien intrusion into the church or a pragmatic development – had a way of being reargued from time to time. One influential advocate of Harnack was to be a scholar who had few theological credentials at all: Max Weber, the pioneer social scientist. His sociology of religion was derivative, and he chose to draw his typology of religious organization from Harnack's own work. In a short time Weber's research would then be cited, in circular fashion, as sociological evidence that sustained the Harnack assumptions.[1]

The category about which Weber organizes his thought on religious societies is that of "domination." "A 'hierocratic' organization is an organization which enforces its order through psychic coercion by distributing or denying religious benefits. A compulsory hierocratic organization will be called a 'church' insofar as its administrative staff claims a monopoly on the legitimate use of hierocratic coercion."[2] This was to be the fate of the early Christian enterprise.

Societies which thrive have in them a strong authority and an organized bureaucracy. A single chief will have the advantage, over collegial bodies, of rapid and clear decision-making. An administrative structure, staffed by technically skilled professionals, will be an efficient means of sustaining authority and carrying out the chief's will. This format of authority, which Weber styles "rational," exceeds in efficiency the two alternative formats: "traditional" and "charismatic."

Its contrast with charismatic authority is stark:

Since it is "extraordinary," charismatic authority is sharply opposed to rational, and particularly bureaucratic, authority, and to traditional authority...Bureaucratic authority is specifically rational in the sense of being bound to intellectually analyzable rules; while charismatic authority

---

[1] Max Weber, *Economy and Society: An Outline of Interpretive Sociology*, ed. Guenther Roth and Claus Wittich, 3 vols. (New York: Bedminster, 1968), 3–62, 212–301, 399–634, 1111–1166. This is more than a translation of the fourth edition of *Wirtschaft und Gesellschaft: Grundriss der verstehenden Soziologie*, ed. Johannes Winckelmann (Tübingen: Mohr [Siebeck], 1956), because it includes other previously scattered sources, and adds a valuable critical introduction by Roth. See especially lxxii–lxxxii. Citations are to the consecutive pagination of the three volumes.   [2] Ibid. 54.

is specifically irrational in the sense of being foreign to all rules. Traditional authority is bound to precedents handed down from the past and to this extent is also oriented to rules. Within the sphere of its claims, charismatic authority repudiates the past, and is in this sense a specifically revolutionary force.[3]

Since a community so governed can survive only in its enthusiastic youth, Weber observes, it must find stabilization if it is to continue, by becoming either rationalized or traditionalized or both. If the former: then norms, training and legislation must ensue. If the latter: then power and advantage will accrue to certain families, classes or ranks. Fiscal responsibility, routine and an impersonal style will replace the utterly personal, *ad hoc* style of the charismatic leader.

The moment for that transformation arrives with the crisis of succession.

[One principal motive for the transformation from charismatic authority to a permanent relationship is] the concept that charisma may be transmitted by ritual means from one bearer to another or may be created in a new person. The concept was originally magical. It involves a dissociation of charisma from a particular individual, making it an objective, transferrable entity. In particular, it may become the *charisma of office*. In this case the belief in legitimacy is no longer directed to the individual, but to the acquired qualities and to the effectiveness of the rival acts.

The most important example is the transmission of priestly charisma by anointing, consecration, or the laying on of hands; and of royal authority, by anointing and by coronation. The *character indelibilis* thus acquired means that the charismatic qualities and powers of the office are emancipated from the personal qualities of the priest.[4]

During rationalization, the prophet customarily is replaced by the priest, who then converts revelation into dogma, fits timeless oracles into a tradition, and moderates the radical ethic into pastoral care.

In Weber's vocabulary, personal charisma becomes office charisma, which is thenceforth much threatened by any reappearance of its ancestor: any genuinely personal inspiration which is prophetic, mystical, ecstatic or miraculous. For that would jeopardize the sovereignty of the organization.

The miracle is incorporated into the regular organization, as for example the miracle of the sacraments. Charismatic qualification is depersonalized; it adheres to the ordination as such and is, in principle, detached from the

---

[3] Ibid. 244.   [4] Ibid. 246–249.

personal worthiness of the officeholder – this was the subject matter of the Donatist controversy. In accordance with the overall scheme, the incumbent is distinguished from the office; otherwise his unworthiness would compromise the office charisma.[5]

Weber thinks Sohm was correct in his characterization of the charismatics. But Sohm's ability to see their decline only in the Catholic Church led him into too narrow an application.[6] It is to be found in all churches. Harnack was correct when he saw that institutionalization was simply the price of survival for any human society. Weber sees it as a continuum rather than an upheaval. But he sides with the consensus by seeing it as a regrettable continuum.

The church was thereby changed from a fellowship of salvation into an institution of salvation. The Spirit was to erupt no longer, now that power was immanent in the institution, especially in its sacraments. Paul and John had seen Jesus as the climactic end of history; the present was already redeemed, and complete. But Luke, typical of the new generation with its loss of nerve, abandoned that view, made Jesus instead the turning point in history, and began to compose a history of the church.

RUDOLF BULTMANN

Another German scholar later stepped into the Sohm – Harnack debate: Rudolf Bultmann, the exegete from Marburg who was tending to be a very influential, if ideological, theologian.[7] He noted that for Sohm, the introduction of order and law had violated the very nature of the church. Bultmann conceived of the church as a transcendent, spiritual congregation of the saints, abiding uneasily in this world under the power of the Spirit in expectation of the final consummation. But as an eschatological community ruled by the Spirit and shunning the world, the church by its nature created regulation and tradition.[8] There was a locus of authority: the utterances of the Spirit-endowed, the charismatic apostles (later, evangelists), prophets and teachers. These chief persons in authority

---

[5] Ibid. 1166. One Weber critic, Robert C. Tucker, has argued that charisma does not really wither with the transition to successors. It survives in the cult of the dead founder. It may be routinized, but it is not depersonalized. "The Theory of Charismatic Leadership," *Daedalus*, 97 (1968), 731–756.   [6] Ibid. 1112.

[7] Rudolf Bultmann, *Theology of the New Testament*, trans. Kendrick Grobel, 2 (London: SCM, 1955), 95–118. This translates *Theologie des neuen Testaments* (Tübingen: J. C. B. Mohr [Siebeck], 1953).   [8] Here he follows Holl against Sohm, ibid. 98.

were those most powerfully endowed by the Spirit, and their primary function was to preach the word of salvation. A second locus of spiritual authority was the congregation itself. The Spirit could be seen at work in miraculous and pentecostal phenomena, and also in the processes of democratic decision-making that provided for an orderly common life. A third element of inspired authority was the tradition which the proclaimed word gradually generated. So Sohm had been quite far from the mark when he denied any spiritual force except in individual charismatics.

But the church had a second, entirely different aspect. Distinct from the eschatological congregation, which is alien to this world and striving for the End, and which is entirely God's handiwork, there was a historical organization: a very human handiwork. The provisions proper to this human assembly were tolerable, even serviceable to the church, but only if they were understood as regulatory, not constitutive. They would become subversive if they were ever regarded as creating the church. And, regrettably, that is what did happen.

The earliest communities did have officers, probably from the very beginning days while they were in process of differentiating themselves from Judaism. Bultmann moves well beyond the consensus when he ascribes to that earliest church order a configuration that was borrowed from the Jews: "The earliest church at first took the form of a synagogue within Judaism, as is well known. As for the Christian congregations in the Hellenistic world, which had developed out of synagogue-congregations or had attached themselves to such, much the same thing holds true."[9] But this organizational model was relatively insignificant, in that it did not derive from the church's special new identity.

At the outset there were officers: elders, called *presbyteroi* in Jewish-Christian churches and *episkopoi* in hellenistic congregations, where they were assisted by *diakonoi*. Informal terms, such as "laborers," "coworkers" and the like, probably were converted later into official designations, but at first they were casual.

The officers were subordinate to the charismatics. They were elected by the membership, whereas the apostles, prophets and teachers were empowered by the Spirit. The officers had an identity and a warrant circumscribed by the local communities that

[9] Ibid. 101.

appointed them, whereas the charismatic preachers had a mission to the entire world. And as officers whose tasks were essentially managerial, they clearly deferred to the personal authority of those whose ministry called the church into being.

But with the passage of time the irreplaceable apostles died, and the second- and third-generation proclaimers of the Word came to display an increasingly enfeebled spiritual endowment. Their work then began to be assumed by others. The proclamation of the Word now became the prerogative of the officers, and they also became the guardians of the sacred tradition of both discipline and belief. It was natural that the spiritual capacity to perform those services adequately came to be associated, not with a direct divine empowerment but with their election and ordination. And the officers became, finally, the authorized leaders of sacramental cult in the church.

The result was devastating for the church's understanding of itself. Thus the human – indeed, often political – process of appointment by the church was interpreted as the conveyance of a divine charisma. The preaching of the church lost its eschatological summons to await and hasten the kingdom, and degenerated into a moral didacticism directed towards the posthumous salvation of the individual. The worship, no longer the celebration of the redeemed, became a supply arrangement for the forgiveness of sins and the provision of immortality. "The future salvation toward which hope is directed comes to be seen less in the completion of the history of salvation and the transformation of the world at the dawn of the new age than the future life of the individual beyond death."[10]

The church had changed from a fellowship of salvation to an institution of salvation. The Spirit became encased within the sacraments, and the gospel was absorbed by the tradition. And the *episkopoi*, *presbyteroi* and *diakonoi*, originally taken to be creatures of the congregation, emerged as its putative creators.

The church then became a different sort of moral actor. Whereas the earliest Christian self-understanding had made faith a total claim on life, with secular concerns left to the state, the new church began to frame competing rules for moral life, and to draw on the Torah for that purpose. A new divine law was in process of being framed. As the Parousia was delayed, Christians needed guidance, not to receive the New Age in their lifetime, but to merit eternal life afterwards.

---

[10] Ibid. 112.

In acknowledging the aboriginal existence of officers in the Christian churches Bultmann had reconstructed history differently from most adherents of the consensus – and more accurately. Their devolution, in the subapostolic period, into sacerdotal officers was a disfigurement of the church no less severe in his mind than in those of others, however. When the church arrogated to itself the power to confer the Spirit through human agency, the Christian community lost its bearings. The new way of life was no longer the demonstration of a salvation already graciously conferred; it could now be only the condition for achieving a future salvation. And, like its purveyors, it would be a sheerly human entity.

Here one sees a typical Bultmann product: meticulous history affected by strong ideology, not in its factual narrative so much as in the interpretation. Actually, his reconstruction of the respective roles of officers and charismatics would turn out to be one of the most accurate of his times. It is Bultmann's assessment of the change wrought between the first and second centuries that skews his story.

Bultmann can side with Harnack in seeing a true order at work in the primitive community, but he is hardly less contemptuous than Sohm in deploring what became of it. In these two widely influential scholars, Weber and Bultmann, the consensus was again mightily reinforced.

HANS FREIHERR VON CAMPENHAUSEN

Hans Baron von Campenhausen's study, which among all works in this century has settled in as a most appealing formulation of the consensus, appeared in the years of reconstruction after World War II. Writing from Heidelberg, where he professed church history, Campenhausen begins his study of church authority with the Lord Jesus himself, who is known by ambiguous and unofficial titles like prophet, teacher, master, and who possesses might and power over demons and sin. He is entitled to deference to his person, not only to his teaching. Yet Jesus holds no office. He is a pure instance of greatest power but he holds no office at all. He is for that reason the root stock on which any Christian office must be grafted.

Jesus has no official status, but he has a mission; he is at the same time the one who is sent and the one who from the start and in his inmost self matches the demands of that mission. He does not, like the ordinary prophet, need to receive God's spirit and endowment; he stands completely on God's side.

Nor is he the holder of any office in the customary sense, he appeals to no official commissioning; for commission and office are combined in his person. Hence there are no ready-made categories under which the distinctive quality of his authority, as this is to be seen in the Gospels, can be subsumed. Seemingly the only effective reality is the demand and promise which stem from God alone, to which Jesus bears witness, and behind which he vanishes in an anonymous humanity.[11]

The Twelve must be distinguished carefully from the apostles. The Twelve were probably designated by Jesus himself. They were held in great respect by the community, but they seem to have played no active or vital part in governance. Though Matthias replaces Judas, no other member is replaced when he dies: so they are to be a first-generation phenomenon only. They are to be eschatological judges, but not rulers during their own lifetimes.

It is the apostles who are the articulate missionary witnesses to the resurrection. They include Peter (possibly the only one of the Twelve to be an apostle), Paul, James, and others. They are plenipotentiaries of the Lord, founders and rulers of congregations. It is they who generate the church. Here von Campenhausen is taking a line ostensibly at variance with many of his predecessors. He describes the apostles as human intermediaries whose mission is actually to beget faith. "The 'Apostles' are earlier than the Church, earlier even than the Church in the limited sense of a sociologically definable entity; and the later view of them in Church history and law is justified to the extent that theirs was an antecedent authority by which the Church itself was established and defined."[12]

The generation that received its faith from these apostles did not find justification simply from a private encounter with God apart from any human mediation. The apostolic mission, therefore, is an exception to the otherwise strict doctrine that no human can be an integral party to any other human's salvation. The conclusion to be drawn from this, however, is that although these men founded and ruled churches, received honor and made decisions, theirs was a unique position, as Jesus' had been. They too had power but no office. For von Campenhausen, one essential feature of office is that it can be handed on to successors, and the apostles had no successors.

It was the appearance of elders that marked the first clear

---

[11] Hans [Freiherr] von Campenhausen, *Ecclesiastical Authority and Spiritual Power in the Church of the First Three Centuries*, trans. J. A. Baker (London: Adam & Charles Black, 1969), 10. This translates *Kirchliches Amt und geistliche Vollmacht* (Tübingen: J. C. B. Mohr, 1953).

[12] Ibid. 13–14.

introduction of officers, and the first fall from grace. They were of Judeo-Christian origin (just as the *episkopoi* and *diakonoi* were gentile-Christian institutions). Acts says that Paul instituted them in his churches, but Paul never mentions *presbyteroi*. That the elders are not therefore pauline is no disqualification, however. Nor that they were a human institution, with no warrant from the Lord. Nor that their nature as conservators of the tradition tended to make them reactionary. The elders, von Campenhausen is quite prepared to admit, were an authentic response to the threat of false teaching in the church. It is only when they overthrew the terms of their appointment and set themselves up, no longer as conservators of the gospel, but as absolute authorities in their own right, that they betrayed their office.

Sohm had rightly seen that the doctrine of Clement was a fundamental deviation from that of Paul. Paul's old arguments for organic unity were, in Clement's strategy, used to legitimate a specific church order: law thereby elbowed spirit aside.[13] What had been a function of community service now was made into a lifelong office. "To this extent it may be said that here for the first time the structures of canon law are included in the category of doctrines and dogma, and given the same sacral and immutable character."[14] Through that one narrow door now entered authority, obedience, institution, formalization, cultic roles, the priesthood – laity division, and an entire sacral system.

The office of elder in the pastoral epistles (which he dates quite late, 100–150 AD, because they describe the church as guided by officers) is not assigned to anyone on the strength of spiritual endowments, since natural abilities are listed among the qualifications for office. In this respect it resembles Jewish rather than Christian notions of leadership. Earlier Christianity did not know offices with secular or practical qualifications. Here too von Campenhausen spies the reassertion of foreign, Jewish influences, drawing the Christian endeavor away from its purest and most distinctive convictions. Office in the pastoral epistles is not derived from the tradition of Paul. "It springs up in the soil of the system of elders, an originally Jewish institution which was taken over at first in a 'patriarchal' form. Renewed emphasis on the idea of tradition now intensifies its authoritarian quality, and at the same time gives it

---

[13] Von Campenhausen acknowledges that Ac, 1 Pt and Js agree with *1 Cl* that *presbyteroi* were of apostolic creation, ibid. 90–92.   [14] Ibid. 92.

more markedly the character of an office. It hereby becomes even further removed from the men of the Spirit within the Pauline congregation."[15]

At this point our author believes he can see the lineaments of three ancient understandings of church which correspond to three great modern church polities. The church order of ancient Rome shares with Catholics a sense of the *episkopos* as a supreme, cultic official. The church of Syria, whose counterpart today is Eastern Orthodoxy, beholds its officers as spiritual examples and mentors. And in the tradition of Asia Minor, recapitulated in Protestantism, the *episkopos* is an ordained preacher of the apostolic message. The Catholic view, for which the others would be a necessary corrective, derives from the pastoral epistles' mistake about what it was the officers were to guard. The Gnostics had been putting round their own *paradosis* = tradition and *diadochê* = succession. The first Catholic reaction in the pastorals puts its stress, not on *paradosis* but on *parathêkê* = deposit. Faith then came to be considered, not as something to be handled, but as a trust to be watched. The notion of office carried with it the notion that non-officers had to be rendered passive. The Gnostics' claim to have a chain of persons preserving their special tradition was met, of course, by the Catholic counter-claim of a succession of officers. Irenaeus deferred to the preserving elders, not merely on the warrant of their position, but on grounds of their teaching and life. But it was more common to honor them simply for the fact of their office. In this way succession of office became identified with right tradition. Indeed, the function of tradition was virtually swallowed up by office, which replaced it as the ground of faith.

As church officers were gaining this recognition, what befell their old rivals, the charismatics? First of all, von Campenhausen will not admit Harnack's classical thesis that the officers and the charismatics were two competing blocs of power. Officers had to possess the Spirit; enthusiasts had to teach the official doctrine. If they had this solidarity with one another, then why did the charismatics break up and disappear? He offers three distinct accounts. The apostles vanished fairly soon, as the retirement of that title from active service served to enhance the awe now reserved for the first missionaries. The prophets, in their turn, were to be a casualty of the conflict with the Montanists. With their claims of absolute authority for their wild

---

[15] Ibid. 116–117.

seizures of the Spirit, the Montanists raised the question of how to distinguish valid prophetic inspiration from demonic possession. The dogmatic formularies that had been devised to cope with the Gnostics were of no help here, for the Montanists were not heretics. It was their predilection for ecstasy which finally brought to the fore an old impatience among Catholics towards any unintelligible prophecy. They came to regard ecstasy and charismatic abandon as suspicious rather than wonderful and reassuring. And so prophecy faded in some disgrace. It was then the turn of the teachers to move to center stage. But they were not the same *didaskaloi* of the old days. "The teachers of the second century are not enthusiasts. They are biblical scholars and theologians, and as such the first conscious champions of an individualist and personalist spirituality within the Church."[16] They taught pupils, not congregations. Their interest in humanistic Judaism led them to a sympathetic attention to pagan scholars. By the end of the second century the teacher, the scholarly expositor of the mysteries, was held in high esteem: a worthy rival, at last, for the bishops. But the teacher was no longer a charismatic. And so the inspired triad disappeared.[17]

Professor von Campenhausen's historical review carries through into an extended contrast between Origen and Cyprian, whom he portrays as paradigms of the two inveterate polarities in the church:

[U]nder cover of the dominant ecclesiastical consensus Origen and Cyprian, the theologians of the Eastern and Western Church, still represent two divergent trends in Christian thinking, both of which were very much alive from the beginning – the authority of the spiritual and the authority of office, the "Gnostic" and the hierarchical self-consciousness, the former associated with the Greek, the latter with the Roman tradition. Each of these feels itself to be the heir to the unabridged tradition, and each affirms the unity of the Church. Cyprian is no more rigidly hierarchical in attitude than Origen is an anti-clerical reformer; neither of them wishes to tear up and destroy the opposing elements but to combine and harmonize them with his own position. In each case, however, the synthesis is only half successful. The old tensions between spirit and office are not to be resolved in this way; they are overcome more on the level of feeling and practice than by arguments on theological principle.[18]

Nevertheless it was Cyprian's view, not Origen's, that would dominate the Western church, and it is this understanding which

---

[16] Ibid. 193.

[17] Interestingly, von Campenhausen does not characterize the gentrification of the *didaskalos* as a fall from gospel integrity.   [18] Ibid. 265–266.

Baron von Campenhausen sees as the pathology the Reformation set out to cure. For Cyprian it is the church, not holiness, which is the concomitant of the spirit. And the *episkopos* holds the church in his power. Elections had become a stylized formality. The bishop alone ordained, forgave, presided or provided presidents at baptism and eucharist, and interacted with other churches. Cyprian's bishop had no rivals: not the charismatics, not even the martyrs. But the power of the keys in his hands had lost much of its Christ-centered, spiritual character. It was orderly, it was official, but it might not master demons and sin.

The flaw which runs like a seismic fault-line across the church from the pastoral epistles to Cyprian and beyond is a lack of any adequate sense of the infinite gulf between the human-rational order and that of the spirit. The officer presides over a sacral society but with a politically pragmatic pastoral style: sensible but secular.

Yet the officer must support his claim to be a religious personage. And that is what reveals the impotence of the tradition of office to von Campenhausen. The outrage is not that offices exist, but that they are pretentiously unilateral in their exercise of authority, and are not engaged in a dialectical relationship with the laity. True power, as it was in Christ and his apostles, had left behind only its vacant shell.

This is a complex and nuanced construct. It attempts to consider office as a legitimate development gone bad, rather than as a violation from the start. Yet as one looks back over the library that had been a-building on our topic since the 1850s, one must remark that despite the fact that the arts and sciences of biblical exegesis and historical research had matured over the years, and despite the increased sophistication of critical method used in these studies, the influence of ideology has, if anything, increased. One is inclined to observe that up to this point – one century after Ritschl – there was still not a Catholic who had seen popular, unofficered sovereignty as the church order of the early Christians, and hardly a Protestant who saw authoritative office as a legacy of the Spirit to chosen leaders. Therein lies a possible lesson. For the argument over office has in fact been an argument over autocracy, and over autonomy, and over anarchy.

Every so often a voice of caution would make itself heard, questioning the most basic tenets of the consensus. It was, for example, accepted as beyond challenge that the church orders of the pastorals represented an authoritarian coup visited upon the free and democratic communities of Paul. Joseph Gewiess, however, raised a doubt about that dogma, a strong doubt.[19] It is true, he admits, that Paul nowhere writes of elders in his churches. But already in his earliest letter, 1 Thessalonians, he mentions those who preside and those who defer. The letter to the Philippians, at the other end of the pauline corpus of letters (whether it be authentic, edited or pseudonymous), begins with an address to the local *episkopoi* and *diakonoi*. The interval between these two documents, Gewiess thinks, might have been one of formalization and development, but it is far from certain that it witnessed a radical transformation.

The record of that period includes 1 Corinthians, Romans and perhaps Ephesians, all of which record a medley of services and empowerments in the community, all of them furnished by divine *charismata*. There is no evidence of two distinct categories of service, charismatic and official: for Paul all ministries are gifts of the Spirit. Gewiess rejects the rule of Knopf: "Wherever people are elected or approved, it is not Spirit and charisms that are in charge, but law and institution."[20] This he considers a conclusion of ideology, not of historical study. The imposition of hands was traditionally associated with charism. There could be no radical opposition between ordination to office and spiritual capacity. Even if one concludes that charismatic gifts were dominant in the pauline congregations, we still do not have adequate evidence to conclude that as societies they were spiritual democracies or anarchies. Some of those very charisms were given for rule and for care. As the literature develops, those duties are seen to comprise instruction, admonition, shepherding and leadership.

It is true that beginning with the pastoral epistles the *episkopos* seems to be accumulating the various roles of ruling and caring. The trend accelerates in Clement. But Gewiess takes issue with those who find no continuity between the later state of affairs and the situation witnessed by Paul, and who therefore claim that the institutions of the second century have no antecedents in those of mid-first century. Paul's inclusion of presidential charisms, and his appointment of the first converts over young communities he was to leave, serves well enough to point the way towards Clement's recollection that the apostles created the bishops and deacons. Clement was writing forty years after the founding of the Corinthian church, and thirty years

---

[19] Joseph Gewiess, "Die neutestamentlichen Grundlagen der kirchlichen Hierarchie," *Historisches Jahrbuch*, 72 (1953), 1–24.   [20] Ibid. 18.

after the deaths of Peter and Paul. His readership both in Corinth and in Rome included living witnesses to what had been done there from the first.

Thus Gewiess argues that it is reasonable to see the beginnings of polity in the early pauline literature. It is already showing signs of a development that will lead eventually towards the episcopate, which as Clement and Ignatius portray it is no less strong and authoritative than Paul himself was. The second-century bishop is a not unworthy successor to Paul's ministry and style.

EDUARD SCHWEIZER

Eduard Schweizer was professor of New Testament at Zürich, and a minister in the Swiss Reformed Church there. His theory, which he both extracts from and applies to the New Testament and early subapostolic writings, is that if one follows the chronological development of the early church from its most primitive documents to those in the early second century, one will observe a steady dissipation of the insight and revolution which were so fiery and hopeful at its brighter days.[21]

Paul, as is now conventional for studies like this one, is put forward as the summit and standard of Christian understanding, against which later documents and doctrines are to be measured. And the threat to Paul's teaching proceeds from Jewish influences which menace the Christian originality of the church. Schweizer records that the Jesus people originally carried on just like the Jews they thought they were. He notes that they did not seem to draw as far away from the mainstream as did some other sects of the day. They seemed to understand themselves simply as converted and newly devout mainstream Jews. Jewish piety flowed unbroken through their fellowship, and indeed retarded their proper consciousness of the radical singularity of their faith. Still, he claims, they were no longer at home.

For it is clear that from the very beginning the Church no longer really lives on temple sacrifice and observance of the law, even if it takes part in them. It hears the Old Testament in the synagogue, and from that it hears God's call; but it hears that call because Jesus' words and Jesus' death have opened the Old Testament to it. It takes part in the Passover, and is thereby

---

[21] Eduard Schweizer, *Church Order in the New Testament*, trans. Frank Clarke (London: SCM, 1961). This translates *Gemeinde und Gemeindeordnung im Neuen Testament* (Zürich: Zwingli, 1959).

reminded of God's redeeming action in Egypt; but that is made actual for it by what it experiences in its own circle at the Lord's Supper.[22]

In retrospect one can see that a breach was inevitable, even imminent. What was to provoke the rupture was not however their proclamation of Jesus as Messiah. Judaism was doctrinally very tolerant. What brought on the crisis was their preference for communion with Gentiles over observance of the Law.

It was Paul who goaded them to know and to act upon their singularity, through the preaching that no salvation was possible but by faith in Jesus. Yet in the postpauline documents we see a fading of that sharp caesura between Israel and the church – and, for that matter, between the church and the world. Christians, despite Paul, remained open to Jewish influences and practices.[23]

The pastoral epistles, which Schweizer regards as especially regressive, are what begin to unravel what Paul had done. They attenuate his polemic against Israel. They present the church as guarantor of the truth, less against Jewish error than against false teachers within the Christian circle itself. They invite believers to think of themselves as sustainers of a social order, not as subversives against it (thus prizing the household and family order more than the Spirit). They imply, through the easy manner in which they draw on Jewish law and hellenistic ethics, that there may be sources of salvation apart from Christian faith. The *Didache* and Clement and Ignatius are even more exposed to Jewish influence than are the pastorals. The church was gradually being overtaken by a sinister reassertion of Judaism, and the form it took was the establishment and exaltation of a hierarchical order that came to function like a new Torah: a law not of the Spirit, however, but of office.

More even than most scholars, Schweizer depicts the founding generation as unstructured. The Twelve were not apostles (that is, missionaries); they were merely witnesses to Christ. Their teaching

---

[22] Ibid. 3k. References to this book are, at the author's request, by chapter and section rather than by page, and refer uniformly to both the German original and the English translation.

[23] Schweizer writes that it cannot "be objected that there was such a strong contrast between Church and synagogue that Christianity could not have taken over anything Jewish after the year 70," ibid. 1c. His examples of borrowing include fasting, a theology of inspiration and a canon of scripture, oral tradition, the tombs of the saints, altars, works of supererogation, intercession of the saints, and succession in ministry. These are mostly influences which Schweizer would judge to be deleterious. They are, however, influences which would not ostensibly have had to enter the Christian tradition after the fall of Jerusalem. It is perhaps easier to make a case for Jewish continuities before then than for Jewish influences afterwards.

was dutiful, but not meant to be decisive. The apostles, who were sent
to proclaim and preach, were similarly not models for anyone who is
to follow them. A certain few of them, like Peter, Paul and James,
were given personal prominence, but even they stood on no eminence
too high above their hearers, for any believing disciple immediately
became the peer of the one who had brought him the faith. Schweizer
writes that "it is natural that those who accompanied Jesus played a
part in the later Church. But of that group of disciples as a school for
Church leaders there certainly was never any thought. This is
suggested by the fact that in the older strata of the Jesus-tradition the
later Church and its order and doctrine do not appear at all – that it
is in fact quite open to question whether the twelve were ever leaders
of the Primitive Church."[24]

Schweizer reads the documents as the consensus does, and he sees
no structures in the New Testament church, except perhaps for the
one passage in the tiny letter, 3 John, where a certain Diotrephes is
excoriated for lusting after presidency: a hint that offices were just
then emerging in the first century, and a foretaste of the incumbents
they were likely to attract. References to *presbyteroi* are, for Schweizer,
evidence that theirs was a cachet of public respect, but not an office.
There are no official teachers, because all are anointed in the Spirit.
Even in Acts, where titles do seem to abound, they are said to denote
functions which are informally and impermanently recognized by the
churches. The offices are an acknowledgement rather than a bestowal
of a charism of service. When, in postbiblical documents, office
hardens into an upper class, and when community decisions are
taken no longer by inspired consensus but have to be put to an actual
vote for majority decision, and when Jewish and secular models and
terminology of hierarchy are emulated, then the church is undergoing
a destructive alienation from its truest self.

The new order, being foreign to the Christian movement, had to be
defended. The argument, in order to be cogent enough to persuade
members to submit to a hierarchy, had to be based, not on the needs
of the building-up of the church (as in Paul), nor on the uniqueness
of the church (as in the New Testament), but on parallels with the
cosmos, the army, the household, and the institutions of ancient
Israel. The *Didache* had given too much allure to ecstasy and
enthusiastic performance (by contrast with the charism of every

---

[24] Ibid. 2i. Schweizer's convictions never show more strongly than when he can assert that
Paul, Peter and James were not men who could command in the church.

believer). With the waning of that movement the leadership passed to the officers. Clement then made order into a rule, and turned the officers from servants into masters. Ignatius saw union with the risen Lord, not as a free and dynamic gift, but as an institutional guarantee. Gospel had been converted – or corrupted – into law.

Schweizer is not all of one mind about what befell the church as it moved from the first to the third generation. At times he describes it as one legitimate emphasis overtaking another. One view, nourished in the pauline communities, stresses the active possession of the Spirit by every believer. The other view, which Schweizer sees in the pastoral and johannine epistles, links the work of the Spirit especially to church offices. These two emphases, that of the free church and that of the institutional church, Schweizer is prepared to describe as needed in a balanced Christianity. But he is clearly more at home with the conviction that when offices were joined with charisms it meant a forfeiture of something distinctively Christian.[25] In the end he concludes that episcopacy, like the observance of Sunday, is simply not to be found in the New Testament. Elders are there, but as a class, not an office. Deacons, he says, are not biblical.[26] The officers that emerged under that title were a later innovation.

What governs the construction of this thesis most is that an attentively Lutheran ideology stands sentinel over every paragraph (though Schweizer, as we have said, belongs to the Swiss Reformed Church). More perhaps than in the earlier writers Linton had studied, Eduard Schweizer begins with the doctrine of justification by Christian faith alone. And with a resoluteness reminiscent of Rudolph Sohm he finds that all the evidence agrees with that doctrine. With that as his standard he separates what is central from what he deems marginal or even deviant. And the conclusion – a non-essential, non-authoritative church order – arrives to surprise no one.

Schweizer is also a devotee of nomenclature studies, though not always a consistent one. When he is making the case that officers are

---

[25] "These ministries have their parallels or their origin partly in Jewish ministries. This is clearest in the case of the elders, who are probably a continuation of the rulers of the Jewish synagogue; though it must not be overlooked that they did not carry out their ministry by any means from the very beginning of the Church, but that their introduction represents a later assimilation to the Jewish forms. More emphatically still, the idea that the elders of Jerusalem are not simply a local body, but that they correspond roughly to the Jewish Sanhedrin, is a very late construction." Ibid. 24i.

[26] Though he does find deaconesses, ibid. 6h.

absent from the earliest churches, the absence of official titles is conclusive. He gives no serious consideration to the possibility that the offices which later emerged as *episkopos*, *presbyteros* and *diakonos* could have been operative then without their eventual titles. But then when this nomenclature does make its appearance, he is easily persuaded that it could not be anything more than a casual description of a function. In early documents Schweizer says titles correspond to offices; in later documents he says titles do not correspond to offices. One would have to notice that the documents present us with a very fluid nomenclature, and sparse information about what various functionaries did in their public roles. It is the work of meticulous scholarship to detect, from studying function, what various titles meant in various documents. Schweizer, who is a very accomplished biblical scholar, regrettably seems to have been guided more by doctrine than by exegesis in that very critical task.[27]

LEONHARD GOPPELT

At this point, understandably, scholars did not straightforwardly offer endorsements of any of their predecessors' formulations. Weber and Bultmann had criticisms and corrections to address to Sohm and Harnack. Yet the points of difference are relatively fine. In fundamentals these men speak in unison. Leonhard Goppelt, a New Testament professor in Hamburg, illustrates this amply. He takes frequent issue with Sohm and Harnack, and with Bultmann and von Campenhausen as well. His own construct, with all its provisos, displays all the main girders and architecture, nevertheless, of the consensus that they all shared.[28]

In Goppelt's theory, the Christian revelation and church were from the start both eschatological and historical, spiritual and pragmatic. For instance, the various forms of inspired *diakonia* = service listed by Paul are supernatural powers, but they are at the same time calls to specific forms or tasks of service. For the integrity of the Christian faith these two aspects must be held in balance. Harnack's sharp differentiation of charism from office, which may have been true for the third generation of the church, does violence

---

[27] Schweizer's work was followed shortly by another that is quite similar: Gerhard Friedrich, "Geist und Amt," *Wort und Dienst*, 3 (1952), 61–85.

[28] Leonhard Goppelt, *Apostolic and Post-apostolic Times*, trans. Robert A. Guelich (London: Adam & Charles Black, 1970), 177–202. This translates *Die apostolische und nachapostolische Zeit* (Göttingen and Zürich: Vandenhoeck & Ruprecht, 1962).

to those functions as they are reported in Paul's time, when they were both charisms and offices.

This is a healthy though tense duality, and Goppelt disagrees with earlier writers who blame the pastoral epistles for unbalancing it. The diversity of services and offices there has not pushed aside its counterpart, the priesthood of all believers. The balance was still holding. It is Clement whom he blames for destroying the synthesis. Clement created the fiction that the offices were of apostolic origin, and as a result were of divine right. After Clement one need not await the Spirit for a *diakonia* to be accomplished; one need only fill the office.

In 1 Clement we actually have existing offices which are to be filled. Here the rule of the Spirit, who offers the charismata and points out new tasks and thus gives structure to the offices, is eliminated. The disapproving silence about prophets and teachers documents this fact. The tension-filled relationship between the spiritual and the historical, the living event and the institution given to the Church from the character of the redemptive event itself, is relinquished and the former is subordinated to the latter.[29]

Clement makes concern for legitimacy eclipse concern for spiritual effectiveness. And what is more, Clement's argument for retaining incumbents in office has become a secular one. Had he argued that God had authorized them and that God would be faithful to his promises and honor his commitment, that might have been over-ridden by an appeal to the freedom of the Spirit, which for Paul would have been a more fundamental principle. But at least it would have been a distinctly Christian argument. Clement instead builds his case on the necessity of world order.

Goppelt stands apart from most exegetes by holding that the pastoral epistles, whatever their authorship, still hold with Paul in their general perspective. But the collapse is merely postponed a few more years. Goppelt agrees with the rest that the churches of Clement and Ignatius are unfaithful to the order of the foundational church.

THE SCHOOL OF SOCIAL ANALYSIS

The contributors to the debate over early church order have been historical scholars: biblical exegetes, experts in patristic literature, or historically oriented theologians. Occasionally a stranger has wandered in, such as Rudolf Sohm whose discipline was the law. Yet

---

[29] Ibid. 198.

he too was a historian by method, even though his subject matter was so different. Max Weber, like Sohm, was an outsider: a sociologist. His contribution, like Sohm's, was the work of an exceptionally brilliant scholar, and despite their want of professional familiarity with theological and ecclesiastical history, both proposed theories that stirred up much sediment from the ancient seafloor beneath the continuing discussion. One would like to think that if they had known more about the Christian church and theological history, their contributions might have been even more enduring.[30]

Quite recently a new cohort of scholars has arrived to address the topic. They are proficient theologically, trained historically, and inclined to apply the methods of social history and development to the early data with a competence not previously seen. Being natives to religious studies, they are critical of the received theories in a way Weber could not have been. Indeed, they have, as a group, put challenges to the consensus that come from an entirely new direction.

GERD THEISSEN

Beginning in the early 1970s the German scholar Gerd Theissen suggested a dramatically new reconstruction of early Christian development.[31] He begins with one massive assumption: that we can disengage from the synoptic gospels the most authentic account of Jesus' preaching, a radically prophetic call for a transformation of Judaism.[32] He summons Israel to be an eschatological community so

[30] Another social scientist, likewise not a theological professional, had applied his social categories interestingly to our problem: Ernst Tröltsch, *The Social Teaching of the Christian Churches*, trans. Olive Wyon (New York: Macmillan, 1931); this translates *Die Soziallehren der christlichen Kirchen und Gruppen* (Tübingen: Mohr, 1912).

[31] Gerd Theissen, *Sociology of Early Christianity*, trans. John Bowden (Philadelphia: Fortress, 1978); this translates *Soziologie der Jesus-bewegung* (Munich: Kaiser, 1977).

[32] Theissen's initial assumption, based on a priority of the synoptics over Paul, resembles an axiom of another social analyst, Norman R. Petersen, who assumes that Paul is prior to Acts and therefore historically more normative. Unlike Paul, who sees himself called to the gentiles, Luke recounts him as typically preaching at a local synagogue when arriving in a new city, and only after rejection there would he work among the local gentiles. Petersen sees this as a theological device in both Luke and Acts: "the rejection of God's agents by God's people in connection with God's sancuaries (synagogues and temple) is the plot device by which the movement of the narrative as a whole is motivated." *Literary Criticism for New Testament Critics* (Philadelphia: Fortress, 1978), 83. What might be questioned is not Petersen's claim that Luke is posterior and hence (when in conflict with Paul) historically inauthentic, but his assumption that it must be so. There is the other possibility: Luke, seeing Paul's repeatedly unproductive approaches to the Jewish diaspora, then decided to enhance that theme in his gospel narrative, while Paul, though prior in publication, might have had his own reasons to downplay his negative treatment by Jewish synagogue

detached from material self-seeking that his message in its raw and potent form could be conveyed only by disciples who abandoned home, family, property and social standing to become wandering, charismatic beggars.

The Jesus-movement arose within Roman Palestine at a time of great instability. Economic recession had thrown many out of work; the rural poor resented the urban elites who accumulated the wealth from their labor; the Roman procurators, Herodian princes and Jewish aristocracy all actively undermined each other's legitimacy; and the various nativist movements that revived Jewish national feeling after a century of careless assimilation to hellenist culture were now all attacking one another as not faithful enough to belong to the True Israel. It was the right time for radical visions of national restoration, such as the Essenes, the resistance fighters and the Pharisees. The Jesus-movement, however, was to have been quite different.

Yet it was soon neutralized. The wandering apostles and prophets were supported by appreciative sympathizers in the towns and villages. But these were disciples of a different stripe. Unlike the detached, marginalized charismatics, they remained rooted in family, class and work. They continued in the normal practices of Judaism, though with a purified spirit. This however produced a tamed version of the Jesus-message, one that was acceptable to this sedentary, second-tier group of disciples. The resulting double standard found its way into the gospels: a compromise ethic alongside the primitive, radical norms; and sacraments as a pantomime of rigorous ascetical discipleship.

In the early days of primitive Christianity in Palestine, the local Jesus people had no community structures. The wandering charismatics were their decisive spiritual authorities. In time, however, those communities grew in size to the point where they might need stable structures of their own. Also, the decision to accept gentile converts without circumcision alienated them from Jewish communities. So they created authority structures: stable, hierarchical offices.

By now the movement was moving from the country to the cities, and with its open welcome to gentile converts it found its widest ambit of freedom in the hellenistic cities. At this point a version of the

communities. At least that alternative possibility must have been considered before Petersen's working principle could safely be pursued.

gospel altogether different from the first, radical call to reform, was crafted by Paul – who in Theissen's account is a breakaway figure, but a disappointing one. It is Paul who formulates an ethic of compromise which Theissen calls "love-patriarchalism." Rather than pursuing the extravagant norms of Jesus and a hope for the miraculous conversion of Israel, Paul called his followers to remain in their social, political, economic and cultural inequalities, to leave society largely as it was, but to create within the church an internalized fellowship.

> In the political and social realm class-specific differences were essentially accepted, affirmed, even religiously legitimated. No longer was there a struggle for equal rights but instead a struggle to achieve a pattern of relationships among members of various strata which would be characterized by respect, concern, and a sense of responsibility.[33]

Naturally, in these more hellenized communities the resident officers quickly replaced the wandering charismatics as the decisive authorities. The itinerant beggars, in fact, quickly fell into disrepute.

Thus Theissen emerges quite on all fours with Sohm in his account of a Christianity fallen so soon into infidelity. What is different is that Paul is now the villain, for he is the creator of these assimilationist communities that surrendered radical freedom for respectability and structure. And the community structures fashioned by the Christians were alien and compromised replacements for the more authentic charismatic wanderers of the first, Palestinian period.

JOHN GAGER

One of the most recent social analysts who are also trained historians and theologians is John Gager of Princeton University. His study of early Christianity poses a direct doubt about the consensus.

> [I]f we accept as a fundamental law the transformation from no rules to new rules, we may not at the same time lament the routinization of the primitive enthusiasm that characterizes all charismatic or millenarian movements in their second generation and sometimes even earlier. If, as Bultmann observes, "the word of the Spirit-endowed, being an authoritative word, creates regulation and tradition," then he lacks all historical justification for his further statement that legal regulation, whether regulative or constitutive, "contradicts the church's nature." Bultmann's "Ecclesia as the

---

[33] Theissen, *The Social Setting of Pauline Christianity*, ed. and trans. John H. Schütz (Philadelphia: Fortress, 1982), 109; see 108–110, 138–140.

eschatological Congregation guided by the Spirit's sway" is a time-bound phenomenon and must give way, indeed it prepares the way for a religious institution with fixed norms of legitimacy. By failing to pursue the full consequences of his own observation about the inevitability of regulations, he and numerous others have simply given up consistent historical analysis. Consequently, a good deal of nonsense has been written about the decline of primitive Christianity into "early Catholicism."[34]

As traced by the scholars of the consensus, the charismatic beginnings of the community were followed by an authoritarian abreaction. But that, says Gager, is only half the story. He sees it as a three-stroke cycle: a subsequent movement of renewal then appeals to the remembered ideas of the founding, and that in turn trips off a repetition of the entire process. The consolidation phase of early Christianity did not extinguish the originating charism. It venerated and preserved its utterances and stories as its scriptures, and these in turn revitalized the church by appealing to values not felt to be adequately sustained in the consolidation. The creation of structures buried the charisma, but only so that it would hibernate and grow towards a second spring and harvest.

Gager cautions against seeing the churches of the New Testament as pure instances of charismatic authority. Jesus himself was a pure, unstructured charismatic. But shortly after Jesus' death his disciples and kinfolk had established communities that were traditional and structured. And they too had their own legitimacy. Paul, who was a convert to their church yet a charismatic in his own right, is an instance of mixed authority: charismatic and traditional. In Jesus and Paul, charism does not separate them – as Weber may have led one to believe – from tradition.

If, for instance, we assume an initial opposition between charisma and office, it will be apparent that neither Jesus nor Paul based his legitimacy on any recognized or official status. But at the same time, their charismatic roles stood firmly within a line of tradition. Indeed, their charisma lay precisely in an authoritative re-evaluation of traditional beliefs and institutions. For this reason, pure charismatic authority is both a theoretical impossibility and a historical fiction. Our earlier discussion...has shown that the successful prophet is one who brings into being a transformation of the old order and a vision of the new.[35]

When congregations moved from charismatic legitimacy sustained by spontaneous manifestations into official legitimacy sustained by

---

[34] John G. Gager, *Kingdom and Community: The Social World of Early Christianity* (Englewood Cliffs, NJ: Prentice-Hall, 1975), 67.   [35] Ibid. 70.

sacramental cult, it was not necessarily a degeneration, for the movement aroused and was countered by vibrant opposition. Montanism, for instance, yearned after the charismatic freedom it felt had gone cold. Monasticism was also a resistance to the blurring of the radical imperatives of Jesus' call.

The canonical scriptures retain, in honored and even idealized form, the account of the church's origins, and thus throughout institutionalization the latent charism provides the legitimacy for future revitalization movements. Consolidation preserves the charism. Gager might have added that the liturgy, like the scriptures, is another canonized institution that re-presents the ancient charism.

BENGT HOLMBERG

Though they are better equipped to address the evidence than Weber was, the modern social analysts tend to honor his genius by using his categories. Bengt Holmberg, in a doctoral dissertation at the University of Lund, begins by pointing out how consistently and dogmatically the earliest communities have been classified as pure instances of charismatic authority.[36] Already at the earliest stages for which we possess evidence, however, the Christian fellowship was invested with elements of traditional and rational-legal (referred to above as "rational-bureaucratic," by Weber) authority. Paul brings to his converts a gospel which has already been formulated, to which all true prophets must conform. He shares with them a cult, including baptism, eucharist, scriptural prayer, the Lord's day, which they adopt – and perhaps adapt; but they do not create the tradition. They confess a faith whose main theological elements are in place: Christ as messianic Son of God, his final arrival at the end, the Spirit as the resident of human hearts. Paul's Christians are inducted into an already formed church, with relationships already fastened in place. Paul and everyone else defer to the Jerusalem church and its resident premier disciples. He has the clear rule of his own foundations. Within those communities there is a variety of functions which, while charismatic, are mostly not "pneumatic," or ecstatic, and are stylized and expected to interact for the community's benefit. There are already members who serve for pay. Though incipient in

---

[36] Bengt Holmberg, *Paul and Power: The Structure of Authority in the Primitive Church as Reflected in the Pauline Epistles* (Lund: Gleerup, 1978).

organization, the churches know a structure of authority with subordination and assigned responsibilities. The structure requires neither coercion nor self-interest in order to function, because all parties accept it as legitimate. Thus Paul's foundations were not instances of pure charismatic authority.

Weber had said that the desire to preserve the unique and transitory blessing of the charismatic founder leads disciples to make it a permanent possession of everyday life by routinizing it. The Sohm view was that only a purely charismatic kind of religion was authentic to Jesus and his followers. Charism and routine are contraries, and when charism devolved into another sort of authority it was denatured. Harnack's view was that the change from charism to office (Weber's rational level) was a deplorable but inevitable degradation. Holmberg disagrees with them both, and with the entire assumption of the consensus that the change was a substantial one. Weber had been mistaken – or misunderstood – to convey a notion of pure social types, all of them mutually exclusive: charismatic, traditional and rational authority. In reality they are usually intertwined.

Charisma need not be traditionalized or rationalized and thereby lose its original identity through routine. Holmberg argues that charism can be institutionalized, and that is not at all the same thing as being routinized. Routine action is action that has lost sight of its inspiring goal. Institutionalization, however, is a stabilized, consensual conversion of relationships into roles and then into custom, duty and office. It need not happen – indeed, it does not happen – by anyone's conscious effort. It is imposed by the sheer logic of group life and group development, and only in retrospect does it become obvious.

When the leader disappears the group is not kept in a state devoid of authority, but with a social construct, whose different parts have a derived, and now independent, authority of their own. The leader's words, his message and example, the rituals and institutions he created now enjoy more authority than before, as he is not there to complete, interrupt or change them. But all these authoritative parts of charismatic group life need to be unified and placed in relation to one another so as to be accessible to the group. This is done by means of a secondary institutionalization which transforms unconsolidated verbal tradition into a body of normative texts, ways of living and a typical ethical "atmosphere" into a formulated code of behaviour and a paraenetical teaching tradition, community rites into organized forms of worship. The most important change is that the former staff of assistants become new leaders of the group, responsible for teaching, decision-making and development.[37]

In Paul's communities the charismatic persons clearly were in the ascendant. Documents dating back to within five years or so from the foundation time show a broad variety of other community roles. The fact that their titles are generic, or that the roles are voluntary, or that they have not assumed the duties later assigned to second-century officers does not justify the conclusion that their communities were unstructured. Indeed, Paul's own letters show a complex social stratification with severe internal stress precisely because established roles were developing into offices. The traditional and rational elements that were always there were consolidating – with the intentional purpose that the charisma be preserved, not replaced.

Why have so many authors read this as the suffocation of an unorganized and spontaneous community? Because, as Holmberg explains it, they have fallen into the fallacy of idealism. They have assumed that historical development was being governed by theological exhortation.

Holmberg offers several examples of how idealism has worked. Paul's list of *charismata* in 1 Corinthians has repeatedly been taken as a description of the local church order. That has led commentators to reconstruct a spontaneous and unstructured congregation without officers. But Paul's itemization of gifts is neither a historical account of what was happening in Corinth, nor even his original plan which he had when he founded the community there. It is an appeal that he has drawn up to counteract what had grown into an unbalanced situation. The actual community in Corinth was overestimating the value of tongue-speaking, and Paul's letter is a corrective. He dampens the excitement to stress that all gifts which upbuild the community are God's gifts, and each is unique. Of course his argument would carry great weight in Corinth. But it is an argument, not a description. Theology and reality interact in the church with a dialectically mutual influence. Paul's text is not even a plan for a model church; it is a strategic move to alter the course of the real church that had already been under weigh in Corinth with a momentum of its own. A responsible reconstruction must incorporate these theological exhortations for what they are: part of the evidence, to be compared with other evidence of what was actually happening.

---

[37] Ibid. 179–180.

Another illustration of idealism refers to Paul's rhetoric about his ranking with other apostles. His theological assertion is that he is the peer of any apostle, or of the "super-apostles," or of the "pillars" in Jerusalem. But the reality was somewhat different. Paul did not actually function according to this theology. For though he might and did dissent and break away from Barnabas, his mentor and senior apostle from Antioch, it is inconceivable that he could or would have behaved similarly towards Jerusalem and the premier apostles there.[38] The reality includes some unarticulated but effective consensual beliefs about the deference due to them, and that evidence must not be subordinated to what Paul says he thinks Jerusalem's role should be. It would be idealistic to construe Paul's theology of apostolate as descriptive. It is not even normative. It is polemic, and corrective.

Holmberg offers a devastating critique of Bultmann, Käsemann, von Campenhausen, Schweizer and other recent sustainers of the consensus for giving emphasis to Paul's theology of charism and interpreting all the factual data in light of it. Paul offers us a reaction to what was happening. The consensus has taken his reaction as the primary datum. It is, rather, secondary to the primary historical situation. They have taken his reactive statements as the structuring principle of the Christian social world, and not as his critique of the existing social structure.

DAVID VERNER

David Verner, in his dissertation at Emory University, applies social analysis in a comparable fashion to the "household duties" prescribed in the pastoral epistles.[39] Those *Haustafeln* had provoked long consideration among scholars of what their sources might have been and what they reveal about social life among the church. Opinions varied: they were borrowed from the Roman-Stoic tradition, and were therefore an alien, non-Christian incubus; they were a reaction against the early egalitarianism of the church, which had seemed socially subversive; they were a scissors-and-paste collage of

[38] "In terms of charismatic authority the Jerusalem church, and the Jerusalem apostles and leaders, are perceived by all actors to be in closer contact than the Antiochene church or Paul with the *fons et origo* of all value in the Church – Jesus himself. Charismatic authority is not defined in a body of tradition, doctrine or law, but is nonetheless effective in history – especially in the history of the Primitive Church." Ibid. 154.

[39] David C. Verner, *The Household of God: The Social World of the Pastoral Epistles* (Chico, CA: Scholars Press, 1983).

fragments from the tradition; or their conservative social order formed the leading message of the pastorals.

The literary genre of the "household code" did endorse the traditional patriarchal family and the stratified society presided over by the affluent in hellenistic society, with roles and duties for fathers, mothers, children, servants and slaves. It found its echo in the station codes by which the pastorals assigned rank and duties to *episkopoi*, *diakonoi*, widows, elders and youth. At first reading the codes appear to reinforce an authoritarian social structure. But closer attention will find, Verner believes, some hints to the contrary. The injunction that *episkopoi*, *diakonoi* and enrolled widows should have been married only once suggests an innovative equality between the sexes which the church would have shared with a contemporary social movement. The fact that Christian slaves were warned not to be uppity reflects some new tension in the traditional roles when both masters and slaves were baptized.

Verner will not agree that the *episkopoi*, *presbyteroi* and *diakonoi*, who are all involved in ruling, teaching and preaching, form an explicit hierarchy. Still, the church is directed by an aristocracy of house-holders who are held in honor. But this is not what the pastorals propose; it is what they assume. Holmberg's doctrine comes to mind here, though with a reverse application. The "household codes" of the church can be mined carefully for material which reflects, not a Christian ideal, but the historical reality which the author wishes to modify. And whoever wishes to reconstruct the scenario of the contextual church must be able to discern what is description and what is prescription.

The social order reflected and defended in the pastoral epistles, says Verner, is one with widely diversified membership in terms of social class: not, as earlier scholars had believed, drawn mostly from the lower classes. Its leadership was recruited among persons to the manor born. What social movement one can perceive comes from a radical direction, in the form of emancipatory tendencies among women and slaves.[40]

---

[40] "The author of the Pastorals is alarmed by the vitality of this movement within his church. He perceives it correctly as a threat to the established order, and fears, no doubt again correctly, that such radicalism will damage the public reputation of the church and thus endanger it. The purpose for which the author employs the image of the Household of God in this context is now clear. He intends to bolster a hierarchical social structure in the church that is being threatened by disruptive forces. The social structure which he is defending has in large part given rise to the disruptive forces, yet they are being fed by certain ideas already

Verner's significance for our purposes is that he reinforces Holmberg's method: to distinguish descriptive from prescriptive evidence, and to reconstruct history from the interplay between them.

The author presents the image of the household not only for descriptive, but also, and more importantly, for prescriptive purposes. In the traditional patriarchal household the householder is expected to exercise his authority in competent fashion, keeping those in subordinate stations properly subject to him and representing his household in the larger community. The other members of the household, typically, women, children and servants, are expected to acknowledge their subordinate positions and to behave accordingly. In the church, the author is suggesting, authority is properly concentrated in the hands of an official leadership that is expected to govern effectively and to represent the church to the world. As in the household, women, slaves, children and young men properly belong to subordinate stations. They should know the limits of these stations and keep within these limits.[41]

WAYNE MEEKS

Wayne Meeks of Yale University more recently contributed his own inquiry into the social structure of early Christian communities.[42] Rather than choosing one among all possible models for the *ekklêsia* = church, he finds that no single one "quite fits": the Greco-Roman city, the synagogue,[43] the philosophical or rhetorical school, the voluntary association or college.

The Christian community understood itself as having strong inward loyalties and an aloofness towards outsiders. It relished a vocabulary of belonging and of family; its initiation rites dramatized a new kinship; despite the conventional and peculiar stratification within the church, there was a rhetoric of unstructured fellowship; and distinctive beliefs about a privileged revelation and a new birth,

present in Christian tradition. He responds by promoting an image of the church that legitimates the established hierarchical structure. In this way he hopes to suppress the forces that threaten it and the radical social values which they represent." Ibid. 186.

[41] Ibid. 182.

[42] Wayne Meeks, *The First Urban Christians* (New Haven: Yale University Press, 1983).

[43] He finds the synagogue the most natural and traditional model. It incorporated features of both household and association, was a closed and cultic community, was a local unit within a worldwide fellowship, followed a worship format similar to that of the churches, and had a belief system out of which the Christian doctrine telescoped understandably. What causes him to hesitate in recognizing the synagogue as the prototype for the church is the fact that Paul never mentions organizing synagogues, that their terminology is different, that Christian women are more active than their Jewish counterparts, and that Christian membership is not ethnic. Ibid. 80–81.

expressed by an in-house *argot*, intensified the community's sense of cohesiveness. Negative judgments about the world, associated with the devil, plus a sense of persecution, further held them as a people with a strong sense of boundaries. They clearly saw themselves as a society apart, a society with its own model.

In reassembling that model, Meeks too has reference to both theological assertions and factual evidence.

A sect that claims to be the unique possessor of what it construes to be a universally desirable value – a monopoly on salvation – does not necessarily welcome free interchange with outsiders; more often the contrary. The cosmic imagery of the Pauline school's baptismal language was used in the admonitions of Colossians and Ephesians specifically to strengthen the internal cohesion of the Christian groups. Yet one of the most obvious facts about the movement associated with Paul and his fellows was the vigor of its missionary drive, which saw in the outsider a potential insider and did not want to cut off communication with him or her. In this respect the ethos of Pauline Christianity is significantly more open than that, say, of the introverted Johannine groups.[44]

Leadership roles in this cohesive society are unofficial in Paul. Like many scholars, Meeks dismisses Acts as an unreliable historical guide, for it projects backwards into the pauline churches a structure that consolidated only later. Meeks accepts the consensus view that roles did not harden into offices until the turn of the century. He differs, however, by disallowing Harnack's theory that the triad of officers replaced the triad of charismatics. He describes a different tripartite pattern of authorities: visible manifestations of Spirit-possession (charismatics), congregational position (officers) and association with apostles or other non-local persons of authority (envoys or deputies). These three groups would claim different sources of authorization: the Spirit, the Spirit through the community and the succession, and higher communities or offices.

Meeks' work will raise most searching questions, less perhaps by his actual historical results (which are, within the consensus, quite conventional) than by his method of social analysis. Just as an earlier biblical criticism had warned scholars away from trying to accommodate the pauline data within Luke's account in Acts, now social critique calls them to distinguish within individual books between what the author sets forth as his ideal and what realities already in place he may be trying to alter.

[44] Ibid. 107.

The social analysts have criticized the purpose, the method and the outcome of the dominant consensus. Motivating the research that had produced the consensus was an abiding conviction that non-episcopal, less liturgical, and counter-clerical churches should rightly find their legitimating ancestry in the church of the apostles. The method which served that purpose was to take prescriptive New Testament texts, especially those of Paul, as descriptive. And the outcome was a portrayal of an ideal community which was demeaned and defiled by the institutions which later overcame it. The challenge to the consensus accepted the account of a simple community format that was later consolidated by offices, law and tradition. But the social analysts saw this as a necessary development which preserved the Jesus-charism, and had within it the ability to absorb secular institutions and turn them to its own distinctive purposes. The church retained the energies of the charismatic past for its own recurrent renewal.

One cannot refrain from noticing that so fresh-minded an academic movement which saw continuities extending forward from the primitive church into its future, could discern few substantial continuities backward into its most obvious antecedent, in terms of community organization: not the Jewish scriptures, but the synagogue.

CATHOLIC ADOPTIONS OF THE CONSENSUS

In quite recent times the ordinary traffic of discussion among partisans of the consensus has lessened, possibly to allow consideration of the new challenges posed by the scholars of social analysis. An entirely new voice has been raised in the meantime. It comes from Catholics whose appeals for renewal in their own church have claimed support in the historical account of early ministries that has been formulated within the consensus.

In many cases theologians have simply incorporated by reference the findings of the consensus, not to use it as an argument for programmatic changes, but to join in the increasingly widespread conviction that the apostolic church was much simpler than what Catholics later made of it. In several instances, however, leading scholars have been more explicit in applying the findings of the consensus. Hans Küng, professor at Tübingen University, used it as historical justification for his call for declericalization. Among

Catholics who favor the ordination of married people and of women, Eduard Schillebeeckx was one of the first to turn to the consensus as a theological instrument to disallow both the standing and the arguments of the hierarchy who have thus far stood by gender and celibacy restrictions. Elisabeth Schüssler Fiorenza, professor at the Harvard Divinity School, believes that beneath the distorted account we have of the first-generation church lies evidence of a brief period of authentic discipleship wherein women enjoyed a prominence and equality that the emergent clergy soon obliterated.[45]

HANS KÜNG

Though Hans Küng had worked primarily as a fundamental and systematic theologian, particularly on topics related to the church, his *The Church*, issued shortly after the Second Vatican Council, stood in part on historical study for which he was indebted to the scholarship of the consensus. He diverges from it in several particulars. He disavows those who see in the New Testament an opposition between two models of church. They favor what they know of Paul, and deplore what later befell his simple, Spirit-governed community tradition. "In this way the history of the Church is disrupted from the first; from the first there were pure and impure currents in it, and its history is the story of a contradiction, of several Churches in opposition rather than of several Churches in unity. In consequence those who take this view are unable to see the post-apostolic history of the Church in a positive light, and are obliged instead to see an increasing falling away from the Gospel, a descent into institution-alism, sacramentalism and clericalism – until perhaps the age of the Reformers, or perhaps until the nineteenth century, or even right down to the present, when at last we are beginning once again to understand what *really* matters."[46]

The disclaimer is all the more needed because of the author's apparent identification with precisely that view. He is appealing eloquently for a notion of ministry by every believer suggested by the New Testament Word, *diakonia* = service.

---

[45] There are Catholics who accept the larger part of the consensus view on its merits, quite apart from any stand on the ordination of women. See, for example, Karl Kertelge, *Gemeinde und Amt im Neuen Testament* (Munich: Kösel, 1972).

[46] Hans Küng, *The Church*, trans. Ray and Rosaleen Ockenden, (New York: Sheed & Ward, 1967), 416. This translates *Die Kirche* (Freiburg: Herder, 1967).

It is not law or power, knowledge [or] dignity but *service* which is the basis of discipleship. The model for the disciples in their following of Christ is therefore not the secular ruler and not the leader scribe, nor even the priest who stands above his people ... the only valid model is that of the man who serves at table.[47]

As we can see in the earliest church, there was no ministry without charism, and every charism was directed towards service. There was a great variety of charisms, perhaps even more diverse than those Paul mentions. There were no clear boundaries between those which empowered one person to be helpful to individuals and other charisms that enabled believers with a more public value; or between that of elder, say, and that of prophet. Those of apostle, prophet and teacher, however, were foremost among them all. Küng believes that in some churches prophets presided, and that only when they were unavailable did that function pass to bishops and deacons (his interpretation of the *Didache* coinciding with that of the consensus). The ministries of *episkopos* and *diakonos* he finds typical of hellenistic churches, while *presbyteroi* are a feature of the quite differently arranged Jewish churches. In fact, since Paul never addresses his often explicit instructions to single officials by title or by name, the assumption must be that officers in authority did not exist.

[Faced] ... with divisions in the community with regard to the settling of disputes within the community, and with regard to the collection for Jerusalem, Paul would have had to address himself to the responsible leaders of the community, if such had existed. But there is obviously no one to whom Paul could say: "Command and teach these things," not even in connection with the Lord's Supper. The community at Corinth to which Paul wrote was a fellowship of charismatic Christians, in which *each* had a responsibility, a specific responsibility according to his charism, and in which *no one* (apart from the apostle) carried an exclusive responsibility for the rest.[48]

Eventually the pauline church model merged with the Palestinian, and the single overseer emerged with authority over the elders and over the entire community. Since the churches with overseers and those with elders had both coexisted, neither was uniquely original; neither had to be normative for the future. When Acts says that there were elders in Paul's communities, and that they were created by the apostles, it is not to be believed. Paul knows nothing of ordination or appointment to office. But how could such an innovation as a humanly appointed hierarchy (which Küng associates with Ignatius

---

[47] Ibid. 392.   [48] Ibid. 403.

in the second century) become an essential model for all time to come? Or was it only a transient arrangement, not necessarily permanent?

Küng cannot find evidence for ordination of ministers at the beginning, especially in the pauline tradition. Then "how is it possible to justify any *special commission by men*, given that each man has received his own charism, his vocation, directly from God[?] Is the inner impulse, the inner motivation for a concrete ministry, in which God's call will be expressed in a man's existence, not sufficient? What is the point of having a human command, a human call, appointment and authorization in addition?"[49]

The mere fact that ordination did become a Christian usage is no answer, nor was the necessity to avoid abuses by a protective establishment, since it is arguable that the institutionalization of charism wrought more harm than good. Appointing ministers brought impoverishment to the church. The only justification is the new need which arose when the Christians finally realized that the Lord would not return imminently, that the church must go on a journey of unknown length, and that it would not be easy to retain the gospel in its original authenticity without some firmer sort of establishment.

But the memory of how variable the offices were at the start might encourage us to envision new forms they might eventually take.

While Ignatius of Antioch's three-tier system may have had its roots in the origins of the Church, this system of offices is not simply *the* original way in which ministries were ordered and shared out. As we have seen, it is the result of a very complex historical development. It is impossible to draw clear theological and dogmatic lines of division between the three ministries, especially between the functions of the *episkopoi* and the presbyters. Such lines were only drawn as the ministries actually developed and their pastoral usefulness was determined. Even if we like to take this threefold division into bishops, presbyters (priests) and deacons as a reasonable development and as a sensible and practical order, these forms which have taken on canonical force, but which are generally the realization of only one possibility among many, should not be taken for dogmatic necessities.[50]

Küng assigns to canonists the task of redesigning the ministries, but one sweeping historical comment is suggestive of what he would have them do. "There is of course today a canon law and disciplinary distinction between the functions of the bishop and those of the presbyter. A theological or dogmatic distinction is impossible to draw not only because *episkopoi* and presbyters were originally differentiated either differently from today or not at all, but because there are no specific episcopal functions which have not, in the course of Church history, been legitimately assumed by priests."[51] The lesson of history for Küng is not that there were no offices, but that they were originally in flux to such an extent that the first years of Christian experience do not impose on us any enduring model of what they must be or do.

EDUARD SCHILLEBEECKX

Eduard Schillebeeckx, O.P., is a Fleming who spent his academic career at the University of Nijmegen in Holland, where he has been professor of theology and of the history of theology. During the bracing season of Vatican II, the Dutch church had caught the imagination of fellow Catholics across the world. They enjoyed bright and liberal bishops, a venturesome presbyterate, an articulate and actively involved laity, an intrepid church press, impressive liturgical experimentation in packed churches, a well-institutionalized and scholarly establishment of higher education, and a benevolent yet unobstructing relationship with the state. Twenty years later the churches were nearly as empty as in the neighboring European churches of the *ancien régime*, and the ranks of the priesthood were depleted to the point where scores of parishes could not be provided with ordained pastors. In their stead, a corps of lay men and women were serving as "pastoral assistants," providing the same range of ministries as ordained priests save that, being unordained, they could not preside at the eucharist or at the rite of confession. Catholics in The Netherlands abruptly discovered themselves in the same (though unexpected) situation as their coreligionists in the Third World: deprived of regular access to these two regular sacraments, not for lack of qualified and willing ministry candidates, but for lack of a pope and bishops willing to accept their qualifications. It was to address this issue that Eduard Schillebeeckx turned to the ancient church for policy guidance.[52]

---

[51] Ibid. 430.
[52] His first major statement on office in the early church was *Ministry: Leadership in the Community of Jesus Christ*, trans. John Bowden (New York: Crossroad, 1981). This translates *Kerkelijk ambt: Voorgangers in de gemeente van Jezus Christus* (Bloemendaal: Nelissen, 1980). This produced an avalanche of criticism on historical and theological grounds, to which

His historical account of early church order follows the dominant consensus faithfully, yet he draws it deftly into several conclusions which are his own theological handiwork. The ministry of "apostle-ship" is the only element of church order established by Jesus himself. The apostles (not the Twelve) and some other activists called prophets founded the earliest churches, but they seem to have consigned to them no fixed pattern of leadership: "[W]ithin the communities, which understood themselves as brotherhoods, without rank or status, spontaneous leaders sometimes came up against the opposition of the brethren ... Although it is recognized as a particular charisma, the gift of leading the community still has no significance as a 'ministry' of the church; it is one of the many services which all the members of the community owe to each other, and each person cannot do everything. Thus originally the leaders of the community do not seem to have had any special name for their ministry."[53] These leaders were known as prophets and teachers in some churches, and as *episkopoi* and *diakonoi* in others. But those were casual designations, not formal titles.

It was only when the Lord's own ministers, the apostles, dis-appeared in 80–100 AD, that leadership came to be reflected upon theologically. At this point the eldest churches took to calling themselves apostolic, by which they meant that they stood in authentic descent from the faith of their founders. There had been apostolic persons: now there were to be apostolic communities. Ephesians shows that the earlier apostles and prophets were succeeded by evangelists, pastors and teachers, with duties of proclamation, leadership and reinforcement of the community. "How one became a leader of the community was not as yet a problem: it was a purely incidental matter."[54]

We learn from Acts that in Jerusalem a local variant was being developed, which was found as well in Asia Minor and Crete: a

Schillebeeckx replied provisionally in "The Changing Meaning of Ministry: The Social Context of Historical Shifts in the Church," *Cross Currents*, 33, 4 (Winter 1983–1984), 432–454; "The Changing Concept of Ministry," ibid. 34, 1 (Spring 1984), 65–82. These translate "De sociale context van de verschuivingen in het kerkelijk ambt", *Tijdschrift voor Theologie*, 22 (1982), 24–59. The Vatican raised pointed objection to his opinion that local congregations could, in the absence of presbyters, ordain their own ministers to preside at the eucharist. See "Judgment on Schillebeeckx," *The Tablet* [London], 19 January 1985, 62–64. He brought out his first book in an considerably new and circumspect edition: *The Church with a Human Face: A New and Expanded Theology of Ministry*, trans. John Bowden (New York: Crossroad, 1985). This translates *Pleidooi voor Mensen in de Kerk: Christelijke Identiteit en Ambten in de Kerk* (Baarn: Nelissen, 1985).   [53] *Ministry*, 9.   [54] Ibid. 14.

college of *presbyteroi* = elders (also called *episkopoi*) who were in charge of the local church. It was an arrangement unknown in Antioch, where we hear only of prophets and teachers. Presbyters are also unmentioned in Paul's authentic letters, plausibly because most of those letters are directed to churches outside Asia Minor.[55] This institution, dating back to the end of the first century, was not then universally found in Christian communities. In fact, different regions at different times display a variety of official structures, Schillebeeckx asserts.

In the pastoral epistles one sees an emergent concern for a stable church order that would be able to survive the threats of disunity. The central resource for that stability was not to be a structured ministry, but the principle of continuity: of a tradition received from the apostles.

The ministry as a service is subordinate to this continuity or succession which is apostolic in content; there must always be ministry in the church for the sake of continuity ... in the Pastoral Epistles the central feature is not the principle of the ministry, much less the structures of the ministry (which remain vague), but *the principle of the apostolic tradition*. This is expressed even in the rite of the laying on of hands, which these letters want to see introduced. For here, too, there is primarily no question of the transference of ministerial authority, but of the charisma of the Holy Spirit, which will help the minister to hand down and preserve in a living way the pledge entrusted to him to make him able to proclaim the apostolic tradition intact.[56]

I Peter testifies to the replacement of the early, charismatic, undifferentiated church order by the institution of presbyteral leadership. The two types of order seem to have coexisted in Corinth – with resulting conflict that Clement tried to resolve by giving priority to the latter type.

In the church as reflected in Matthew, the charismatic order remains in power, and is defended by strong sayings against anyone ruling among the disciples. The *Didache* shows no elders, and even its *episkopoi* and *diakonoi* seem subordinated to the prophets and teachers who preside at the eucharist. The record suggests, however, that churches without elders tended to disappear during the second century, or to have succumbed to Gnosticism. The churches of the johannine literature did have elders, but without any special

---

[55] Schillebeeckx seems uncertain of geography, mentioning the letter to the Galatians as being directed to Asia Minor. Ibid. 15; *Church*, 84.   [56] *Ministry*, 17–18.

authority. All authority belonged to the Spirit, and had been bestowed on all believers, without any discrimination in favor of elders. Since these churches also vanished after the first century, the institution of elders, somewhat by default, became standard practice.

Whatever the identity or nomenclature of its leaders – prophets and teachers, or elders, or *presbyteroi-episkopoi* – the churches expected them to preside at the eucharist. But this was not a status or a rank. In the early and formative centuries they were not a corps set apart, as clergy vs. laity, or as "orders" (though the stratification of the empire, with its senatorial and equestrian and other orders, would later be a model for the Christian hierarchy). Theirs was a function: an assignment by the community to organize for their Christian peers (all of them were their equals) the eucharist to which the community had an apostolic right.

Schillebeeckx's historical construct continues, though rapidly, through all the succeeding centuries. But it is the treatment of the New Testament church and its immediate progeny that sinks the pilings for the theological edifice he wishes to erect.

Now it has emerged from the theology of the ministry in the first millennium that the sacramental substance or nucleus of *ordinatio*, appointment to an office, lies in the fact that as a minister a believer is recognized and accepted by the church (the local community and its leaders) and is called to the service of the ministry in and for a particular community, along with the gift of the Spirit which is bestowed in such an instance.

Anyone who in [a time of need] was required by the community to preside over the community (and thus at the eucharist) *ipso facto* became a minister by the acceptance of the local church: he was instituted, i.e. became the authorized leader of the community ...

[I]n emergencies all ministers can take the place of the team leader and perform his ministry without supplementary "ordinations" being needed.[57]

What of the fact that the legitimacy of such leadership is blocked by higher authorities in the church today? Schillebeeckx undercuts this by finding that all authority at a level higher than the local church is a questionable innovation.[58]

He attempts to be more explicit about his interpretive method than most contributors to the consensus had been. He does not

---

[57] Ibid. 82, 51–52, 69. This conclusion was the point at which the Vatican most sharply took offense, and Schillebeeckx's later edition, *Church*, is much more circumspect.

[58] Ibid. 73–74; *Church*, 42–45. Schillebeeckx is sometimes ambiguous about what he takes to be the right meaning of "local church": the single congregation at worship, or the cluster of congregations in and around a city. See criticism by Walter Kasper, "Ministry in the Church: Taking Issue with Edward Schillebeeckx," *Communio*, 10 (1983), 185–195.

acknowledge any era as classical, as presenting a model church against which other church orders are to be compared. Instead, we must learn what is normative for the church by assessing the many periods of its development.[59] Though he does not advert to it, Schillebeeckx's principle can lead to two entirely divergent applications. If no single period provides the archetype for all others, one would review the many variations an institution had undergone, and attempt to discern in the constancy, the resiliency, the trajectory of the institution what showed itself to be central, and what peripheral. This would require astute historical analysis. A second method of applying the very same principle would regard as non-essential any feature or element that was missing in any period. This application requires very little historical astuteness. The former application obliges one to consult every period in order to ascertain a sort of flowing consensus. The latter method gives a veto power to every single era.

Schillebeeckx disavows the second application. Yet his clear preference for the earliest church, which he joins the consensus in portraying as unstructured and without officers, functions as his warrant for prospective reforms in our own time.[60]

ELISABETH SCHÜSSLER FIORENZA

Elisabeth Schüssler Fiorenza, professor of New Testament at Harvard Divinity School, propounds a somewhat different method of interpretation which she entitles a "Feminist Critical Hermeneutics of Liberation."[61] The Bible, she states, does not offer us an acceptable doctrine or model of church, for it is compromised by pervasively androcentric and patriarchal assumptions. Even the New Testament cannot provide us with an archetype of authentic Christian community, for it is the carrier of oppression and exploitation which have dominated the Christian church as early as the first century. Yet it does harbor some elements which, if correctively treated, can serve as guides.

Previous feminist scholars had used different procedures to separate out what was acceptable in scripture from what needed to be

---

[59] See *Church*, 5; "Changing Concept," 82; "Changing Meaning," 435.
[60] See, for instance, *Ministry*, 67.
[61] Elisabeth Schüssler Fiorenza, *In Memory of Her: A Feminist Theological Reconstruction of Christian Origins* (New York: Crossroad, 1985).

discarded. Whatever discriminated against women was man's word; whatever promoted equality was God's Word. The "usable past" was the ore; the "unusable past," the slag. The vision of the classical prophets was the acknowledged standard, and all other biblical texts were authoritative insofar as they agreed with it. Fiorenza disagrees with these and other interpretive devices which attempt to sort through biblical data by extracting some standard or absolute principles or essential truths.

> The historical-theological insight that the New Testament is not only a source of revelatory truth but also a resource for patriarchal subordination and domination demands a new paradigm for biblical hermeneutics and theology. This paradigm must not only shed its objectivist pretense of disinterestedness but also its doctrinal neo-orthodox essence-accidents model of interpretation. All early Christian texts are formulated in an androcentric language and conditioned by their patriarchal milieux and histories. Biblical revelation and truth are given only in those texts and interpretative models that transcend critically their patriarchal frameworks and allow for a vision of Christian women as historical and theological subjects and actors.[62]

It is the practical interests of women in their current struggle for power, freedom and independence which must provide the norm for any critical reinterpretation of the biblical documents. "I would therefore suggest that the revelatory canon for theological evaluation of biblical androcentric traditions and their subsequent interpretations cannot be derived from the Bible itself but can only be formulated in and through women's struggle for liberation from all patriarchal oppression."[63]

Schüssler Fiorenza displays greater candor than Schillebeeckx in displaying her principles of historical analysis. However, she shares with him and the other partisans of the consensus the operative conviction that scripture and other sources of the Christian past will yield acceptable guidance for the church only if interpreted in light of the socio-political doctrines and ideological agenda of the present. Thus feminist scholars do not so much derive from the ancient record, as apply to it, their judgments of what real oppression and true liberation are.

Even with this method, she discerns in the past one ideal model of church: Jesus and his earliest egalitarian community. Jewish documents from Jesus' time disclose a society in which women were imprisoned in economic and social roles that a patriarchal religious

[62] Ibid. 30.   [63] Ibid. 32.

tradition had actively endorsed. Following on the heels of some earlier movements for reform, Jesus (according to our most primitive accounts) went out of his way to be inclusive of society's victims in his retinue: the destitute poor, the sick and the crippled, tax collectors, prostitutes: the impure, the estranged and the resourceless formed the majority, says Schüssler Fiorenza, of his following. Theirs was a fellowship without rank or precedence or privilege. "The all-inclusive goodness of Israel's God calls forth human equality and solidarity."[64] Women were treated as equals. Indeed, they were the ones who sustained and organized the disciples when the men defaulted. And the women provided the impetus for innovation: Schüssler Fiorenza construes the stories of the Syro-Phoenician (or Canaanite) woman and of the Samaritan woman as evidence that women were the first non-Jews to enter the Jesus movement.[65]

In the texts that derive most directly from Jesus, sayings on family and social roles are given a counter-cultural stress: there must be no father-authority, and no gradations of status among the disciples.

It was not long before the social pressures from Jewish and Roman culture closed in on this radical and subversive movement. The salience and accomplishments of women and of freed slaves in the foundational communities was gradually suppressed: not only in the church, but even in the church's own documentary remembrance of its honeymoon years. According to Schüssler Fiorenza's reconstruction, the house-church was the normal clustering at first, and the mistress of the household was responsible for the community and for its gatherings. The community was patterned, however, not after the patriarchal household, but after the cultic *collegia* = associations wherein women and slaves enjoyed equal standing with all men. Being a true community of equals, this primitive church would not tolerate stable roles or offices. Instead, tasks were alternated, in acknowledgement that every member shared equal endowment. Women served as *episkopoi, presbyteroi* and *diakonoi*, as well as in all charismatic roles: apostle, prophet, teacher. Widows enjoyed equal standing with *episkopoi*, and some women's groups formed churches unto themselves. But when women began to be subjected once again to male domination, the men who wrote and edited the documentation of the time began to expunge from the record all remembrance of the earlier egalitarian usages. Thus the New

[64] Ibid. 132.   [65] Ibid. 138.

Testament needs to be interpreted, not by reading the roles it describes, but by restoring them to what a feminist sense of justice knows they must have been.

It had been conventional to make Paul the champion of a free and unstructured Christianity, and to assign the spoilsport role to authoritarian Jewish traditionalists. The pauline treatment of women makes him less a hero in this interpretive scheme. Schüssler Fiorenza takes the independent view that the pauline tradition itself bears the marks of the gradual retreat from the early egalitarianism of Jesus. Paul's early outbursts that all distinctions of race, bondage or gender had been annulled – a teaching so forthrightly in conflict with prevailing social norms – gave way to more cautious injunctions. Women ought to desist, he said, from prominent roles in worship, and slaves from pressing for emancipation, lest the Christian church be burdened by a reputation for indecency or revolt. Paul begins to reintroduce family and household metaphors. His calls for emancipation start to become generic, while at the same time he begins not only to tolerate but even to encourage various specific forms of subordination. He insists that the new Spirit will induce persons held within unequal relationships to treat one another graciously (Schüssler Fiorenza calls this "love-patriarchalism"), but it sounds less and less compelling. Gradually, as the church flinched at the radical social change it had introduced, patriarchalism was re-established, for the alleged needs of the church if it was to survive in society. Equality was now to be an internalized virtue, not a social structure.

House-churches were absorbed into city organizations, known as "the household of God." Officers took over the leadership from the affluent (house-hosts) and the influential (charismatics). Apostles and prophets were merged into bishops. Women were marginalized. Montanism, with its spontaneity, and Gnosticism, with its prominence for women, were late eruptions of the old inspiration. Some of the gospels, in opposition to the postpauline literature, emphasized Jesus' call to sacrificial leadership and to renunciation of privilege in community. But the communities where these gospels were read out had been restructured under the oppressive control of officers to whom all classes, sexes and races had by then been subordinated.

Schüssler Fiorenza's thesis, in its method and its outcome, is perhaps the most authentic reappearance of Rudolph Sohm's theory which had appeared nearly a century earlier. Hers differs, of course, in its selection of androcentric and patriarchal oppression, instead of clerical domination, as the principal defection from Jesus' gospel. But this only shows how hers is a variant of the consensus, not a departure from it. That consensus continues, as we have now traced it across six centuries, with variations that are never radical, to construe the earliest church as unorganized in structure, spontaneous in ministries, free of authority figures or roles or offices, and thereby the normative ideal for a restored and authenticated Christian church order today. Now it is time for us to appraise its validity.

CHAPTER 5

A search for a new hypothesis

At this point it is timely to review and assess the consensus which, despite the bewildering number of variants with which it has been formulated, constitutes an enduring and influential project that still secures the acceptance of most scholars today.

THE PRESUPPOSITIONS OF THE CONSENSUS

The consensus is grounded first of all upon a commitment to rigorous respect for a critical, scientific use of the New Testament and the earliest Christian documents. First textual criticism allowed scholars to reconstruct from the many manuscripts (all copied centuries after the originals) what the primitive published text was most likely to have been, relieved of errors and amendments later introduced. Next came historical criticism, with which one could determine which books must have been written after the careers of the persons presented as authors, and what passages were added after the first edition. Study of literary forms and of editorial techniques later allowed scholars to discern the stylistic conventions and the theological purposes of various genres of ancient Christian literature, to trace their changing doctrinal contexts, and thus to elicit the preoccupations and agendas, and thereby the more subtle and implied meanings, of their successive editors.

Gradually scholars reconstructed the likely course of development followed by documents which, through sometimes lengthy oral transmission and then continuing revision at the hands of diverse editors, underwent alterations in both shape, message and emphasis en route from original utterance to canonical publication.

Beginning with the collection of books received within the church, biblical scholars first categorized the divergent narrative accounts and the differing theological purposes – sometimes complementary, sometimes in conflict – which gave a second dimension to the literature. Then by tracking those divergences across time and place, they rendered still further dimensions explicit, to the point where the corpus of earliest Christian literature could be projected, as maps are in a complex atlas, and yield up not a single, flat message, but a highly contoured and scaled multidimensional account of how the producing community had fared historically and evolved theologically over the course of its first century of existence. Since those who wrote and edited that literary corpus had neither the perspective nor the conviction nor the intention to tell a story with all those developmental factors showing, it took the meticulous application of several critical methods to get beneath the surface of the text and reconstruct reliably the fascinating course of its emergence. For those who regarded Jesus himself, and the first generation(s) of the Christian venture as somehow normative for all their later disciples, this offered an access to that privileged time which, though reconstructed from the canonical scriptures and their earliest extant sequels, was believed to be substantially more correct and helpful than the sacred text flatly and naïvely read without this contoured perspective.

And when they did read the documentary record in this fashion, what did the artisans of the consensus find? They found that the closer one drew to Jesus himself, the less evidence there was of structure or offices among his following. The early gospel materials are decidedly egalitarian. Among the disciples there is to be no pride of rank, as there typically is among heathen rulers. They are to teach all peoples what they have learned, but no one is to claim or accept the title or deference that the scribes bore as teachers. No "first seats" are available to preferred disciples: only a closer share in the Master's service and suffering. As for Jesus, the talk is the talk of a king but the voice is the voice of a prophet: no establishment, no sinecures, no favorites, no magic. And no talk of any future organization. The word church = *ekklêsia* does not even appear in the gospels save in a single passage which, like the allusions to sacraments in John, embodies the preoccupations of much later editors, not those of Jesus himself.

Among the literature attributed to Paul, when those which are certainly from his pen (Romans, 1&2 Corinthians, Galatians, Philippians, 1 Thessalonians, Philemon) are separated from those which are either surely or probably the work of others

(2 Thessalonians, Colossians, Ephesians, 1&2 Timothy, Titus, Hebrews), a noteworthy difference appears. Paul himself depicts a community wherein the leading figures are divinely gifted apostles, prophets, teachers, healers, etc. Those whose efforts distinguish them in the service of the church are designated by functional, generic terms: coworker, servant, overseer. By contrast, Acts and the later New Testament books begin to use titles and to trace them to appointment or election within the community. The latest books – the pastoral epistles – are even more markedly institutional, and promote a church wherein the charisms of the Spirit seem to have been domesticated into a humanly devised institution.

The evidence from the closing years of the first century implies some open stress between the free and charismatic categories of the early New Testament documents and the regimented and official scenario that must have arisen later. The *Didache* depicts a church wherein *episkopoi* and *diakonoi* exist, but seem somehow secondary in rank and role to the charismatics who are venerated as carriers of Jesus' prophetic inspiration. But the *Letter of Clement* (1 *Clement*), speaking with asserted authority from and for Rome, claims ultimate rights for elected and ordained elders who, once instituted, hold stable office and powers to which other community members are bound to defer. Shortly thereafter Ignatius of Antioch polemically (and successfully) lays down as the official structural authority of each local church a hierarchy of officers: one presiding bishop = *episkopos*; next, a college of elders = *presbyteroi*; and lastly a corps of deacons = *diakonoi*.

The documentary evidence, critically read, implies a substantial change in the leadership, authority sources and (as the consensus firmly believes) the inward character of the community, within the eighty years or so during which the divinely inspired, unregimented charismatics were being replaced by the uniform echelons of institutional officers.[1]

Thus the course of events has been reconstructed, with the aid of critical methods that have been perfected during recent years. At this

---

[1] It seems not to have been noticed that other shifts of role and influence may have been as significant as the rise of the *episkopos* to governing presidency. The *presbyteroi* were also transformed: from a corporate status to an individual one, from citywide counselors to presiders of satellite congregations. Another unnoticed issue: was it because the *episkopoi* and *diakonoi* became professionalized before the *presbyteroi* that they ascended to a more strategic influence first?

point the consensus then has stern recourse to a further, particular rule of scholarly method: where the record is silent, the historian is not free to fill the lacuna. Especially after a showing of such shift and change over a brief period of time, one must not presume any constancy of tradition that would allow one to project the settled usages of later times back into the primitive record. Thus, for instance, if Paul never mentions *presbyteroi* we must infer that there were none in his churches. The same rule applies as well to place as to time. The fact that some usage is evidenced in one locality does not authorize us to infer that it exists in other churches. If James is the only individual whom the New Testament names as presiding over a local church, we must not assume that Rome or Antioch had a similar officer. We must either accept it as a singular practice in Jerusalem, or hypothesize that it may have passed on to the immediately influenced churches in Judaea, but then dead-ended when these Christian communities were either disbanded in the chaos of 68–70 and 131–135 or lost to the Ebionites shortly thereafter.

Then arise several theological axioms. One – so fundamental that it scarcely finds open expression – is that the founding era of the Christian fellowship is normative. These beginnings, unlike any other stage in Christian history, are classical and privileged, and the church of the present is accountable for its fidelity to the primitive discipleship of Jesus' first followers. Therefore what we make of the earliest record has governing importance for how our church conducts itself today.

Another theological presupposition of the consensus holds that Jesus radically broke away from Israel. The old religion, characterized by the Law and the temple-priesthood and political kingship, was hardly better than the other religions of the earth, save for what it brought forth in Christianity. Jesus established a prophetic reign that offered what Israel had never offered: salvation as a free gift to the individual who accepts him by faith. So utterly did he call his followers to set aside all hope in human contrivance or accomplishment that before long some members of the movement began to flinch and to lose the courage to believe so boldly. In what was a devastating apostasy, they took Jesus as a reformer instead of a founder, and began to construct a compromise with the Jewish usages of their past. The great threat to the primitive church came from these judaizers, whom Paul rightly exposed for their vain hope that the gospel of salvation through faith alone could survive any companion doctrine of salvation through approved rituals or accredited personages. That was a struggle which has endured, for authentic Christianity in every age is obliged to purge itself of residual, inauthentic notions of institutionalized churchcraft that presume to invest human rituals or officers with the power of the Spirit.

There has been, beneath the surface of this discussion, a propensity to color the Judaism of Jesus' time with the qualities Protestants found most retrograde in the Catholic Church. "We have here the retrojection of the Protestant–Catholic debate into ancient history, with Judaism taking the role of Catholicism and Christianity the role of Lutheranism."[2]

AN ASSESSMENT OF WEAKNESS

To what extent, one is obliged to ask, are these working principles of the consensus – its rules of method and its axioms of theology – subject to weaknesses that might compromise its conclusions?

As for the methods of critical establishment and exegesis of the texts, the scholars of the consensus may be faulted only for not having followed them rigorously enough. For they have often been selective and arbitrary in their use of higher criticism. Let several illustrations suffice. There has been a persistent circularity of argument in reference to the pastoral epistles, because of their undeniable provision for authoritative church offices. This has been offered in evidence as a chief reason for designating them, not merely as inauthentically pauline, but as of very late origin, quite possibly towards the middle of the second century. But then it is asserted that because the pastorals are such late documents, the church offices they present must also be of very late origin. This is obviously a circular argument.

---

[2] E[dward] P. Sanders, *Paul and Palestinian Judaism* (Philadelphia: Fortress, 1977), 57. See A[lf] T[homas] Kraabel, "The Roman Diaspora: Six Questionable Assumptions," *Journal of Jewish Studies*, 33 (1982), 463–464; "Greeks, Jews, and Lutherans in the Middle Half of Acts," *Harvard Theological Review*, 79, 1–2 (1986), 147–150; also Morna D. Hooker, *Continuity and Discontinuity: Early Christianity in its Jewish Setting* (London: Epworth, 1986). Jacob Neusner has argued that even when a sympathetic Christian scholar like Sanders deals with rabbinical sources for purposes of comparison with Paul, he fails to study them in their own right but sees in them only what is of interest to his pauline agenda: "The Use of the Later Rabbinic Evidence for the Study of Paul," in *Approaches to Ancient Judaism*, ed. William Scott Green, 2 (Chico, CA: Scholars Press, 1980), 43–60.

Even more problematic to the consensus have been the letters of Ignatius of Antioch, who emphatically attributes the faithful survival of the churches to their deference to a hierarchy of local officers: the *episkopos*, the *presbyteroi* and the *diakonoi*. The first recourse to critical method rejected the entire corpus of Ignatian writings as forgeries. Then, when Ignatius' authorship had been vindicated, critical methods were invoked to designate as spurious all passages that treated of officers. After the authentic roster and texts of seven Ignatian letters was established beyond much quarrel, the argument shifted course. First the entire story of Ignatius' journey and martyrdom was denied. Later, when that possibility was closed, the dating was challenged and moved from about 110 AD to mid-second century. One does come away with the suspicion that it was the conclusion, not the critical methods, which was in control.

The period of scholarship under review here – from the early nineteenth century until the present – has witnessed wave after wave of increasing sophistication in biblical and patristic scholarship. Older assumptions and conclusions have been overturned repeatedly. Not a few of the underpinnings of the consensus have been shown by advances in method to be of balsawood rather than of oak. Yet, as Olof Linton noticed more than a half-century ago, that seems to have made no difference or led to any profound re-examination of the consensus. Resistance to some of the ancient evidence seemed clearly more dogmatic than historical. The determined way in which scholarly criticism was put into fitful and controlled service suggests that the framers of the consensus were also open to the rebuke they had always directed against the papal, patriarchal and episcopal churches: that they were defending a system, not writing critical history.

A further remark: the partisans of the consensus have yet to adopt the most recent critical methods of the social analytic school. These latter have argued persuasively that some of the pivotal texts in this debate were intended strategically, and cannot be understood unless we can infer what the situation already was and how the author wished to alter it. Thus, when ancient oriental writers state that there must be no lusting after any "first chairs" within the Christian community, one might infer, not that there were no honored ranks in the churches, but that there were, and they were sometimes filled by men who had come to be served rather than to serve. And one might infer, not that rank and love of rank were late deviations in postapostolic times, but that rank and its attendant problems had been present at least since the Sons of Thunder were first recruited on the beach. In a word, the writers put a spin on their statements, which we must now calculate.

What of that other, particular methodological rule that later evidence can never be used to fill in earlier lacunae? Or that reports from one locale cannot justify generalizations about churches at a distance? Here one must make several cautionary remarks. We are aware that this was a traditional movement: one quite conscious of the authority of its divinely inspired foundation. What Christ Jesus had established, and what his closest disciples did by way of precedent, carried decisive authority. Those precedents were so decisive, in fact, that there had to be a temptation to fabricate them in order to give credence to later ventures. Thus the custom of assigning apostolic authorship to so many publications. And thus, the consensus would argue, Clement unhistorically tells the Corinthians that the apostles provided for self-perpetuating colleges of local elders, whereas it was really his own doing.

When one considers further the custom of pseudonymity in ancient Christian writing, it becomes clear that while it was sometimes used as a device to legitimate unorthodox innovation, it was also used to signal congruity and continuity with established teaching. It is thus an open question whether Clement's attribution to the founders was intended to justify a spurious change of his own, or rightly to dignify an abiding custom. As Joseph Gewiess has reminded us, Clement was writing only three decades after the deaths of Peter and Paul, and the Corinthian church had been founded only ten years earlier than that. He was writing to an audience that included plenty of people whose membership went back to the foundation. We have to reckon, then, that his claim that the system of elders dated back to the apostles conformed to actual recollection, and was no fiction on behalf of some new arrangement. Thus Clement's evidence given from Rome in the nineties might well be approached as valid evidence for the existence of *presbyteroi* in the Corinthian church even during the time Paul was writing 1 & 2 Corinthians. That would, of course, raise the question why Paul did not refer to them. And that question needs to be faced. In a period so brief, in a scatter of communities so actively linked by apostolic and evangelical and epistolary and delegate connections, in an environment where precedent – especially the precedent of Jesus, the apostles, the founders or their deputies, and of certain chief churches – received so much deference, the fact that an earlier text is silent about a usage described in a later text can indeed imply that an innovation had occurred. But that is not the only possible inference. It is not unreasonable or unscientific to inquire whether the usage might have been present earlier, yet for some plausible reason have left no mark on the record.

The *argumentum contra silentium* must also be tempered by the episodic character of the New Testament documents and their earliest sequels. The gospels were not intended to pass on information about the communities of disciples after Jesus no longer moved among them. They display editorially some of the preoccupations and controversies and perspectives of the emergent church, but in ways that are indirect and partial.[3] Nor are the other primitive books all that systematic. Most of them contain epistolary literature, with topics limited to what was crucial and contentious then and there. Even the books which are letters that drift into treatises, like *1 Clement*, or which are treatises made to look like letters, such as Romans, are polemic and deal with vexed issues, not the broad span of Christian life. Such information as they offer regarding community organization is all by way of *obiter dicta*. In fact, the only books which do set out to prescribe what community organization should be and

---

[3] This is exemplified by the findings of Gerd Theissen, one of the most distinguished of the sociologists of the Jesus-movement. He identifies the synoptic gospels as the most primitive source for information about the earliest disciples, and concludes: "At first, wandering charismatics were the authorities in the local communities. In any case, local authorities were unnecessary in small communities. Where two or three were gathered together in the name of Jesus (Mt 18.20), a hierarchy was superfluous. Problems were resolved either by the community as a whole or by wandering charismatics who happened to arrive" (*Sociology of Early Palestinian Christianity*, trans. John Bowden [Philadelphia: Fortress, 1978], 19–20; this translates *Soziologie der Jesusbewegung* [Munich: Kaiser, 1977]). The underlying assumption is that Christians could have formed their own structured communities only rather late when they were excommunicate from the synagogues. This ignores that the formation of distinctively oriented synagogues was quite normal in Palestinian Judaism in the first century. Indeed, it was the only normal way for Jews to form communities; to have rejected such a tradition would have been so abnormal that one would expect it to have been recorded in the synoptics as one of Jesus' points of teaching. Here the silence bespeaks social continuity, not dissidence.

It is Theissen's analysis that the Christian leaders and community were marked by alienation from both public and Jewish social forms. "Two tendencies towards social segregation emerge clearly here: tendencies towards inter-cultural segregation from the Gentiles, and tendencies towards intra-cultural segregation from other Jewish groups," ibid. 84. Of Paul and his charismatic rivals in Corinth: "All these people had left behind that social world in which they once lived. A great religious unrest, doubtless connected to the social conflicts of that era, turned them out onto the highways and made of them roving itinerant preachers, outsiders and 'outlaws'." *The Social Setting of Pauline Christianity: Essays on Corinth*, ed. and trans. John Schütz (Philadelphia: Fortress, 1982), 58.

do are Acts, the pastoral epistles and the *Didache*. And these are disparaged as unreliable evidence of the early churches.

Nevertheless, the argument continues, surely the fact that something as important, as central, as crucial as an official church order goes virtually unmentioned in the very earliest Christian documentation must mean that it did not exist. But what if the officers were not very important then? What if they were not at the center of things, not crucial? Both the consensus and its critics have assumed all along that church officers (their presence or their absence) would have to be very important, and so they have either affirmed or denied their primitive existence. Neither side seems sufficiently to have contemplated the possibility that they were there all along, but did not count for much. It is a hypothesis they should not have overlooked.

The possibility that church officers might have existed, but as a peripheral cadre of people, in the earliest churches invites us to take a fresh look at the theological axiom that the apostolic church must be normative for all future churches. For the unexpressed but always operative understanding was that in matters which were characteristic of the church, which composed and preserved her specific identity, which bore the Lord's purposeful imprint – in those, but not in lesser matters, the apostolic norm was authoritative. Apostolic marital status or hair styles or suggestions regarding widows did not touch upon the church's character and mission closely enough to impose themselves as a pattern for later ages. The question must be presented, then, both to those who affirm the consensus and to the nay-sayers (for both parties share this conviction of the apostolic patterns as normative): was the pattern of community order, role and office or leadership crucial enough to the church then for it to be an imperative for all churches later? Our task is not only to reconstruct what their usage actually was, but to ascertain as well how integral it was. For want of having considered that question, the consensus limps upon the leg of this theological axiom.

One might also reply, of course, by turning the argument from silence in exactly the opposite direction. We know that Christian Jews discontinued the fulfillment of kashrut, or dietary regulations, of sabbath observance, of submission to the authority of the Sanhedrin, of the rule of non-intercourse with gentiles. The New Testament bears heavy witness to these radical and highly controverted departures from Jewish practice. It is reasonable to doubt that an abandonment of the traditional community organization would have taken place without leaving any trace of controversy in the record.

There is a further problem raised by the virtually unquestioning belief that the very earliest Christian community must be the pattern for all ages to come. The apostolic generation must be normative.

The question arises: granted a scientific finding that a hierarchy of officers somehow replaced an anarchy of charismatics during the first and crucial age of the church, how are we to evaluate that shift? Was this a defection from a pristine, inspired model? Why could it not be considered, alternatively, as the outcome of a maturing process that brought the church into a seasoned durability?

Was it a bad change? Indeed, if it was a change was there any alternative but for it to be wrong? Was it a sort of progeria, whereby the church pathologically rushed into precocious decrepitude? Why could it not have been, instead, the closing of its fontanelle and the limbering of its motor skills? If one is to take the earliest discipleship as portrayed in the scriptures for one's norm and model, is it to be the fishermen on the Sea of Galilee or the network of established churches flung round the shoreline of the Mediterranean that is its affirmative point?

The consensus has said that the institutionalizing of the first century was a shrinking back from radical discipleship. The change was deplorable. The proper goal of perpetual reform in the church is to discredit and delegitimate that very credence in human authorities and rites which has threatened Christian fellowship since before the story of Jesus ever found its way onto paper.

But the consensus itself has provided the elements that build easily into another interpretation of that history. Stresses on the very young and defenseless unity of the church obliged the early Christians to develop an instrumentality to cope with heresy and schism. The ruling episcopate, many admit, was that development – sadly entailing high costs of autocratic governance as the price of communal survival. Even if one were to take such a dim view of church officers, if such structures really were an implied necessity for the first-generation church to survive through time – a need to be appreciated only as crisis actually threatened – how can we say that it is an alien development?

It has been rightly pointed out that the Catholics and Orthodox and Anglicans have some explaining to do. If they cannot trace their church order any further back than the second or third generation of

Christians, how can they repose their confidence upon it as constitutive of the authentic church? But the supporters of the consensus must then face a question that is also vexing. If the church could not hold faithful to authentic discipleship in that charismatic freedom which is constitutive of the authentic church for any more than one or two generations, how can the Lord confessed by that church inspire much confidence? Or, to put it somewhat differently: is the church of the first days more likely to be in authentic continuity with a church guided by the protégés of the apostles in the latter decades of that same century, or with a church re-created by Europeans fifteen hundred years later?

A last presupposition – the theological axiom that a Christian community is better off without privileged offices – must meet with several criticisms. It is a difficult generalization to support, for while church officers seem not to have been salient in the early conflict with judaizers, most scholars (even those who do so with regret) agree that they provided essential leadership in the crises to follow, against Gnosticism, Montanism and the Marcionites. But the weakest feature of this ideological axiom is its very strength. It is not merely one principle among four or five others. This is the governing principle, the axiom which forecloses any theory or conclusion from the evidence except that which the consensus, with such a shifting diversity of procedures, always manages to produce.

An alternative hypothesis

The Protestants who have constructed, revised and defended the consensus have been, on the whole, more accomplished historical scholars than their Catholic and Anglican antagonists. It is not unfair to conclude, however, that it was often not their scholarship but their churchmanship which governed their theory, at least on the subject at hand. In this both sides seem to have been at fault.

Both sides have also failed to consider another hypothesis.

It is impossible to understand primitive Christian worship unless in continuity with Jewish worship. So much of what we might consider to be distinctively and creatively Christian was in fact an outgrowth of its Jewish antecedents: the blending of word and gesture into sacrament, the weekly holy day, the calendar of feasts, the daily rhythms of prayer, the reading of scriptures followed by exposition, the sacred meal, ritual initiation through baptism, anointing, the laying-on of hands: this and so much else derive from the Jewish tradition. And we continue to discover other ancestral links, as when some of the most ancient Greek liturgical chants were traced back to Hebrew melodies.[4]

The Bible of the earliest Christians was that of Jesus – and of Israel. Its collection of books, its exegesis, its customs of homiletic application: all were Jewish. Fasting, charismatic prophecy, burial practices, ethical norms and ethical inquiry, veneration of the tombs of the saints, catechesis about the identity and roles and titles of Jesus, the centrality of Jerusalem, dedicated celibacy, impediments to marriage: these were some of many other usages which Jews brought with them to their discipleship of Christ and shared with their gentile brothers and sisters.

Appreciation of this massive cultural continuity from Judaism to primitive Christianity is relatively recent for Christians. For one thing, "Judaism" has tended to signify either ancient Israel as recoverable from the Old Testament, or rabbinic Judaism and its later unfolding. It was precisely the intermezzo of the Second Temple period, which flowed directly into our apostolic age, that was least familiar to us for it had produced so little documentation.

Also, the primal importance of Paul, whose letters represent the earliest documentary access we have to the first Christians, has been skewed by misunderstanding. Luther's odium for things Jewish, plus the abiding anti-Semitism which Christians have kept vigorous from age to age, have construed Paul to be a single-minded opponent of Jewish usages. His hostility to Judaizers in 1 Thessalonians, Galatians and the earlier chapters of Romans has been designated as the central point of his preaching. Also, biblical critics have discredited the complementary account of Paul given by Luke in Acts, which portrays a Paul and a church wherein Jewish theology, practice and influence remain quite prominent. The sum of this is that Paul has been presented, with some manhandling of evidence, as one who

---

[4] W[illiam] O[scar] E[mil] Oesterley, *The Jewish Background of the Christian Liturgy* (Oxford: Clarendon, 1925); F[rank Stanton Burns] Gavin, *The Jewish Antecedents of the Christian Sacraments* (New York: Macmillan, 1928); C[lifford] W[illiam] Dugmore, *The Influence of the Synagogue upon the Divine Office* (London: Oxford/Milford, 1944); Louis Bouyer, C.Orat., *Liturgical Piety* (Notre Dame, IN: University of Notre Dame Press, 1955); Roger Beckwith, "The Daily and Weekly Worship of the Primitive Church," *The Evangelical Quarterly*, 66, 2 (April 1984), 65–80; 3 (July 1984), 129–158.

presented Christianity precisely as a rejection of Jewish identity and usage.[5]

Since our faith is based on the understanding that Jesus did a New Thing, we tend to look for innovation rather than for continuity. Yet our increasing familiarity with the course of Israel's experience through the Jewish scriptures now makes us more aware of a series of drastic New Things wrought in Israel that repudiated some earlier tenets of faith, yet reinforced rather than severed ties with the tradition. In the sixth century BC, the exile opened Judah to the wider world and begot the discovery that there was but a single God, Yahweh their Lord; that this God was therefore creator of all peoples and indeed of the heavens and the earth and all that lived within them; and that the Jews were henceforth not the enemies of other nations but the bearers of neighborly tidings about their creator. This was as New a Thing as you could imagine. Yet although it repudiated so much of what the Hebrews had previously believed, it invited them to renew their connections with the past though in order to walk in a direction they had not previously anticipated. When, in the second century BC, the Wisdom of Solomon dawned upon the Jews with the shocking proclamation of continuing life after death in either the heavenly court or the underworld, that was a New, New Thing. And it invited people, not to reject their past, but to reconstrue and redirect it.

So with Jesus. It was a Jewish view, not a Christian view, that Jesus tore away from the people and traditions of Abraham, Isaac and Jacob. And if this be so in so many other usages, might it not be worthwhile to investigate whether and to what extent community organization among the earliest Christians might display and even be illuminated by continuities with its past?

Granted, the breach with their ancestral loyalties that the earliest

---

[5] Jacob Jervell has been arguing that if Acts be taken seriously, it may provide evidence that although Jewish Christian population in the church was waning through the later years of the first century, its intellectual influence was never stronger than in the last decades. The Paul of Acts is a religiously observant Jew; all the missionaries are Jewish; there is no church presented as all-gentile; and in the pauline churches it is the gentile believers who must accommodate the sensibilities of the Jewish Christians. Jervell points out that Romans 9–11, which predicts the eventual salvation of Israel, represents a late turn by Paul from his earlier hostility to Jewish conservatives among the Christians. Churches like Corinth and Rome, evidently quite influential in the network, remained strongly influenced by their Jewish Christian membership and theology during the late first-century period when Acts was written. See *The Unknown Paul: Essays on Luke-Acts and Early Christian History* (Minneapolis: Augsburg, 1984); also *Luke and the People of God: A New Look at Luke-Acts* (Minneapolis: Augsburg, 1972).

Christians eventually accepted was severely disruptive. They had had no previous contemplation of a bond with their Lord that was not ethnic. Yet precisely in the midst of chaos – and for them it was a chaos with economic, social and cultural elements – continuity is what saw them through. The concurrent transition of Jews who refused Jesus' messianic claims was no less wrenching, as they lost their political independence, their temple and its attendant levitical and priestly castes, and their biblically understood hopes, yet made their way forward into rabbinic Judaism. They too preserved their continuity by refashioning older institutions into the patriarchate, the academy, the synagogue and the rabbinic corpus. The same thing may be said of the two cohorts of Jews: that two crises in one century sent off into two divergent directions. They coped with the crisis of discontinuity by an institutional continuity. The forms were not dramatically changed, though they began to function differently in ways that took considerable time to be manifest.[6]

Scholars have been correct when they resisted reading into the silences of the primitive documents the Christian preferences of later, much more developed times. But what about the antecedent practices with which the earliest Christians themselves had been raised?

Let us, in order to entertain such an alternative hypothesis, approach the material from a different direction.

THE FORMATIVE ANCESTRY OF A MOVEMENT

Every story should start at the beginning, but for the historian the beginning may already be too late.

Any movement or institution which thrusts itself forward onto the human scene will be identified and appraised by the purposeful innovations that it introduces. Consider some examples. Paul of Tarsus argued that gentiles need not be circumcised in order to follow and worship Jesus of Nazareth, and in the churches that answered to him this novel view became a major loyalty issue. Virtually all Protestants followed Luther's rejection of celibacy as a prerequisite for clerical ordination, and this was stabilized as a primary agenda item in their reform. The drafters of the United States Constitution, conscious advocates of liberty and burdened by the Independence

---

[6] Roger Brooks, "Judaism in Crisis? Institutions and Systematic Theology in Rabbinism," in *From Ancient Israel to Modern Judaism: Intellect in Quest of Understanding*, ed. Jacob Neusner, Ernest Frerichs and Nahum Sarna (Atlanta: Scholars Press, 1989), 3–18.

doctrine that all men are created equal, gave the freedom of the land to all.

To understand these and similar historical changes we must be familiar with the older ways which their founders rejected. Innovation is known by contrast with what went before. But we must also understand what continued to make those older ways sensible and attractive enough for many of their contemporary adversaries to stand by them as by a more authentic tradition. Thus the historian must know the antecedents of any innovation in order to grasp what is specific and distinctive about its changes.

But there is a further reason for beginning before the beginning: subtler, and usually more profound. Every enterprise, even if it is most creative, prolongs many of the older ways unchallenged, and therefore often unnoticed. Because these continuities are uncontroversial the record tends to be silent about them. Consider some examples. The New Testament several times carries Paul's injunction that fellowship in Jesus' name should close over the ancient cleavages between Jew and gentile, male and female, master and slave. That he spent himself so tirelessly to bring the first imperative of that program to actual fulfillment is spread all over the record; it looms out as what many readers understandably think was chiefly characteristic of Paul's work. But is it any less significant – though it was then less noteworthy – that he never pursued the rest of his program to comparably radical conclusions? Or that Luther and some of his fellow Reformers shared the traditional view that clergy ought not be freebooters, and should be ordained only to some assured work assignment? Or that the US Constitution originally withheld the franchise from women, slaves and unpropertied men (and, effectively, from emancipated blacks, prisoners and the illiterate)?

For a comprehensive understanding the historian must grasp both the creative innovations and the uncontested continuities. We must search out what was most characteristic because it was a change, but we must also be aware of what was characteristic since it involved no change – indeed, because the idea of changing it never arose.

For both those reasons we must familiarize ourselves with the formative antecedents of any movement: the institutions and customs and convictions established in the past. It is ironic that in order to enjoy this pluperfect perspective on the past of the past, we usually need the vantage for ourselves of a timepoint well removed into the future.

Thus may it have come to pass that our remoteness from the first Jesus-people is precisely the advantage we require to comprehend better what they may have meant by acknowledging elders and prophets and deacons in their midst. And to do so, we must begin well before Jesus appeared in Nazareth.

The very earliest disciples of Jesus were Jews native to Galilee and Judaea. The character of the group and of its customs was subjected to a series of shocks when – almost unwillingly – they were obliged to incorporate new classes of membership that were increasingly alien to the charter disciples: first Greco-Roman Jews, then proselyte Jews (converted gentiles), then Samaritans, then God-fearers (sympathetic gentiles admitted to "associate status" with Jews), and finally out-and-out gentiles who had no previous nexus with the people of Israel. After some decades of strain and dispute the gentiles began to gain the ascendancy over the Galilean and Judaean proto-Christians, a shift that was consolidated by the transfer of primacy from the church at Jerusalem to the church at Rome.

This metamorphosis took up much of the first century, a period that later Christians have consistently regarded as privileged, even normative. As documentation has increased and our ability to decipher it has matured, it has become easier to track the course of church development through that tumultuous period. Historians are not of one mind when they come to study that trajectory. Some scholars prefer to see it as evolutionary. It took, as they read the documents, a good length of time for the community to work out its characteristic lineaments. Therefore the end of the trajectory represents a community that had settled into its authentic form. Other scholars have taken Jesus' personal mastery as the event of purest, surest inspiration and revelation. They have worked to get behind the later records and reconstruct what must have been the very earliest form of discipleship. These two views are at odds with one another. One takes the mature and final form of the New Testament as normative; another tries to reconstruct the pure and primitive teaching of Jesus, and regards later developments as possibly degenerative. But whether the first century was, for followers of the Way, a time of consolidation or a time of compromise is a question we need not resolve or even enter at the threshold of our study of the ancient sources. We shall be looking to all phases in this period as instructive and significant.

The antecedents of this Christian movement, then, must be sought in Judaism in Galilee and Judaea, yet as heavily influenced by the far-flung network of Jewish communities elsewhere, and indeed by the hellenistic culture in the Roman empire.

THE CULTURAL ANTECEDENTS

The mainstream tradition from which Christianity emerged was, of course, that of the people of Israel. As a continuum, that tradition begins to be recoverable for us with the exodus events of the thirteenth century BC. This is as far back as historically accessible narrative reaches, though it is over-reached by earlier materials about Canaan and Egypt which were put to theological use in the story. The exodus from Egypt and the entry into Canaan are followed by somewhat more than two centuries of truculent co-existence with the resident tribes. Just when the covenant-bound confederation of Yahweh-worshipers swells to a force to be reckoned with, it is nearly overwhelmed by a competing group of immigrants, the Philistines, and against this threat tribal jealousies bow to the need for a single standing military force, and therefore to a monarchy. The kingdom of Israel would last nearly three hundred years and finally succumb to Assyria. Its southern sister, Judah, would survive her by more than a century, before falling to Babylon. This was a period of inward national consciousness, and much influenced by prophets who were hostile to the foreign ways. Israel was nevertheless much beholden to other traditions, particularly to the more advanced Canaanite culture, of which it was in this period so often the emulator and the vassal. But because it was the prophets whose teaching held heavy influence on those who eventually edited the received record of that time, those Egyptian and Canaanite contributions, those of the hellenistic empires of Greece, Egypt and Syria and lastly that of Rome, are only covertly represented in the story.

Every people becomes fascinated with its own past just when its future is put at hazard. So it was that during the sixth-century exile the Jews began to gather, to re-edit and to reconstrue the documents of their past. Indeed, community reading of the newly collated scriptures became a central act of worship for postexilic Jews. They were a subject population throughout the period: first of Babylon and then of Persia. Despite their sensitized national consciousness, though, the Jews were absorbent of the dominant cultures. The fact that Aramaic, a cousin-tongue of their Hebrew, became the diplomatic language of the time gave them an advantaged access to international culture. Their long-cultivated scribal tradition provided a cadre of trained candidates for the imperial civil services. So the province of Judah came through this age considerably accommodated to Persian ways.

When Alexander and his Successors engulfed the Jews with their rule, their taxation and their rescue mission from barbarism, there was stiff resistance, at times to the death. Yet it could not stem the flow of hellenism into the Jewish cultural stream. The scattered Jewish communities throughout Mesopotamia, Arabia and the Mediterranean, settlements of mercenary contingents or of released war prisoners, and the ethnic neighborhoods of the great cities were even more exposed than were the homeland Jews of Galilee and Judaea, but even the patriotic Maccabees bred the Hasmonean line of priest-kings in Jerusalem, which became thoroughly hellenized and yet dominated Jewish society. Not even the subsequent resistance movements, such as the Pharisees and the Essenes, could purify themselves entirely of the Greek ways.[7]

[7] "On the whole, it emerges that Hellenism also gained ground as an intellectual power in Jewish Palestine early and tenaciously. From this perspective the usual distinction between Palestinian and hellenistic Judaism needs to be corrected. Here it is not only used misleadingly as a designation of subject-matter and in a false contrast as a geographical concept, but tends to give a mistaken account of the new situation of Judaism in the hellenistic period. From about the middle of the third century BC *all Judaism* must really be designated '*Hellenistic Judaism*' in the strict sense, and a better differentiation could be made between the Greek-speaking Judaism of the Western Diaspora and the Aramaic/Hebrew-speaking Judaism of Palestine and Babylonia." Martin Hengel, *Judaism and Hellenism: Studies in their Encounter in Palestine during the Early Hellenistic Period*, trans. John Bowden (Philadelphia: Fortress, 1974), 1:104. This translates *Judentum und Hellenismus: Studien zu ihrer Begegnung unter besonderer Berücksichtigung Palästinas bis zur Mitte des 2. Jahrhundert vor Christus* (Tübingen: J. C. B. Mohr, 1969).

Subsequent critics claim that Hengel overstates his case, or at least exceeds the evidence when he portrays hellenization to have made inroads among the Jews during the second and third centuries BC. See the reservations by Arnaldo Momigliano in *Journal of Theological Studies*, n.s. 21 (1970), 149–153. Fergus Millar's "The Background to the Maccabean Revolution: Reflections on Martin Hengel's 'Judaism and Hellenism,'" *Journal of Jewish Studies*, 29, 1 (Spring 1978), 1–20, argues "that the evidence shows how un-Greek in structure, customs, observance, literary culture, language and historical outlook the Jewish community had remained down to the earlier second century, and how basic to it the rules reimposed by Ezra and Nehemiah had remained," 20. See also Shimon Applebaum, *Judaea in Hellenistic and Roman Times* (Leiden: Brill, 1989). John Collins has pointed out that Hengel the historian "has not entirely shed the negative view of Judaism which has been endemic in Christian biblical scholarship," "Judaism as *Praeparatio Evangelica* in the Work of Martin Hengel," *Religious Studies Review*, 15, 3 (July 1989), 226–228.

"[W]hile Hellenization may appear to have triumphed in the rabbinic period, such a victory may have impinged more upon the externals of Jewish life than on the inner workings of religion and culture." Eric M. Meyers and James F. Strange, *Archeology, the Rabbis and Early Christianity* (Nashville: Abingdon, 1981), 93; see also 102.

The hellenistic empires were in their turn swallowed up. Even before Pompey's acquisition of the land in 63 BC, Jerusalem had begun to draw upon Roman influence. Earlier Syrian overlords, and even their own Maccabees, had paid court to those new and promising ways, and the most venerable Jewish institutions once again took on a new foreign tincture in order to survive.

The Jewish culture of Jesus' time, and of the time of his apostles and their early successors, is an ancient Hebrew heritage that had, in making its way along, adapted to much that was Egyptian, Canaanite, Babylonian, Persian, hellenistic (whether of a Ptolemaic persuasion from Egypt or of a Seleucid one from Syria) and Roman. Scholars have traced other influences: Philistine, Hittite, Ugaritic. But those seem somewhat fainter. In fact, no other culture was able to impress itself on the culture of Israel unless it also enjoyed a dominance that was military, political and economic.

A religious movement sprang up in the name of Jesus in Galilee and Judaea. It secured adherence from an ever-widening arc of believers round the Mediterranean basin. The older the movement became, the more cosmopolitan its membership and character. The old believers – Palestinian Aramaic-speakers – were soon enough outnumbered by newcomers who arrived from ever greater cultural distance. The neophytes, however, were all initiated and amalgamated into a tradition that was explained to them as ancient, and this process of indoctrination was one that the old believers continued for some time to control.

Soon enough it was settled (though not without conflict, and not unanimously) that the followers of the Way need not submit to the Torah, or at least that they need do so only selectively. Nevertheless, it quickly became clear to them that only in Israel had the Father's plan been long underway. New believers from Carthage and Lyons and Edessa could all consider themselves heirs of Abraham, subjects of a new David, disciples of the prophets of Israel and Judah. So whatever the innovative pressures in this church that was recruiting helter-skelter, it had to hold itself loyal and beholden to this confluence of traditions I have been sketching out, at least as it grasped those traditions through its own historical perspective.

The question we have to ask of the evidence is as follows. Were there forms of community organization that such a movement would have been likely to inherit? Were there patterns of leadership and dynamics of worship and usages of money and set roles for officers that had become so traditional as to become virtually instinctive? Further, were these patterns so entrenched in Palestine and so widely practiced by Jews that they would inevitably have been accepted and perpetuated by those of increasingly Greco-Roman exposure and experience who came along to join them? If such deeply traditional patterns of community organization and office among late Second Temple Jews can be verified, then we would enjoy a considerable advantage when we turn to study the records of the earliest Christians.

Imagine the impossible task of any future scholar trying to reconstruct the internal political history of almost any institution in America in ignorance of *Robert's Rules of Order*, the format by which virtually all meetings are conducted. The wardens of a Congregationalist church in Newport, a teamsters union in Chicago, a chapter of the Disabled American Veterans in Dubuque, a town meeting in Vermont, a mothers' club in San Luis Obispo: all of them run their meetings pretty much the same way, Robert's way. The book is a traditional item of community organization, entirely familiar to the nation, and for that very reason it is so taken for granted that it is rarely mentioned. By the same token, any familiarity which we can gain with similarly familiar antecedents of the earliest Christians will help us to construe better the ways that they were following – because they were the only ways they knew of forming a community.

Any innovative movement may reject components of an earlier tradition. To the extent that early Christians broke with theirs, and created organizational patterns that were distinctive, we shall best be able to see that by reference to the repudiated tradition. We would then inquire what it was that led the young movement to insist on its own ways of doing things. But when the record is silent or all but mute on any aspect of how the Christians arranged their affairs and provided themselves with church officers, it is safe as an initial assumption to suppose that the traditional patterns may have been carrying on. We may thus be able to fill out the portrayal of that young church – though cautiously – in some places where the record is fragmentary or puzzling.

Were there such polity patterns: so traditional, so familiar, so regular as to be instinctive, or even inevitable? We must explore the possibility that there were, and that they were embodied in the Jewish synagogue.[8]

[8] Credit must be given to a very learned if disorderly scholar who long ago argued that the synagogue was the model for the early church: a committed Dutch Calvinist of a Pietist persuasion, Campegius Vitringa. See his *De Synagoga Vetere Libri Tres*, 2 vols. (Franeker: Johannes Gyzelaar, 1696); *Archisynagogus observationibus novis illustratus* (Franeker: Strick, 1685); *Liber de Decemviris otiosis synagogae* (Franeker: Gyzelaar, 1687).

CHAPTER 6

Jewish community organization in the later Second Temple period

To begin with, our sources for evidence should be identified. The period we mean to study here, roughly the last century before the destruction of Jerusalem in 70 AD, is not as bountiful as one might wish it to be in primary sources on the Jews. We can, if we are cautious about it, include materials somewhat earlier and somewhat later than the period, to the extent that they may reliably attest to a situation that was culturally stable. The sources include: (1) the latest postexilic Jewish scriptures, especially in their Greek versions, and the apocrypha; (2) the works of Philo of Alexandria; (3) the Christian scriptures, insofar as they attest to Jewish practices without Christian adaptation; (4) the works of Flavius Josephus; (5) inscriptions referring to Jews (with caution since they are often difficult to date); (6) papyri referring to Jews; (7) Qumran and the other Dead Sea documents; (8) rabbinical documents (with very few exceptions I have left aside the Amoraic literature as too late, accepting that even in the Mishnah, published under Judah the Patriarch at the end of the second century, there are materials that reflect changes from the Second Temple times, and that if used carefully it is still a valuable witness to our period); (9) references to Jews in the documents of gentile contemporaries.

A further cautionary word must be entered here regarding the Mishnah. It is a very problematic source to use critically, not only because it was compiled more than a century after the close of the Second Temple period, but also because much that it presents is, if read literally and not obliquely, so fanciful. To illustrate: in a period when the Temple had been in ruins for more than a century with no realistic prospect of restoration, the rabbis of the Mishnah dwell at length on the detailed proprieties of Temple management.

The same Mishnah also frequently mentions the community chief = *rosh ha-keneset* and the community servant = *hazan ha-keneset*:

officers of the synagogue. There was nothing fanciful about the synagogue, since at that time it had long been the basic unit of community to which Jews commonly belonged. Here was a point of reference known to every reader. An entry in the Mishnah may not be sufficient evidence that any particular function of those offices actually existed, but it does sustain the inference that such institutions existed, and existed widely, and with a fairly stable identity. When the functions as described are paralleled by first-century evidence from Philo and Josephus (themselves problematic but independent witnesses) and the funerary inscriptions, they are that much the more removed from fancy. The synagogue format we shall attempt to reconstruct cannot be established as uniform or universal. It can, one has reason to believe, be proposed as typical, and that is the most that need be asserted.

Opinions vary greatly about when the synagogue first appeared in Jewish history (it should be understood that the word "synagogue" refers primarily to an organized community, and only secondarily and much later to a building where the community assembles). Some early rabbis taught that seasonal public readings of the scriptures dated back to Moses, and that synagogue buildings were in use in Babylon during the exile.[1] Philo and Josephus in the first century AD had identified Moses as the originator of synagogal readings.[2] Scholars have given no credence to these traditions, for no corpus of publicly accredited scriptures existed in Moses' thirteenth century, and no evidence of any synagogue buildings as early as the sixth century is known.

One respectable but unnoticed opinion would see the beginnings of the synagogue in Judah even before the sixth-century exile. The successful purge of Josiah (640–609) had swept away most local shrines = *bamot*. The temple itself, besides being defamed by the hardly forgotten perversities of the royal family and the priesthood, was very remote geographically from most villagers. This would naturally leave a dearth of legitimate places for worship. There are some hints of regular, perhaps sabbatarian, meetings under the aegis of dissident prophets, where Jews could "seek the face of the Lord," listen to the prophetic teaching and pray together. In any case, there were already diverse services that a local community then would

---

[1] *Mishnah* (hereafter *M.*) *Megillah* 3:6; *Babylonian Talmud (hereafter T.B.) Megillah* 29a, 32a; *Palestinian Talmud* (hereafter *P.T.*) *Megillah* 4:75a.
[2] Philo, *Mos.* 2:215–216; *Op.* 128; Josephus, *C. Ap.* 2:175.

have had to provide for itself, and thus would need to organize and meet. In all this, some see the beginnings, even before the exile, of the synagogue.[3]

A more common theory holds that the shock of losing all their familiar reassurances of the divine predilection – the land of Israel, the city of Jerusalem, the monarchy of David, the temple of Solomon – must have created in the Babylonian exiles a need to recover their traditions. Assemblies to listen to the now revered prophetic oracles, and some newly edited Torah, and to join in prayer, would have been an obvious expedient.[4] Other scholars cannot find enough evidence in the record to justify this reconstruction. They would see the emergence of aristocratic elders = *presbyteroi* and notables = *archontes* in the early Persian period, when there are recollections of popular assemblies for reading and prayer under Ezra in the fifth century.[5] A formalized body of Jewish governing elders is not actually mentioned until the time of the Seleucid king Antiochos III the Great (223–187),[6] and evidence from inscriptions and papyri of established synagogue communities cannot push verified instances back much earlier than that.[7]

Still more conservative commentary has noted that when the books of Maccabees describe in detail the Syrian efforts, midway through the second century BC, to extirpate every native institution and observance precious to the Jews, no mention is made of

[3] Leopold Löw, *Gesammelte Schriften*, ed. Immanuel Löw (Szegedin: Ludwig Engel, 1898), 4:1–12; Louis Finkelstein, "The Origins of the Synagogue," in *The Synagogue: Studies in Origins, Archeology and Architecture*, ed. Joseph Gutmann (New York: Ktav, 1975), 3–13.
[4] Julius Wellhausen, *Israelitische und jüdische Geschichte*, 6th edn. (Berlin: Georg Reimer, 1907), 194; Jean-Baptiste Frey, C.S.Sp., *Corpus Inscriptionum Iudaicarum* (hereafter *CII*): *Recueil des inscriptions juives qui vont du IIIe siècle avant Jésus-Christ au VIIe siècle de notre ère* (Rome: Pontificio Istituto di Archeologia Cristiana, 1936–1952), 1:lxviiiff; George Foot Moore, *Judaism in the First Centuries of the Christian Era: The Age of the Tannaim* (Cambridge: Harvard University Press, 1927), 1:283.   [5] Neh 8; 9; 13.
[6] Mentioned in Josephus, *Ant.* 12:138.
[7] See Emil Schürer, *The History of the Jewish People in the Age of Jesus Christ*, revised English edn. by Geza Vermes, Fergus Millar, Matthew Black and Martin Goodman (hereafter Schürer, *History²*) (Edinburgh: T. & T. Clark, 1973–1987), 2:200; Charles Guignebert, *The Jewish World in the Time of Jesus*, trans. S. H. Hooke (New York: Dutton, 1939), 50–51, 74; Martin Hengel, *Judaism and Hellenism: Studies in their Encounter in Palestine during the Early Hellenistic Period*, trans. John Bowden (Philadelphia: Fortress, 1974), 1:25–26; Hengel, *Jews, Greeks and Barbarians: Aspects of the Hellenization of Judaism in the Pre-Christian Period*, trans. John Bowden (Philadelphia: Fortress, 1980), 43 (this translates *Juden, Griechen und Barbaren: Aspekte der Hellenisierung des Judentums in vorchristlicher Zeit* [Stuttgart: KBW, 1976]); Samuel Safrai, "The Synagogue," in Safrai and Menahem Stern, eds., *The Jewish People in the First Century: Historical Geography, Political History, Social, Cultural and Religious Life and Institutions* (Assen: Van Gorcum, 1974), 2:910–912.

synagogues. From that some infer that even this late into the hellenistic era the synagogue had not yet become a common establishment for homeland Jews, though it had for some time existed among their more cosmopolitan and free-thinking peers in the dispersion.[8] An alternative explanation might hold that by this time the local political-economic-religious assembly had become so universal in Syrian territories that it could not have been viewed as peculiarly Jewish. Or, the synagogue was implicitly assailed in the determination to destroy all copies of the sacred texts which by then were likely to be the centerpiece of the Sabbath assemblies.

How is it that scholars disagree this widely on the origins of so common an institution? They all examine the same evidence, yet differ by as much as six centuries about when the synagogue became the received structure of Jewish community life.

Each of them identifies the synagogue with some component and then looks to find that one component in full and mature form. Some look for gatherings to read from the canon of sacred scriptures. Others look for a hierarchical political system wherein a central college of elders exercises rule over the nation from Jerusalem. Still others look for a community-owned physical plant, or even for a time when such a structure would be called a synagogue. One might as well look for priests and church buildings among Christians, and conclude that Christianity did not originate until the fourth century after Christ.

THE SCOPE OF COMMUNITY

The synagogue was an institution that, as it matured, took on lineaments which were political, liturgical, educational, financial, eleemosynary and ethnic. But its true nature cannot be reduced to any one of these aspects. Still less can it be identified with the particular form or functions any of them was eventually to assume.[9]

It was a form of community organization. Its political form tended to be presbyteral: that is, it was influenced (though not always

[8] Moriz Friedländer, *Synagoge und Kirche in ihren Anfängen : Eine Studie zur Geschichte des Sabbaths und der Synagoge in der Diaspora* (Amsterdam: Philo, photoprint of 1908 edn.), 53–78. Friedländer notes that Onias' express motive in building a temple at Leontopolis in Egypt was to unite the Jews of the dispersion whom he found doctrinally disunited because of their independent places of worship and their tradition of free interpretation of scripture (Josephus, *Ant.* 13:66).
[9] This has been seen by Solomon Zeitlin, "The Origin of the Synagogue," in Gutmann, *The Synagogue*, 14–26; Schürer, *History*[2], 2:207–209; Safrai, "Jewish Self-Government," in Safrai and Stern, 1:381–382.

governed) by a class or college of elders. Whether they lay under a despotic sovereign or a distant overlord, or had a measure of autonomy; whether the elders were actually senior in age or were of aristocratic lineage or were adroit technocrats: the elders were to be reckoned with as guardians of the tradition and of the people. Among a people where prayer was neither as ancient a tradition nor as strategic a national resource as sacrifice had been, local communities during this period had found themselves held together against a threatening world by prayer, when they were sheltered no more by tribal boundaries nor by royal borders. They were a people who had lately acquired a library – one of the only national treasures left to them, and itself only recently assembled – that preserved oracles and tales and laws which the God who laughed at the very notion of other gods had settled upon them, and which could be heard by and explained to the humblest countryman. Their farthest-flung settlements had dues to pay: taxes to rulers, levies for the temple, percentages to the priests and Levites. And so they devised for themselves a system of assessing and collecting and sequestering and transferring those funds. There was always the peace to be kept, particularly internal civility between the families who might ravage a town with a blood feud. And they required a reverent peace with God, for one person's flouting of the Law might visit devastation on a whole area: God sometimes acted with mighty gestures. There were the widows and orphans and aliens and others beyond the shelter of kin; all these had to be provided for. Everyone needed certain public amenities which only the rich could afford if purchased privately. In foreign countries Jews had to have their own settlements lest they cease to be Jews. In the larger cities, various neighborhoods easily filled with Jews who immigrated with different dialects and customs, and found solidarity in familiar association with their own kind.[10]

All of this was synagogue: not all at once, nor in every locale. But this evokes the complex of services and arrangements that Jews progressively found it best to provide for themselves through a stable community organization.

These various activities tended with time to be the responsibility of different people, whether through sinecure or training or election or

---

[10] Acts 6:9 records a Jerusalem synagogue with a predominance of émigré members from Cyrenaica and Alexandria. Roman synagogue names suggest comparable memberships from Judaea, Phoenicia, Proconsular Africa, Cyrenaica and North Lebanon. Frey, *CII*, 1 :lxxvi – lxxx; Harry J. Leon, *The Jews of Ancient Rome* (Philadelphia: Jewish Publication Society, 1960), 135–166.

assignment. Yet each was the concern of all, and the community created ways of popular expression and decision-making and accountability which kept even the most technical services as a communal concern. And the diverse activities leant upon one another: scripture understanding governed jurisprudence, leadership affected prayer, the prosperity of the treasury was a function of inter-familial politics.

What I refer to as a synagogal way of life was so integrated, so omnicompetent, so communitarian that our distinctions between public and private, or between sacred and secular, or between the person and the community – all of them distinctions so needful for our wisdom about the world – would be largely inapplicable. It was a society where various people were in charge – often many people – but ultimately they answered to the community for the entirety of its needs and interests.

The Persian, hellenistic and Roman periods did not constitute an era when Jewish communities, whether left to themselves in Palestine or living in isolated villages or ethnic neighborhoods in gentile lands, enjoyed full autonomy in the direction of their own affairs. But such self-determination as their rulers did allow came to be exercised in the synagogue. If, for example, they were subject to an activist government, then the local community might have to restrict its program accordingly, and might occupy itself mostly with matters of worship. But if, under a few major constraints of imperial policy, a Jewish community was left to manage itself, then the synagogue might generate the full apparatus of a civil municipality.

Before examining the synagogue one must recall the political fortunes and memories of the Jews at the latter end of the Second Temple era. By the time of Jesus' appearance in public, the Jewish homeland was entering into its seventh century of subjugation to foreign powers (that is, from a Jewish perspective). There had been one intermezzo of freedom, when internal quarrels in Seleucid Syria to the north, military impotence in Ptolemaic Egypt to the south, and the unwillingness of Rome to allow those two powers to prolong their ancient feud (in which the buffer province of Judaea was usually one item of contention) permitted the Jews a very brief opportunity to rule themselves (142–63 BC). But even that period under the Hasmoneans saw Judaea as a client state between its two large neighbors.

It was a period when widely scattered Jewish settlements were appearing throughout the hellenistic world. By mutual understanding they constituted, along with their homeland kinfolk, a united world Jewry. Some were conscript or mercenary soldiers who served in all-Jewish fighting units and were given homestead rights, as in Egypt and Arabia. Some were deportees for whom the overturn of their captors brought release from political imprisonment but no need or desire to be repatriated, as in Babylon. Some were descended from clusters of manumitted slaves, or were merchants or craftsmen who found better fortune abroad, in prosperous centers like Antioch, Alexandria, Corinth, Rome.

Despite occasional attempts such as that under Antiochos IV Epiphanes (175–164 BC) to oblige Jews to conform to the state religion, this was an era when they were left to themselves. Provided they collected and forwarded their taxes, sent detachments of troops when required, referred specified cases of highest judicial consequence for higher review, and observed ceremonial courtesies towards their masters, Jews encountered little disposition to assimilate them. Indeed, as the Greek and later the Roman cities evolved an increasingly privileged status of citizenship, resident ethnic populations such as the Jews were generally unwelcome as full members of the cities, and were left as political enclaves: separate, and far from equal.[11]

Throughout this period, then, though Jews lacked sovereignty they were left sufficient privacy to be able – indeed to be obliged – to manage their own communities. It was not untypical for Julius Caesar to affirm that "it has been decided by me and my council under oath, with the consent of the Roman people, that the Jews may follow their own customs in accordance with the law of their fathers."[12]

---

[11] Even the Jews of Alexandria, who were numerous and of ancient residence there, were excluded from citizenship. It had previously been thought that an edict of Claudius (41–54 AD) recorded by Josephus (*Ant.* 19:280–285) granted the Jews this status, but a more reliable, official copy preserved on papyrus explicitly leaves them as a resident enclave = *politeuma: Corpus Papyrorum Judaicarum* (hereafter *CPJ*), ed. Victor A. Tcherikover, Alexander Fuks and Menahem Stern (Cambridge: Harvard University Press, 1957–1964), no. 153; see nos. 150–159. This is carefully discussed by Shimon Applebaum, "The Legal Status of the Jewish Communities in the Diaspora," in Safrai and Stern, 2:434–440. For further bibliography see Josephus 9:583, Appendix Q.

[12] Josephus, *Ant.* 14:214: *zēn kata ta autôn ethē. Ant.* 16:163: *edoxe moi kai tôi emôi symbouliôi meta horkômosias, gnômēi dēmou Rômaiôn tous Ioudaious chrēsthai tois idiois ethismois kata ton patrion autôn nomon.* See also Philo, *Flacc.* 74. In like vein, Jews had been patronized by Cyrus and his Persian successors (Ezra 6), some Seleucids (1 Macc 6:55–60; 2 Macc 11:22–33), and Claudius (Josephus, *Ant.* 19:280ff; *CPJ*, no. 153).

It was only natural as the Jews went about organizing their communities in ways they considered appropriate, that no matter how traditional or separatist they imagined themselves to be, their exposure to Greco-Roman society would inevitably draw them somewhat in its direction. This held true whether it was simply an assimilation of vocabulary (as when Philo describes the Essenes as a club, or hellenistic association = *thiasos*); or presenting themselves to outsiders in ways familiar to them (the patriotic tract, 2 Maccabees, is itself written in a very stylized hellenistic Greek); or even adopting gentile customs outright (the gymnasium became an avenue of access to Greek and, in rare cases, possibly Roman citizenship for those enrolled).[13] The Mishnah uses about 200 loan-words from Greek and Latin; the Talmuds, 4,000.[14] The Jews, despite themselves, absorbed hellenism.

They cross-bred their ancestral polity with such international forms as seemed to be harmonious and, to boot, publicly appealing. There was no lack of models. The hellenistic and the Roman city = *polis*, the army = *stratia*, the sovereign's court and those of his subordinates and emissaries = *sunklêtos/philoi/consilium*, ethnic enclaves = *politeumata*, civic associations = *thiasoi/eranoi/collegia*, settlements = *katoikiai*, villages = *kômeis*: all were familiar examples of social organizations to which Jewish communities everywhere could and did conform themselves, with rather parallel results in the homeland and in the dispersion.

There is still – or again – today a serious historical opinion that the Greek-speaking Jews of the Roman world developed a new form of community organization which was fairly uniform from one Diaspora city to the next. That social organization, it is thought, was basically Greco-Roman.[15] On the contrary, whatever the measure of assimilation to outside social structures, the burden of evidence is persuasive that the predominant model for social organization in the synagogue, during the period when it could have been influential

---

[13] Tcherikover in *CPJ*, 1:40–41; no. 153.
[14] See Philip Blackman, *Mishnayoth* (New York: Judaica, 1964), 7:105, 107–123. Selections from the Mishnah will be drawn or adapted from this edition and translation. See also Saul Lieberman, "Greek of the Synagogue," in *Greek in Jewish Palestine: Studies in the Life and Manners of Jewish Palestine in the II-IV Centuries C.E.* (New York: Jewish Theological Seminary, 1942), 29–67.
[15] A[lf] T[homas] Kraabel, "Unity and Diversity among Diaspora Synagogues," in *The Synagogue in Late Antiquity*, ed. Lee I. Levine (Philadelphia: American Schools of Oriental Research, 1987), 49–60.

upon the founding generation of Christians, was inveterately Jewish. Let us try to discern what were the consistent structures of those Jewish communities within that milieu.

THE ASSEMBLY

In their own nomenclature, the Jews *were* an assembly. The cultic and political act of a solemn and formalized convention of the whole population – men, women and children – was felt to be so typical and representative that, by metonymy, it provided the popular designation whereby one referred to the Jews.

In the accounts of the premonarchic period the assembly = *'edah* = *synagôgê* is a common synonym for the people, especially in Exodus, Leviticus, Numbers and Joshua. The expression fades in the literature of the monarchy, where "Israel," "Judah," "House of Judah" are preferred. But in the later postexilic literature an even stronger expression for assembly = *qahal* = *ekklêsia* is used to designate the people.[16] The expressions are also current in the apocryphal writings like 1 *and* 2 *Enoch* and the *Psalms of Solomon*.[17] And the custom is attested in the Jewish inscriptions.[18] Philo writes: "For when the whole multitude came together with harmonious oneness to give thanks for their migration (the exodus), [the Lord] no longer called them a multitude or a nation or a people but an 'assembly'."[19] There are early rabbinical usages which also designate the people as an assemblage.[20] Of course there were other, surrogate, expressions used to refer to the people, but the array of terms that depict Israel as a convened assembly (and *synagôgê* is a very common one) is used with such frequency that there must have been something archetypical and constitutive about such gatherings.

And that is the case. The Hebrew scriptures describe critical national events as transacted in plenary assembly = *ekklêsia* = *synagôgê*:

1 For taking corporate military decisions:
   (a) at Mizpah, to avenge the crime at Gibeah of Benjamin (Judg 20:2; 21:5, 8);

---

[16] For example, Neh 7:66; Mi 2:5; 1 Macc 4:59; Pr 5:14. Several texts in Dt use it in this sense, e.g., 23:2–4.   [17] *1 Enoch* 53:6; *2 Enoch* 68:7; *Ps Sol* 17:44 (17:48, old versification).
[18] Shürer, *History*[2], 2:429, no. 12; *CPJ*, no. 473 (quite late, however).
[19] Philo, *Exod.* 1:10. This work is extant only in an Armenian version, but the translators see here the Greek original: *plêthos synagôgês*.   [20] These include *tsibur*, *keneset*, *chaberah*.

   (b) attacked by Moab and Ammon, Judah consults the Lord (2 Ch 20:5, 14);

   (c) Israel is obliged to release captives and booty from Judah (2 Ch 28:14);

   (d) the Maccabean rebels deliberate how to relieve Galilee and Gilead (1 Macc 5:16);

   (e) Bethulia deliberates how to respond to Holofernes' siege (Jdth 6:16);

   (f) the pioneers returned to Judaea face the order to dismiss their foreign wives (Neh 8–10).

2 For ratifying the covenant:

   (a) under Moses (Dt 4:10; 9:10; 18:16; 23:1, 2; 31:30);

   (b) under Ezra (Ezra 10:1, 8, 12, 14; Neh 8:2, 17).

3 For acclaiming rulers:

   (a) Solomon (1 Ch 28:2, 8; 29:1, 10, 20);

   (b) Jeroboam (2 Ch 10:3);

   (c) Joash (2 Ch 23:3);

   (d) Simon (1 Macc 14:28).

4 For hallowing:

   (a) David receives the ark (1 Ch 13:2, 4);

   (b) Solomon dedicates the temple (1 Kgs 8:14, 22, 55, 65; 2 Chr 6:3, 12–13; 7:8);

   (c) Hezekiah renews Passover (2 Ch 30:2, 4, 13, 17, 23–25).

5 For receiving communications:

   (a) Moses commands the Law to be read out every seven years (Dt 31:9–13);

   (b) Jeremiah delivers his oracle that Babylon will take the land (Jer 25);

   (c) Messages from Rome and Sparta (1 Macc 14:19).

6 For bestowing official honors:

   (a) on Yahweh (1 Ch 29:20);

   (b) on heroic neighbors (Sir 31:11; 39:10; 44:15);

   (c) on Judith (Jdth 6:14–20).

7 For judgment, especially of capital crimes:

   (a) adultery (Ezk 23:46);

   (b) sabbath-breaking (Num 15:32–36);

   (c) folly (Pr 5:14).[21]

---

[21] See Klaus Berger, "Volksversammlung und Gemeinde Gottes: Zu den Anfängen der christlichen Verwendung von 'ekklesia'," *Zeitschrift für Theologie und Kirche*, 73 (1976), 174.

This is not, of course, to be treated uncritically as a historical reconstruction. What it does witness is a cumulative conviction that the plenary assembly was the rightful venue for all major events in and of the community of Israel. Whether in fact or in symbol, it had been the ancient usage that the people had to be convened for certain acts too momentous to be left to rulers alone. The word that characteristically designates these rallies – *qahal* in Hebrew, *ekklêsia* in Greek – derives in each language from the verbal root meaning "to call, to convene." In the late Second Temple period there were many kinds of event that would, at various levels, require an *ekklêsia*, and the witness and assent of the popular assembly. The gathering was no mob event. It was convened by elders or other public officers to address some issue which tradition would not permit them to resolve on their own unratified authority.

For what purposes was an entire community convened, in the period under study? For one thing, high community officers continued to be either elected or presented for acceptance within the assembly. Leviticus had described Moses as convening the entire community for the sacring of Aaron and his sons as priests. Philo and Josephus both elaborate on the scene by having the assembled people ratify God's choice.[22] Herod presents his three fractious sons to a general assembly in Jerusalem and asks for acceptance of them as kings and as his heirs apparent.[23] Later, when Herod himself dies with certain death warrants still outstanding, his sister Salome withholds the news from the military long enough for the prisoners to be freed, then calls out a formal army parade and surrounds them with a full assembly of the people, and only when that stage is set does she announce the king's death and his choice of successors. Had there been any disposition among the military to take matters into their own hands, she adroitly squelches it by calling for a formal acclaim of the new regime, company by company, in the presence of the assembly.[24] When Josephus arrives in Galilee to quiet the growing sedition there he presents himself as appointed by the assembly of Jerusalem.[25] On a more local level, there is evidence that assemblies

[22] Lev 8:3, *pasan tên synagogôgên ekklêsiason*. Philo, *Mos.* 2:143, *meta tês hapantos tou ethnous gnômês*. Josephus, *Ant.* 3:192, *synêinoun têi tou theou cheirotoniai.* [23] Josephus, *B.J.* 1:457–460.
[24] Ibid. 1:665–669.
[25] Josephus, *Vita*, 341, 393, *hypo toi koinou tôn Ierosolymitôn*. Elsewhere Josephus states he was commissioned by the community leaders in Jerusalem, 28ff, and by the Sanhedrin, 62. There is thus the possibility that the authority of the assembly was invoked without a formal meeting, but by an act of the council of elders who could speak for the assembly.

would gather to elect their own leaders and officers: the Mishnah, for example, speaks of treasury officials being chosen by a majority of the assembly.[26]

Hecataeus of Abdera, a contemporary of Alexander the Great, in about 300 BC describes the Jewish assemblies as remarkably acquiescent to priestly leadership: "It is [the high priest], we are told, who in their assemblies and other gatherings announces what is ordained, and the Jews are so docile in such matters that straightway they fall to the ground and do reverence."[27] It is possible that the reading and the exposition of the holy books was one of the less stressful agenda items of the Jewish assemblies. The *Letter of Aristeas* takes up the older tradition that royal letters must be read out there,[28] but much more frequent were the presentations of Jewish scriptures (one must remember that in a society where few, even of the aristocracy, were literate, the act of reading was always vocal and public).

Philo recounts that each sabbath day the Jews would assemble in their prayer houses = *proseuchai* and sit in ranks according to order and seniority to hear the scriptures read out. Then they would be expounded by a priest or an elder after which all joined in the discussion, until the late afternoon.[29] Both Christian and rabbinical sources record this as a regular Jewish observance, and note that it was also the appropriate setting for community prayer.[30] The same practice was observed by the Therapeutae, a community of Jewish ascetics Philo admired, save that the explanation was regularly given by their chief elder, and women attended behind a screen.[31]

We also know that at least some synagogal groups had communal suppers. For the Essenes, who actually lived together and thus were daily commensals, maintaining a common table and bread-sharing, this was a principal bond of their community.[32] In fact, a candidate was made to undergo three years of probation and only after that, when he had taken his initiation oaths, was he admitted to the community table. He would then forswear, for the rest of his life, any

---

[26] *M. Shekalim*, 5:2.

[27] From his *Aegyptiaca*, quoted in Diodorus Siculus, *Bibliotheca Historica*, 40:3, in Menahem Stern, ed., *Greek and Latin Authors on Jews and Judaism*, 1 (Jerusalem: Israel Academy of Sciences and Humanities, 1974), 26ff.   [28] *Letter of Aristeas*, 42.

[29] Philo, *Mos.* 2:216 (where he ascribes the practice to Moses); *Som.* 2:127; *Hyp.* 7:12–13.

[30] Lk 4:16–30; Ac 13:14; 15:21; 17:1; 18:4; *M. Megillah*, 1:1–2; *M. Berakoth*, 4:7.

[31] Philo, *Vit. Cont.* 30–32. The senior elder was *ho presbutatos*.

[32] Philo, *Hyp.* 11:5, 11–12; Josephus, *B.J.* 2:129–133. Philo says they have a *koinē trapeza*, and *syssitia*; he describes them as *homotrapezoi kath hekastēn hēmeran*.

other sustenance but what the community would provide.[33] The Therapeutae had periodic festal banquets at which the president led them first in prayer and then, as the meal progressed, in a consideration of various biblical questions, ending with a round of hymns.[34] But there is also evidence of an ordinary practice of plenary suppers by the membership of ordinary synagogues.[35]

The assembly continued to serve as the setting where momentous community policies were either agreed upon or at least set forth for public acquiescence. Joseph the Tobiad, before dispossessing his uncle, the high priest Onias, of his hereditary tax-farming prerogative, thought it well to call an *ekklêsia* in Jerusalem to allay public suspicion that taxes were about to be increased (they were).[36] Whether or not Josephus' account is historically accurate, he tells us that Simon the Ethnarch, sire of the Hasmonean dynasty, expelled the Syrian garrison from the Jerusalem citadel and determined to reduce that fortress, lest it ever again be occupied by foreigners and used to menace the temple next door. For such a move, which would also deprive the Jerusalemites of their refuge of last resort, he called an assembly to secure public consent.[37] Herod, after a long journey devoted to cultivating the patronage of the sometime consul Marcus Agrippa at heavy expense to the treasury, summoned an assembly on his return, gave a warm account of his political success on their behalf, and then rebated to them a fourth of their annual taxes.[38]

Petronius, the Roman legate to Syria, arrived with orders to install a statue of Caligula in the temple in Jerusalem. He soon saw that it was a gesture likely to provoke a rebellion, and he convened a sizeable assembly at Tiberias to assure the Jews he would ask that the order be rescinded.[39] In the wake of outrage and massacre by the maladroit procurator Gessius Florus (which eventually ignited the Jewish revolt of the sixties) the high priests hurriedly called an assembly to appeal to the Jerusalem populace not to provoke him further.[40] A while later in the catastrophe which unfolded, when Jerusalem had fallen under the control of the Zealots who would

---

[33] Josephus, *B.J.* 2:137–145; Philo, *Quod Omn. Prob.* 86.
[34] Philo, *Vit. Cont.* 40; 60–80.
[35] Julius Caesar, in a rescript transcribed by Josephus, refers to common meals = *syndeipna* among the Jews as one of their specifically acknowledged and protected national customs, *Ant.* 14:215–216. An Egyptian document apparently records contributions by Jews to one of a series of feasts = *poseis*, but this may be for a dining club, not an entire synagogal community, *CPJ*, no. 139.   [36] Josephus, *Ant.* 12:163ff.
[37] Ibid. 13:215–217; *B.J.* 1:150; but compare 1 Macc 14:37.
[38] Josephus, *Ant.* 16:63–65.   [39] Ibid. 18:279–283.   [40] Josephus, *B.J.* 2:319–320.

surely incite Rome to annihilate them all, an assembly was called by Ananus, the most senior of the high priests, who shamed the gathering into an attempt to oust the Zealots.[41] After the fall of Judaea, a pogrom against the Jewish residents of Antioch was instigated at a plenary assembly of the citizens, and it required a stern appearance by Titus at another *ekklêsia* to quell it.[42]

The realities of political life, then, occasionally required that the entire population be formally convened and satisfied on matters that might otherwise drive a wedge between rulers and people.

There was another requirement of the public peace which claimed public witness: the settlement of graver questions of justice. Messiah, when he came, would judge nations and tribes in solemn assembly.[43] Capital crimes sometimes required a trial in assembly, as that of which Susanna stood accused.[44] Lawsuits between Jews could also be adjudicated before the public forum.[45]

When the silversmiths at Ephesus rouse the populace and fill the theater with their protests against Paul's disrespect for Artemis, it is the clerk/scribe = *grammateus* of the city council, whose prerogative it is to summon all parties to trials, who scolds the crowd for being illegitimately assembled, and reminds them that they are free to raise their complaints before a proper *ekklêsia*.[46] That is, of course, an episode involving the legal process of a Roman city, but in this period the Jewish processes are quite similar – including the possibility of mob violence. Once when Herod was bent upon doing away with two of his ambitious sons, he was obliged by Augustus to arraign them in Beirut before a select court of notables who gave in an ambiguous and inconclusive verdict. He returned to Caesarea, turned up some co-conspirators, and put them on trial before a city assembly, where they were battered to death by the crowd. Under cover of that show of public support Herod forthwith proceeded to execute his sons.[47] Shortly before his death a group of rabbinical students hacked down a great golden eagle he had erected in the temple. Rather than risk public sympathy for them in Jerusalem he changed the venue to Jericho and secured from the assembly there a sentence of death.[48]

[41] Ibid. 4:151, 162ff.   [42] Ibid. 7:46ff, 106ff.
[43] *Ps Sol* 17:44 (see n. 17).   [44] Sus 28, 41, 60.
[45] So, for instance, in the community at Sardis: Josephus, *Ant.* 14:235.   [46] Ac 19.
[47] Josephus, *B.J.* 1:540–551; *Ant.* 16:367–394.
[48] Josephus, *B.J.* 1:647–655; *Ant.* 17:149–167. One text describes the court as a bench of notables; the other, as a popular assembly. It could have been both together; or this could be another instance of a court speaking with the authority of the assembly.

In 73 AD, after the last vestiges of rebellion had been erased in Palestine, several hundred *sicarii* = daggermen slipped into Alexandria and began to bully the Jewish residents there into a renewal of the revolt. They assassinated a few dignitaries who opposed them. The rest of the community leaders saw where this was leading, convoked a general assembly, denounced the outside agitators, seized them on the spot, pursued and arrested those who had evaded the meeting, and handed them all over to the Roman authorities (all this, according to Josephus.[49]

Our knowledge of the Jewish community in assembly during this period is sketchy. At times it is difficult to reconcile Philo's picture of leisurely Torah discussions with Josephus' tales of crowds crying for blood.

About their scripture study and their judicial gatherings we are fairly well informed. Where deliberation of public policy is at stake our picture blurs. What does seem clear is that the local assembly was taken as a microcosm of the full assembly of all Israel. The residual authority of each synagogue was vested formally and fully in its membership in assembly. By the time of the late Second Temple that authority had been hedged by superior claims of superior synagogues and occasional synodal bodies, and had effectively been exercised locally by various officers, collegial and individual. In theory, however, the local assembly was competent to resolve virtually any issue it decided to address, and any local deputies had to act in the name of the assembly. Like the Electoral College in the United States of America, the Jewish assemblies legally retained impressive prerogatives even while they were receding in actual importance. But by the end of the Second Temple period there were echelons of select people on whom most of those prerogatives had effectively devolved. It was the responsibility of those personages to convene the assembly when they thought it appropriate, and to control its agenda and the freedom of the floor. Thus the assembly could be used, and it was used. But a free-spoken public convention where no conclusion could be reached until consensus had arisen from among the common people – such a democracy seems not to have been functioning at the close of the period under study here.

[49] Josephus, *B.J.* 7:409–419.

Superior authority for a synagogue

Much was required of Jews anywhere who wanted to live as a community. And if communion among one's close neighbors was such a part of one's life, presumably there would need to be some kind of comity binding the far-flung synagogues together in a worldwide network. The evidence suggests that there was. In fact, there were two ways of doing it.[50]

It had been an ancient understanding among the Jews that their settlements formed a hierarchy of jurisdiction. The old land lists in scripture speak of "towns with their villages,"[51] and of "cities with their towns and outlying villages."[52] The larger settlements had a relationship to their subordinates that was described as parental. Thus there were mother cities = *métropoleis*,[53] with towns called "daughters."[54] Larger towns, in their turn, could be called "mother towns" in relationship to their village dependencies.[55]

It is interesting that many of the texts which in the original Hebrew speak of "towns with their villages" emerge in the Greek translation as "cities with their villages." The hellenistic gradation recognized only cities and villages, not towns. It is also possible that the translators were already moving towards the peculiarly Jewish classification, evident in the Mishnah, of two sorts of settlement: those with synagogues (and thus cities) and those without synagogues (villages). Jews in settlements too small for a community organization would resort as members to that of the mother town.[56]

Since the Roman government organized its municipalities according to a traditional subordination it would have been congenial for Jewish communities to observe the established hierarchy, and for

---

[50] Obviously Jewish communities were rarely free to arrange their forms of self-government as they pleased. Various despots either disenfranchised them or laid their governing bodies under alien officials. Empires might allow these bodies to function but would inhibit their authority. Often these overlords would demand control of what they would call civil matters and leave what they called religious matters to be settled by the Jews: a division of activities the Jews would never consider natural. Through it all, the Jews coped and adapted and survived. What we are after is not just how inter-community jurisdiction actually worked, as crimped by these impositions, but how, whenever the interference was relieved, it tended by tradition to reassume its native character.

[51] Josh 15:32, 36, 41, 44; 19; Num 21:25 (the villages are *synkyrousai* = subordinated to their rule), 32; 1 Ch 7:28–29.   [52] Josh 15:45, 47.   [53] 2 Sam 20:19.

[54] Neh 11:25; Judg 11:26; Ezek 16:46; 1 Macc 5:8, 65.

[55] See Schürer, *History*[2], 2:187–189.

[56] See Safrai, "Jewish Self-Government," 412–413. M. *Sotah*, 9:2, for instance, seems to subordinate a town without a court to one with a court.

the most part they probably did. But where the Roman world-view did not coincide with theirs they seem to have gone their own way. Thus, though on a Roman organizational chart Sepphoris could be the chief seat of Galilee, and Caesarea the chief city of Judaea, both of these were heavily gentile cities then, and were correspondingly reduced, by the end of the Second Temple period, in the Jewish table of accountability.

The mother of mothers, of course, was Jerusalem, and all synagogues looked to the Great Council there as to an ultimate authority. In the second century BC the book of Judith portrays the council in Jerusalem directing military defenses in Galilee, and receiving requests for variances from the requirements of the Torah.[57] Its literary contemporaries, the books of Maccabees, show the insurgent leadership consulting with the Jerusalem elders about defensive measures that would affect the entire province.[58] Within our period it is the Jerusalem elders who commission Josephus as commander of all Galilee.[59] Judicial matters of a graver or a more complex nature were to be referred to that council as to the ultimate court.[60] Torah issues were to be resolved there.[61] And though the ordinary line of authority would proceed from Jerusalem to the other great regional capitals, the Sanhedrin enjoyed a sort of eminent domain that permitted it to bypass intermediate cities. Thus, in sending Saul with orders to the Damascus community to expel any Christians there – an undertaking in which Antioch, as metropolis of Syria, had a clear right to function as the intermediary – Jerusalem was ignoring the normal chain of command, as was apparently within its power to do.[62] The seat of authority had a significance of its own. Thus, although the Sanhedrin could imaginably convene elsewhere than in the land of Israel, it was thought that there were some issues of such national gravity that they could be settled only on home ground.[63]

---

[57] Jdth 4:8; 11:14.   [58] 1 Macc 12:35–37; 2 Macc 13:13.
[59] Josephus, *Vita*, 28, 62.   [60] *M. Sanhedrin*, 11:4; Josephus, *Ant.* 4:218.
[61] *M. Peah*, 2:6.   [62] Ac 9:1–2, 21; 22:5; 26:12.
[63] Josephus, *Ant.* 14:90–91. Josephus notes that this re-established aristocracy in the land, which the people heartily preferred to the rule of one man. A[lf] T[homas] Kraabel, "Social Systems of Six Diaspora Synagogues," in *Ancient Synagogues: The State of Research*, ed. Joseph Gutman (Chico, CA: Scholars Press, 1981), 79–91, relies on archeological evidence to claim that at least in the western Diaspora synagogues were relatively remote from each other and and to stipulate that they were autonomous, even of Jerusalem. Though his method is fascinating, his conclusions would not easily apply to our period, since the synagogues older than the second century AD number less than half a dozen; most of Kraabel's evidence is from the fourth century and later.

This pattern of relationships, whereby one Jewish community was accountable to another, one might call metropolitan. It is to be contrasted with another pattern which one might call synodal.

When Josephus took up his command in Galilee he co-opted seven elders from each of the ten major cities or towns and formed of them a council of notables, seventy in number, to facilitate his control of the region. The local communities were not disestablished, but they were made accountable to and through a representative regional body that had no populace of its own, no local *ekklêsia* behind it. This was no great innovation. A century earlier the proconsul Gabinius had visited a Judaea ravaged by warlords, and he divided it into five districts, each with a capital and each with a *synedrion* = council. These councils were apparently not the metropolitan elders who were already in place, but representatives from the entire district.

That kind of arrangement seems to have been a response to crisis or disorder. Perhaps the separatist tradition among synagogues was so strong that it took menace to make them willing to submit to a synodal superior, which would be more activist, more likely to impinge on their independence than the metropolitans had been. And perhaps this is why there is so little evidence of synodal authority in the context most natural for it: the larger cities.

We do know that Jerusalem had a council of elders that was different from others in that it seems to have had no local community to serve. It is theoretically possible that in a large city all the synagogues, according to the metropolitan principle, were subordinated to one: the "first synagogue," so to speak. There is little in the record to turn our minds towards that suggestion.[64] We do know that some members of the Sanhedrin may have lived in the surrounding towns.[65] It is not improbable, then, that it was somehow formed of elders who already belonged, in virtue of residence – and might continue to belong, for some purposes – to one of the many synagogues in the vicinity. This would make it, if not representative of the far-flung Jewry over which it presided, at least synodal, in some token fashion, for the city as a whole.

In Alexandria we know that the Jews had a large residential

---

[64] At Side on the Pamphylian coast a certain Isaac put it out that as commissioner of the "first synagogue" there he had much improved its buildings and furnishings. But this would most easily be taken to designate the eldest of the Jewish foundations in that city, and we cannot know whether all subsequent ones had a filial relationship to it. *CII*, no. 781.

[65] Mk 15:43, Joseph of Arimathaea; *M. Taanith*, 3:6.

population, and many synagogues,[66] but that for some time they lived under a central governance. Strabo records that an ethnarch had been imposed upon them, with virtually full powers of rule over them as a political enclave.[67] *Aristeas* says that even before they had an ethnarch the Alexandrian Jews composed a single community, with elders and assembly.[68] At the decease of the ethnarch Augustus abolished that office and authorized a central council of elders which forthwith took and retained control.[69] One assumes that this body was somehow representative of the many Jewish congregations in the city. The fact that Alexandria was said to have had one great synagogue building with seventy-one golden chairs for a council of elders leaves a trace of plausibility for a "first synagogue" there, with a population that was one of several local communities.[70] That the overstructure by itself did not always succeed in bringing a fractious population into consensus might be inferred from the emperor Claudius' irritated command to the Alexandrian Jews "not in future to send two embassies as if they lived in two cities."[71]

Antioch, the other great city in the eastern Mediterranean with a substantial Jewish population, has not yielded enough evidence for safe conjecture about an umbrella organization during our period.[72]

Rome is the city where Jewish residents have left behind copious epigraphical evidence about their community and its organizations. A very few peculiar items in those inscriptions have prompted some historians to conclude that there was a central Jewish authority there. Others find the evidence inconclusive, as do I.[73] But whatever the outcome of that debate, an important point is here to be grasped.

The advantages of some coordination between the many synagogues of a large city are many and obvious. Each had to remit its contributions annually to Jerusalem, and could do so more securely

---

[66] Philo, *Leg.* 132, 156; *Flacc.* 47.　　[67] Quoted in Josephus, *Ant.* 14:117.

[68] *Aristeas*, 310.

[69] Philo, *Flacc.* 74 (to be preferred to the version in Josephus, *Ant.* 19:280–285). Some read this text to say that Augustus himself appointed the elders, but I do not see that as a necessary reading, nor would it have gone down with the Jews quietly. It would hardly have been a way to give a large and touchy ethnic minority a sense of their own destiny. On Alexandria, see Tcherikover in *CPJ*, "Prolegomena."

[70] *Tosefta Sukkah* 4:6. Cf. Josephus, *Ant.* 12:108. On Jewish communities in Alexandria see Applebaum, "The Organization of the Jewish Communities in the Diaspora," in Safrai and Stern, 2:473–476.　　[71] *CPJ*, no. 153, ll. 88–92.

[72] But see the discussion in Applebaum, "Organization," 485–486.

[73] The debate is lengthy. For the existence of a central authority are Juster, Krauss, La Piana, Guignebert, Baron, Applebaum. Against it are Schürer, Frey, Momigliano, Leon. For summary arguments see Leon, 168–170; Applebaum, "Organization," 498–501.

by joining with the others. Governments at the municipal, provincial or imperial level had to be dealt with, and would require representatives with credentials from the entire local Jewish population. Common cemeteries would require joint management, as would other shared activities such as schools. Judicial decisions would occasionally clamor for an appellate jurisdiction nearer than Jerusalem. The need for at least informal consultation and periodic concerted action would appear inescapable. At least in Jerusalem and Alexandria we know of formal synodal authorities in existence. Yet we are unable to conclude that they took an activist stance in governing the local synagogues under them. As for the other cities, if they had such compelling reasons to centralize, and even if such centralization did exist in some informal and fluid fashion, it must have faced an inveterate and formidable reluctance from the individual synagogues, a centrifugal force that resisted any loss of autonomy. It is plausible that some coordination between the synagogues of a large city was inevitable, and one might interpret the silence of the record as a sign that the coordination was informal, and that it was possibly kept that way by the constituent synagogues as a strategy of independence.

A synodal form of authority would seem to have been a more imposing threat to community independence than was the metropolitan form. It seems, for the most part, to have met acceptance in times of stress when unification is usually more urgent and tolerable. One is left with a sense of clannish separatism and localized loyalty, even between neighboring communities. Ordinarily the worldwide network was loosely woven, and there was apparently a decent reluctance to use such superior authority.

THE PROGRAM OF A SYNAGOGUE

Next we must try to ascertain the range of activities and services which a Jewish community at this time would have provided for itself. Archeologists have excavated some synagogue buildings from the late Second Temple period, but often they have been undifferentiated structures. Documentary and epigraphical sources are more complete in telling what a variety of operations they might have housed.

The one activity that every synagogue, by definition, had to sponsor was meetings: meetings of the assembly, of the elders, of the notables.[74] The assembly met regularly to hear the scriptures: most anciently on the sabbath, and perhaps on Mondays and Thursdays besides.[75]

These meetings to read and expound the scriptures appear to have had a twofold effect during the Second Temple period, especially in the Diaspora. First, they were the seat of a catechetical tradition in Jewry. At a time when no central agency, even in Jerusalem, seems to have exercised a magisterial authority, a widespread, common-law tradition of normative belief was being formulated across the network of synagogues. Second, since attendance was open to gentiles, this teaching tended to emphasize the ethical features of Judaism that would have direct appeal to the hellenistic mind. Thus the institution of synagogue indoctrination served to unite the people by a standard doctrine, but it tended to be an exoteric doctrine that accentuated universalist themes, rather than those of Jewish exclusivism.[76]

Jewish communities also fostered civil associations and craft guilds, which would utilize any meeting facility that the synagogue might have.[77]

Another closely related activity, as we have seen, was the administration of law and of criminal and civil justice. Every synagogue had to deal internally with alleged violations of Torah, and with litigation between members of the community. This would entail judicial sittings, fines and other punishments.[78]

At this time the school was coming to be a standard feature of communities. There was a common distinction in Hebrew between the meeting house, or house of assembly = *beit ha-keneset*, and the school house, or house of inquiry = *beit ha-midrash*.[79] In smaller communities both activities must have been conducted on the same premises.[80] Philo even makes the point that the prayer houses of the

---

[74] Quite commonly the echelons of the community were ranged on benches according to rank: Mk 12:39 and parallels; Lk 11:43; 20:46.
[75] Ac 13:14–15, 27; 15:21; *M. Megillah*, 1:1. There is evidence of daily scripture study in synagogues, though possibly as a school activity rather than as one in assembly: Ac 17:10; J 18:20.
[76] Dieter Georgi, *Die Gegner des Paulus im 2. Korintherbrief: Studien zur religiösen Propaganda in der Spätantike* (Neukirchen-Vluyn: Neukirchener Verlag, 1964), 86–100; John J. Collins, *Between Athens and Jerusalem: Jewish Identity in the Hellenistic Diaspora* (New York: Crossroad, 1983), 142–163.
[77] For an illustration of an association meeting in a Jewish prayer-house, see *CPJ*, no. 138. On craft guilds see Applebaum, "Organization," 476–482.
[78] Mt 23:34; Ac 22:19; *M. Sanhedrin*, 1:1; 3:1; Schürer, *History*², 2:225ff.
[79] Sir 52:23.   [80] *M. Terumoth*, 11:10; *M. Menachoth*, 10:9.

Jews are schools [81] Already in this period the language of the assemblies for scripture and prayer had diverged from that of the house of study. The former had turned to the vernacular, and the scripture texts would be read out in either Aramaic or Greek, or at least translated after a reading of the Hebrew. The schools seem to have dealt in the original languages, and hence would have Hebrew itself to teach. Also, the accumulation of scrolls and codices would put any decent-sized community on its way to maintaining a library.[82]

Most communities also needed to preserve their stores of important documents. These would include any charters of privilege, and communications from government officials, or from Jerusalem, or from other Jewish communities. There would be copies of the synagogue's proceedings, chronicles and resolutions of honor.[83] For its member families, the community might preserve deeds, contracts, marriage agreements, wills, manumission papers and the like. The synagogue could come to be an official repository and source of authentication for official and private documents, and so it had to offer the services of a notary.[84]

Other valuables might also be deposited in a community stronghold. The temple in Jerusalem had long performed this service and any local synagogue that was secure might be called on to do the same,[85] as well as to hold in escrow objects of disputed ownership.[86]

Jewish law bade every adult male pay a half-shekel annually. One of the most frequently protected rights of Jewish communities was to transmit these temple taxes to Jerusalem, a right that was to be eroded only later under Christian rule. Central governments did not like to see money flowing regularly across borders except to their own capitals; the fact that this was allowed the Jews shows how much of

---

[81] Philo, *Mos.* 2:216: "For what are our places of prayer (*proseuchtêria*) throughout the cities but schools (*didaskaleia*) of prudence and courage and temperance and justice and also of piety, goodness and every virtue by which duties to God and men are discerned and rightly performed?"

[82] Jean Juster, *Les juifs dans l'empire romain: Leur condition juridique, économique et sociale* (New York: Burt Franklin, photocopy of 1914 edition), 1:474–475.

[83] Ibid. 475–476.

[84] For an instance of a will deposited in a Jewish archive, see *CPJ*, no. 143. For a registered copy of a burial inscription in Phrygia, see *CII*, no. 775; in Smyrna, no. 741.

[85] 2 Macc 3:10 states that Hyrcanus the Tobiad had some of his wealth on deposit in the temple. Josephus, more than two centuries later, says that in the melee of the Roman invasion the wealthy had brought their valuables to the temple for safekeeping, *B.J.* 6:282. *M. Erubin*, 10:10 mentions a synagogue which had a bolted inner door. See also Schürer, *History*², 2:279–281; Lieberman, 172.   [86] *CPJ*, no. 129; *M. Arachin* 9:4.

a sticking point it was with them.[87] It also implies that their communities had the facility to hold these offerings until they were remitted: a treasury belonging to the synagogue. In fact, the theft of any such "sacred revenue" was considered a sacrilege in Roman law, especially if it was kept in a synagogue building, where all deposits were protected by this legal status.[88] There were other forms of public money that would also need the safety of a local treasury. Sometimes the community or its officers had the task of tax collection for the government.[89] There were also various charity funds out of which the poor, the kinless and the aliens had to be supported.[90]

It seems also that local communities may have kept some of the priests' dues in kind from harvests, and have found a way to store the produce.[91] Some Jewish communities were given preferential access to certain required food commodities, which may have brought a victuallers' market of sorts under community auspices.[92]

One public amenity of special value to a Jewish settlement was a water supply and a facility for bathing, since their social cohesiveness and the needs of ritual purity would make a gentile bathing facility unattractive. These baths were commonly maintained at community expense, as were public water taps and fountains.[93]

A common duty of hospitality obliged every community to house travelers, and common buildings they had lay open to this usage. One such building, on Mt. Ophel in Jerusalem, was fitted out

---

[87] Ex 30:15; Josephus, *Ant.* 16:281. The Mishnah describes the coffers used in local communities to provide the required coinage for this tax; they resembled those used for this purpose at the temple: *M. Shekalim*, 2:1; 5:6; 6:5; 1:3. Philo mentions the first-fruits payments as still being made and conveyed to Jerusalem; where done, this must have required a conversion into money: *Spec. Leg.* 1:78; *Leg.* 333. See Schürer, *History²*, 2:288.

[88] Juster, 1:377–385; 424–427; Josephus, *Ant.* 16:162–165.

[89] Josephus, *B.J.* 2:405–407; E. Mary Smallwood, *The Jews under Roman Rule: From Pompey to Diocletian* (Leiden: Brill, 1981), 32–33.

[90] 2 Macc 3:10.

[91] The storage of harvest produce in the temple was said to have given rise to a legal issue when fieldmice in the bins escaped and began to gnaw the sacred scrolls, *M. Kelim*, 15:6. That similar storage occurred in local synagogues seems implied by *M. Sabbath*, 18:1.

[92] Josephus, *Ant.* 14:259–261. The Talmud later discloses a custom of Jewish inspectors to watch over market honesty, Safrai, "Jewish Self-Government," 417.

[93] *M. Nedarim*, 5:5; *M. Taanith*, 1:6; *CII*, nos. 754, 1197; Louis Robert, "Inscriptions grecques de Sidè en Pamphylie," *Revue de Philologie*, 32 (1958), 43ff. Two synagogues in Arsinoë, Egypt, paid water bills to supply each with the equivalent of four fountains, possibly providing households of the Jewish neighborhood with their water supply, *CPJ*, no. 432. The later synagogue in Sardis also provided a bountiful water supply: 11 gallons a second by one reckoning: W. H. Buckler and David M. Robinson, eds., *Sardis VII* (Leyden: Brill, 1932), 37–40, no. 17.

specifically to house pilgrims.[94] Those in even more critical need than the ordinary wayfarer might find shelter too. The sick and the aged might need hospices and it appears that some synagogues maintained such facilities.[95] In hellenistic Egypt Jewish prayer houses were granted the same privileges of legal asylum that Egyptian temples enjoyed.[96] And in that gesture of final hospitality, synagogues were expected to provide and to watch over burial places for their dead.[97]

An early talmudic passage expects every Jewish community to provide for common use " a law-court competent to scourge, a prison, a charity fund, a synagogue and a public bath, a public latrine, a doctor and artisan, a scribe, a slaughterer and a teacher of children."[98]

One must remember that we have drawn upon evidence from documents that span several centuries, some of which (for example, the Mishnah) are of uncertain historical meaning, while others report on Jewish communities scattered at great distances, and possessed of different needs and resources. No single synagogue is likely to have included all these elements in its program. What the evidence does illustrate is the array of services and functions that any Jewish community of the period might provide for its membership. The evidence is not plentiful enough to indicate how widespread many of these elements actually were, or whether they were ordinary or optional. The reports portray an institution which was to provide for the full span of the commonweal of an ethnic community that enjoyed, either by choice or by necessity, only limited participation in the enterprises of the public society, and largely had to fend for itself religiously, economically, hygienically, financially, socially and governmentally. To infer from that picture, it is plausible to see many, if not most, of the activities and services as likely in the program of all but the very small synagogues of the time.[99]

---

[94] Its inscription reads: "Theodotus the son of Vettenus, priest and community chief, son of the community chief, grandson of the community chief, built this synagogue for the reading of the Torah and the study of the commandments, and the hostel and the rooms and the water installations, for needy travelers from foreign lands. The foundations of the synagogue were laid by his fathers and the elders and Simonides," *CII*, no. 1404; further, nos. 694 (Stobi), 979 (Er-Ramah). See also Safrai, "Relations between the Diaspora and the Land of Israel," in Safrai and Stern, 1:192.   [95] Juster, 1:476–477.

[96] F. Wilhelm Dittenberger, *Orientis Graeci Inscriptiones Selectae* (Leipzig: S. Hirzel, 1903–1905), I, no. 129; CII, no. 1449. Asylum may also have been involved in *CPJ*, no. 129.

[97] *CPJ*, no. 138.   [98] *T.B. Sanhedrin*, 17b; *P.T. Kiddushin*, 4:68b.

[99] See Shaye J. D. Cohen, *From the Maccabees to the Mishnah* (Philadelphia: Westminster, 1987), 111–115.

THE SYNAGOGUE BUILDING[100]

We do not know what proportion of synagogue communities did acquire land and construct buildings. The documentary evidence suggests that this was common, but the archeological evidence is still sketchy. In some areas, like Egypt, such a building was known as a prayer house = *proseuchê/eucheion/sabbateion*.[101] Philo and Josephus follow – ordinarily though not exclusively – the same nomenclature,[102] and similar usage is also known in Rome.[103] Philo notes that the Essenes call their holy places "synagogues," or meetings, and the New Testament seems to follow that usage also.[104] Other sources generally use that term to designate the community itself.[105] Some simply called the building "the holy place."[106] The Mishnah regularly styles it a meeting house = *beit ha-keneset*,[107] while gentile writers refer to it as a prayer house.[108] The evidence seems to show that buildings appeared in the Diaspora well before they became common in Palestine. It was in the late Second Temple period in Palestine that the name for the community became the name for its building = *synagôgê*, and that its emergence as the scene of worship, scripture study and Hebrew schooling coincided with the rise of Pharisaism.[109]

Some of the establishments that have been excavated are imposing, for instance, at Masada, Dura-Europos, Sardis, Capernaum, Mt.

---

[100] Levine's *Synagogue in Late Antiquity* is a reliable presentation of contemporary research and speculation on the synagogue building.

[101] *CPJ*, nos. 129, 134, 138, 432 (*eucheion* is used as a synonym in this document); *CII*, nos. 1432, 1433, 1443, 1444; *CPJ*, no. 1532a. See also Jeanne and Louis Robert, "Bulletin épigraphique," *Revue des Etudes Grecques* (hereafter *BE*), 1983, nos. 281 (Samaritan) and 434.

[102] For instance: Philo, *Flacc.* 49; *Mos.* 2:216 (*proseuchtêrion*); Josephus, *Vita*, 277, 293; *Ant.* 16:164.   [103] *CII*, no. 531.

[104] It is often difficult, when a text locates an event *en têi synagôgêi*, to know whether it means "in the meeting" or "in the building." But New Testament usage seems to imply the latter: Mk 1:21, 39; 3:1; 6:2; Lk 13:10; J 6:59; 18:20; Ac 9:20; 14:1; 17:17.

[105] Philo, *Quod Omn. Prob.* 81; *CII*, no. 1404.

[106] *CII*, nos. 694 (Macedonia), 867 (Gerasa), 966 (Gaza). Frey finds this usage familiar in Palestine, *CII*, lxx, n. 3. See Josephus, *B.J.* 4:408.

[107] For instance, *M. Megillah*, 3:1, 2.

[108] Thus Juvenal (Stern, *Greek and Latin Authors*, no. 297); Cleomedes (Théodore Reinach, *Textes d'auteurs grecs et romains relatifs au judaïsme* [Hildesheim: Georg Olms, 1963 photocopy of 1895 edition] no. 121); Apion (Josephus, *C.Ap.* 2:10); *CII*, no. 532.

[109] Martin Hengel, "Proseuche und Synagoge: Jüdische Gemeinde, Gotteshaus und Gottesdienst in der Diaspora und in Palästina," *Tradition und Glaube: Das frühe Christentum in seiner Umwelt*, Festgabe für Karl Georg Kuhn zum 65. Geburtstag, ed. Gert Jeremias, Heinz-Wolfgang Kuhn and Hartmut Stegemann (Göttingen: Vandenhoeck & Ruprecht, [1971]), 157–184.

Ophel. Others, such as that in Berenice in Cyrenaica which had an amphitheater among its properties, are known through written records. Most of the early structures thus far excavated appear to have been converted residences – an intermediate step between meeting in a member's home and possessing community real estate.[110] Whatever the size of a synagogue's physical plant, it enjoyed considerable immunity before Roman law. Frey summarizes well, regarding the community:

> They practiced their religion in freedom and enjoyed the right of association with all that it entailed: the right to meet; to hold property, particularly buildings for worship and land for cemeteries; to administer community funds and to amass contributions destined for transmittal to the religious center of Judaism. This was so, despite the restrictive way in which Augustus had again explicitly confirmed, in a general edict, the liberties which Caesar had awarded all Jews throughout the empire.[111]

As regards the buildings, their legal protection was substantial. It is true that in some cities, as in Rome where synagogue buildings were for a long period not permitted within the *pomerium*, the enclosure of the central city proper, discrimination kept them off at a distance. This may also have been by choice, for better access to an open water source.[112] But as an *aedes sacra*, or sacred edifice:

1 it was called a religious property = *religionis locus*;
2 theft of funds or of documents was classified as a *sacrilegium*;
3 it could retain ancient rights of asylum, or sanctuary;
4 it was immune from most intrusions by civil authorities (though troops could be quartered there);
5 no symbols of other religions could be imposed upon it;
6 any destruction or vandalism was a crime.[113]

It is well to keep in mind, however, that excavated synagogues from as early as the first century AD are still rare.[114] The possession of real estate by congregations may have become more common only in succeeding centuries. When one confronts this disparity between abundant documentary references and sparing archeological remains it seems reasonable to conjecture that during our period synagogues

[110] Kraabel, "Social Systems," 81.
[111] Frey, "Les communautés juives à Rome aux premiers temps de l'église," *Recherches de Science Religieuse*, 20 (1930), 276.
[112] The synagogue in Philippi seems to have convened outside the walls by the river, probably in the open air, Acts 16:13.   [113] Juster, 1:456–472.
[114] Delos, Masada, Gamla, Herodium, Capernaum I(?).

must often have convened in the open, in the land of Israel, or in private premises in the Diaspora: most typically, in the home of an affluent member.[115]

The evidence available allows us to make sparing but significant inferences for our purpose. The first followers of Jesus typically belonged to a local synagogue. In a Jewish town it would have comprised the full population. Villages would be likely to resort to a nearby town-synagogue of which their village was a traditional dependency. Residents of a city with significant Jewish population would have had their pick among synagogues according to neighborhood, preference of dialect or immigrant origins. The synagogue assembly was, in theory, omnicompetent for its own ordinary affairs. In fact, it was answerable to higher authority, Jewish and Roman, and it exercised a governance through its own officers that could be more titulary than supervisory. The activities they would typically have undertaken would include scripture reading and inquiry, prayer, election of officers, and disciplinary proceedings. Services rendered by the synagogue might have included collection and remittance of taxes and levies, social welfare for the dependent and indigent, hospitality to travelers, Hebrew school, custody of documents and valuables, and water provision for ritual and possibly domestic purposes. Their gatherings would have been in members' homes or in the open or at an all-purpose meeting house. In brief, the instrumentality for virtually all communal aspects of life beyond the family – religious, civic, economic and educational – was found in their local synagogues. For most Jews it was perhaps the only organization to which they would ever belong.

[115] See Joseph Gutmann, "Synagogue Origins: Theories and Facts," in his *Ancient Synagogues*, 1–6. Also G[eorge] H. R. Horsley, ed., *New Documents Illustrating Early Christianity, 1978* (North Ryde, NSW: Macquarie University, 1983), 94; *New Documents, 1979* (1987), 111.

CHAPTER 7

The officers of the synagogue

Who then constituted the official personnel of a typical synagogue community in the later Second Temple period?

THE ELDERS

Israel's earliest memories portrayed her as a presbyteral people. Local settlements had a class of men called elders = *zeqênim* = *presbyteroi*. Though in earliest times they may typically have been older men, one did not become an elder just by becoming elderly. Theirs was a socio-political status. Their precise function was to give wise counsel, and to legitimate community policy, whether they actually formulated it or only ratified it. Elders were collegial. The Greek Bible frequently converts the Hebrew plural of "elders" into a corporate singular word: council of elders = *gerousia* = *presbyterion*. They are also functionally described as a council = *'etsah* = *boulê*.

In the literature of premonarchic Israel it is the elders whom Moses first alerts about the vision of the burning bush, the passover and the covenant.[1] They surround the great leaders, like an operatic chorus, in the great scenes: Joseph, in the cortege marching to Jacob's burial; Moses, celebrating victory, quelling Korah's revolt, promulgating the Law; Joshua, mourning for the defeat at Ai, and making his deathbed address.[2] They provide a legitimating presence when the covenant is ratified or renewed, and when the priests are invested.[3] They act with authority, as when they must sacrifice for the people's inadvertent sins, decide upon tribal strategy, bear the penalty when that strategy fails, or recruit tribal leaders.[4] And to them will fall the

---

[1] Ex 3:16; 4:29; 12:21; 19:7.
[2] Gen 50:7; Ex 18:12; Num 16:2, 25; Dt 27:1; Josh 7:6; 23:2.
[3] Ex 24:1, 9, 14; Dt 5:23(20); 29:10(9); Josh 9:2 (8:33); 24:1; Lev 9:1, 3.
[4] Lev 4:15; Num 22:4; Josh 9:11; Judg 21:16; 8:14, 16; 11:5–11.

228

administration of covenant law.[5] In its memories of the nomadic days, Israel sees its elders as authority figures within the clans: dominated by the great captains of Yahweh, filled with their spirit,[6] yet already existing as a group and thus needing to be included as the people's traditional representatives. Before Moses was, elders are.

One of the first concerns of the monarchy was to compete successfully with the older tribal loyalties. Like the French revolutionaries two centuries ago and the new African heads of state two decades ago, Solomon attempted to edge aside the traditional local leadership by officials sent out from the new central regime.[7] But the elders endure as the ineradicable representatives of the cities, towns and villages.[8] When elders are found associated with the king, it may be to give him political assent,[9] or to surround him at a significant moment,[10] or to lend support to his adversaries,[11] or to serve as his emissaries.[12] But most typically elders have turned their wisdom to service as counselors.[13] That they remain a traditional power to be reckoned with is shown by the fact that the classical prophets appeal to them.[14]

Though these texts depict the elders of Israel and Judah in an idealized role, they are obviously written to draw upon a legitimating authority inherent in that office that had an abiding historical reality in the context in which those texts were later edited and published.

With the removal of the monarchy and its forceful centralizing pressure, elders re-emerge as the natural authorities at the local level. The events of reconstruction, which was national in scope but focused on Jerusalem, necessarily include elders in the cast.[15] Indeed, it is they who hold and exercise the authority to rebuild the temple. But later, especially in the Maccabean period, they are once again the policy-makers in the towns and villages[16] and, most prominently, in Jerusalem.[17] They have become the men of the Law.[18]

As the Second Temple period is drawing to a close, Jewish communities are still provided with a *gerousia* – a college of *presbyteroi*

[5] Dt 19:12; 21:2–6, 19; 22:15–18; Ruth 4:2–11.   [6] Num 11:16–30.   [7] 1 Kgs 4.

[8] 1 Sam 15:30; 16:4; 30:26; 1 Kgs 20(21):8, 11; 2 Kgs 10:1, 5.

[9] 2 Sam 3:17; 5:3; 19:12.   [10] 1 Ch 15:25; 21:16; 1 Kgs 8:1; 2 Kgs 23:1.

[11] 2 Kgs 6:32.   [12] 2 Kgs 19:2; Is 37:2.

[13] 2 Sam 12:17; 17:4, 15; 1 Kgs 12:6–24; 21(20):7, 8; 1 Chr 12:20; 2 Chr 10:6–13; 32:3; Ezk 7:26; Ps 104(105):22; 118(119):100.

[14] 2 Kgs 6:32; Is 3:14; Ezk 14:1; 20:1–3; Jo 1:2.   [15] Ezra 5:9; 6:7–14; 10:8, 14.

[16] Pr 31:23; Jdth 4:8; 11:14; 15:8.

[17] 1 Macc 7:33; 11:23; 12:6, 35; 13:36; 14:20, 28; 2 Macc 1:10; 4:44; 11:27; 13:13.

[18] Sir 38:33–34.

– that serves the community as its *boulê*. How large was such a group? There is evidence, both direct and indirect, that the college of elders in Jerusalem, also called the Sanhedrin, numbered seventy (plus the high priest who presided).[19] There is late evidence that the great synagogue building in Alexandria held seventy-one thrones for its elders and president.[20] Philo makes it a point that this was the number of elders assembled by Moses, thus strengthening the supposition that even in his time his city maintained a *gerousia* of seventy.[21] The Mishnah, with an eye to the same tradition, says that this number is required for major national policy decisions, such as the declaration of war.[22] The regional council convened by Josephus for the governance of Galilee was of the same size.[23]

Yet we also learn of councils of different sizes. Josephus states that the city of Tiberias had a council of 600 members.[24] The Mishnah prescribes 23 members as the proper *gerousia* for a town of 120 or more Jews.[25] A gentile settlement in Cyrenaica, plausibly organized similarly to those of Jews there, had 53 elders.[26] It may be that, with

---

[19] *1 Enoch* inveighs against seventy shepherds assigned by the Lord to his sheep, who slay and consume them instead. This is often read as a satire on the Jerusalem council, 90:20–27. In the last days of the temple after virtually all of the elders had been eliminated by the Zealots, they set up a mock trial for Zacharias, an uncooperative aristocrat, and dragooned seventy men to sit as judges: plausibly in imitation of the Sanhedrin, Josephus, *B.J.* 4:336.

[20] *Tosefta* (hereafter *T.*) *Sukkah*, 4:6; *T.B. Sukkah*, 5lb. On one occasion the prefect, in pursuit of the entire body, managed to find thirty-eight of them in their homes, Philo, *Flacc.* 74. At one point, in 12 AD, the Alexandrian Jewish community was upgraded by Augustus and, instead of continuing under the rule of a single ethnarch, it was put under a council of elders, which some have thought was appointed by the emperor or prefect, *Flacc.* 74. Even were that so (the text seems ambiguous) the Alexandrian situation is unusual. *Aristeas*, 310 and Josephus, *Ant.* 12:108 speak of the Alexandrian Jewish community = *politeuma* as having a *gerousia*. Surely neither that nor any other sizeable settlement of Jews during this period could have gotten on without a bench of elders, regardless of what civil recognition may have been given or withheld by their Roman rulers. Thus I would construe Augustus' action as an empowerment of a *gerousia* already in place. One might object that the Jewish community in Rome seems to have had no central body of elders, but the Jews there never seem to have formed, as far as we know, an over-arching *politeuma*. Each of the synagogues there, just as each of the synagogues in Alexandria (Philo says they were numerous and scattered throughout the city, *Leg.* 132) surely had its own bench of elders. In fact, one might say that because the Roman Jews apparently had no city-wide council, they did not think of themselves as one community. See Jean-Baptiste Frey, C.S.Sp., *Corpus Inscriptionum Iudaicarum : Receuil des inscriptions juives qui vont du IIIe siècle avant Jésus-Christ au VIIe siècle de notre ère* (Rome: Pontificio Istituto di Archeologia Cristiana, 1936–1952) (hereafter *CII*), 1:lxviiiff.   [21] Num 11:16; Philo, *Sob.* 19; *Mig.* 201.   [22] *M. Sanhedrin*, 1:6, 5.

[23] Josephus, *B.J.* 2:570–571; *Vita*, 79.   [24] Josephus, *B.J.* 2:641.

[25] *M. Sanhedrin*, 1:1, 6. For judgment of a capital crime a court of twenty-three was required. Charles Guignebert, *The Jewish World in the Time of Jesus*, trans. S. H. Hooke (New York: Dutton, 1939), 51–52, is sceptical of these figures in the Mishnah.

[26] Shimon Applebaum, "The Organization of the Jewish Communities in the Diaspora," in Samuel Safrai and Menahem Stern, eds., *The Jewish People in the First Century: Historical*

the exception of Jerusalem and certain other metropolitan communities, synagogues abided by no obligatory size for their rosters of elders. As we shall see, a shift in the status and role of elders may have made that not very important.

How were elders designated? There are many references in the literature to the procedure for accession to other Jewish offices. Priests succeeded by heredity. Scholars, at least soon after the period we are studying, were ordained by the senior sages. Many synagogue officers were chosen by election. But how one came to be an elder, a member of the synagogue council, we are not told. The stature of one's family seems to have counted for more than did a personal career record of shrewd judgment. Philo makes the point that age alone did not qualify one to be an elder, and many have taken this to be an apology for the system with which he was familiar: a system wherein social prestige was what hoisted a person into the office.[27]

We know that after the Hasmoneans assumed both the kingship and the high priesthood they saw to it that the Jerusalem *gerousia* was dominated by priests. In a later day the Pharisee scholars, particularly after the patronage of Queen Alexandra (76–67 BC), eventually gained a significant number of seats on the council. What this surely means is that the Jerusalem council, the most authoritative of them all, was reflective of the shifts of influence and affluence among the community.[28] The fact that Herod, who had no difficulty putting high priests out of office, exterminated the existing council upon his entry into Jerusalem as king, suggests that those men were the nobility, not short-term office-holders, and that they must have expected to enjoy that dignity throughout their lifetimes.[29]

Geography, Political History, Social, Cultural and Religious Life and Institutions (Assen: Van Gorcum, 1974), 1:467.   [27] Philo, *Mig. 201; Sob.* 7; *Abr.* 270, 274.
[28] "In talmudic literature the word *bouleutēs* (city councillor) is often synonymous with 'man of wealth'," Applebaum, "Economic Life in Palestine," in Safrai and Stern 2:663, n. 3.
[29] Josephus, *Ant.* 14:175; 15:5. Guignebert concludes: "The aristocratic character of the Sanhedrin makes it possible that its members did not change from year to year, and were not elected, but that they were co-opted for life…" 52, agreeing with Emil Schürer, *The History of the Jewish People in the Age of Jesus Christ*, revised English edn. by Geza Vermes, Fergus Millar, Matthew Black and Martin Goodman (hereafter Schürer, *History*²) (Edinburgh: T. & T. Clark, 1973–1987), 2:211. Safrai, "Jewish Self-Government," Safrai and Stern, 391, concurs, as does Tcherikover, *Corpus Papyrorum Judaicarum* (hereafter *CPJ*), ed. Victor A. Tcherikover, Alexander Fuks and Menahem Stern, (Cambridge: Harvard University Press, 1957–1964), 9–10. Frey believes that elders were elected each year by the assembly, but his conjecture rests on standard procedures in Greco-Roman associations, not on Jewish evidence, *CII* 1:lxxxv. Also, although the literature regularly teaches that sagacity and perspective equip a person for counsel only in later years, we see examples like Josephus himself, who was given high responsibility at the age of 30. Bloodlines counted. See Philo,

The known prerogatives of the councils of elders were extensive. They continued to honor their own public servants and their gentile patrons and benefactors.[30] They took action on behalf of the community: deciding on resistance or surrender in warfare;[31] sending or receiving embassies between the courts of the great rulers;[32] collecting and transmitting taxes;[33] electing judges and empaneling themselves to give judgment.[34] They were the interpreters of the Law, on matters such as sabbath regulations, calendar, priestly purity and prerogatives, and probate.[35] They still served as legitimating witnesses: for instance, when Herod announced the betrothals he had arranged for his grandchildren.[36]

There is much evidence that either *en banc* or in panels the elders continued to mete out justice. Local courts were imprisoning robbers,[37] and scourging violators of the law.[38] They also resolved civil disputes between members.[39] The court of Alexandria galvanized the local *ekklêsia* to eliminate the dangerous rebels who had come from Judaea.[40] When young Herod, as governor of Galilee, exterminated the brigands in his territory without holding trials or taking prisoners, he was haled before the high priest and the Sanhedrin, as was James, the brother of Jesus and chief of the church in Jerusalem, a century later, on quite other charges.[41]

In sum, the elders as a college were expected to be both statesmen and jurists: representatives of the people's interests to outsiders, while maintaining lawful discipline within the community.[42] To a considerable extent, the colleges of elders had long since taken from the plenary assemblies most decisions on public policy, save on those rare

---

Op. 103–105; *Exod.* 2:31; *Mig.* 201; *Sob.* 20; *Leg. All.* 3:191; *M. Avoth, 5:21; M. Kinnim,* 3:6; Josephus, *B.J.* 3:396.　　[30] Philo, *Leg.* 133; Lk 7:3.　　[31] Jdth 4:8.
[32] The Jerusalem council formally welcomed both Ptolemy IV Philopater (*3 Macc.* 1:8) and his arch-enemy Antiochos III the Great (Josephus, *Ant.* 12:138). It dispatched intercessory missions to Augustus (*B.J.* 2:80), to Lucius Vitellius and to Cestius Gallus, both legates in Syria (*Ant.* 18:88; *B.J.* 2:533). It held parley with Lucius Petronius, another legate (Philo, *Leg.* 229, 239). Their counterparts in Alexandria sent deputations to Caligula (*Leg.*) and probably to Trajan and to Hadrian (*CPJ*, nos. 157–158).　　[33] Josephus, *B.J.* 2:405.
[34] Sus 5, 41, 50.
[35] *M. Erubin,* 8:7; *M. Rosh Hashanah,* 2:5; Josephus, *Ant.* 20:216; *M. Middoth,* 5:4; *M. Kethuboth,* 13; *M. Peah,* 2:6; *M. Eduyoth,* 7:4.　　[36] Josephus, *B.J.* 1:556–559.
[37] Ibid. 2:273. It is not clear whether the councils here mentioned are Jewish.
[38] Mk 13:9; Mt 10:17–18; Lk 21:12; Mt 23:34; Lk 12:11; Ac 22:19. See chapter 6, note 97.
[39] Mt 5:21–26; Lk 12:57–59; 18:2.　　[40] Josephus, *B.J.* 7:412.
[41] Josephus, *Ant.* 14:168; *B.J.* 1:210; *Ant.* 20:200. Herod emerged, with the help of political pressure, unscathed. James was executed by stoning, but Ananus was later deposed from the high priesthood for having convened this capital trial in the procurator's absence.
[42] See Philo, *Jos.* 63, 76, 79; Josephus, *Ant.* 12:39, 49.

occasions when it seemed requisite to have a show of action by the fully assembled *ekklêsia*. The formal rights of the assembly remained, but except for religious assemblies and festal banquets, the gatherings of the entire community had gradually been replaced by gatherings of the elders. The residual popular prerogatives were still there, but they were held in abeyance. When an officer did convene the assembly, there was still enough potential power resident in the people there that it might rise up to proceed further than had been requested; hence a plausible reluctance among the elders to undergo that risk.

However, there is also much to suggest that by the latter part of the Second Temple period the elders also had yielded power. Naturally, they had always had to accommodate the sovereign. But apart from the Sanhedrin in Jerusalem, which had briefly shared sovereignty, this was nothing new. The shift of prerogative at this time was towards a new echelon of notables that emerged from within the *gerousia* and in some respects was due to overshadow it. The same process of centralization which had drawn authority upward from the assembly to the elders simply continued on, and lifted that authority higher still.

THE NOTABLES

As the presbyteral ranks became depleted in talent through re-cruitment by family succession instead of by merit, it is possible that a smaller group emerged and took to itself, in fact perhaps even before then in official right, the initiative in providing for the interests of the community. A ruler to whom a large body was assigned as official counselors would and perhaps did tend to select an inner group of the more agreeable or reliable voices. In other circumstances a traditional body like the *gerousia*, which seems not to have been restricted by a *numerus clausus*, might swell to an unwieldy size, and be persuaded to delegate much of its work to an executive committee.

Perhaps something of this sort occurred in the Jewish colleges of elders. By the time our period arrives, a new term is emerging to designate a select personage of the synagogue: *archôn*, which in this usage I would render as "notable."[43]

---

[43] The literature of hellenistic Judaism is replete with titles of influence that are difficult to differentiate. They seem generic, almost interchangeable: *archontes*, *prôtoi*, *prôteuontes*,

The book of Judith reports that, besides having a body of elders, Bethulia had three notables who, as a triad and also through their chief alone, convened the elders and presided.[44] They were themselves elders, and their chief served as spokesman for all the elders and for the town.[45] Here, in the literature of the mid-second century BC, we have a picture of a council of elders with an inner circle of leadership and initiative: notables.

Philo, who often refers to *archontes*, usually is designating authorities in general, as distinct from common folk.[46] However, he also uses the word as a title, to specify an officer different from an elder.[47] In this precise sense of notable he seems to include several public responsibilities,[48] but that he does have specific functions in mind is clear from his contempt for the custom in some regions of choosing them by lot rather than by election.[49]

Josephus also distinguishes notables from elders.[50] In his narratives, however, he tends to keep them apart from one another. Indeed, as a man of action and a romancer of men of action, he rather favored the notables. They tend, unlike priests or elders, to stand at the head of some enterprise rather than in choruses. When he assumed his Galilean command he chose seventy elders – seven from each city – as a coordinating force, and made them notables for all Galilee.[51] Here again one sees the smaller group extracted from the larger: notables as an elite among elders. Some have detected here an unguarded historical disclosure that whatever the traditional theory might have been, a village of moderate size in Josephus' time may have had a governing group of seven men. Elsewhere Josephus describes Moses chartering all cities with a complement of seven rulers, and describing them as the ordinary bench of judges in a civil case.[52] Since neither provision appears to have existed in biblical or

---

hêgoumenoi, hêgemones, proêgoumenoi, dynatoi, dynatôtatoi, megistanes, epimelêtes, stratêgoi, gnôrimi, episkopoi, hoi en telei, epistatai, prostatai, etc. The terms are often used, without reference to any specific office, to denote prominent persons in an upper echelon of influence. In the matter under discussion here, one of these terms emerged as a technical title for an office in the synagogue.   [44] Jdth 6:14–15; 7:23; 6:16, 21; 8:9.

[45] Ibid. 8:10; 7:30; 8:28; 13:18ff; 14:6; 15:4.

[46] Philo, *Post.* 98; *Spec. Leg.* 1:121, 226, 307; 2:226–227; 3:183; 4:184; *Mos.* 2:235; *Praem.* 97; *Flacc.* 117.   [47] Philo, *Det.* 134; *Mig.* 116; *Mos.* 4:214; *Flacc.* 76, 80; *Leg.* 5.

[48] Philo, *Spec. Leg.* 4:21.   [49] Ibid. 151–157.

[50] Josephus, *Ant.* 4:186; 7:28, 78. For Josephus, *hêgemones* and *archontes* are equivalents; see, for instance, *Ant.* 7:276–278; 341–342.   [51] Josephus, *B.J.* 2:570–571; *Vita*, 79.

[52] Josephus, *Ant.* 4:214; *Archetôsan de kath hekastên polin andres hepta* ... See also 4:287. Some scholars see traces of a ten-ruler norm: Stern, "The Province of Judaea," in Safrai and

other documentary sources, it has seemed to some that Josephus was drawing on the custom familiar to him.[53]

Jewish inscriptions regularly denominate both elders and notables. In Rome, while many burial inscriptions identify the incumbent as a notable, only a single stone honors an elder, despite the fact that we know the synagogues there had colleges of elders.[54] Berenice in Cyrenaica had a Jewish community that memorialized only notables as its leaders, without any reference to elders. If the latter exist, they are not assigned prominence in the direction of the synagogue.[55] In Alexandria we learn of both elders and notables from *Aristeas* and from Philo,[56] and a combination of evidence tells us that the Jewish community in Antioch harbored both sorts of dignitary.[57] Jerusalem too is reported to have had both notables and elders.[58] The same distinction is memorialized in Pamphylia.[59] Inscriptions of this period, latinizing *presbyteroi* into *seniores/maiores* and *archontes* into *primates*, seem to reflect the continuing distinction.[60] Curiously, notables are missing from the Mishnah. A Christian document written a while afterward states explicitly, however, that the Jews in Antioch elected their notables annually at Sukkoth in the month of Tishri, the first of the Jewish year.[61]

All of this goes far to verify that from within the traditional council of elders had emerged a category of executive committeemen called *archontes*. This was no longer a generic title encompassing all

Stern, 1:345; Charles Guignebert, *The Jewish World in the Time of Jesus*, trans. S. H. Hooke (New York: Dutton, 1939), 53. Such a ten-man group may be reflected in Eccl 7:19 (third century BC).

[53] Thus Schürer, *History*², 2:187; Safrai, "Jewish Self-Government," 379; Safrai, "The Synagogue," 933. There are also late, talmudic references to seven councilors in a city: *P.T. Megillah*, 3:74a; *T.B. Megillah*, 26a–b.

[54] See Frey, *CII*, 1:lxxxvii – lxxxviii; also no. 378.

[55] *Corpus Inscriptionum Graecarum* (hereafter *CIG*), nos. 5361–5362a/b. See Jeanne and Georges Roux, "Un décret du politeuma des juifs de Bérénikè en Cyrénaïque au musée lapidaire de Carpentras," *Revue des Etudes Grecques*, 62 (1949), 281–296. Also Schürer, *History*², 3:94; Applebaum, "Organization" 486–487.

[56] *CPJ*, p. 9, n. 24; Philo, *Flacc.* 74, 80, 117.

[57] Josephus, *B.J.* 7:47; M. Schwabe, "Greek Inscriptions found at Beth She'arim in the Fifth Excavation Season," *Israel Exploration Journal*, 4 (1954), 252–253. [58] Ac 4:5.

[59] Louis Robert, "Inscriptions grecques de Sidè en Pamphylie," *Revue de Philologie*, 32 (1958), 36ff.

[60] See Hans Lietzmann, "Zur altchristlichen Verfassungsgeschichte," *Zeitschrift für wissenschaftlichen Theologie*, 55 (1914), 130–132. I would think that *CII*, no. 681 belongs to a notable.

[61] Pseudo-Chrysostom (thought to be Pontius Maximus), "De Nativitate Sancti Joannis Baptistae," in *CII*, 1:lxxxvii; Schürer, *History*², 3:99.

influential persons in the community.[62] Notables are distinctly identified. It is possible that the chief officers were also notables,[63] but they need not have been. Whether or not the synagogues took their cue from the well-established hellenistic system, in both government and private associations, of electing *archontes* annually, the fact that some Jewish notables were honored in their epitaphs as having served twice or thrice strengthens the inference that they were elected for a term, though whether by the *ekklêsia* or by the *gerousia* we could not tell. If it was of note that a notable served several terms we may take it that there was some real turnover in the board of notables, more perhaps than in the *gerousia*. Some inscriptions identify notables who served "for life." Was this because they had a satisfied clientele, or because even this more merit-oriented position failed to escape entirely the influence of aristocracy? There were some who already carried this title of *archôn* when they died as children, and other youngsters who died as "notables-designate" (these latter usually were the children of synagogue notables), an indication that there may have been "seats" on those benches traditionally occupied by representatives of certain principal families.[64]

There has been some puzzlement about several epitaphs inscribed with the definite article: "N. the notable." One opinion is that synagogues may have had a single officer with this title at one time. More likely, however, the Jews may have used the title for the first-ranking member of a board of notables.[65]

---

[62] The New Testament, however, which is not always precise about official Jewish nomenclature (especially Luke-Acts), does use *archontes* sometimes in the generic sense of "notables, authorities": Mk 10:41–45 and parallels; Mt 5:25; Lk 18:18; 23:13, 35; 24:20; Ac 3:17; 4:5; 13:27; J 3:1; 7:26; 12:42; 1 Cor 2:8. In the same generic sense *prôtoi* designates public leaders of indeterminate office: Ac 13:50; 25:2; 28:17. Likewise *hêgemones* and *hêgoumenoi*, Mk 13:9.   [63] *CII*, nos. 265, 347, 553.

[64] Ibid. lxxxviii – lxxxix; Schürer, *Die Gemeindeverfassung der Juden in Rom in der Kaiserzeit nach den Inschriften dargestellt* (Leipzig: Heinrichs, 1879), 19–25; Harry J. Leon, *The Jews of Ancient Rome* (Philadelphia: Jewish Publication Society, 1960), 173–179; Lietzmann, 116; Jean Juster, *Les juifs dans l'empire romain : leur condition juridique, économique et sociale* (New York: Burt Franklin, photocopy of 1914 edition), 1:443–447. In his conjectures about notables, Frey relies overmuch on the supposed conformity of synagogue structures to those of hellenistic associations, but there is evidence enough without that to inform us of their existence and basic role. See his "Les communautés juives à Rome aux premiers temps de l'église," *Recherches de Science Religieuse*, 20 (1930), 269–297; 21 (1931), 129–168.

[65] Thus in Jdth 8:9 Uzziah, who is the principal among three notables, is called "the notable." Philo notes that in Athens, where ten notables served the city at one time, the first among them, whose name is used to tag their year in office, is simply called *ho archôn*, *Abr.* 10. In the fourth century a gentile well informed in matters Jewish refers to the Patriarch Gamaliel ben Jehuda as the notable of the notables, *ton tôn archontôn archonta*: Menahem Stern, ed., *Greek*

The picture as it emerges is of a community wherein authority has moved progressively upward. The community assembles frequently, but most often to be exposed to the ancient scriptures. The community welfare would periodically be matter for discussion, yet the elders would now be cautious about allowing such open discussion to move too near anything like a synagogal free-for-all. There was always the possibility of a formal assembly to take some solemn step, but most Jews may have heard of such gatherings more often in the sacred books than they could remember from their own experience.

The council of elders had assumed responsibility for the community welfare. Since the elders tended to be those who were socially more prominent, their policies might tend towards conservatism. Yet since these were men who had had to maintain influence within the larger community they were perhaps more at their ease in compromise and adaptation within the public culture.

Yet a third group had now succeeded in taking to itself a position of effective governance. While on the level of theory, courtesy and formality effective deference belonged to the assembly and then to the elders and lastly to their agents the notables, on the practical level it had probably reversed. The *archontes*, who might be disposed to regard the community as unable to understand many issues, and might think the elders as loath to decide some matters because of self-interest, had emerged as the ones able to prompt their fellow Jews to adopt their initiatives. Sometimes they would simply go forward themselves without ratification, for the community had already acquiesced in letting them act in its name.[66]

THE SENIOR ELDER

With this idea, then, of the synagogue community, its various echelons of policy-making authority, its program and its physical plant and real estate, let us learn what we can about its various officers. The first personage of the synagogue is the *gerousiarchēs*. Scholars are virtually unanimous in identifying this official as president of the *gerousia* = council of elders of each community.[67]

and Latin Authors on Jews and Judaism (Jerusalem: Israel Academy of Sciences and Humanities, 1974–1980), 2, no. 504.

[66] For example, in the first centuries BC and AD the Jewish community in Berenice in Cyrenaica awarded public honors to benefactors on the vote of its college of notables, without reference to either elders or assembly: *CIG*, 5361–5362a-b.

[67] Schürer, *History*[2], 3:98–100; Frey, *CII*, 1:lxxxv; Guignebert, 217; Juster, 1:442; Leon, 181–183; Applebaum, "Organization," 493; Baruch Lifschitz, "Fonctions et titres

Some report that he ranked second among all officers, though they are not in agreement about who ranked first.[68] In any case, it would be a position of high and unique dignity.

But is this widely accepted thesis reliable? If there were a president of the council of elders, why is that position unmentioned in the Bible, the apocrypha, Philo, Josephus, the papyri and the Mishnah? Also, since the evidence shows rather clearly that it was another officer, the community chief, who was the executive and the public representative of a Jewish community, would this not have created a basic tension, even struggle, between two officers whose titles both implied primacy?

The existence of this office is attested by numerous inscriptions: sixteen from Rome, one from near Ostia, one from near Pozzuoli, two from Venosa in Apulia, one from Marani near Naples, one from Beth She'arim in Galilee (the epitaph of an Antiochene), one from Tiberias and one from Apamea in Syria.[69] That the title existed, and existed widely, is undeniable. There are, however, several other possible explanations of the role that harmonize more easily with the evidence.

The evidence, as we say, is virtually all epigraphical. We have no documents that describe a *gerousiarchés* at work. It is clearly a title of honor, since gravestones like to mention that the deceased is related to such a personage. And inscriptions several times make much of the fact that the deceased, a *gerousiarchés*, was kind to others, respected and loved widely, a friend to all.

There are two more plausible construals of this title. One would see him as the seniormost among the elders. By this period the elders themselves were being transformed gradually from functionaries into dignitaries.[70] We know that deference to seniority was natural and well known at this time. Ananus, who played a prominent role in Jerusalem during the revolt, is described by Josephus as "the eldest

honorifiques dans les communautés juives: Notes d'épigraphie palestinienne," *Revue Biblique*, 67 (1970), 59; Schwabe, "Greek Inscriptions," 252–253.

[68] Leon says the *archisynagógos*; Frey, the *patêr synagógês*.

[69] *CII*, nos. 9, 95, 106, 119, 147, 189(?), 301, 353, 355 (disputed by Leon), 368, 405, 408, 425, 504, 511, 733b, 533, 561, 600, 613; *Corpus Inscriptionum Latinarum*, 10:1893; Jeanne and Louis Robert, "Bulletin épigraphique," *Revue des Etudes Grecques* (hereafter *BE*), 1959, no. 730; Lifschitz, 59; *CII*, no. 803.

[70] This distinction for elders is well made by Pierre Benoit, O.P., "Les origines apostoliques de l'épiscopat selon le Nouveau Testament," in *L'évêque dans l'église du Christ*, ed. Humbert Bouëssé (Bruges: Desclée de Brouwer, 1963), 25.

among the high priests."[71] Among the Therapeutae it was the senior elder who was central in the community's honor.[72] And in the temple priesthood notice was taken of the dean, the eldest among the priests.[73]

One of the few facts we do know about the *gerousiarchês* is that those whose age is known from their epitaphs include no young men, as contrasted with the notables and the elders. Three died at ages 54, 65 and 80. Several others left grown children to mourn them. It is more plausible that this specifically Jewish office (though there were hellenistic *gerousiai* we know of no gentile *gerousiarchês*) was one of deference, not of presidency.

This would help us interpret a single epitaph on an *archigerousiarchês* in Rome.[74] In a city with a goodly number of Jewish synagogue communities, this old man would have enjoyed the seniority to outrank all the elders put together.

As initiative and power rose, by a sort of capillary action, from the elders to the notables, it is not easy to believe that the latter would have left in existence an office which had the prerogative of convening the council of elders, with its ancient and traditional dignity, an office which would always stand as a threat to the solidarity of the community. The evidence allows us to suppose that one officer alone presided, and that it was the community chief, who continued nevertheless in matters of courtesy to defer to the one who most embodied what elders were supposed to represent. Should any community fall upon difficult days of internal dissent or contest between the various forces there, one infers that the dignity of the dean, or senior elder, might then have strategic importance and allow him to intervene in a more activist mode than usual.

A second interpretation of the *gerousiarchês* grows out of the fact that there was a general custom of referring to this personage without the definite article. Thus one was typically "a" rather than "the" *gerousiarchês*. The title might signify, therefore, not an officer or a seniormost member, but a leading elder. The component -*arch*-, when

---

[71] Josephus, *B.J.* 4:151: *ho geraitatos tôn archierôn*. He describes Jeshuah as "oldest next after Ananus," 4:238.   [72] Philo, *Vit. Cont.* 31.

[73] *M. Taanith*, 2:1. One might see a parallel in the *av beit din* = the dean of the court whom the Mishnah regularly ranks right after the high priest (as distinct from the *segan ha-kohanim* = prefect of the priests who served as temple adjutant). The dean was a dignitary who enjoyed seniority and honor; he was not a functionary. In the rabbinical period this title continued on to designate the dean of the sages, ranking next to the *nasi* = patriarch.

[74] G[eorge] H. R. Horsley, ed., *New Documents Illustrating Early Christianity, 1976* (North Ryde, NSW: Macquarie University, 1981), 73.

used as a prefix or a suffix, sometimes means the chief X and sometimes means a leading X. Thus the *stratopedarchês* is a camp commander and the *architriklinos* is a head waiter and the *archilêstês* is the robber chieftain; yet the *politarchês* is a political official, but not always one in a specific position, and an *archiereus* might be the high priest but might instead be a member of a prominent priestly family. In this sense of the title, the *gerousiarchês* = senior elder would be a personage, but not an officer of the synagogue. While the evidence is too laconic to decide which of these senses is the more likely, or indeed whether either of them is correct, it does seem clear enough to show that the senior elder was not an officer, or that if he was, there is no way of knowing what function he had, since the role of the *archisynagôgos* is unambiguously presidential.

THE COMMUNITY CHIEF

The common understanding of the *archisynagôgos* = community chief may also deserve some review. Emil Schürer, one of the great historians of early Jewish community life, has had the most influential say in the matter. Our most plentiful source of information on this office comes from inscriptions, and Schürer was the first to use this source systematically to study the structure and organization of synagogues.[75] Once he had decided that the *gerousiarchês* was the presiding officer of the elders, he concluded that this would establish him as president of the synagogue in its entirety. He then had to find some other *raison d'être* for the *archisynagôgos*. This officer, he opined, "had accordingly nothing whatever to do with the direction of the congregation in general. Instead, his special responsibility was to attend to public worship. He is called *archisynagogus* not as chief of the congregation, but as leader of its meetings for worship."[76]

Jean-Baptiste Frey, who set out to collect and publish all known inscriptions relating to Jews, accepted Schürer's thesis and reinforced it. When Frey lists the officers of administration of the Jewish community, the *archisynagôgos* is not even mentioned. He then creates a second level, those who deal only with religious services, and lists him there. His reason is that the title is very familiar in Greco-Roman associations, and in that context it identifies the officer responsible for religious ceremonies. "It is not from *synagôgê*, meaning 'community'

---

[75] Leon, 168.　　　　[76] Schürer, *History* 2, 2:435; 3:100.

that the *archisynagôgos* derives his title, but from its other meaning: 'gathering'. He is not at all 'the spiritual leader of a community of believers'; he merely presides over its religious assemblies."[77] That, he concludes, is also the role that this title identifies in Jewish communities. As distinct from those who form what one might call the civil administration, he describes "those who form what one might call the Jewish clergy... The administration is lay... and its competence extends to religious questions as well as to civil, financial and judicial matters. The 'clergy', by contrast, is firmly kept, one might say, in the sacristy. The archisynagogue is the religious master of ceremonies: his responsibilities are purely liturgical and operate within the synagogue. He has, in virtue of this office, no part in administration, and no teaching function."[78]

Actually, the evidence for this assumption is not primarily epigraphical. Frey notes that the inscriptions tell little if anything about the office. He argues, firstly, by assuming that the *gerousiarchês* must be the community president. Then, secondly, he draws an analogy from the gentile use of the title, which was liturgical. Thirdly he notes that in modern usage the rabbi of a synagogue is engaged for its cultic activities by a lay board.[79] Schürer had raised one further argument: that in the New Testament we see this officer in a liturgical context. In Luke, when Jesus heals a crippled woman in a synagogue, the *archisynagôgos* is indignant because it is a breach of the sabbath.[80] Acts recounts that at Antioch in Pisidia Paul and his fellow visitors were invited at sabbath service, by the *archisynagôgos*, to speak after the readings.[81]

The common view has supposed that this officer would have been elected: annually, because that was the custom in Greco-Roman associations. And this reconstruction, established nearly a century ago, has been accepted by virtually all scholars since then.[82] It is now time to give the evidence a review.

[77] Frey, *CII*, 1:xcvii. He is opposing Théodore Reinach. [78] Ibid. ci.
[79] Frey notes with approval a recent Fascist decree (he was writing in Rome in 1930) which favored lay dominance over the rabbinate, ibid. n. 7. [80] Lk 13:14.
[81] Ac 13:15. Schürer also notes that later rabbinical commentary gives this officer the task of orchestrating the scripture readings. Actually, Acts uses an extraordinary plural: *hoi archisynagôgoi*. Like the category of high priest, possibly this had become a title that applied to both present and past incumbents; see n. 174 below.
[82] Thus, for example, Guignebert, 218; Juster, 1:450; George Foot Moore, *Judaism in the First Centuries of the Christian Era: The Age of the Tannaim* (Cambridge: Harvard University Press, 1927), 1:289; Leon, 171. Applebaum, however, has some reservations about the prevailing interpretation, "Organization," 492.

The inscriptions show us that the office existed throughout Jewry. We find mention of it in Jerusalem and Caesarea in Judaea, in the Fayum and Lower Egypt, in Antioch, Apamea, Beirut, Tyre and Sidon in Syria, in Phrygia and Lycia and Caria, in Ephesus, Ionia and Aegina on the Aegean, in Corinth in Achaia, in Lower Moesia, in Brescia, Venosa, Capua, Porto and Rome in Italy.[83] First off one notices that amid so many instances, no single incumbent is said to have served "twice" or "thrice" in office. It is extremely unlikely then that it was filled by annual or frequent election. One *archisynagōgos* gives notice that he was in office four years and rebuilt the entire plant, which he had found in dilapidated condition. The time span appears to be mentioned, however, not as a term of office so much as evidence of rapid accomplishment from the very beginning of his service.[84] Several are presented as "lifetime" incumbents. Scholars have taken this to be an honorific title, but one might be more specific and see it as the title of an *archisynagōgos* who had retired: *emeritus*.[85] There are several instances recorded of the office having passed on from father to son, and even to grandson, suggesting that this could become a family profession.[86]

In several inscriptions we learn that an *archisynagōgos* has been responsible for significant building improvements, either as a donor

---

[83] *CII*, nos. 1404, 1414 (Jerusalem); Lifschitz, "Fonctions et titres," 58–59 (Caesarea); *CII*, nos. 803, 804 (Apamea and Antioch in Syria); Lifschitz, ibid. (Beirut); *CII*, nos. 991 (Tyre and Sidon); 1531 (Fayum; if, as Frey supposes, *hêgemôn* is here to be taken as a surrogate title); 1441 (Xenephris in Lower Egypt: *prostantes*, another synonym); 766 (Acmonia in Phrygia); 759 (Synnada in Lycia); 756 (Myndos in Caria); 741, 744 (Smyrna and Teos in Ionia); 722 (Aegina); 681 (Oescus in Lower Moesia); 100 (*prostatês*, another synonym), 265, 282, 336, 365, 383, 504 (Rome); 548 (Porto); 553 (Capua); 584, 587, 596 (Venosa in Apulia); 638 (Brescia). Robert, *BE* 1980, no. 230 (Corinth); 1981, no. 428 (Ephesus). A few of these, which are all difficult to date, may be too late to shed light on the Second Temple period. But even with that cautionary note, one sees here the synagogue functionary most often attested in the inscriptions.

[84] *CII*, no. 722. See Horsley, *New Documents, 1979* (1987), 113.

[85] *CII*, nos. 744, 766. The latter inscription, from Acmonia, mentions two *archisynagōgoi*, thus making it plausible that the one who is *dia biou* is emeritus, while the other is his successor in office. Ages on epitaphs are 72, 53, 70, 50.

[86] *CII*, nos. 584, 1404. One *archisynagōgos* has a son who went on to become a *gerousiarchês* = senior elder, no. 504. The one infant *archisynagōgos* in the record might be understood as the scion of a family that had made of this work a profession, if not a sinecure: not as a youngster of three years who had already been designated for future office, *CII*, no. 587. The coexistence of several *archisynagōgoi* could be explained by a plurality of synagogues in a town or city (thus Mark 5:22), or the presence of both active and retired together (Acts 13:15; *CII*, nos. 803, 1441), in the same way that one then referred to "the high priests" in Jerusalem. We do not encounter senior elders side by side in the same way because that is, by definition, an honor from which one does not retire (unless one accepts Frey's reconstruction of no. 533).

or as the community executive or as both.[87] That would seem to bring this officer well out of the sacristy. If one imagined synagogue buildings to be exclusively dedicated to scripture reading and prayer, then a merely religious functionary might be given responsibility for the upkeep of the fabric. But as we have seen, they were multipurpose community centers. Neither the synagogue as a community nor the synagogue as a physical plant can legitimately be bisected into "religious" and "civil" components, to suit a perspective that would only have bewildered the Jews of this period. And if the *archisynagôgos* had his hand that far into the treasury, he was no minor functionary.

Turning to the New Testament evidence one encounters this title five times. Jairus, *archisynagôgos* in one of the villages or towns on the western shore of the sea of Galilee, has his daughter restored to life by Jesus.[88] The narrative does not allow us to infer anything about his role. The official noticed by Schürer is indeed presiding at sabbath services; we cannot tell how much farther, if at all, his responsibilities would go, as is the case with the one who invites Paul to speak.[89] But several narratives in Acts are helpful. Paul's preaching at sabbath services in the synagogues of Corinth provoked great resentment which was only intensified when one *archisynagôgos*, Crispus, went over to the Christians with his household. Later, when the proconsul snubbed an angry Jewish delegation because their complaints about Paul dealt with matters he thought they should settle among themselves (here too one sees how outsiders fail to grasp the Jewish view in which all matters are integrated), they fell to beating Sosthenes, (possibly the successor) *archisynagôgos* of the community, after leaving the judgment hall. We cannot know whether it was because he was their spokesman and had put the case too timidly, or whether he too was thought attracted to the dissidents. But it is clear that the two men were of strategic importance to the communities they served.[90]

This office is not mentioned by Philo or by Josephus, though it is possible that *archisynagôgoi* may have been included among the elders and notables that Josephus was always presenting in clusters, for the incumbent of this office could be, and perhaps was, simultaneously an elder and also a notable.[91]

---

[87] *CII*, nos. 548, 722, 744, 766, 803, 1404, 1531.

[88] Mk 5:21–43; Matthew's version omits Jairus' name, and calls him an *archôn* = notable, 9:18–26; Luke uses both titles, 8:40–56.   [89] Lk 13:14; Ac 13:15.

[90] Ac 18:1–17. In 1 Cor 1:1 Paul later writes with "brother Sosthenes," but there is no clue whether this be he of the bruises.   [91] *CII*, nos. 265, 553, 681(?).

The early Mishnah material knows this officer as the *rosh ha-keneset*.[92] The later talmudic materials would transmogrify the title into *rabbi*, but only after a thorough redefinition of the office had occurred in the wake of the destruction of the commonwealth.[93] Traditions change only with inertia, however. In the early second century Hadrian (117–138), who is somewhat familiar with the nomenclature of elders in the newer Christian movement, knows but two officers of the Jewish community: the patriarch, and synagogue chiefs.[94] And more than a century after that, easterners who held Alexander Severus (222–235) in contempt for his favoritism towards Jews used to call him, by way of insult, a high priest and a synagogue chief.[95]

What emerges from the evidence is an enduring perception from within the Jewish people that this officer, the *archisynagōgos*, was not simply a master of religious ceremonies. He was the executive of the local community, acting under the formal oversight of the elders but the more active superintendence of the notables. He presided over the community, he convened it for its activities, he superintended its staff. It was a position of some permanency, and one in which fathers might hope to see their sons succeed them. The community chief was, if not the most prestigious member of his community socially, the one who worked, often professionally, as the man at the forefront of his people. As broad as were the interest and the programs and services of his community, so broadly reached the breadth of his responsibility. If he presided at worship, it was because he presided at all community functions.

FEMININE TITLES OF OFFICE

Some who know the records well may wince at the gender-exclusive terminology employed thus far. For the sources reveal references to various dignitaries and officers of synagogue communities in the feminine gender. We read, apparently, of female elders and com-

---

[92] *M. Yoma*, 7:1; *M. Sotah*, 7:7–8.

[93] A Greek synonym for *rabbi*, *didaskalos* = teacher, also serves in the transition, *CII*, nos. 1266, 1269, 1414.

[94] Théodore Reinach, *Textes d'auteurs grecs et romains relatifs au judaïsme* (Hildesheim: Georg Olms, 1963 photocopy of 1895 edition), no. 182.

[95] *Scriptores Historiae Augustae*, "Alexander Severus," 28:2; in Stern, *Greek and Latin Authors*, 2, no. 521.

munity chiefs.[96] Also present are several references to mothers of synagogues, but these must be considered separately. As regards all the rest, the record is silent about any public leadership exercised by women. Indeed, it is with some wonderment that Philo describes how the Therapeutae admit women into their sabbath assemblies, though they come only to listen, not to speak, and are situated behind a high partition.[97]

Females had a presence in many of the synagogue activities, but we can find no support for the supposition that they acted as officers. What these feminine titles seem to denote is that the women are married to men in those positions, and theirs is a consortial form of dignity.[98] This may be seen even more clearly in certain titles which are or are not feminized. There was absolutely no participation by females in the Jewish priesthood, yet there are epitaphs of Jewish

---

[96] Feminine elders: *CII*, nos. 581, 590, 597 (*presbiterēs*; all from Venosa in Apulia), *Corpus of Jewish Inscriptions*, ed. Baruch Lifschitz (New York: Ktav, 1975) (hereafter *CII²*; this is a slightly edited photocopy of the Frey original, but with a prolegomenon in which the editor adds some entries), nos. 692 and 731c (*presbytera*; Thrace and Cisamus); Robert, *BE* 1982, no. 493 (*presbeteressa*; Tripoli in Africa) (also *SEG* 27 [1977], 1201); A. Ferrua, S.J., "Antichità cristiane: Le catacombe di Malta," *Civiltà Cattolica*, 100, 3 (1949), 505–515 at 513 (see also Ross S. Kraemer, "A New Inscription from Malta and the Question of Women Elders in the Diaspora Jewish Communities," *Harvard Theological Review*, 78, 1–2 (January–April 1985), 431–438).

Feminine community chiefs: *CII²*, no. 731c (*archisynagōgissa*, from Cisamus in Crete), *CII*, nos. 741 (*archisynagōgos*, from Smyrna in Ionia), 756 (orthography conjectured, from Myndos in Caria). Louis Robert, "Inscriptions Gréco-Juives," *Hellenica*, 1 (1940), 25–27, would also see *archēgissa*, *CII²*, no. 696b (from Thebes in Achaia/Thessaly), as designating a community chief's wife, because it is the feminine form of *archēgos* which, because it is the equivalent of the Latin *principalis*, is the feminine form of *archēgos* which, because it is the equivalent of the Latin *principalis*, he identifies as chief. However, he relies upon an inscription in Moesia, *arcisinagogos et principalis* (*CII*, no. 681); if the two titles are distinct, and not synonymous, I would take the latter to be an alternate title for *archōn*, and *archēgissa* to be a notable's wife. [97] Philo, *Vit. Cont.* 32.

[98] Thus also Frey, *CII*, lxxxvi, n. 2 and Samuel Krauss, *Synagogale Altertümer* (Berlin: Harts, 1922), 144. Bernadette J. Brooten, *Women Leaders in the Ancient Synagogue: Inscriptional Evidence and Background Issues* (Chico, CA: Scholars Press, 1982), in the absence of evidence that these women were not functioning officers, concludes that they must be accepted as such (including female priests). All other intepretations, she writes, are guided by a bias which does not wish to see women as synagogue officers. Shaye J. D. Cohen, "Women in Synagogues of Antiquity," *Conservative Judaism*, 34, 2 (1980), 23–29, reaches a similar conclusion. Their construal of the evidence seems to take little account of the patterned exclusion of women from the public domain in mishnaic culture. Brooten expects that nomenclature referring to females be interpreted similarly to when it refers to males. This ignores much of what we already know about the culture, however. How is it likely in a culture where women were legally forbidden to be counted as members of the worship fellowship, to study Torah, to join in the communal recitation of grace (and by many rabbis, to read Torah in public), that women could have been officers of the community's public affairs? See Judith Romney Wegner, "Woman and the Public Domain," *Chattel or Person? The Status of Women in the Mishnah* (New York: Oxford University Press, 1988), 145–167.

priests in the feminine.[99] On the other hand, we do not find memorials to scribes or assistants in that gender. This is probably because it is not the function as held by a woman that authorizes these titles, but the honored status of the husband. Scribes and assistants do not rank quite high enough for this sort of honor to be shed upon their partners.

Some years later one encounters records of Christian *episcopae* and *episcopissae*, who are bishops' wives.[100] Similarly, many spouses of the nobility in various countries will through marriage acquire a corresponding courtesy title. Paradoxically, the more inaccessible a title and office was to a woman as incumbent, the more attractive it was to adopt its title as a consort. And the more it correlated with family tradition rather than personal skill, the more it would provide a title by which families would care to be known. I would regard this as a possible key to understanding the various child-titles found in these records. Thus, a "child-notable" would not be a three-year-old already designated for office in later life, but would be "the notable's son," much as a squire's tenants would have addressed his son as the "young master."

THE ASSISTANT

If anyone were to qualify as Frey's *le sacristain* in the synagogue it would be the assistant. Some of the memories of shrine and temple worship among the Hebrews note that men of the tribe of Levi served its worship activities under the priests, who were the elite of their tribe.[101] In the period we are studying, those assistants were remembered by different names. Philo wrote of "those of the second order, the temple assistants = *neôkoroi.*"[102] Josephus uses the

---

[99] *CII*, nos. 315 (*hierissa*, Rome), 1007 (*hiéreia*, Beit She'arim in Galilee), 1514 (*hierisa*, Leontopolis in Egypt). There are feminine titles, such as *prophêtis* (Lk 2:36), which are to be taken in the proper, not consortial, sense, but these are not titles of office.

[100] Also, a Christian *hierissa* is a priest's wife; Robert, *BE* 1971, no. 695 (near Jaffa). For a later survival of this usage of *presbytera* and *episcopa* see Brian Brennan, "'Episcopae': Bishops' Wives Viewed in Sixth-Century Gaul," *Church History*, 54 (1985), 311–323.

[101] Num 1:48–54; 3:5–13; 8:20–26; 18:20–32; 35:1–8; Dt 18:1–8; 1 Ch 23–26. The role of Levites as a second-level staff of the temple may be true only of the Second Temple, as a result of the Josian reform and/or the Ezra settlement. Earlier texts give the Levites a non-subordinated role in connection with shrines. See Roland de Vaux, *Ancient Israel: Its Life and Institutions*, trans. John McHugh, 2nd edn. (London: Darton, Longman & Todd, 1965), 364–366. This translates *Les institutions de l'Ancien Testament* (Paris: Cerf, 1958).

[102] Philo, *Spec. Leg.* 1:156; see also *Mos.* 2:276. Philo saw many social entities ranked in orders: *Leg.* 74, 328.

same title as well as a synonym, *hypêretês*.[103] The early rabbinical literature knows them by their Hebrew title, *hazan*.[104]

At the close of the third century BC Antiochus III the Great ordered that two thousand Jewish families then resident in Mesopotamia be sent to resettle in Phrygia, a subject kingdom which was then restive. He instructed his satrap in Phrygia to provide public food rations "to those engaged in the public service," an expression that designated the Levites who then continued to provide for public worship, not only in the temple, but also in the local communities.[105] The rebuilt temple and its services were quite remote from the lives of these deportees, most of whom had probably never seen Jerusalem, but the characterizing word in the imperial rescript is the verbal cognate form of *hypêretês*, and may indicate to us that the Levites, whose duties had been largely ritual, were at this time being replaced by the newer *hazanim*, who earned their bread by a fuller program of community service.[106] Even in the Second Temple period Josephus noted that Moses wished every Jewish settlement to have two *hypêretai*, and that they were of the tribe of Levi.[107] The evidence suggests that all but perhaps the smallest synagogue communities had at least one *hazan* to assist the community chief.

Under the superintendence of the community chiefs they would serve as masters of ceremonies at scripture readings.[108] In judicial proceedings they would serve as officers of the court, summoning those under accusation and scourging those under sentence.[109] They

---

[103] Josephus, *B.J.* 1:153; 2:321. Philo, in his turn, may also have known this title as synonymous, *Sac.* 132. In late Second Temple days the high priest had at his disposition a prefect = *segan* = *stratêgos* responsible for public order in the temple, aided by subordinate *stratêgoi* and troops of temple gendarmes = *hypêretai*. Though they were primarily temple police, the high priest's role as president of the Sanhedrin put them indirectly at the disposal of this body, with power of physical arrest, detention and punishment: Mk 12:12 and parallels; 14:1 and parallels, 43, 65; Mt 27:62; 28:11–12; Lk 22:4, 52; J 7:32, 45–46; 18:3; 12:22; 19:6; Ac 4:1; 5:17–26, 40; 6:12; 23:2.
[104] *M. Succah*, 4:4; *M. Tamid*, 5:3.
[105] Josephus, *Ant.* 12:152: *tois eis tas chreias hypêretousi*. Abraham Schalit has identified these functionaries as Levites: "The Letter of Antiochus III to Zeuxis Regarding the Establishment of Jewish Military Colonies in Phrygia and Lydia," *Jewish Quarterly Review*, n.s. 50 (1959/1960), 289–318, esp. 310–316.
[106] An even larger role by Levites in the creation of synagogue worship is reconstructed by Morton Smith, "Jewish Religious Life in the Persian Period," in *The Cambridge History of Judaism*, ed. W. D. Davies and Louis Finkelstein, 1 (Cambridge: Cambridge University Press, 1984), 256–261. [107] Josephus, *Ant.* 4:214.
[108] Lk 4:20; *M. Yoma*, 7:1; *M. Sotah*, 7:7–8.
[109] Mt 5:25; *M. Makkoth*, 3:12. Local communities must have been able, on occasion, to provide a squad of volunteer police, as is likely in Ac 22:19.

appear to have served as clerks in the treasury function of the community.[110] Where there were teachers on the staff they may have assisted as pedagogues,[111] and in the absence of teachers they themselves may have carried that responsibility.[112] Available references to the *hazan* are not plentiful, but what we do have suggests that, just as the community chief was the overseer of the full range of a community's activities, so his assistant could be put to work in any part of that program.

The Therapeutae and the Essenes are synagogal communities somewhat out of the ordinary, but from them we gain further suggestions about the assistance provided. At the community meals of the Therapeutae, young men waited on the tables. Among the Essenes, each community had someone in charge of hospitality for travelers. These were communities whose adherents were all professing an intense dedication to service. Hence the roles and vocabulary which in ordinary synagogues depicted the *hazan*, or factotum, here designate volunteer members.[113]

Those who interpreted the mandate of the *archisynagôgos* as exclusively liturgical have seen the work of his assistant as correspondingly limited. But here too the evidence is too broad to make such a reading of it persuasive.[114] The post of *hazan* was most likely the first one among the offices of a synagogue to become stipendiary. Even poorer communities unable to pay a full-time chief might find a salary for a *hazan*, who would then have become a combination choir director, sacristan, master of ceremonies, janitor, Hebrew

---

[110] *CPJ*, no. 129.   [111] *M. Sotah*, 9:15 says that a *hazan* is inferior to a teacher.

[112] *M. Sabbath*, 1:3 says that when children are reading on a sabbath, the *hazan* might look in on them to monitor their progress, but he may not read along with them (for that is his ordinary work).

[113] Philo, *Vit. Cont.* 70–71 (cf. 50); *Jos.* 241; Josephus, *B.J.* 2:124–127. The literature of the period introduces a fourth synonym: *diakonos*. Philo describes the table attendants as *hypêretai* and as *diakonoi*. Nemias, a man buried in Syria, is memorialized as *AZZANA KAI DIAKONOS*, *CII*, no. 805, while his Roman colleague Flavius Julianus is remembered as a *YPERETES*, ibid. no. 172, and a Jewish association in Egypt enjoyed the services of some *archypêretai*, *CPJ*, no. 138.

[114] See Juster, 1:454; Moore, 289–290; Frey, *CII*, xcix. The Talmud, which we are purposely refraining from using as a major source for this period, refers often to the *hazan* in a context of worship, but this was a point of emphasis with the rabbis. Another factor which has influenced some historians to interpret the *hypêretês* as a merely liturgical minister is comparison with the usage of Greco-Roman associations, which used the title for functionaries on the liturgical side, and their temples, which used the title for servants. But the Jews had their worship more integrated into total community life, and in other instances displayed a readiness to use a common gentile word in their own quite distinctive way.

teacher, hostel manager, bailiff, caterer, plumber, clerk, scribe, welfare officer, penal officer and gravedigger. Where Jews constituted the entire population of a village, or existed as a *politeuma*, or autonomous ethnic enclave, the synagogue *was* the community, and the *hazan* its basic municipal employee. He was no magnate. No woman had it put on her gravestone that she was a *hazanissa*. But these were men who truly were the servants of all their fellows.[115]

FATHER AND MOTHER OF THE SYNAGOGUE

There is another synagogal designation which seems to have no sign of existence before the late Second Temple period, that of father of the synagogue = *patêr synagôgês* and mother of the synagogue = *mêtêr synagôgês*.[116] Whereas the title of senior elder seems to have been exclusive to the Jews and is found nowhere else, here we encounter a designation with no Jewish roots, one that was taken over and adapted from hellenistic, particularly Roman, usage. In associations connected with the mystery cults, a *patêr* or *mêtêr* would be an initiate of the most advanced degree. In some professional groups it might be a title or a synonym for the president. In most contexts it served as a title of honor for a person the *collegium* wished to felicitate.[117] It seems to have been taken up by the Jews in its sense of patron, with a further

---

[115] See Leon, 190; Applebaum, "Organization," 466; Safrai, "The Synagogue," 935–937.

[116] There is however evidence that it continues afterwards, and prominently. See, for instance, Severus of Majorca, *Epistola de Judaeis*, a fifth-century Christian document. It refers to two prominent Jews in the town of Magona (present-day Mahón in Minorca) who became Christians. "Judaeorum populus maxime cujusdam Theodori auctoritate et potentia nitebatur, qui non solum inter Judaeos, verum etiam inter Christianos ejusdem oppidi et sensu et honore saeculi praecipuus erat: siquidem apud illos legis doctor, et (ut ipsorum utar verbo) pater patrum fuit; in civitate autem cunctis Curiae muniis exsolutus, et Defensor jam exstiterat, et jam nunc patronus municipium habebat... [it then goes on to describe another] vir honestus, et non solum inter Judaeos, verum etiam in civitate usque adeo praecipuus, ut etiam nunc Defensor civitatis electus sit, Caecilianus... Caecilianus autem cum esset Judaeorum pater, habito cum Florino fratre suo aeque Judaeorum patre seniore consilio, hujusmodi (sicut agnovimus) verbis synagogam adorsus est: Ego (inquit) cum sim in honore synagogae post Theodorum primus, non sicut juvenis Galilaeus..." *Patrologiae Latinae Cursus Completus*, ed. J.-P. Migne, 20:733, 734, 741. The text is interesting in its portrayal of two ethnic communities in one town, each with its own organization and a shared municipal enterprise. The *Codex* of Theodosius records an award of certain privileges by Constantine in 331 to "hieros et archisynagogos et patres synagogarum et ceteros qui synagogis deserviunt," 16, 78, 4.

[117] Jean-Pierre Waltzing, *Etude historique sur les corporations professionelles chez les romains* (Louvain: Charles Peeters, 1895) 1:446–449; Franz Poland, *Geschichte des Griechischen Vereinswesens* (Leipzig: Teubner, 1909), 371–373.

difference, that they appear not to have conferred it upon gentile benefactors but only on their fellow Jews.[118]

The title "father of the synagogue" is attested by inscriptions and papyri from Rome, Ostia, Brescia, Smyrna, Oxyrhynchos in Egypt and Setif in Mauritania.[119] The facts that this title is given more accolade in inscriptions than are other titles, and that it is often mentioned in relation to some large public benefaction, and that it is associated with social and political prestige, all suggest that this was an honor given to especially helpful patrons and philanthropists. It would thus designate a dignitary rather than a functionary.

The title "mother of the synagogue" is attested by inscriptions from Rome, Brescia and Venosa.[120] Virtually all scholars have taken this to designate the female counterpart of the father: that is, a woman being honored in her own right. In favor of that interpretation is the fact that the dignities were borrowed from hellenistic society where women enjoyed a level of emancipation that Jews did not emulate, yet which at least those in the dispersion must have assimilated to some degree. And, as already mentioned above, this title might be quite different from others in the feminine because it derived from the one sort of prominence a Jewish woman could have even in a community where she could not aspire to official leadership: prominence of wealth and social position. Women were denied public office but they could and did (albeit usually through male proxies) own and dispose of property.

Still, there remains reason for doubt. Hellenistic usage did not necessarily confer the title of *mêtêr* on the wife of a *patêr*.[121] This would suggest that in a gentile context the male and female titles could be held separately and in their own right. But in the one Jewish instance where both spouses are identified, both hold the title.[122] Also, there are some variants in the feminine title that may indicate they are consortial. Alexandra of Venosa is called, not *matêr*, but *pateressa*, a derivative of the male title similar to others that were given

---

[118] However, the Jewish honoree need not have been of the same community, for some held the title in more than one synagogue: *CII*, nos. 508, 523.

[119] Ibid. nos. 88, 93, 319, 494, 508, 509, 510, 535 (same person as 510), 537, 533, 739; *CPJ*, no. 473 (late third century); *CIL*, 8:8499. Juster, I :449, n. 2 cites a number of other references, all of which are blind leads. [120] *CII*, nos. 166(?), 496, 523, 606, 639.

[121] Thus Auxanius was father and patron of the city of Venosa (Venusia), but Faustina his wife, on her separate epitaph, seems not to have been honored as mother of the city, *CII*², nos. 619c, d. She is called simply *mêtêr*, which Lifschitz sees as an honorific, yet it is a common ascription for a woman who has raised a family. [122] *CII*, no. 166.

consortially to wives: *archisynagôgissa, hierissa, episcopissa*. Thus, at least with the scant evidence before us, it may presume too much to assert that mothers of the synagogue held their positions in their own right. Here too they may have been honored as partners of their husbands.[123]

THE SCRIBE

Another officer of the community was the clerk, or scribe = *grammateus*. Part of our task is to untangle the role of this functionary from the many traditional usages of this common title.

With the monarchy had come the need in Israel for scribes = *sopherim*. Their skills in reading, writing and translating gave them monopolistic access to the entire civil service, a career they made sure to pass on to their own sons by enrolling them in the royal schools for scribes. With the exile and dispersion many of these found employment in the bureaux of the growing empires, but a few turned their talents and interests to a new concern of their own people: the sacred books of Israel and Judah.[124] It was they who edited, copied, studied and interpreted the scriptures. When the disaffection from politics in the second century BC spawned new reform movements such as the *Hasidim* and the Pharisees, their loyalty to the tradition caused the founding of new, more flexible scribal academies, which at the end of the Second Temple period allowed the Pharisees to dominate the profession of those who interpreted the Torah.

In our period a Jew might be a scribe in the service of the king; for example, one reads in an Egyptian papyrus of a Jew who served as scribe under the regional Egyptian chief scribe.[125] Or a Jew might be a lifelong student of legal interpretation; it is such scholars whom the gospels present repeatedly as "the scribes." With reference to the Law, the term "scribe" had wide application. It might refer to a simple copyist who produced the scrolls. Or it might refer to one of the great sages.[126] And, in a culture where written transactions were

---

[123] Even in Greco-Roman associations, a *mater* often held the title through marriage: Waltzing, 1:430.

[124] See Hilaire Duesberg, O.S.B., *Les scribes inspirés: Introduction aux livres sapientiaux de la Bible* (Paris: Desclée de Brouwer, 1938–1939). Early postexilic scribes who worked on the sacred documents may, like Ezra, have been priests, continuing the yet older priestly function of interpreting the Law. As it developed, however, this office did not remain a priestly prerogative. [125] *CPJ*, no. 137.

[126] All the great sages from Ezra to Simon the Just were known in the rabbinical literature as *sopherim*.

few but crucial, any town would have a scrivener available to draw up official documents for unlettered citizens. In all these senses, the Hebrew *sopher* had become the hellenistic *grammateus*.

None of these is to be confused with the scribe of the synagogue.[127] Just as the Sanhedrin in Jerusalem had its own scribe,[128] so every synagogue would need one. His tasks would be to draw up the minutes and acts of the assembly, elders and notables, to draft outgoing correspondence, to preserve incoming correspondence and all else that was in the archive, to act as clerk of the court, to function as notary and, probably, to be of counsel to members who were preparing important legal papers.[129]

Virtually all evidence of individual scribes is to be found in epitaphs, of which the most by far (25 out of 26) are from Rome.[130] Six are identified as scribes of named Roman synagogues. No one seems to have questioned whether the simple designation *grammateus* on the epitaph necessarily means that this was a synagogue officer, especially since there were so many ways to come by the title.[131]

The ages at death indicate that this was not a position one assumed only in advanced years: 22, 24, 27, 35, 37, 45, 50, 70. No one is described as having served several terms: it does not seem therefore to have been elective, at least in the sense that after a short term one really had to strive for re-election. The remembrance of scribes-designate (died ages 19 and 24)[132] and of child scribes (died ages 6, 7 and 12)[133] prepares one to believe that this was another position which families liked to hold through the generations. One scribe buried his son, a scribe, at the age of 24, and his surviving son, a notable, promptly designated his own son for that office.[134]

The office of scribe was one of professional competence and prestige. In many communities it was perhaps held *gratis* as a part-

---

[127] Frey, *CII*, xciii; Juster, 1:447–448; Leon, 183–186; Applebaum, "Organization," 495.

[128] Josephus, *B.J.* 5:532; the Mishnah says two scribes, at least for trials, *M. Sanhedrin*, 4:3.

[129] Most of this must be conjectured from what is known of the literary traffic of the synagogue program. Cf. also Gert Lüderitz, *Corpus jüdischer Zeugnisse aus der Cyrenaika* (Wiesbaden: Ludwig Reichert, 1983), 21–24.

[130] *CII*, nos. 7, 18, 24, 36, 53, 67, 99, 102, 121, 122, 125, 142, 145, 146, 148, 149, 180, 221, 225, 279, 284, 318, 351, 433, 456, 800 (Bithynia).

[131] One epitaph, on an infant girl, concludes: "I, Victor the scribe, made this." Frey peevishly comments: "Ce 'grammateus' ne donne pas une haute idée de ses capacités littéraires: il n'y a guère de mot qui soit écrit correctement," *CII*, no. 102.

[132] Ibid. nos. 279, 121.

[133] Ibid. nos. 146, 180 (the usual modifier *nêpios* is absent, but this youngster clearly had not entered office), 284 (likewise, this young *grammateus* is also a *mellarchôn*); 122 (records a child scribe but no age).   [134] Ibid. nos. 145, 149, 146.

time service by a well-connected community member (several scribes were relatives of notables).[135]

What should a judge do, asked Philo, when the case before him is so complex and obscure that he cannot see a fair resolution of it? Send it up to more discerning judges, he thought.

And who should these be but the priests, and the head and leader of the priests? For the genuine ministers of God have taken all care to sharpen their understanding and count the slightest error to be no slight error, because the greatness of the King whom they serve is seen in every matter ... Another possible reason for sending such cases to the priests is that the true priest is necessarily a prophet, advanced to the service of the truly Existent by virtue rather than by birth, and to a prophet nothing is unknown ... [136]

Thus from Alexandria, before the catastrophe of 70. From Rome, well after that catastrophe from which with exquisite finesse he had extricated himself, Flavius Josephus, a priest himself, was also convinced of priests' special gifts.

Could there be a finer or more equitable policy than one which sets God at the head of the universe, which assigns the administration of its highest affairs to the whole body of priests, and entrusts to the supreme high-priest the direction of the other priests? These men, moreover, owed their original promotion by the Legislator [Moses] to their high office, not to any superiority in wealth or other accidental advantages. No; of all his companions, the men to whom he entrusted the ordering of divine worship as their first charge were those who were pre-eminently gifted with persuasive eloquence and discretion. But the charge further embraced a strict supervision of the Law and of pursuits in everyday life; for the appointed duties of the priests included a general supervision, the trial of cases of litigation, and the punishment of condemned persons. Could there be a more saintly government than that?[137]

Most Jews thought there could be: or at least a more credible one. It is striking how decisively the priesthood vanished from the scene of power after the fall of Jerusalem in 70, like that other great institution

---

[135] Ibid. nos. 125, 145, 146, 284. No. 800 commemorates a scribe who was an elder (or an elder's son) and also *epistatês tôn palaiôn* (either the superintendent of the aged or an official of a district by that name: thus Applebaum, "Organization," 484), or perhaps the equivalent of a *gerousiarchês*.   [136] Philo, *Spec. Leg.* 4:190–192.

[137] Josephus, *C. Ap.* 2:185–188; also *Ant.* 11:111; 14:41, 404.

of hereditary office, the davidic monarchy, had been disestablished when Jerusalem fell nearly seven centuries earlier.

The execution of the leading figures of the priesthood by the desperate rebels, and the devastation of the temple itself by the exasperated Roman troops, had struck a fierce blow at the operational base of priestly influence. Yet that alone need not have extirpated the priestly ascendancy. Jewish identity re-emerged later. Why was priestly leadership no longer part of it?

One reason which is well acknowledged was the take-over of Torah interpretation by the Pharisee scholars. Rabbi Johanan ben Zakkai and the band of scholars who escaped Jerusalem with him founded a yeshiva at Yavne (later it moved to other places like Usha, Sepphoris and Tiberias) which reconstituted a council of seventy (plus two presiding) to give continuance to the Sanhedrin as the authority of the chief *keneset* or synagogue of world Jewry. Unlike the Sanhedrin, which had ended as an unstable alloy of priests and sages, the academy of scholars did contain some members who were priests, yet as a bloc appear to have enjoyed no significance.

But another adjustment, less noticed, and well before the events of 70 AD, presaged all this. The local synagogues had already chosen to deny priests any special privileges or position. We must realize that it need not have been thus. The priesthood had anciently been associated, not simply with sacrificial worship, but with the interpretation of the Torah and with judicial discipline. Jonathan, Simon and John Hyrcanus were thought to have consolidated their rule, which was gained through the Maccabean revolt, by taking on the high priesthood also. Yet in the villages and towns and cities, where priests in plenty dwelt and were available, a totally lay synagogue organization had long since decided it needed no legitimacy which the priests could give.

Priests did exist, probably, wherever Jews had settled. Where family mausolea existed, we can find them buried together.[138] There are also individual priests interred.[139] Priestly females have been memorialized at Beth She'arim and Tiberias in Galilee, at Leontopolis in Egypt and at Rome. As already noted, a *hierissa* was the wife or the daughter of a priest.[140]

---

[138] As at Beth She'arim, *CII*, nos. 1001, 1002.

[139] Also at Beth She'arim, Lifschitz, "Fonctions et titres," 63; at Rome, *CII*, nos. 346, 347, 375.

[140] Frey writes: "*hierisa*, littéralement *prêtresse*, ne peut signifier, dans le cas présent, qu'un membre de la famille sacerdotale d'Aaron," *CII*, no. 315 (Rome); see also nos. 1514

As such, priests were not officiants at any synagogue activity.[141] There were still some rituals explicitly assigned to them by the Law, and these they presumably retained: receiving the five-shekel redemption money for each first-born son,[142] reciting certain blessings at worship services,[143] receiving tithes on produce,[144] and performing certain purification rituals.[145]

The *kohanim* = *hiereis* = priests would form a cadre of identifiable members in any synagogue, to whom biblical imperatives reserved certain ritual actions, but to whom no further deference on the part of the community is in evidence. They had minor hereditary prerogatives but cannot be considered officers of the community. Jerusalem, as it turned out (and Leontopolis, where another temple, acceptable to local Jews though anathema in Jerusalem, functioned until 73 AD), was not merely the only place where priests might preside at sacrifices; it was the only place where they presided at anything.

The one exception of which we are aware is in the Qumran documents, records of a devout hieratic community (or communities) that rejected what the Jerusalem priesthood had made of itself, yet which honored priests and Levites above any other category of member. Priests ranked highest as a category, above even the elders.[146] The ruling council had a certain number of seats reserved for them.[147] A community was segmented into small cells of ten persons and each was headed, preferably, by a priest.[148] Priests and Levites were listed first on the annual census, led the initiation rites, held first seats in the assembly, had special responsibility for fidelity to the group covenant and, according to one scroll, were expected to be leaders in battle, issuing commands and blessings and curses.[149] Some records show the priests as forming a group apart, the "House

---

(*hierisa*; Leontopolis), 1007 (*hiereia*; Beth She'arim). See Louis Robert, "Epitaphes juives d'Ephèse et de Nicomédie," *Hellenica*, 11/12 (1960), 381–384 (Tiberias).

[141] *M. Menachoth*, 13:10 (also 1:3, 4; 3:3) holds that they could officiate only in the temple, but we must understand this as *parti pris*, from a rabbinical source, confirming what had already become the case.   [142] Ex 13:14; Num 18:15–16.   [143] Lev 9:22; Num 6:22.

[144] Num 18:26.   [145] Lev 14:1–32; Mk 1:44; Mt 8:4; Lk 5:14; 17:13.

[146] This is specified in the *Scroll of the Rule*: 1QS 6:8ff. Similarly, along with the Levites, in the *Damascus Document*: CD 4:1–4. In the *Rule Annexe* they share this primacy with the heads of family of the community: 1QSa 1:2, 15–16, 23–25; 2:3. But they still hold an edge on them in rank, 2: 14, 17, 21.

[147] Three out of the College of Fifteen, 1QS 8:1–4; four priests and Levites out of ten in the College of Judges, CD 10:4.   [148] 1QS 6:3–5; CD 13:1–7.

[149] 1QS 2:19–20; 1:16–2:18; 6:8; 5:2, 9; *War Scroll*: 1QM 7:9–9:9.

of Holiness for Aaron,'' and to have reserved to themselves final authority in matters of justice and property.[150]

More must be said later about the innovations that later Jewish separatist groups introduced into their synagogue communities. The remarkable precedence they awarded to priests and Levites shows by dramatic contrast how different it was in mainstream Jewish synagogues, where they were integrated into the ranks as much as possible.

OTHER OFFICERS

Let us proceed to identify other synagogue functionaries of which we have evidence. It must be remembered that a Jewish community could be quite large or quite small, with lavish or with meager resources. In the smaller synagogues there was probably no limit to what the community chief might call upon members to do without stipend or title, or what he might add to the job description of the assistant. Large synagogues with elaborate programs might appoint or elect officers to bear specific responsibilities, and then any of those posts might later disappear with a shift of leadership or emphasis or budget. Besides the offices already mentioned, none is very widely attested in the sources. We must assume a certain diversity of custom and fluidity of structure, and that the prestige associated with these minor offices was so modest that people did not think to include them in the interesting but terse *curricula vitae* of their gravestones.

One must wonder at the absence of evidence for the office of treasurer. The temple is remembered to have had treasurers and comptrollers and auditors in abundance.[151] It was a financial task that any community would have to fill, but it seems to have been the charge of one or another of the officers in place: perhaps a notable, or the community chief himself. Schürer was persuaded by the Mishnah that there had to be an almoner in each synagogue because of the obligatory collections and distributions to the indigent.[152] The absence of any record of almoners implies that this was not a

---

[150] 1QS 9:5–7. Not so in CD, but in the latter the overseer of the community himself must be a priest, 14:6–8. Philo's accounts of the Essenes make no mention of priestly precedence: *Quod Omn. Prob.* 75–87; *Hyp.* 8–11. Josephus records only that a priest says a prayer before the community meal, *B.J.* 2:131, and (in an obscure passage) that priests prepared the bread and other victuals, *Ant.* 18:22. Philo's description of the Therapeutae makes no mention of priestly members.   [151] *M. Shekalim*, 5:2.

[152] Schürer, *History* 2, 2:437; *M. Demai*, 3:1 and *M. Kiddushin*, 4:5 speak of almoners = *gavei tsedekah*, but away from the Sanhedrin this may not have been a separate office, at least by this name.

formalized office, or at least that it was a function included within the duties of an existing office, perhaps that of assistant under super-intendence by the chief.

THE COMMISSIONER

On the financial side we do, however, encounter the *phrontistês* = commissioner. In general usage the word means administrator, manager, trustee.[153] The office existed among Jews in a wide scatter of places: Palestine, Egypt, Pamphylia, Porto and Rome.[154] Several incumbents (in Caesarea and Side) are thanked for substantial ameliorations in the synagogue buildings, and several others (in Rome) have held heavy honors in their communities: father of the synagogue, or two and three times a notable. Most plausibly the commissioner was charged with the synagogue's physical plant. It was natural as one of the responsibilities a council of affluent elders or notables would first want to take from the other officers and entrust to more seasoned and competent hands. Feeding widows is one thing; vaulting a roof, quite another. This surmise is strengthened by the one set of inscriptions from the Greek island of Aegina, where the title itself does not appear, but the participle of its cognate verb does. The community chief, Theodore, had managed the affairs of the synagogue for four years and had rebuilt their collapsed meeting house. Theodore, Jr., given the management of finances, had adorned the entire building with mosaics.[155] Whether or not the community chief or the younger Theodore ever assumed the title of commissioner, it is clear what that line of work was: capable stewardship of the fabric.

[153] Thus *CPJ*, no. 432, a papyrus from Arsinoë in 113 AD, is the financial report to the auditor from the four water *phrontistai* of the city.

[154] Lifschitz, "Fonctions et titres," 59–60 (Caesarea); *CII*, nos. 919 (Jaffa); 918 (Alexandria, or a synagogue of Alexandrians in Jaffa?); 781 (Side); Robert, "Inscriptions grecques," 36ff (Side); *CII*, nos. 337, 494 (Rome); Robert, *BE* 1982, no. 499 (Porto). Robert, *BE* 1974, no. 641, suggests this office may also be entitled *pronoêtés* and *mizoteros* (Tiberias).

[155] *CII*, nos. 722, 723. The two men are described as *phrontisas* and *phrontizôn*. Juster identifies this title as a synonym for the *archisynagôgos*, 1:451, and much debate has ensued: see Frey, "Les communautés juives," *RSR*, 21:145–146. What one must be able to distinguish is the responsibility from the office. The former was much less formal, and presumably more widespread. See also Applebaum, "Organization," 497.

THE TEACHER

There are relatively few attestations of teachers, though the school was an ordinary part of the synagogue program. The common title is *didaskalos*, and we encounter it in Jerusalem, Beth She'arim, Venosa and Rome.[156] That one of these teachers is also honored as a "disciple of the law" evokes the character of the schooling expected of them.[157]

THE READER

The principal proceeding in the worship of an assembled Jewish community was the reading and exposition of Scripture. As we have seen, this would take place with the community chief presiding and the assistant getting out the scrolls and serving as master of ceremonies. Although Philo says that a priest or elder would do the reading,[158] this is not confirmed by other evidence. In general, both the act of reading and the opportunity to construe the text seem to have lain open to anyone present, though in so stratified a society deference may have been paid to rank and seniority. A very few burial records do memorialize Jews as readers, leaving us with the not improbable impression that in some synagogues the task grew into an office.[159]

This concludes the description of the personnel and organization with which a Jew in the late Second Temple era might be familiar in his or her own community. The community itself was responsible for its own welfare, and at critical junctures would be convened to act corporately on matters of great significance. It was the elders who held traditional responsibility to promote and endorse wise judgments and policy for the community. Their dean, the chief elder, representing the longest draw on the past tradition, was held in special honor. At this time, however, most ordinary governance had been gathered securely into the hands of a board of notables who actively superintended the community's welfare, interests and

---

[156] *CII*, nos. 1266, 1268, 1269; 1158; 594; 333.

[157] *CII*, no. 333. Lifschitz writes of these *didaskaloi*: "Il s'agit évidemment d'une distinction honorifique," "Fonctions et titres," 63. While that might be understood of the title *nomomathês*, I am not persuaded that the title of teacher, which in other contexts might suggest a community chief as spiritual leader, or a rabbi (thus Frey or his editors, *CII*, nos. 1266, 1269), need be construed out of its ordinary meaning. See Leon, 193. The New Testament displays the title *didaskalos* often, but with a quite different meaning, as we shall see.   [158] Philo, *Hyp.* 7:13.

[159] *CII*, nos. 798 (*anagnôstês*: Nicomedia in Bithynia); 896 (qireh: Jaffa).

program. Also of high rank were the father and mother of the synagogue, whose patronage had helped the community to meet its needs better than common resources might have allowed.

Presiding over the community, and over both its echelons of governing notables, was the community chief, who was the executive of the community's activities and program. His assistant was expected to provide or to facilitate all these activities under the direction of the community chief, and not infrequently he was obliged to perform paraprofessional services which more affluent synagogues could provide through professional staff. Every community would call on various members *ad hoc* to help with the program, and it was their duty to lend a hand without title or compensation. But as a higher level of development made it possible, certain offices could be assigned to the more skilled members, and perhaps with stable appointment. The offices of which we have evidence include those of the scribe, the commissioner and the reader. Most communities would have had some priests resident among them, and for certain statutory occasions they would have had ritual duties to perform, though for individuals and families more than for the synagogue as a community.

SELECTION OF OFFICERS

How were these leading figures in the destiny of Jewish communities chosen? One of the political strategies to which Greek and Roman democrats resorted, as a way of deflecting partisan power build-up, was the selection of key office-holders by lot. The Jewish political tradition, thought Philo, followed a higher path.

Some legislators have introduced the system of filling magistracies by lot, to the detriment of their peoples, for the lot shows good luck, not merit ... Can it be right to make masters and rulers of whole cities and nations out of persons chosen by lot, by what we may call a blunder of fortune, the uncertain and unstable? In the matter of tending the sick lot has no place, for physicians do not gain their posts by lot, but are approved by the test of experience. And to secure a successful voyage and the safety of travelers on the sea we do not choose by lot and send straight away to the helm a steersman who through his ignorance will produce in fine weather and calm water shipwrecks in which Nature has no part. Instead we send one whom we know to have been carefully trained from his earliest years in the art of steersmanship ... These things Moses, wise here as ever, considered in his soul and does not even mention appointment of rulers by lot, but determines to institute appointment by election ... There should be a free choice and an unimpeachable scrutiny of the ruler made by the whole people with the same mind. And the choice will receive the further vote and seal of ratification from Him who confirms all things that promote the common weal, even God who holds that the man may be called the chosen from the race, in which he is what the eye is in the body.[160]

Philo was romancing. In his time Rome ruled Greece and the emperors ruled Rome, and they made none of their personnel assignments by lot.[161] Among the Jews, leaders were chosen by merit, but who assessed those merits was a matter of some finesse. There had long been a strain between the ancient theory of populism and the social reality of aristocracy, and that strain was creating a tension in the community organization we have been studying. But what allowed Philo this bit of puffery that public figures were chosen by a show of hands? In many – possibly most – cases the effective discernment and politicking would have been settled before the actual election, while the formality of election continued to be honored.[162]

Historians of the synagogue have been in long debate over which if any of the notables and officers were elected. That is perhaps due to very different pictures they may have of what an election is. Let us set aside, from the outset, the priests, who were (despite the pleas of Philo and Josephus that they served by merit) to the temple born. Let us set aside also the senior elder who, if my discernment of his role be correct, would succeed to that title by whatever reckoning of seniority was customary. Apart from these, if we ask which notables and officers were elected by a show of hands, I think it safe to say that they all were. If, however, one asks which notables and officers were

---

[160] Philo, *Spec. Leg.* 4:151–157.

[161] In ancient, classical Athens the entire ruling *boulê* was not continuously in session, but delegated everyday government to one of the ten tribal *prytaneiai*, which then every day elected by lot its *epistatês*, who throughout that day directed the entire state. See Franz Poland, E. Reistinger and R. Wagner, *The Culture of Ancient Greece and Rome*, trans. John Henry Freese (London: Harrap, [1926]), 282–284.

[162] Philo's expression for election is the classical Jewish term: *cheirotonein, cheirotonia*. The biblical and hellenistic-Jewish vocabulary used a variety of terms for the act of selecting persons for office: *apodeiknymi, kathistêmi, hairein. Cheirotonia* brought the added connotation of extending one's hand in a gesture of election. There is a convergent sense in which this word-root denotes the act of extending one's hand over a candidate's head in a way that effects either election or inauguration and possibly both together. See G[eoffrey] W. H. Lampe, *A Patristic Greek Lexicon*, s.v. *cheirotoneó, cheirotonia, cheirothesia*. This is not to be confused with the rite of laying both hands on the head, the *smichah*, by which one prepared an animal for sacrifice: *M. Megillah*, 2:5; *M. Chagigah*, 2:2; *M. Kiddushin*, 1:8; *M. Menachoth*, 9:7–9; *M. Tamid*, 7:3. See also an extraordinary treatise by John Selden, a jurist and man of erudition in Caroline England: Joannis Seldeni, *De Synedriis et Praefecturis Juridicis Veterum Ebraeorum*, 1 (Amsterdam: Boom & Someren, 1679), ch. 14.

elected by an assembly or a council that gathered for elections without any preliminary caucusing, and only thus discovered who would be their choice, then I think it safe to say that none of them was.

We know that the elders were men of station and family, whose presence on that council must have involved some years of delicate discussion, grooming and anticipation: "carefully trained from his earliest years in the art of statesmanship," as Philo had said. When the day came for a man to be co-opted into that establishment, presumably for life, there were no surprises.

With the notables it must have been somewhat different. There was a tradition that elders chosen out for representative responsibility were elected by their peers, and for a time.[163] We have already noted that after the close of our period Jews were said to be electing their notables annually for one-year terms, and the evidence of two- and three-term incumbencies implies that something similar may have been customary in Second Temple days.[164]

The community chief did not sit in a chair from which, no matter how frequent the electoral procedure, he was likely to be quickly unseated. The position was filled only at long intervals, since it was presumably awarded until retirement, and the selection process must have been lengthy and sometimes contentious. When and where it became a full-time occupation, and stipendiary, there was the natural tendency for it to become professionalized, and for it to become a family tradition.[165]

The election of a father and/or a mother of the synagogue was a different affair altogether: an infrequent event and a delicate one (since one presumes they held the honor for life, and without rivals), but not one to affect future interests and policy.

The assistant, more than any other officer, would have had to be acceptable to the community chief, and, indeed, recruited by him. This would be an election surest to follow upon nomination.

The scribe, if a man of the establishment, was surely the creature of the elders and notables, and tended to serve for years once installed. If he were a professional, and stipendiary, his selection must

---

[163] Thus in the second century BC tale of Susanna, two elders had been selected that year as judges, 5.
[164] Similarly, comptrollers in the temple treasury were to be elected by the congregation = *tsibur*, though it is unclear exactly which congregation that was, M. *Shekalim*, 5:2.
[165] After the destruction of Jerusalem the seventy-two elders of the reconstituted Sanhedrin would elect the head of the yeshiva, M. *Yadayim*, 3:5. See ch. 8, n. 55.

surely have been in the gift of the community chief, to whom he would be accountable.

It was probably otherwise for the commissioner, who would have been a man of the establishment, one of their own, and imposed upon the administration.

The selection of a reader, or readers, must have been one of the lighter choices made by the community chief, and one about which it would be congenial to take counsel with the elders and notables.

Thus, in anticipation of the "free choice and unimpeachable scrutiny" whereby electors raised their hands to empower someone for community office and service, there were surely well-understood yieldings to patronage and to possession.[166]

The most volatile force in the community was the most powerful: the board of notables. Since its membership turned over regularly and offered the most frequent political choices in the synagogue, that college must have been the most responsive to shifts in influence and emphasis. One might also presume that the relations between the notables and the community chief were potentially temperamental. His presidency and longevity were poised over against their superior but ephemeral policy powers. Also, a president put in place by a board of notables representing a stable, consistent majority among the elders could one day discover a long-term shift in dominance, and a reverse of emphasis in the group to whom he was most accountable.

Yet another strain – one that became visible in the Jerusalem Sanhedrin – surely had its counterpart on the local level. The traditional elders – aristocratic, established, prestigious – were being challenged by the devout – those who cultivated the Law and scholarship. The priesthood, which in Jerusalem was an effective

---

[166] A much later recollection of emperor Alexander Severus (222–235), who was favorable towards the Jews, is included in the *Scriptores Historiae Augustae*. Alexander, in a mood of civil service reform, wonders why, when both the Jews and the Christians give early notice of their candidates for office (which, with his imperfect acquaintance, he called that of priesthood: a Roman misunderstanding), the same practice would not make good sense for prospective governors of provinces, to ascertain what the public thought of them. "Dicebatque grave esse, cum id Christiani et Judaei facerent in praedicandis sacerdotibus, qui ordinandi sunt, non fieri in provinciarum rectoribus, quibus et fortunae hominum committerentur et capita," Stern, *Greek and Latin Authors*, 2, no. 523; *SHA*, "Alexander Severus," 45:7. Granted that the exacerbated relations between Jews and Christians at that time must have discouraged either group from copying the other (at least knowingly), it would seem that this common practice was due to common tradition, not imitation. Thus advance notice of candidates for synagogue election in our period seems plausible, though we cannot know whether it was of persons still under scrutiny or of persons who had the nod and required only a voting session to take office.

third force, seems not to have counted for much in local communities. The diversity of program in any synagogue would allow each group a sector of preference and ascendancy, but in the choosing of notables and of the community chief this cleavage must sometimes have widened.

THE SYNAGOGUE PATTERN: HOW BORROWED, HOW NATIVE?

The resemblances in nomenclature and in structure between what we have been discerning here and the social organizations in the hellenistic world are manifold and striking: so much so that scholars are much drawn to filling in the blank spaces in Jewish social history by borrowing from Greco-Roman models. Yet the Jews had a way of adapting and assimilating without adopting many institutions or institutional elements unchanged. Hence a need for caution in drawing parallels. To offer but a single illustration of this, let us look at one of the most inveterate traditions in Jewish society: presbyteral authority.

The Persian empire of the new Achaemenian dynasty was the first to incorporate the Jews into its society and rule after they had been swallowed up by the Babylonians. It was a divinely sponsored, autocratic regime, and no one has professed to see democratic premonitions in Persepolis or Susa. Yet in the Persian court the sovereign relied on four councils. A council of princes, which served as a crown council for matters of state policy, included the leaders of the feudal families that had hoisted the royal house to power, together with foreign princes and resident exiles, even from defeated or hostile peoples. A council of sages was entrusted with most judicial matters, with or without the sovereign presiding. A council of warriors gathered the highest military officers to formulate decisions and strategies for warfare. And a palace privy council, whereon the queen sat with considerable influence, gave the king some purchase upon the smaller yet very significant world of his own retinue. Thus, an absolute monarch sat in the midst of specialized aristocratic bodies and took his decisions in conciliar style. Plato wrote admiringly of their tradition of free and frank speech in these meetings.[167]

---

[167] Plato, *Laws*, 3:694b; also Herodotus, *History*, 4:97; Ezr 7:14; Esth 1:14. See Morteza Ehtécham, *L'Iran sous les Achéménides: Contribution à l'étude de l'organization sociale et politique du Premier Empire des Perses* (Fribourg: St-Paul, 1946). The offices and style of the Persian court are reflected also in 1 Esdras.

After Alexander mastered Persia and left his missionary work to
the Successors, oriental tradition was blended into Greek polity,
which required more public involvement in the workings of power.
Homer's great hero Odysseus, "sharing the wine of council," had
journeyed through a saga marked by great community deliberations.
The story opens with one assembly of Ithacans, crests with an
assembly of Phaiacians, and closes with another assembly in
Ithaca.[168] Indeed, in the great Greek communities it was in the
assembly of enfranchized men (*apella* in Sparta; *ekklêsia* in Athens)
that the greatest decisions were to be made: about war, or bonds with
other peoples, or elections. But in time the effective governance
devolved upon the council of elders (*gerousia* in Sparta; *boulê* in
Athens). Administration was in the hands of magistrates elected by
and from the people (*ephoroi* in Sparta; *archontes* in Athens), who in
turn superintended various commissioners for specific public projects
(*epimelêtai*), and stipendiary officers who carried out their policies.
The magistrates, or notables, functioned by division of duties: one
protecting family affairs; another, military affairs; another, the
welfare of foreigners; others, the judiciary. Election of officers was by
cheirotonia = show of hands.[169]

The hellenistic kingdoms, so influential in Jewish life at home and
in the great dispersion settlements of Syria, Egypt and Babylon, were
a strange amalgam of Greek populism and oriental despotism. The
army, conscripted round an old guard of Macedonian mercenaries,
insisted on holding occasional *ekklêsiai*, but few plenary assemblies
were permitted, as not suiting the king's tastes. The aristocratic
penumbra of the Persian court reappeared: the king's counselors
were called the "friends," and the highest-ranked among them were
called the "kin," and they enjoyed formalized courtesies of intimacy
with him. Autocrat though he was, the Seleucid or Ptolemaic king
would hold court surrounded by his *synedrion/symboulion* = council,
and take account of their opinions before rendering judgment.[170]

Roman hegemony was to bring yet another tradition into the
blend, and it strengthened the trend towards at least more formal
popular involvement. The lowest/highest authority in ancient Rome
had been the popular assembly = *comitia* which from the beginning

---

[168] Homer, *Odyssey*, 13:9; 1:372–373; 2:10; 8:16–17; 16:376–377; 24:420. The assembly in
Homer is the *agorê* (epic form of *agora*).   [169] See Poland, *Culture*, 280–290.
[170] See, for instance, 2 Macc 14:5; 4 Macc 17:17; Jdth 6:1, 17; 11:9; also 4 Macc 5:1; Da
6:7–8; *1 Esdras* 8:11; Josephus, *Ant.* 13:77, 114.

of the republic began to elect magistrates. The elders = *senatus*, numbering 300 first and later swelling to 600, were an ancient patrician body that slowly and grudgingly began to take in plebeian members, and eventually absorbed high magistrates after their terms of office. The *comitia* retained certain basic prerogatives such as the right to declare war or peace, but the senate was the seat of most authority which even under the empire was still formally observed. Out in the provinces, governors were also obliged to hold court with counselors = *assessores* and to convene occasional assemblies.[171] Beginning with Augustus, emperors formed for themselves a select *boulê/synedrion/consilium* = council of aristocratic advisors called *amici* = friends. This served increasingly as the sovereign's council of state, and during times of troubled succession it acted as a stabilizing agent of continuity. Here, as back in Persia, bold and blunt talk was expected.[172]

One might wonder how patterns of social organization at the imperial level could affect the habits of Jews huddled in small towns. There probably was very little direct influence, but the patterns we describe are more generalized in their usage. It is simply the case that the sovereign's court left more records behind, and thus it is a privileged source of evidence from which to infer cautiously how communities at all levels might have been structured in that world.

Much closer to home were the Greco-Roman associations = *thiasoi/eranoi/collegia* that pervaded hellenistic society. Military brotherhoods, athletic unions, youth groups, religious sodalities, guilds of artisans or laborers or businessmen: all were independent, voluntary membership groups, and their organization conformed to a common model: indeed, it was in some respects controlled by law. The general membership in this period was coming to a certain ennui about the transaction of business at plenary assemblies = *ekklêsiai/synodoi/synagôgai*. Deliberative business was left to a council of

---

[171] Porcius Festus took counsel with his *symboulion* before deciding what to do with Paul, Ac 25:12.

[172] Frank Frost Abbott, *A History and Description of Roman Political Institutions*, 3rd edn. (Boston: Ginn, 1911); George Willis Botsford, *The Roman Assemblies from Their Origin to the End of the Republic* (New York: Macmillan, 1909); John A. Crook, *Consilium Principis: Imperial Councils and Counsellors from Augustus to Diocletian* (Cambridge: Cambridge University Press, 1955); Poland et al., *Culture*, 293ff; Josephus, *Ant.* 13:165, 261–266; 14:117; 16:163; 19:248; *B.J.* 3:83; 6:237; Reinach, nos. 190, 324; Stern, *Greek and Latin Authors*, 2, nos. 282, 293; Erwin R. Goodenough, *The Jurisprudence of the Jewish Courts in Egypt: Legal Administration by the Jews under the Early Roman Empire as Described by Philo Judaeus* (New Haven: Yale University Press, 1929).

elders = *gerousia* = *presbyteroi*, who in turn left much management in the hands of the annually elected officers = *archontes*. In the Greek tradition, the president was entitled *archisynagôgos* or *prostatês*. The Romans preferred the corporate presidency of a college of masters = *magistri*. Commissioners for *ad hoc* projects were *epimelêtai*. Each association would have a secretary = *grammateus* and a treasurer = *tamias*. Fathers and mothers = *patres* and *matres* were elected as an association's affectionately honored patrons. All of these personages were elected regularly by a show of hands = *cheirotonia*. The servant of the association was variously called *hypêretês/diakonos/pais*.[173]

Here, it might seem, we have the script and all the roles. The average Jewish community had simply to write in its own *dramatis personae*.[174] Yet despite the detailed resemblances, the Jews were not simply imitating an existing model, however socially compelling it may have been.

There were differences. The suspicion of power which made regular elections and short terms of office desirable in gentile society seems to have been less conspicuous among the Jews, who abided longer incumbencies. The elders themselves, who in many societies were elected for terms, were stable personages in the synagogues. The ambit of concern for a college of elders in a hellenistic city or association was particular and limited. For a Jewish council it comprised the entire welfare of the people. The most significant communications which a Jewish assembly might convene to hear were not letters of amity or curial rescripts, but regular passages from the Torah. For even the most democratic among them, neither the assembly nor the elders nor the president nor the king was ultimately authoritative: their God was Lord over them all.[175] The Jewish counselors, more than their gentile namesakes, carried the burden of consistency with their brethren elsewhere in Jewry, as well as with their deceased brethren who had preserved the faith. And with them there could be no doubt that among their many social involvements, this one was paramount. Although in effect the elders and notables were a counterpoise to the power of the community chief, in their

---

[173] Poland, *Geschichte*; Waltzing, *Corporations*.

[174] Some, like Frey, have been perhaps too ready to see hellenistic associations as the chosen model for the synagogue, *CII*, 1 :lxxxiiff.

[175] Klaus Berger, "Volksversammlung und Gemeinde Gottes: Zu den Anfängen der christlichen Verwendung von 'ekklesia'," *Zeitschrift für Theologie und Kirche*, 73 (1976), 167–207.

mind's eye they were the latest beneficiaries of that charismatic spirit with which Moses had left his lieutenants inspirited.

There is also much, at a level of analysis, that shows forth in the two systems as similar: a conservatism in form, while power is being reallocated; a residual legitimating role for traditional bodies that have yielded real decision-making freedom; an ability of elders and officers to embody their people and to act for them; a repeating strain between aristocrats and communalists.

The conviction with which we emerge is that the Second Temple period Jews were able to adapt elements of an alien social structure to the point where they became legitimately continuous with their ancestral customs. In this instance of presbyteral authority, the graft was hellenistic but the stock was Hebrew. After all, they worshiped a God whom they imagined as surrounded with elders and notable-spirits: in fact, they envisioned a heavenly *ekklêsia* with whom their earthly assembly was in communion.[176]

THE SYNAGOGUE: A COMPELLING PATTERN

As a final exercise, we might hold up against this pattern of synagogue organization what we can reconstruct of separatist Jewish groups which were purposely attempting to be distinctive.

We are in possession of a variety of contemporary documents which appear to describe various sectarian movements of the Second Temple period. Philo and Josephus describe the Essenes and the Therapeutae. A trove of manuscripts recovered in the Dead Sea area, which are generally considered to be the archive of a central Essene settlement at Qumran, has been construed by one later analysis to be a library collection reflective of numerous communities, possibly from another vicinity.[177] It is to be expected that eventually scholars will be able to classify the documents into identifiable groupings. For the present, however, it must suffice to take them, along with what Philo and Josephus tell us of sectarian community organization, as an undifferentiated cluster of evidence about sects of the time. Granted

---

[176] Sir 24:1–2; Wsd 5:5; *1 Enoch* 47:3; *2 Baruch* 56:3.

[177] The point made here is, of course, more focused if one holds that the Dead Sea documents are all Essene. Norman Golb has argued against identifying the Dead Sea documents as the archive of a single Essene community. His controversial hypothesis is that they are a library brought from Jerusalem, and represent an amalgam of sectarian sources. *Proceedings of the American Philosophical Society*, 124 (October 1980), 1–24.

this conservative restraint, what continuities and discontinuities can we discern in these documents left behind by Jews who intended to go their own ways?[178]

What did the groups call themselves? More than two dozen titles appear in the documents. Generally they are variants on *yachad* = community ("the holy community"), *'edah* = congregation ("the congregation of Israel"), *etsah* = council ("the council of the good"), and *sôd* = assembly ("the assembly of the saints"). There is a curious and obvious refusal to use the traditional Hebrew social vocabulary, though the sense of the expressions used matches the terms current among their Jewish contemporaries.[179] The movements are critical of the present state of the people, and aim to establish a new covenant with the Lord, to invite recruits to swear fidelity to the Law of Moses. Since entrants were all Jews, the clear implication is that other Jewish communities had defected from fidelity to what Moses commanded.[180]

There is mention of settlements belonging to the communities. The membership, "the Many," would sit in plenary assembly:

1 to receive grievances between members;
2 to accept into membership or to reject a candidate after training;
3 to dispose of property and revenues, which were held in common;
4 to decide whether to absolve repentant members;
5 to regulate the common life;
6 to celebrate ritual suppers.[181]

Decisions in assembly were to be by majority vote.[182]

As has already been seen, priests and Levites held positions of high honor and authority, at least in some communities. Elders were present and were to be treated with deference, but they do not appear to have had any role in governance.[183]

There is an elite group. One document describes it as fifteen men, including three priests, exemplary in their dedication to the Law.[184] Another describes a college of ten elected men, including four priests

---

[178] Such a reconstruction must remain very tentative. Our evidence from this movement is fragmentary. The documents are not thoroughly consistent with one another. Also, we cannot be certain to what degree they are idealized, and to what degree they reflect actual practice.
[179] 1QS 9:2; 1QSa 1:1, 20; 1QSb 4:24; 1QH 4:25; Philo says they call their holy places "synagogues" (instead of *proseuchai*, as he would say), *Quod Omn. Prob.* 81.
[180] 1QS 5.
[181] Josephus, *Ant.* 18:22; 1QS 6:1, 15–16, 20; 8:19, 26; Josephus, *B.J.* 2:143; 1QS 6:8–13, 20.
[182] 1QS 5:2–3; Josephus, *B.J.* 2:146.   [183] 1QS 6:8.   [184] 1QS 8:1.

or Levites. They are to administer justice, and cooperate with the overseer to collect funds for the poor, needy, dying, fugitives, captives, kinless virgins, unwanted spinsters.[185] Yet a third variant seems to describe a larger but still select council to dispense justice.[186]

A single overseer = *mevaqqer* presides. He is to:

1 teach the Many the ways of God and the Law;
2 control recruitment;
3 examine and train novices;
4 control financial transactions;
5 preside over the Many;
6 hear grievances.[187]

He is assisted by an "overseer of the revenues of the many."[188] And over all the community settlements there is a single overseer for all the camps.[189]

The members are grouped into cells of ten persons each, for devout reflection and discussion, preferably with a priest as leader.[190]

To generalize further would exceed what the documents permit us to conclude. What we see in these sectarian documents is dissident communities making every effort to follow a distinctive way of life. They regard their fellow Jews as unfaithful to Moses' call. Their communities are designed and presented as rigorous and radical regimes that have broken with what they regard as the unfaithful practices of mainline Judaism. Even the vocabulary is chosen to avoid the use of terms reminiscent of the ordinary path. Yet despite this purposeful and conscious effort to dissociate from what other Jews are doing, we encounter in the sectarian program the old familiar organization. There are a popular assembly (rather stronger), a select group for both policy and discipline, a single presiding officer, common meals, regular scripture reading and exposition, a system of discipline with accountability, a welfare program, a distant superior authority, a common treasury (though more bountifully supplied), baths, a prayer house, a cemetery.

We behold a paradox: for dissidents bent upon a new departure, the sectarians devised a community remarkably conformed, in its

---

[185] CD 10:1–4; 15:4; 14:12–16; Philo, *Hyp.* 11:13.   [186] 1QSa 1:25; 2:14, 17, 21.
[187] CD 13:7–8; 14:7–8; 13:11–13; 15:5–15; 1QS 6:14–15; CD 13:15–16; 14:7–8; 9:22.
[188] 1QS 6:20; Philo, *Hyp.* 11:10.
[189] CD 14:8–11. Another leading figure is mentioned: the prince of the congregation = *nasi ha'edat*, 1QSb 5:20; 1QM 3:15; 5:1. He is more an apocalyptic than an historical figure.
[190] Josephus, *B.J.* 2:146; CD 13:1–7. The cell leader also is once called an overseer, 13:5.

most fundamental lineaments, to the traditional pattern. So tenacious was that pattern of community organization in Jewish synagogues as the Second Temple era drew to a close. It was this firm and fast tradition that was to be both heritage and point of departure for another dissident group about to emerge within Jewry, to follow a new Way which was not all that New.

In concluding this account of the synagogue and its organization during the period when it might have served the earliest Christians as precedent and model for their communities, we should look once more at the nature and quality of our evidence to be sure that we are not asking more of it than it can vouch for.

The evidence reviewed is very disparate. There are significant variations in genre between late Jewish scriptures and apocrypha, in both Hebrew and Greek, on the one hand, and the Christian gospels on the other; between the Qumran documents and the funerary inscriptions; and between the politically manipulated history of Josephus, the philosophically infused history of Philo and the aloofness from history of the Mishnah.[191] Also, we know there were some clear differences between Jewish practice in Eretz Israel and in the Diaspora. Further, the sources available represent very different eras: they belong to periods as different as the Hasmonean hegemony and the rule of the Flavians, and they are divided most abruptly by the catastrophic changes that differentiated Jewry after 70 AD from what had gone before.

From this miscellany of evidence we could never reconstruct a single, uniform pattern of synagogue organization throughout all of Jewry, homeland and Diaspora, during and after the Commonwealth, in villages and metropolitan centers. But that was never our undertaking.

What we do claim to have discerned is a pattern that is typical rather than uniform. The fact that the evidence is so very disparate is itself a striking advantage for any attempt to discern features of community, program, services and offices. Precisely because they are found so broadly attested across time, place and circumstance, they are likely to have been typical, if not invariable. And the fact that many of these features have been retained by breakaway groups within Judaism strengthens the plausibility of their having been

---

[191] See Jacob Neusner, "Beyond Myth, after Apocalypse: The Mishnaic Conception of History," in *The Social World of Formative Christianity and Judaism*, Essays in Tribute to Howard Clark Kee, ed. Neusner et al. (Philadelphia: Fortress, 1988), 91–106.

continued by those Jews whose beliefs in Jesus quickly set them apart as dissidents.

The evidence shows that the offices of elder, synagogue chief and assistant are more widely evidenced than those of senior elder, scribe or commissioner. As for the program of a synagogue, common provision for the welfare of the indigent, for reading and discussion of the scriptures and for remittance of taxes show forth as more typical than provision of a kosher market or custody of documents. There are institutional elements that seem more standard; others, that are more marginal.

The question we put to the mass of evidence is, in the end, quite circumscribed: was there a tradition of community program, services and offices so typical in Jewish synagogues throughout the period of Christian origins that we could ascertain whether the Christian communities telescoped out of that predecessor tradition, or went their own way with innovative structures (or freedom from structures) of their own?

The structures we have managed to sketch out thus far suggest a positive answer to that question. But it can be no more than a provisional answer. Examination of the Christian evidence will have to tell us whether or not there was such an initial continuity. If there was – if the church did initially follow the synagogue model – then that fact would add yet further confirmation to the durable yet flexible character of the synagogue, typical enough to be retained by what was arguably the most powerful defection from Israel for centuries.

CHAPTER 8

Community organization in the early Christian settlement

We lack direct evidence that the first Christians assembled to read and consider the scriptures. Yet scholars without exception accept that they did. On what grounds? Because we can assume that the practice attested later can be projected backwards into the first century documentation? No. It is because this practice was established in the Jewish synagogue from which Christians emerged, and later reappeared, after a hiatus in specific information, in the churches of later years. This has justified the assumption that it must naturally have been a continuous practice all along, and indeed one so thoroughly native and natural to the communities that it somehow escaped comment.

That is the same method to be used in studying the continuous existence of community offices, which has been a matter of considerable debate.

When we turn our inquiry from the Jewish to the earliest Christian communities, the resources are not the same. There are virtually no inscriptions referring to identifiable Christians before the third century. No papyrus collections have survived. The Christians of the first, say, four generations had no Philo or Josephus to lay down a corpus of literature that would be theirs. Not until well through the second century were dissident sects emerging that would leave us a polemical literature, nor can we gain access to very early alternative Christian communities, such as the Qumran documents reveal in the Judaism of the time. The new religion elicited only a few brief notices from gentile writers, none of which bespeaks much knowledgeable familiarity with the movement. Remarkably little comment is found in the documents of contemporary Jews (and what we can find, in Josephus, is discounted as being later insertions by Christian editors).

Compared with the variety and plenty of extant sources on Judaism of the first century AD and the first half of the second century, our access to Christianity at that time is meager indeed. The canonical scriptures, Clement's Letter to the Corinthians, and perhaps part of the *Didache* are all that we can claim unarguably from the first century. The Christian scriptures themselves do not offer full yield for our purposes, since much of the information they contain reflects Jewish, and not Christian, custom. The sum of other Christian documents up until the midpoint of the second century amounts to a library that at most only doubles the volume of what we have in the New Testament. Add to all this the fragments that appear later in Irenaeus, Eusebius and several other cinder-sifters, and that is the end of it.

In our reconstruction we shall, for reasons set forth in chapter 6, be treating Acts as a problematic but not misrepresentative source on the early church, the pastoral epistles as neither very late (second-century, as some have wished) nor distorting, and the seven-letter corpus of Ignatius as authentic and dating from 110.

With so little evidence available we are naturally drawn to see an entire species in every jawbone fragment. The desire to reconstruct a church order from this period which laid down the authoritative precedents for the generations shortly to follow, and which stands as uniquely classical for every Christian age, is understandable. It must be tempered by our suspicion that these were people too unmoored from their past, too scattered from one another, too charismatic in leadership, to have abided by any single pattern or to have developed along a single trajectory.

Christian historians have of course been helped to fill in the early picture from what they knew of later times. The evidence we have of the fourth- and fifth-century communities is abundant, and it reveals certain forms that were then becoming dominant. The beguilements of reading later usages back into an undefined past have led to much myth and mischief, however.

In our case we must be alerted to the very valuable patterns of the hellenistic Jewish community customs in which the earliest and most influential Christians were raised. Those were men and women seized by the excitement of what they considered God's great new Act in their midst. But whatever the creativity of the new believers and their liberation from usages of their past, those established ways of living were too deeply rooted for us to ignore them when trying to fill in this sketch of the earliest Christians.

A word about method is in order at this point. The very earliest

Christian writers have left behind scant evidence of organized congregational life, programs, services or usages. By the turn of the second century, however, there were official structures in place that appear at first sight to be innovative. Put most schematically, the church of the New Testament and the church of the "Apostolic Fathers" appear to embody, respectively, charismatic and official traditions of leadership that are characterized by associated contrasts: lay vs. clerical, congregational vs. hierarchical, voluntary vs. professional.

Scholars have generally interpreted this discontinuity between the early generations in loyal conformity with their own views about the sixteenth-century Reformation. Some, because they acknowledge apostolic succession and ordained office as essential to authentic Christianity, have claimed to see enough hints and harbingers of office in the New Testament to verify a radical continuity between the two periods (and indeed between the polity then and the polity in their present church). Scholars of a contrary loyalty and interpretation have seen a radical discontinuity and have taken the earlier, "unofficered" church as their inspired norm.

Let us go about it in an entirely different way. Instead of examining the two earliest Christian periods, let us try to relate three stages, beginning with the Judaism that was the context and departure-point of the first Christian discipleship.

Instead of projecting official structures backwards from the second century into the first, or refusing to acknowledge any structures in that period for which there is no explicit and convergent evidence, let a third method be tried. Let us begin with a hypothesis: there is an antecedent likelihood that the first Christians, being Jews, organized themselves in the familiar and conventional ways of the synagogue. This does not assume that they were conservative and conventional: only that their energy and dissent flowed into new priorities, new convictions and new styles of behavior more than into new institutions. Allowing for shifts in nomenclature and for distinctively Christian developments in how a community of belief functioned, let us see whether the fragmentary evidences we do have from the earliest Christian period fit congruently onto the synagogue template, as archeologists who recover only a few sherds can compare them to the traditional pottery forms to identify their original shape. Then let us see whether the synagogue structures and offices go on to develop plausibly and continuously into the third period, over the crest of the first century into the second.

Rather than fastening on each item of evidence in its own right, as heretofore, let us see whether, taken all together, they allow themselves to tell a story of continuity of structure amid turbulence and innovation in the functions and styles of office. If the evidence allows us to reconstruct the earliest Christian period as a cantilever connecting the synagogue of the first century to the church of the second century, it will go far to sustaining the hypothesis.

Two questions would then face us. If the traditional offices of the second-century church are descended from those of the hellenistic synagogue, then why are their incumbents so strikingly insignificant in the biblical authors' memory of their communal experience? And why do officers eventually emerge with such strength and significance in the second century?

Another methodical word of caution is in order before one approaches these documents. Meyers and Strange, noting the difficulty archeologists have in distinguishing Christian from Jewish artefacts in the Palestine of late antiquity, observe that the Christians were slow in developing their own repertoire of physical identifiers.

Our discussion of Jewish tombs, burial practices, and views of afterlife has reinforced our methodological assumption that a study of the earliest Christian remains in Palestine means studying Jewish remains. Given this fact that Christianity did not develop its own symbolic vocabulary of signs and symbols until the fourth century, we must, so it seems, depend on Jewish remains in order to understand the context of early Christianity.[1]

The literary evidence, however, suggests that the early Christians did create one distinctive kind of sign: continuing the familiar practice of any Jewish faction, they quickly developed their own institutional vocabulary. But one must be quite careful to observe its method and tempo of development.

Vocabulary has a way of becoming stylized. This is a widespread human experience. A devout and purposeful woman gathers others of like generosity to live and work in a community. Their style is frugal and unadorned: they simply tie white kerchiefs about their heads. Four centuries later those muslin bandanas have evolved into

---

[1] Eric M. Meyers and James F. Strange, *Archeology, the Rabbis and Early Christianity* (Nashville: Abingdon, 1981), 169.

starched linen headgear that is neither frugal nor unostentatious. What was intended to preserve the past has in effect discontinued it.

It is much the same with words. Feminism that is not all that feminine; a Servant of the Servants of God who expects to be obeyed; waiters who are always in a hurry: words have a way of turning around without meaning to. Often a word is put to use in its original sense. For instance, Jewish synagogues and Christian churches had staff members called *hypêretai* = *diakonoi* = servants. In time the Christian *diakonoi* evolved into powerful administrators. Their title then had taken on new overtones. It no longer came across like "employee," or "assistant." When translated into other languages it could no longer be replaced with an equivalent word, for to call these executives "servants" would be incongruous. And so *diakonos* could not be translated at all: it was simply brought across as "deacon."

When we deal in a single traditional language, therefore, as functions change, titles may not. They can become stylized instead, and it becomes very important for a historian to know just what functions a title connotes in a particular era or context.

Let an appropriate illustration serve. Some ancient societies acknowledged the corporate sagacity and authority of older men. Ancient Israel called such a person a *zaqen* = an elderly person. In time many Jews came to speak Greek, and they called such a community authority *presbyteros*, the direct Greek equivalent of *zaqen*. But in the meantime the *presbyteroi* had begun to be not all that old, since an aristocracy of wealth and family had replaced the eminence of age and experience. The first Christian *presbyteroi* seem to have been cut from a different cloth: they were exemplary, activist believers who were ready to exert themselves in the new movement. Then as the church expanded into the suburbs and villages those who carried that title were no longer members of a corporate policy group: each one found himself presiding over a satellite parochial community of his own. Just when that change was being transacted, the word was put to an altogether new use, yet ironically one that restored it somewhat to its native meaning: it was used to refer to the generation of "elders" who were the extant living link of the third and fourth generations with the apostles.[2] In the literature of no more than a century, then, one is obliged to discern behind this single

---

[2] Papias, 3:3; Irenaeus, *Adversus Haereses* (hereafter *Haer*), 2:22:5; 4:27:1, 2; 4:30:1, 4; 5:5:1; 5:33:3; 5:36:1, 2; Eusebius of Caesarea uses the word in both senses: *Historia Ecclesiastica* (hereafter *H.E.*), 5,4,1; 5,4,2; 3,39,4.

technical term three or four successive and coexistent realities: some retentive of the word's original meaning, and others now become quite stylized.

There are other words familiar to this tradition that have shifted in their reference: *chêra* = widow ≫ dedicated ecclesiastical woman, *martus* = witness ≫ martyr and torah = Law ≫ five books of Moses. One must also, contrariwise, be alert to the opposite: when functions continue virtually unchanged but are given a new title. This, we shall observe, was the case for several synagogue offices which Christians retained, but preferred to call by alternative names.

THE NAME OF THE MOVEMENT

It is usually revealing what a group resolves to call itself at the outset. The evidence shows considerable diversity among the first Jesus people. The earliest letters, for example, are addressed to "*hoi hagioi* = the holy ones" or to "the assembly of God," or to "the assembly of God the Father and of Jesus Christ."[3] The book of Revelation uniformly speaks of the group as *douloi* = slaves. Some authors use formulas all their own: James is addressed to "the twelve tribes of the Dispersion"; 1 Peter, to "all those living as aliens in the Dispersion ... who have been chosen"; 2 Peter, to "those who have received a faith as precious as our own"; Jude, to "those who are called."[4] They are "God's people" in Hebrews.[5] In Antioch the group began to be known as *christianoi* = Christians, and this continued as an identifying name by which the group could be known to outsiders.[6] They were also known in some outside circles as Nazareans.[7]

Very early, however, the dominant title used within the group was simply *hê ekklêsia* = the assembly.[8] Throughout the literature the

---

[3] 1 Cor 6:1; 2 Cor 1:2; Phil 1:1; Col 1:2; Eph 1:1; 2:19; Hb 13:24; 1 Cor 1:2; 2 Cor 1:1; Ignatius of Antioch, *Letter to the Philippians*, address; Ignatius, *Letter to the Smyrnaeans*, address. (Hereafter his letters to the Ephesians, Magnesians, Trallians, Romans, Philadelphians, Smyrnaeans and Polycarp are identified as *IEph*, *IMg*, *ITr*, *IRo*, *IPhld*, *ISm*, *IPol*.)
[4] Js 1:1; 1 Pt 1:1; 2 Pt 1:1; Jd 1.   [5] Hb 4:9.
[6] *Letter to Diognetus* (hereafter *Dg*), 1; Pliny the Younger, *Letters*, 10:96–97 (to and from Trajan).
[7] Ac 24:5; the *Birkat ha-Minim* version found in the Cairo Geniza. Ray A. Pritz, *Nazarene Jewish Christianity* (Leiden and Jerusalem: Brill & Magnes, 1988).
[8] 1 Th 1:1; 2 Th 1:1; Phlm 2; Clement of Rome, *Letter to the Corinthians* (hereafter *1 Cl*), address; *IEph*, address; *IMag*, address; *IRom*, address; Polycarp, *Letter to the Philippians* (hereafter *Pol*), address. *Ekklêsia* has descended into the romance languages, through the Latin *ecclesia*: *église*, *iglesia*, *chiesa*. The Germanic languages have drawn their equivalent

local community is called "the assembly" with no further modifier except the designation of locality: typically, "the assembly dwelling in *X*."[9]

The word *ekklēsia* was, as we have seen, in current Jewish usage. Originally a virtual synonym for *synagōgē* = meeting, it had been differentiated by the Greek Bible. *Synagōgē* served to translate *keneset*, and was used to designate local communities; *ekklēsia* translated *qahal*, and was used to designate plenary gatherings of the community. By metonymy the two terms could be and often were exchanged. Christian usage takes full advantage of the metonymy and prefers to use *ekklēsia* = assembly to mean community, both local and worldwide. In Christian usage the word rarely designates an actual meeting.[10] This choice of title seems to be purposeful. The Christian community systematically avoided the continuation of the even more traditional term, *synagōgē*. Acts 20:28, quoting from Psalm 73, replaces *synagōgē* with *ekklēsia* precisely in order to make it applicable to the Christian community. In the gospels and Acts the customary usage is almost entirely suppressed: *synagōgē* is almost never used to designate a Jewish community.[11] Instead, following Palestinian usage it refers to Jewish meeting houses. The usual word elsewhere in Jewry for meeting house = *proseuchē* is, in turn, never used in the New Testament for that purpose. It is rare for these Christians to speak of their own communities or gatherings as *synagōgai*.[12] In fact *synagōgē* is used pejoratively: "the *synagōgē* of Satan," "the *synagōgē* of villains."[13] Paul, the most frequent user of *ekklēsia*, never once writes the word *synagōgē*, nor do the deutero-pauline letters.

Clearly the Christians were beginning to differentiate themselves from other Jewish communities – by nomenclature, not by structure

word from the Greek *kyriakē* = the Lord's: *Kirche*, *kirk*, church. In every case the word is not translated, just passed on.

[9] 1 Cor 14:26; 2 Cor 8:23; Ro 16:23; Js 5:14; 3 J 9–10; Ac 16:1; *1 Cl*, 54:2; *IEph*, 1:3; *IPhld*, 10:1–2; *IPol*, 8:1; *Shepherd of Hermas* (hereafter *Hm* [Mandate], *Hs* [Similitude], *Hv* [Vision]), *Vision* 2:4:3.

[10] 1 Cor 11:18; Ac 7:38; *ITr*, 3:1. Acts sometimes uses *to plēthos* = the entire group to refer to an assembly: 6:2; 15:12, 22; 21:22; see also *Hm*, 11:9. In a way this expression supplants their reference, as Jews, to themselves as a people = *dēmos*.

[11] Exceptions: Ac 6:9; 9:2; 26:11; see *Hm*, 11:9.

[12] Js 2:2; *Hm*, 11:9; *IPol*, 4:2; Epiphanius, *Adversus Haereses*, 30,18,2. The first two documents are from Judeo-Christian authors.

[13] Rv 2:9; 3:9; *Letter of Barnabas* (hereafter *B*), 5:13 (quoting Ps 21:16); 6:6. By contrast, when a favorable allusion is to be made, the word used is *ekklēsia*: "the *ekklēsia* of my brothers," "the *ekklēsia* of the holy ones" (quoting Ps 42:3; 22:23), *B*, 6:16.

– at a very early date.[14] This was a practice of Jewish sectarian groups which, as we shall see, became customary as the Christians chose a distinctive vocabulary to denote institutions which were not all that distinctive.

Jewish communities were accustomed, and even obliged, to tolerate a diversity of doctrinal views. In large cities, such as Alexandria or Jerusalem, there were enough *synagôgai* that they could sort themselves out by preference. Pharisees, Sadducees, Zealots, Therapeutae, Essenes and those of any other sect = *hairêsis* could congregate with those of their own persuasion. But in towns and villages, especially in the Dispersion, a single Jewish community might have learned to abide sometimes strenuously held partisan doctrines. The early Christians benefited by that tradition, and engaged their fellow Jews in agitated debate for some time, when they were referred to as one more *hairêsis*.[15] They were sometimes allowed a long stretch of time to argue for their own understanding of the scriptures. But there is also evidence that after they had expressed themselves a while in any one community things came to a breaking point, and they could no longer participate as members.[16]

Obviously the first point of annoyance was their claim that Jesus was the Messiah. In Jerusalem this claim would have had a particularly insulting aspect, since it implied grand criminal fault in the highest authorities there. The associated claim that Jesus had been raised from Sheol would have made their preaching all the more repugnant to Sadducees. Their interest in a spiritual renewal would, for the Zealots, have been a political distraction. The new band of believers wore out their welcome in their synagogue communities and simply banded together in separate communities of their own, as did the other sects. They replicated much of the customary Jewish practice and, whether they had by then shirked the word or not, they were a network of *synagôgai*.

It was later that they provoked a much more violent cause of dissociation, by accepting into some of their communities table-fellows who were not Jews: Samaritans, "God-fearers," gentiles. At first they were circumcised as part of their initiation; when that was

[14] See also Robert Murray, *Symbols of Church and Kingdom: A Study in Early Syriac Tradition* (Cambridge: Cambridge University Press, 1975), introduction, esp. 18.
[15] Ac 24:5, 14; 28:22; see 5:17; 15:5; 26:5.
[16] Ac 6:9; 18:4; 19:8; 5:12; J 9:22; 12:42; 16:2. See Steven Katz, "Issues in the Separation of Judaism and Christianity after 70 C.E.: A Reconsideration," *Journal of Biblical Literature*, 103, 1 (1984), 43–76.

discontinued, the provocation could not but be intense. It was at this time that they were faced, not only with rejection far sterner than the conventional sects directed towards one another, but with a radical separation. Now they no longer fit into anyone's categories within the people of God.

The question is repeatedly asked: did the Jews banish the Christians or was it the Christians who severed the tie? It now appears that the question itself has been poorly put. Both the pharisaic Judaism that survived the catastrophe of Jerusalem's (twice-repeated) desecration and the Jewish-gentile Christianity that surprised itself by abandoning an ethnic identity were under strong challenge to identify themselves with Israel of the past. The presence of each group as an aggressive contender for legitimacy was a stimulus for the other to define itself as exclusively as could be. Their relationship was not so much that of an establishment and a rebel: one group in quiet possession resisting an outsider group that contested the field. The synagogue and the church were two innovative rivals who simultaneously and energetically framed their biblical canon and interpretation, moral code and liturgical usages, in attentive conflict with one another, in a definitive season of self-definition for both peoples.[17]

During that first period of a Christianity with exclusively Jewish membership, with the single-minded goal of bringing their entire people to welcome Jesus as the risen Messiah, it is not unlikely that when and where they became estranged from their communities they would have hived off into synagogues of their own. It was after the later and (at least in its social consequences) more drastic development that the Christians would have begun to reach for a name of their own. The choice was always from among the alternatives offered by the Jewish nomenclature, but almost always a variant less used in the Jewish mainstream. It would need to be traditional

---

[17] Evidence for this has been presented helpfully in some of the essays edited by E. P. Sanders et al., in *Jewish and Christian Self Definition II: Aspects of Judaism in the Greco-Roman Period* (Philadelphia: Fortress, 1981). Lawrence H. Schiffman sees self-definition at issue in Jewish ethical rule-making and in liturgical formulae: "At the Crossroads: Tannaitic Perspective on the Jewish-Christian Schism," 115–156. Joseph Blenkinsopp argues effectively that competitive struggle had spurred Jewish sectarian rivals during the Second Temple period to formulate self-legitimating rules of biblical interpretation (in order to claim continuity with the prophets), and then to canonize explicit rosters of sacred scripture. The process as he describes it seems to have continued into the period and the rivalry we are studying here: "Interpretation and the Tendency to Sectarianism: An Aspect of Second Temple History," 1–26.

enough to assert their claims to authentic continuity, but enough "their own" to represent the new identity they were stumbling into. Thus the tendentious rejection of *synagógé* and adoption of *ekklésia* (which was the harbinger of a general avoidance of the standard Jewish vocabulary for offices, activities and functions even when hardly changed from the tradition) signaled a threshold of self-awareness that their communities were now going to stand by themselves while consciously claiming continuity with the past.

One must appreciate what it meant for a Jew to quit or be put out of his or her synagogue. One lost all public standing in one's hereditary society, all welfare benefits, all recourse to a judiciary for the protection and enforcement of rights and debts, all means of sending taxes and tithes to Jerusalem, all access to marital arrangements, any facility for obtaining or authenticating official documents, the amenities of ritual purification, bathing and water supply, hospitality and succor when sick or journeying, political advocacy or clout in the face of municipal or imperial power. Worship and schooling were easy enough for the dissident Christians to provide for themselves, even without public premises or buildings. But we must not underestimate the social, economic, emotional and political costs incurred in this stubborn following of loyalties. Clearly they would have begun to duplicate the traditional synagogue program as best they could. There is, as we shall see, evidence that they did. But those who departed from established communities, with vested wealth and recognized status in the larger society, were taking their chances with a new community that had little stored wealth but many new obligations.

Very likely the expected contributions of the average member had to exceed what he or she had given in the past. Motivation had to be robust: strong enough even to support the communistic economy recorded of the very first Jerusalem group. One imagines communities with a lower share than before of landowners, and a greater proportion of widows and other welfare claimants. If the cautionary tale of Ananias and Sapphira (Acts 5) made a profound impression on the whole *ekklésia*, there were surely many others who worried about the future of their households in this enthusiastic movement, and hesitated to commit their entire financial and social stake to its survival.

How much more severe the break, however, when these "synagogues of the Nazareans," or whatever they were called, agreed one by one to admit the uncircumcised. Every gathering they held was defiled; every supper they shared, inedible; every teaching they formulated, no longer able to be considered. They were no longer of Israel: they forfeited the recognition of both the Jewish and the Roman authorities. Both Jewish and gentile members went into a legal and social underworld to comfort each other.[18] It is in such a situation that Christian documents (like Acts) can now speak of "Jews" and "Greeks," and see themselves as a third and distinct entity.[19] The name they preferred for that entity was *hê ekklêsia* = the assembly.

The movement itself was known intramurally for a while as the Way = *hê hodos*.[20] Eventually it would require some general name which could enclose, not simply a local community, but the entire fellowship of believers from city to city. As Jews they had simply called themselves Israel. Eventually – but this was well into the second century – they could speak of themselves as "the New Israel," but many years and disappointments would have to bring them to that point.[21] In the earlier days of sharp and costly estrangement, the preferred title of *ekklêsia* also served, as *synagôgê* had not usually served the Jews, to name the worldwide fellowship of *ekklêsiai*. The *ekklêsia* was not only the local community assembled; it was the great solidarity of Jesus-believers.[22]

It is timely to note now three ways in which the Christians – much like the Jews – managed their nomenclature. First, an early variety of words gave way eventually to a standard nomenclature. For instance, *'edah* = congregation, *qahal* = *ekklêsia* = assembly, *keneset* = *synagôgê* = meeting, *yachad* = community, *etsah* = council, *sôd* = assembly, *to plêthos* = the whole are some of the traditional titles to refer to the people of Israel. Eventually the local community came to be known properly as *keneset* = *synagôgê* = meeting. The other words continued

---

[18] Philip Francis Esler has well argued that a salient purpose of Luke was to reassure Jewish Christians that they had made a legitimate choice to remain Christians at the cost of losing communion with Judaism, and also to reassure Roman Christians that their religion was essentially compatible with allegiance to Rome; *Community and Gospel in Luke-Acts* (Cambridge: Cambridge University Press, 1987).

[19] *hoi hellenisteis kai hoi hebraioi* = the Hellenists and the Hebrews was a way of describing cohorts within their group; "Greeks and Jews" referred to outsiders; Acts 6:1.

[20] Ac 9:2; 19:9, 23; 22:4; 24:14, 22.

[21] Peter Richardson, *Israel in the Apostolic Church* (Cambridge: Cambridge University Press, 1969).

[22] 1 Cor 11:22; 15:9; Phil 3:6; Col 1:18; *IPhld*, 5:2; *B*, 7:11; *Hv*, 2:4:1; *Martyrdom of Polycarp* (hereafter *MPol*), 8:1; 19:2.

in use, but they had become synonyms while the selected term, no longer generic, had become a technical title: a name, not a designation. Another characteristic in this development is that the competing sectarian vocabularies, which had to entitle organizational elements that thoroughly resembled their counterparts in the other groups, avoided whenever possible using the official names the other groups had selected as theirs. Hence the *archisynagôgos* of the synagogue and the *mevaqqer* of Qumran; the *episkopos* of the Catholics and the *epimelêtês* of the Gnostics.

Partisans of the nineteenth-century consensus have interpreted the distinctive vocabulary of the Christians as a token of innovation. Richard Hanson has observed that

the fluidity and wide-ranging use and meaning of the terms chosen by the Church to describe its main official ministries make the search for predecessors of these ministries in Jewish institutions and in Greek or other pagan society an almost futile one. Inspector (*episcopus*), assistant (*diaconus*), older man (*presbyteros*) – these are names of such wide use and general application that scholars ought to be convinced that they are chosen to describe new and untraditional functions rather than that they were modifications or re-interpretations of offices or functions already existing in Jewish or pagan society.[23]

But the evidence shows that the Christian development of titles follows the Jewish customs rather faithfully. The title of the community chiefs may serve as an illustration. At first they are called *presbyteroi* or *episkopoi*, or *hêgoumenoi* or *poimenes*: sometimes sharing a common designation with the elders and sometimes having one of their own. If, as seems natural, the first community chiefs continued to be called *archisynagôgoi*, that title has faded from the record because of its too-clear identification with the Jewish synagogues, as well as with Greco-Roman associations. When the strategic role of the president gave the office more prominence – in a word, when superintendence = *episkopê* shifted away from the college towards the chief – then one of the descriptors was converted into a title, a name: *episkopos*. The remainder words, like shepherd or elder or presider, remained in use but now they were analogous, not titulary. This characteristic process whereby a variety of terms gives way to one;

[23] Richard P. C. Hanson, *Studies in Christian Antiquity* (Edinburgh: T. & T. Clark, 1985), 120–121.

the one is converted from a generic descriptor to a title; and the title is selected so as to differentiate the group from rival groups: all this is very traditional in Judaism and betokens continuity more than it does innovation. At a time when the Jewish world was alive with competing religious movements, each striving for distinctive self-definition, gestures of differentiation were, paradoxically, evidence that the movements were all involved in a simultaneous task.[24]

THE AGENDA OF THE ASSEMBLY

If this new and beleaguered movement chose to call itself "the assembly," what were the activities it undertook with full membership convened and present?

Paul, Acts and *Barnabas* report meetings to discuss and adopt community policy.[25] The issues requiring resolution all have to do with relations between the communities. Since the Christian communities lacked the legal standing which both Rome and Jerusalem acknowledged in the synagogue communities, there is no record of meetings to resolve issues of civil welfare.

We know that letters written between communities were read out at assembly, as were those from venerated leaders like Paul and Ignatius.[26] These letters were then copied and circulated and began to accumulate into a corpus that evolved into the shared library of all communities.[27] There is no record from this period that the scriptures (the Law, the prophets and the writings) were read, or that the gospels were being circulated and read out, but it is a reasonable surmise that they were. Here was a group whose founders in every city had made themselves *personae non gratae* at synagogue meetings by being first on their feet to explain what the scriptures *really* meant. When, for their pains, they were finally unwelcome in their communities for being intolerably contentious, and chose (or were obliged) to keep company by themselves, nothing could be more certain than their immediate need to meet and pore over those

---

[24] Dominique Barthélemy has shown how Christian and Pharisaic canon-making proceeded side-by-side as another tactic of self-definition: "L'état de la Bible juive depuis le début de notre ère jusqu'a la deuxième révolte contre Rome (131–135)," in *Le canon de l'Ancien Testament: Sa formation et son histoire*, ed. Jean-Daniel Kaestli and Otto Wermelinger (Geneva: Labor et Fides, 1984), 9–45.

[25] Gal 2:14; Ac 14:27; 15:2, 4; 21:22; *B*, 4:10. [26] Ac 15:31; 1 Th 5:27.

[27] Col 4:16; *Pol*, 13.

scriptures to their own satisfaction. Thus the primeval act of the postexilic synagogue – indeed, perhaps its most typical act – had to be continued by the Christian dissidents. And as the anecdotes about Jesus were circulated, there can be no doubt that they found pride of place in the assembly readings.

The Jewish custom of exhortation and discussion was also continued. Community leaders – apostles and elders – took the lead, and the fact that Paul bids women be silent listeners in those discussions suggests that in at least some communities they had found their voice.[28]

There are abundant references to the communities being met for prayer. Also, the confession of sins seems to be an act that was somehow made a public rite, and therefore incorporated into the community assemblies. This may also have been the occasion for collections for other, indigent communities.[29]

That there were common meals is not open to doubt. But the record is strewn with an assortment of evidence. We read of the Lord's supper, the sharing of the cup and loaf, the breaking of bread, the *eucharistia* = thanksgiving, the common table, the *agapê* = love meal.[30] Were these all simply synonyms for the ritualized sabbath meals which every Jewish household and religious fellowship observed? Were they designations of synagogal banquets that were also a tradition? One must appreciate that, though increasingly unwelcome, Jewish Christians continued for a good while to join their compatriots in the temple and synagogue observances. But during those earliest days of community stress, the only worship situation where they might arrange to find themselves exclusively in sympathetic company was at the domestic sabbath suppers. It was inevitable that those suppers would become the treasured occasions for worship among the Jesus people. They would and did also serve as the most appropriate occasions to evoke the Lord's death, and his suppers with the disciples before and afterwards.[31] When Christians were finally no longer participating in synagogue meetings they brought home the service of readings, preaching, discussion and prayer and amalgamated it with the domestic supper. Thus several

[28] 1 Ti 2:11; Ac 5:42; 20:7; *2 Cl*, 17:3; 1 Cor 14:34–35; 1 Ti 1:18.
[29] 1 Cor 11:2–16; 14:23, 26; Ac 12:12; *IEph*, 5; 13:1; Js 5:16; *Didache* (hereafter *D*), 4:14; 14; 1 Cor 16:1.
[30] 1 Cor 11:20–34; 10:16–17; Ac 2:42, 46; 4:32–35; 20:7–12; *IEph*, 5; *D*, 7, 9, 10, 14; *Dg*, 5:7; Jd 12; *ISm*, 8:2.   [31] 1 Cor 11:24–25; Lk 22:19; 24:28–35.

narratives clearly decribe these two activities as combined.[32] But among the various accounts of community meals may be allusions to other, less ritualized meals, with a strong emphasis upon solidarity between haves and have-nots.

The Jewish synagogue communities knew two types of common meal: the fellowship meals shared by the full assembly, and the domestic sabbath meals eaten by households. Those two traditions both enjoyed Christian continuation, but as the domestic ritual meal becomes an observance of the full assembly (though in a home, for they have nowhere else to go), the two kinds of meal are (until one eventually absorbs the other) difficult to distinguish in the record. Since the account in 1 Corinthians, with the strongest injunctions to sharing among rich and poor, unequivocally refers to the Lord's supper and to Christ's body and blood, it is not easy to separate out two clearly distinctive meal formats.

These celebrations came eventually to be separatist, when transferred from sabbath eve to that of Sunday, the Lord's day. But there are also exhortations to hold frequent assemblies, presumably on weekdays. The memoir of Polycarp's death tells us that his bones were recovered and that the Christians in Smyrna gathered to celebrate "the birthday of his martyrdom" where they were interred.[33]

Baptism is mentioned in conjunction with the community suppers, but it remains unclear whether those meal gatherings were the ordinary venue for baptisms (if the latter required, by preference, running water), or whether baptisms required an assembly at all.[34]

The election and inauguration of community officers was another event that seems commonly to have transpired in assembly. Elders and deacons were so selected, as also representatives to be sent out on missions of preaching or negotiation. Paul's allusion to prophecy associated with Timothy's appointment implies an assembly for either prayer or eucharist.[35]

Whatever arrangements the communities made for internal discipline, certain judgments of a grave nature could be debated and delivered in plenary session. Paul writes to the Corinthian Christians

---

[32] Ac 20:7–12; *D*, 14; *IEph*, 5; symbolically in Lk 24:13–35.
[33] 1 Cor 16:1; *D*, 14; 16:2; *IPol*, 4:2; *MPol*, 18.
[34] *ISm*, 8:2; *D*, 7–10; cf. Ac 8:38; 9:18.
[35] Ac 14:23; 6:2, 5; 8:14 (Paul and Barnabas are commissioned at a prayer meeting, Ac 13:2–3, and report to an assembly on their return, 14:27); Ac 15:2, 22, 30; 1 Ti 1:18; 4:14.

of a punishment imposed on one offender by "the majority," and instructs them to deliver a recalcitrant, incestuous member over to Satan in full assembly.[36]

We learn, then, of many activities the Christians of this period are said to have undertaken in assembly: public policy debate, reading of scriptures and of community correspondence, exposition and exhortation, prayer, sacred fellowship meals, appointment and installation of officers, major judicial decisions, and perhaps baptisms. The earliest description of the community program of the newly converted may serve also as the agenda for their assemblies. They were faithful to the teaching of their leaders, the fellowship, the breaking of bread, and the prayers.[37]

If we compare this pattern to that of the Jewish synagogues, we note two differences. First, there is an absence of activities relating to the civil order, since Christian communities did not enjoy status as self-governing political enclaves. Second, the lack of public buildings kept all Christian assemblies in private homes, and combined some of the assembly activities with the domestic meal which may not previously have been an observance of the full gathering.

We have seen that the Christian Jews were given a very formative push off onto their own when local synagogues could no longer contain them. Those Jewish communities were not particularly narrow in their ideologies. As a community defined by ethnicity they had had no choice but to live and let live among fiercely partisan factions. We see no such willingness to tolerate diversity within the circle of the new movement. Paul inveighs against faction-building in his communities and considers it grounds for expulsion. The pastoral epistles are also intransigent about doctrinal unity, and Jude, Clement and Ignatius are, if anything, more peremptory.[38] As the social analysts would remind us, this insistence on unity is strong evidence that there was diversity and factional dispute in early days. But it was more of a threat to the *ekklêsia* than it could have been to an ethnically bonded *synagôgê*.

One must bear in mind that the principal identity of a Jew was to be son or daughter of Abraham and Sarah. All one's loyalties and debates were functions of that identity. Pharisees and Sadducees who

---

[36] 2 Cor 2:6 (*tôn pleionôn*); 1 Cor 5:4. [37] Ac 2:42.
[38] 2 Th 3:14; 1 Cor 1:10–12; 3:4; 11:18; Gal 1:8–9; Ro 16:18; 1 Cor 5:3, 11–12; 16:22; 1 Ti 1:3–7, 20; 4:1–11; 2 Ti 2:14–24; Tit 3:10; Jd 8; *1 Cl*, 51:1; 57:1; *IEph*, 3:2; *IMg*, 4:6; *IPhld*, 4; 8:1; *ISm*, 8:1; *IPol*, 2:1.

were impatient adversaries could stand side by side when confronting the gentile world. One had no choice: you could not easily drum anyone out of a group whose defining unity was ethnic. For the Christians the case was now otherwise. Their identity rested upon choice; they were not to the *ekklêsia* born. And after they took the drastic step of becoming multiracial, all ethnic identity had to be forfeited. Their unity rested, not upon a kinship of blood, but upon one of understanding: an understanding of what the God of Israel had accomplished in Jesus and how they were to respond. For them, doctrinal differences were far more ominous than for the Jews, and hence were regarded with much higher alarm. This was a community that was immensely less sanguine about pluralism and free thought. Such a change in their concerns made less difference in the agenda of their gatherings than in the tenor and priorities of their common life.

THE APOSTLES

Before studying the officers who served these communities, we must turn our attention to one group of leaders who loomed large in ways that differentiated the Christian assemblies from their Jewish antecedents: the apostles.

When a local community saw any of its members go forth with their sponsorship to serve as itinerant preachers, the bearers of this trust could be called *apostoloi* = delegates. That was how Barnabas and Saul first came into this title.

In the church at Antioch the following were prophets and teachers: Barnabas, Simeon called Niger, and Lucius of Cyrene, Manaen, who had been brought up with Herod the tetrarch, and Saul. One day while they were offering worship to the Lord and keeping a fast, the Holy Spirit said, "I want Barnabas and Saul set apart for the work to which I have called them." So it was that after fasting and prayer they laid their hands on them and sent them off.[39]

Their journeys took them through Cyprus, Pamphylia, Pisidia and Lycaonia, after which they reported to the home community what they had accomplished.

The pauline and lucan literature records other such apostles. Epaphroditus is an apostle of the assembly in Philippi, sent to work under Paul's direction. Andronicus and Junias (possibly Julia?) are

---

[39] Ac 13:1–3. They are called apostles in 14:4, 14.

The apostles

apostles imprisoned after long service, and Paul sends to Corinth two other apostles working in his retinue. Paul was peeved to discover that apostles from somewhere were circulating in his territory with a deviant doctrine. The *Didache* mentions itinerant apostles. It states that they are to be received with reverence but provided with a maximum of two days' food and lodging. Perhaps by this time the hospitality of the communities had been strained by vagrant missionaries in whom the Spirit had flickered low.[40]

Apostolic delegates were supposed to enjoy the good will due their sponsoring community. Still, the record tells us that Christian apostles were not merely community appointees. They were charismatics who, whether through a personal call or some prophetic summons, went forth as appointed by God. Hence a much higher sponsorship that their home churches might accept and accredit but not initiate. In this they differ from apostles = *apostoli* = *schelichim* sent out by the chief authorities of rabbinical Jewry in the early years. Jesus' own designees were acknowledged as sent prophetically or messianically by him as for the Lord (and later, by the Lord himself when Jesus' divine sonship came to the fore). Because of the utterly singular lordship of Jesus, a unique authority was acknowledged in his closest disciples who were to be the founders ("pillars," they are called[41]) of the early Christian communities. However many were the men and women closest to Jesus, all four gospels at one point or another stylize them as twelve men (though the names in the lists do not entirely match). The Twelve are remembered as a group after Jesus' departure, and since their significance among the believers now makes "disciple" an awkward title, they are honored as apostles of Jesus, and are so presented in some later gospel accounts. Acts likens them to the ancestors of the tribes of Israel, in that a vacancy in the group needed to be filled in order to leave the classical number intact (as, with the waning of Simeon, the Hebrew tribe of Joseph was split into Ephraim and Manasseh). There was of course an incongruity for in the story of Matthias' election to the place of Judas the prerequisites for nomination (that one have been a veteran of the long march with Jesus and have been a witness to his resurrection) assured that this could not be a group that would long endure.[42]

It may well be that the most vital of Jesus' inner circle did go forth as itinerant preachers. Apart from Peter, and perhaps John, there is

---

[40] Phil 2:25; Ro 16:7; 2 Cor 8:23; 11:5, 13; 12:11; *D*, 11:3–6.   [41] Gal 2:9; *1 Cl*, 5:2.
[42] Ac 1:15–26.

virtually no documentary record of the work done by any of these twelve called apostles. What has caused the title to glow with such brilliance in the Christian firmament is its very determined and successful appropriation by Paul.

His first visit to Jerusalem as a new and still suspect convert had proved an embarrassment to the Christian leadership there. He reawakened some of the violent local animosity that Stephen had so maladroitly brought down on their heads, and confirmed their distrust of hellenistic Jewish Christians. He had had to be sent home quietly.[43] His next journey to David's city, bearing relief funds from Antioch, might have raised his credit there,[44] as would news of his first apostolic journey (except that, to Jerusalem ears, the stories of the riots he had provoked at Iconium and Lystra would only have revived those misgivings). Paul's next appearance there, arguing on behalf of the liberal Antioch policy towards gentile converts, brought home a generous enough compromise.[45]

But at that point Paul determined never again to be so accountable to the conservative council of apostles and elders in the mother city. As of his second journey he redefined himself: no longer an apostle of God drawn prophetically from the Antioch community, but as an apostle of the risen Lord Jesus directly. He could not, of course, claim to be one of the Galilean veterans, but he offered his own redefinition of the title. He was an apostle of the Lord Jesus in virtue of his visionary encounter on the road to Damascus. It is this claim, imposed through both his letters and the lucan books, and eventually on the Jerusalem establishment by dint of his clear success in the field and their dependence on his financial support, that canonized for later Christian assemblies Paul's notion of an apostle of the Lord.

It is no exaggeration to say that Paul's transformation between his first and second journeys was the counterpart, in importance, of his earlier conversion experience. At this time came the parting of ways with Barnabas, his advocate and ally from earliest days. Now he would work only with subalterns, not peers. His letters are studded with unbashful assertions that he was commissioned by the Lord Jesus personally, and therefore he can claim an authority subordinate to none other in the church.[46] Paul asserts his right to command and

---

[43] Ac 9:26–31.   [44] Ac 11:27–30; 12:24–25.   [45] Ac 15.
[46] 1 Th 2:4–6; 2 Th 3:6, 12; 1 Cor 1:1, 17; 9:1–5; 12:9–11; 2 Cor 1:1; 5:20; Gal 1:1–22; 2:7–8; Col 1:1, 25; Phlmn 8; Ro 1:1, 5; 11:13; 15:16. The deutero-pauline letters continue the theme: Eph 1:1; 3:7; 1 Ti 1:1; 2:7; Tit 1:1, 3; 2 Ti 1:1, 11.

to judge, with the expectation that he will be obeyed.[47] He prefers to plow no one else's field, and resents the intrusion of any other apostles on his soil.[48] It is the duty of the churches to provide for his financial needs, and he reminds them of this even when he forgoes their support.[49] Indeed, one might say that Paul enjoyed an even wider ambit of independence than either Peter or John who, as long as they operated out of Jerusalem, seem to have been accountable for their work to the local elders. The strong position there of James, brother of Jesus and community chief but not an apostle or one of the Twelve, suggests another pattern of authority where community officers, even in the presence of apostles of the Lord, held their own.

Paul's attitude towards Jerusalem was drastically changed.[50] He had gone there, now no fresh convert but an apostle of sixteen or seventeen years' experience, to answer for his practices, and had come home with their decision, explained by their own envoys, not by Barnabas and himself. For a time he had worked, so to speak, under their aegis,[51] but then came the change. Seven or eight years later he would write to the Galatians of "the reputed leaders" there, "not that their importance matters to me."[52] His account of the negotiation in Galatians 2, so much more self-vaunting than Luke's in Acts 15, claims that it was he, not Antioch, that had been under scrutiny, and that even then he was not quite answerable to Jerusalem, since his divine commission made him Peter's peer. Paul looks now to no human tribunal; he is answerable to the Lord only.[53] Obviously the network could not handle many persons in circulation with this kind of credentials, for they would eventually collide.

It is not without significance that the churches in Corinth and Galatia received the most lengthy and heated lectures on the subject of apostolic authority, and that the letter to the Philippians is the only pauline document without a single mention of it. The former

---

[47] 1 Th 2:6; 2 Th 3:6–15; 1 Cor 5:3; 7:12; 14:37; 2 Cor 10:6, 8; 13:10; Phlm 8.
[48] Ro 15:20; 2 Cor 11:5, 13; 12:11.
[49] 2 Th 3:7–9; 1 Cor 9:4, 14; 2 Cor 11:7–8; 12:13; Phil 4:10–18.
[50] Esler argues well that Paul's estrangement from Jerusalem was much sharper than presented by Luke-Acts, where Peter and James are presented as patrons of a reconciliation with the Hellenists (Acts 6) and of acceptance of God-fearer gentiles (Acts 10), two trends which in fact Jerusalem resisted. *Community and Gospel*, 131–163. Norman R. Petersen doubts the historicity of Acts' account that Paul typically approached local Jews in their synagogues, and only when rebuffed there, preached to gentiles. His mission, at least after breaking with Barnabas, was immediately to gentiles. *Literary Criticism for New Testament Critics* (Philadelphia: Fortress, 1978), 81–92.   [51] Ac 16:4.   [52] Gal 2:2–6.
[53] 1 Cor 4:4.

communities had had the most energetic quarrels in his absence, and the latter had been the most docile and devoted. Paul's apostolic claims were in direct proportion to the challenges raised against his controversial policies. He was more than willing to argue his case on its merits, but if that did not carry the day he produced his fall-back argument that was procedural. It was conflict that elicited this show of authority, in a loosely networked community that was desperately in need of unity.

And it turned out to be fateful that the area of Paul's influence – the Christian "fertile crescent" from Antioch through Asia and Greece to Rome – was, apart from Egypt, the homeland for the New Testament and the venue for later Byzantine and Latin Christianity. By the time Clement in Rome, Ignatius of Antioch and *Barnabas* in Alexandria were echoing it, this high apostolic doctrine received from Paul was clearly normative in those Christian communities, when there were no more apostles of the Lord alive.[54] Bringing all this to bear now on our study of local community leadership among Christians, we shall appreciate those alterations they underwent, especially in the first century, from what had been normative in synagogue communities.[55]

THE ELDERS

As soon as early converts in any locale became unwelcome enough in their own synagogues and numerous enough to cluster into a community of their own, they would require elders. During that period when they might have coexisted as local synagogues themselves, elders would have been *de rigueur*. There is always the possibility that the earliest clusters formed community, not after the model of the synagogue, but after that of sages and their pupils. These

---

[54] *1 Cl*, 5:2; 42:1–2; *ITr*, 3:3; *IRo*, 4:3; *B*, 5:9; 8:3.

[55] It is particularly interesting to compare the scope of higher authority acknowledged by the earliest Christian communities to superior churches and the apostles, with the authority enjoyed by the new patriarch = *nasi* in Yavne, Usha, Sepphoris and Tiberias, his sanhedrin, court and apostles. The destruction of the ancient authority in Jerusalem had left a vacuum in worldwide Jewry, one which Johanan ben Zakkai's academy and authority were gradually to occupy, but only over the course of several generations. See Hugo Mantel, *Studies in the History of the Sanhedrin* (Cambridge: Harvard University Press, 1961). On the background of *apostolos* in hellenistic Greek see K.H. Rengstorf, *s.v.*, in *Theological Dictionary of the New Testament*, 1 (1964), 407ff; Hans von Campenhausen, "Der urchristliche Apostelbegriff," *Studia Theologica*, 1 (1947), 100; W. Schmithals, *The Office of Apostle in the Early Church* (Nashville: Abingdon, 1961); F. Agnew, C.M., "On the Origin of the Term *Apostolos*," *Catholic Biblical Quarterly*, 38 (1976), 49–53.

chaburoth = devout scholarly fellowships were in some respects the model for Jesus and his disciples. But if this form of community was the case for the first Christians, it left no imprint upon the documents, nor on the successor assemblies of which we do have knowledge. Therefore we must suppose the synagogue pattern as normal from the start.

It has been an exegetical commonplace that elders are absent from Paul, and evidently a construct of Acts. But this ignores a continuity of which Paul can be seen as the earliest witness. That there were certain persons in positions of leadership is made clear to us by Paul in his earliest letter, to the Thessalonians: "We appeal to you, my brothers, to be considerate to those who work so hard among you as your leaders in the Lord and those who admonish you. Have the greatest respect and affection for them because of their work." The leaders are *proïstamenous hymôn* = ruling over you. That is not a technical term, but it may plausibly imply the kind of responsibility which elders commonly had.[56]

Acts refers repeatedly to elders in the Jerusalem community, and mentions them in Lystra, Iconium, Pisidian Antioch (Paul's early foundations) and Ephesus. If the pastoral epistles are indeed directed to Ephesus and Crete, copious references confirm their existence in those communities. Paul addresses elders in Philippi and describes them to the Thessalonians. Clement's entire letter concerns the elders in the Corinthian assembly; the *Shepherd of Hermas*, likely written in Rome, has much comment on elders; James, 1 Peter and 2 & 3 John all mention them; and Ignatius deals with elders in Ephesus, Magnesia, Tralles, Philadelphia and Smyrna.[57]

The evidence before us says that during the organization of a new community the elders were appointed by the apostle or founder. Paul and Barnabas are reported to have done so on their first journey.[58] Clement says the apostles appointed them in the cities and towns where they preached, having "tested them by the Spirit."[59] The pastoral epistles seem to imply that the selection of elders was a

[56] 1 Th 5:12–13. André Lemaire writes, "Ainsi le premier témoignage que nous avons d'une communauté paulinienne nous montre à sa tête des hommes jouant un rôle spéciale et qu'il faut apprécier comme tels," *Les ministres aux origines de l'église* (Paris: Cerf, 1971), 76.
[57] Ac 11:30; 15:2, 4, 6; 16:4; 21:18; 14:23; 20:17; Phil 1:1 (*Pol* also deals with elders in Philippi, 5:3; 11:1); 1 Th 5:12–13; Js 5:14; 1 Pt 2:25; 5:1–4; 2 J 1; 3 J 1; *IEph*, 2:2; 4:1–2; 20:2; *IMg*, 2, 3, 6, 7, 13; *ITr*, 2:1–2; 3:1; 7:2; 13:1; *IPhld*, address; 4; 5:1; 7:1; *ISm*, 8:1; 12:2; *IPol*, 6 (Polycarp also writes of his Smyrnaean presbytery, *Pol*, address).
[58] Ac 14:23.   [59] *1 Cl*, 42:4–5.

prerogative of Paul's major deputies after the time of founding.[60]
There is a hint that prophets may have played a part in validating
candidates for community office, just as occurred when Saul and
Barnabas were received as apostles. But in the case of elders, being
community officers they would still require designation by the
communities.[61] Eventually the responsibility for appointing elders
reverted to the local assemblies.[62] The vocabulary of appointment is
consistent, whether by community insiders or outsiders, and it follows
faithfully the terminology that had been conventional for synagogue
appointments.

> *cheirotonein* = choose, elect by extending hands
> *kathistêmi* = appoint
> *apodeiknymi* = make, proclaim, appoint
> *cheireis epitithêmi* = lay hands on.[63]

As the selection became a matter for local choice, the requisite
qualities for elders are specified by several writers.

[He] must have an impeccable character. Husband of one wife, he must be
temperate, discreet and courteous, hospitable and a good teacher; not a
heavy drinker, nor hot-tempered, but gentle and peaceable, not avaricious,
a man who manages his own household well and brings up his children to
obey him and be well-behaved: how can any man who does not understand
how to manage his own household take care of the Church of God? He
should not be a new convert, in case pride should turn his head and he incur
the same condemnation as the devil. It is also necessary that he be held in
good repute by outsiders, so that he never falls into disrepute and into the
devil's trap. (1 Timothy)[64]

[E]ach of them must be a man of irreproachable character, husband of one
wife, and his children must be believers and not liable to be charged with
disorderly conduct or insubordination. [He] has to be irreproachable since
he is God's representative; never arrogant or hot-tempered, not a heavy
drinker or violent, nor avaricious; but hospitable and a lover of goodness;

---

[60] 1 Ti 5:17–22; *1 Cl*, 44:3; Tit 1:5.
[61] 1 Ti 1:18; 4:14. All such texts in 1&2 Timothy undergo the difficulty that we cannot be sure
just what Timothy's status was supposed to be. Was he an apostle of the assembly in Lystra
or of a band of prophets there (2 Cor 8:19–23; Ac 16:1), or a factotum for Paul (1 Cor 4:17;
Phil 2:19; 1 Th 3:2), or an elder (1 Ti 4:12–14)?
[62] *D*, 15:1; *IPhld*, address. Ignatius says they were appointed by the judgment of Jesus Christ
and the ratification of the Holy Spirit; had church personages been party to the choice, they
too would most likely have been mentioned.
[63] *cheirotonein*: 2 Cor 8:19; Ac 14:3; *D*, 15:1. *kathistêmi*: Tit 1:5; *1 Cl*, 42:4, 5; 43:1; 44:3; 54:2.
apodeiknymi: *IPhld*, address. *cheireis epitithêmi*: 1 Ti 4:14; 5:22; 2 Ti 1:6.
[64] 1 Ti 3:2–7. He writes of an *episkopos*.

sensible, upright, devout and self-controlled; and he must have a firm grasp of the unchanging message of the tradition, so that he can be counted on both for giving encouragement in sound doctrine and for refuting those who argue against it. (Titus)[65]

Men who are meek and not lovers of money, and true and approved. (*Didache*)[66]

[They] must be compassionate, merciful towards all men, turning back the sheep that have gone astray, visiting all the sick, not neglecting a widow or an orphan or a poor man: but providing always for that which is honorable in the sight of God and of men, abstaining from all anger, respect of persons, unrighteous judgment, being far from all love of money, not quick to believe anything against any man, not hasty in judgment, knowing that we are debtors of sin. (Polycarp)[67]

The injunction, several times repeated, that elders who were not at all elderly should still command respect, testifies in another way that it was an office intended, not for time-servers, but for the exemplary, no matter what their age.[68] These are high ideals. They would probably not have needed such articulation if standards were not somehow at risk. It is likely that in the heady days of first founding, the elders were the reliable members of the new community. It was a clear attempt to reform the synagogue tradition: no more aristocracy of heritage, no assured representation of affluent families, no need to provide for political balance or to include men with civic clout. As the communities aged, the tides of politics and the necessities of the social order had to pull on those presbyteries, and when the boards of elders became self-replacing the community needed these ideals held up before its eyes. While there is no clear evidence of election of elders by the assembly, the Jewish precedent would raise a presumption in its favor. Also, the fact that Clement had to contrive such varied and forceful arguments against the unseating of elders by the Corinthian community implies a continued claim by the assembly to control membership on the board of elders even at the end of the first century.

The early second century, in fact, produced some acidulous criticism of the opportunists and the arrogant who had become elders. Polycarp alludes to Valens, a Philippian elder now out of office whose greed had caused him to abuse his station = *locus*.[69]

---

[65] Tit 1:6–9. He writes of *presbyteroi* and *episkopos*.
[66] *D*, 15:1. The text mentions *episkopoi* and *diakonoi*.
[67] *Pol*, 6:1. He writes of *presbyteroi*.   [68] *IMag*, 3; 1 Ti 4:12.   [69] *Pol*, 11:1.

Ignatius had previously warned the Smyrnaean office-holders not to let station = *topos* (= *locus*) puff them up.[70] 3 John has a sour comment on the hostile officer in one church, "who enjoys being in charge of it," and is expelling good folk arbitrarily.[71]

The wryest critique, however, is to be found in the *Shepherd of Hermas*. Hermas is told in a vision to let the church rulers = *hēgoumenoi* know that they should be righteous and steadfast. The point is made that higher honor in the community should be given, not to the elders, but to the heroes who have suffered for the faith.[72]

I say to you that are rulers = *proēgoumenoi* of the church and that occupy the first seats = *hoi prōtokathedritai*: do not be like the sorcerers. They carry their drugs in vials, but you carry your drug and poison in your heart. You are case-hardened, and you will not cleanse your hearts and mix your wisdom together in a clean heart, so as to obtain mercy from the Great King. Beware, children, lest these divisions of yours cost you your life. How can you wish to instruct the Lord's elect, while you yourselves lack instruction? Instruct one another, therefore, and be at peace among yourselves.[73]

The *Shepherd*'s revelations express contempt for ambitious church-men who hanker after high office. Those who contend for the first seats are fools. "In the commandments [of the Lord] there is nothing about first places, or about glory of any kind, but about long-suffering and humility in man."[74] Ordinary human politics had somehow come home to roost in the preferment process of the elders.

The usual title for elders is the traditional one: *presbyteros*. Interestingly, the earliest Christian literature never refers to them as a *gerousia*: possibly to shun the synagogal vocabulary, possibly because their ideal profile so ignored age that this word would have heightened the incongruity, or possibly because Christian elders rather quickly assumed duties that were individual, not only collegial. A second term often used is *episkopos* = overseer, a synonym with some but fewer synagogue overtones. Acts, Philemon, the pastoral epistles, Clement, the *Shepherd* and the *Didache* all use this title.[75] Jesus was also called an overseer and the Twelve were said to have an

[70] *ISm*, 6:1.
[71] 3 J 9–10; the man is *philoproteuōn*. The capacity to act with such personal arrogance suggests a community chief more than an elder.   [72] *Hv*, 2:2:6; 3:1:2.
[73] *Hv*, 3:9:7–10. In another passage, when Hermas hesitates to take his seat before the elders have assumed theirs, he is told to sit down and be done with it, ibid. 3:1:8.
[74] *Hm*, 11:12; *Hs*, 8:7:4, 6. He who seeks the first seat = *thelei prōtokathedrian echein*; pride of place is called *prōteia*.
[75] Ac 20:28; Phil 1:1; 1 Ti 3:2; Tit 1:7; *1 Cl*, 42:4, 5; 44; *Hs*, 9:27:1–2; *D*, 15:1.

episkopê.[76] Ignatius uses the title in an altered sense, as we shall see when treating of the community chief. That these are both titles already in the first century, and are both used of elders, can be seen in the several *loci* where they can be used interchangeably. The elders of Ephesus who journey to Miletus for a farewell visit with Paul are described both as *presbyteroi* and as *episkopoi*. *Titus* presents a profile for office that employs both titles. And Clement describes the *presbyteroi* as having received an *episkopê.*[77] For this early period, then, they are used interchangeably.

In addition to these two titles, the early literature has recourse to a variety of synonyms to refer to community elders. Sometimes they are called rulers = *hêgoumenoi* but this expression may have too many overtones of the Sanhedrin to be attractive to most of our authors.[78] *Barnabas* writes of them as lords = *kyrioi.*[79] One of the most interesting synonyms, one used particularly to illuminate the title of *episkopos*, is shepherd = *poimên.* Paul lays this duty on the Ephesian elders:

Be on your guard for yourselves and for all the flock = *poimnion* of which the Holy Spirit has made you the overseers, to feed = *poimainein* the Church of God which he bought with the blood of his own Son. I know quite well that when I have gone fierce wolves will invade you and will have no mercy on the flock. Even from your own ranks there will be men coming forward with a travesty of the truth on their lips to induce the disciples to follow them.[80]

It was a most serviceable synonym, which lent a double set of overtones to *episkopos*: those of pastoral gentleness and those of stubborn defense. Paul elsewhere speaks of the charismatic gifts of shepherds and also of pilots = *kybernêseis.*[81] The author of 1 Peter, an elder addressing his co-elders, directs their attention to Christ who is shepherd and overseer of their own souls:

Give a shepherd's care to the flock of God that is entrusted to you: watch over it, not simply as a duty but gladly, as God wants; not for sordid money, but because you are eager to do it. Do not lord it over the group which is in your charge, but be an example for the flock. When the chief shepherd = *archipoimên* appears, you will be given the unfading crown of glory.[82]

---

[76] 1 Pt 2:25; Ac 1:20.   [77] Ac 20:17, 28; Tit 1:5, 7; *1 Cl*, 44.
[78] Hb 13:7, 17, 24. Also *1 Cl*, 1:3; 61. The term in Clement is ambiguous, possibly denoting civil rulers. But in the context of his letter, which is a call to obedience within the Christian assembly, and of his description of the *hêgemonia* which is conferred with a divine *exousia*, and of a divinely directed *boulê* – hardly what a Roman churchman under the shadow of Domitian would write about civil rulers – I think we may take it as referring to church elders. Also *Hv*, 2:2:6.   [79] *B*, 19:7.   [80] Ac 20:28–30.
[81] 1 Cor 12:28; Eph 4:11.   [82] 1 Pt 5:2–4; also 5:1; 2:25.

Not unnaturally the *Shepherd of Hermas* uses the image in a passage which seems directed at the elders:

Become of one spirit, and heal those evil clefts and take them away from among you, that the owner of the flocks may rejoice concerning them. For he will rejoice, if he find all things whole. But if he find any part of the flock scattered, woe unto the shepherds. For if the shepherds themselves shall have been found scattered, how will they answer for the flocks?[83]

Here also we see early evidence that there were some who found the office a sinecure, and others determined that it should not become one. There are numerous texts which describe the office as a *leitourgia* = public charge, or *diakonia* = service.[84]

What was the scope of the elders' public role which made the office both demanding and alluring? It is already implicitly set forth in the rosters of qualifications presented above. The elders held authority in the assemblies. Their duties seem to have included preaching and teaching, as also the control of community finances, admonition and rebuke when unity was at risk, appointment of officers and endorsement of apostles, care for the sick and for the community's dependents. Their rank deserved honor and (a point raised even more emphatically) obedience.[85]

The elders are described as a group. They are a *presbyterion*, like a *synedrion* or an entourage. They are visualized as a council in session with the community chief, and thus a ruling council for the full assembly.[86]

We can see the descendants of the *gerousia* of the synagogue community, though with some significant alterations. The selection and character of incumbents is supposedly depoliticized. Their authority has been restricted, since they carry no authority in the civil sphere. Yet their authority has also been enhanced, since the group is now totally a voluntary one and internal discipline and unity have become issues of high concern. No longer can an elder be a patrician policy-maker. These elders are to share actively in the day-to-day work, with a sustained energy and self-sacrifice, and a high

[83] *Hs*, 9:31:4–5. Here, as so frequently in the documents of the period, the strain in the churches was dissent and division.
[84] For instance, *1 Cl*, 44:2; 2 Ti 4:5. 2 Ti 2:24 similarly calls the elder a slave = *doulos* of the Lord.
[85] *Hv*, 2:4:3; 1 Th 5:12; 2 Ti 4:2; Tit 2:15; Hb 13:7; Acts 11:30 (the most salient evidence for financial responsibility is the constantly recurring warning that greedy men should be disqualified for this task); 1 Th 5:12–13; Ac 20:29–30; 1 Ti 4:14; Js 5:14–15; *Pol*, 6:1; 1 Ti 5:17–22; 1 Ti 4:12; 1 Pt 5:1–11; Hb 13:17; *1 Cl*, 54:2; 57:1; *IEph*, 5:2; *Pol*, 5:3.
[86] *ITr*, 2:1–2; *IMg*, 2, 13; Ac 15:2–12; 21:19; *IPol*, 7:2; Ignatius, passim.

expectation of ardor from their constituency. In return for this the community, under no compulsion but its own will, is held to render loyal, compliant obedience.

Several formal changes bear further witness to turnings in the Way. There is no hint anywhere of a *gerousiarchês* = senior elder. A community wherein seniority had been abolished as a basis for rank would have no room for an *Älteste*. Also, although in a few instances the elders themselves are referred to as notables = *archontes*, the context makes clear that this is another synonym, like *hêgoumenoi*, and not a title.[87] With all elders expected to take an activist role in leadership, there seems to have been no call for an executive committee or formalized inner elite.

This presents us with the much-debated question of whether there was a community chief. But in order to resolve that issue one must first account for two somewhat distinctive and historically crucial roles in the early Christian communities.

THE PROPHETS AND THE TEACHERS

On the occasion of their baptismal initiation it was not unusual for new Christians to undergo a psychic convulsion that was taken as token of possession by the Holy Spirit.[88] Some of the phenomena which ensued reminded the community of the tales of the ecstatic prophets of Israel, and were viewed with awe. For example, many converts emerged with what was called the gift of tongues: incoherent speech which believers regarded as an utterance of the Spirit and which only certain gifted persons claimed to construe. Two of the most esteemed sequelae to this seizure by the Spirit were prophecy and teaching.

PROPHETS

Prophecy was especially desirable since the return of the charism had been an object of national hope.[89] The earliest Christian texts are quite precise in their understanding of how it functioned. A prophet was able to discern within the hearts of humans what their true state of conscience was, and to discern within human affairs what God had in mind to do. Anna, the old woman who identifies the infant Jesus brought into the temple, is a prophetess.[90] Jesus' dinner hosts are

---

[87] *1 Cl*, 60. [88] For instance, Ac 10:44–48; 11:15–18; 19:6.
[89] 1 Macc 4:46; 9:27; 14:41; J 6:14. [90] Lk 2:36.

reassured he cannot be a prophet because he seems not to know the sinful reputation of the uninvited woman who approaches him, whereas the Samaritan woman says he *is* a prophet because he knew her history of marital infidelity.[91] Caiaphas is said to have inadvertently uttered an *ex officio* prophecy, and Jesus is taunted to play the prophet by identifying who struck him while he was blindfolded.[92] Agabus the prophet knows there is a famine coming, and that God wants the Antioch community to send relief to his home area. Later he discerns that Paul will be captured and imprisoned.[93] A group of Antioch prophets discerns that God wants Saul and Barnabas to go on the road as apostles.[94] Another band of prophets has prayed and given utterance over Timothy at the time of his appointment, which one may take as presaging what his future service was to be.[95] Paul, who was himself both a prophet and a teacher, describes the prophetic charism: "But if you were all prophesying when an unbeliever or someone uninitiated came in, he would find himself put to the test by all and judged by all and the secrets of his heart revealed; and so he would fall down on his face and worship God, declaring that God is indeed among you."[96]

Prophecy is typically accounted for as an utterance of the indwelling Holy Spirit.[97] Among the manifold gifts of the Spirit, only that of being an apostle is consistently ranked ahead of prophecy.[98] Paul thinks it is a gift one might well aspire to: certainly in preference to tongues, which he describes as fascinating but unintelligible.[99] Indeed, prophecy is so intelligible that it confronts people in an unnerving and threatening way, and many of the references to it carry allusions to the fact that a prophet's lot is not a happy one.[100] Nevertheless, he warns, the Spirit is not to be repressed nor prophecy treated with contempt.[101] In Matthew the promise is made that whoever welcomes a prophet will have a prophet's reward.[102]

Despite the very respectful treatment given Christian prophets in the New Testament, mild misgivings do begin to appear. Not all those who say, "Lord, Lord, did we not prophesy in your name?"

[91] Lk 7:39; J 4:19. [92] J 11:51; Mt 26:68. [93] Ac 11:27; 21:10.
[94] Ac 13:1-3. [95] 1 Ti 1:18; 4:14.
[96] 1 Cor 14:24-25; see also v. 37; Acts 13:1; 1 Ti 2:7.
[97] 1 Cor 12:10; Eph 3:5; 1 Ti 4:14; 2 Pt 1:21; Ac 2:17; 11:27; 19:6; 21:10; Rv 22:6.
[98] 1 Cor 12:10, 28; 14:1; Eph 2:20; 4:11. Apostles and prophets are mentioned in tandem by Lk 11:49. [99] 1 Cor 14, esp. v. 39.
[100] Mt 23:37; Lk 11:49; Ac 21:10; Rv 11:3-10; 16:6; 18:24. [101] 1 Th 5:20.
[102] Mt 10:41; also Rv 11:18.

will find admission into the kingdom. False prophets will arise. This concern is elevated from one of private destiny to one of community welfare, for prophetic discernment is relied upon in the community for policy decisions regarding such things as money and personnel. It is a gift intended to build up the community, but in the wrong hands it is at best confusing, and at worst it can be destructively divisive.[103]

If one then turns to the Christian literature of the subsequent generation or two, those misgivings have ripened. To begin with, most of the writers are absolutely mute about the existence of Christian prophets. For Clement, Ignatius, *Barnabas*, Polycarp, his Smyrnaean memorialists, *Diognetus* and Pseudo-Clement, the only prophets in sight are the Hebrew writers who foresaw Jesus.[104]

Christian prophets are mentioned in only two of the documents, and in ways that are clearly cautionary. The *Didache* says they fulfill a *leitourgia* = public charge for the community and should be held in high honor. Indeed, the text says that elders and deacons deserve honor because, *like* prophets, they have their public functions.[105] With priority even ahead of the poor, prophets tried and true should receive tithes of food, money and clothing.[106] But on the subject of which prophets were tried and true, the *Didache* has much more to say, as does the *Shepherd*. Both passages require display.

But concerning the apostles and prophets, act according to the ordinance of the gospel. Let every apostle, when he comes to you, be received as the Lord. But let him not remain more than a single day or, if need be, a second day. But if he remains three days, he is a false prophet. And when he departs let the apostle be given nothing more than bread, to supply him until he next finds lodging. If he requests money, he is a false prophet. When a prophet speaks in the Spirit you should neither put him to the test nor interpret what he says: for every sin shall be forgiven except this one. Yet not everyone who speaks in the Spirit is a prophet: only he who walks in the ways of the Lord. From his ways therefore the false prophet can be distinguished from the prophet. Whenever a prophet, speaking in the Spirit, shall command you to set out food, he alone may not eat of it; otherwise he is a false prophet. And if a prophet teaches the truth but does not follow it himself, he is a false prophet. And every prophet tried and true, whose life shows forth to the

[103] Mt 7:22; 24:24; 1 Ti 1:18; 4:14; Ac 13:1; 1 Cor 14:4; 14:29–32; Rv 2:20.
[104] *1 Cl*, 12:8; 17:1; 43:1; *IMg*, 8:2; 9:3; *IPhld*, 5:2; 9:1–2; *ISm*, 5:2; 7:2; *B*, 1:7; 2:4; 4:4; 5:6, 11, 13; 6:2, 4, 6, 7, 8, 10, 13, 14; 7:4; 9:1; 11:2, 4, 6, 9; 12:1, 4, 8, 10; 13:4; 14:2,7–9; 16:9 (this last reference is ambiguous, but I take the passage to speak of the full range of the gifted person's experience rather than of the present time only); *Pol*, 6:3; *MPol*, 12:3; 16:2; *Dg*, 11:6; *2 Cl*, 11:2. See also *Hv*, 2:3:4; *Hs*, 9:15:4; 9:16. Here the dyad, "prophets and apostles," designates Hebrew prophets, not Christian: *IPhld*, 9:1; *Pol*, 6:3; *ISm*, 7:2 is comparable. [105] *D*, 15:1–2. [106] Ibid. 13:3–6.

world the mystery of the community, but does not teach you to act as he does: this one shall not be judged by you. He shall have his judgment in the sight of God, for prophets in ancient days did likewise. Whoever shall say in the Spirit, "Give me silver or anything else," do not listen to him. But if he tells you to give to others who are in want, that utterance must stand above anyone's judgment. (*Didache*)[107]

"How then, sir," I said, "shall we be able to tell a prophet from a false prophet?" "Listen," [the Shepherd] said, "to what I shall tell you of both kinds of prophets, true and false, and how you are to test them. Test the man who has the divine Spirit by his life. First, he who has this spirit is gentle, tranquil and humble, and abstains from the wickedness and vain desire of this world, and treats himself as inferior to others, and does not give prophetic answers to people's questions, nor does he give utterance in private (the Holy Spirit does not speak on demand), but speaks when God prompts him. Next, when the man with the divine Spirit comes into an assembly = *synagôgê* of righteous men who have faith in a divine Spirit, and intercession is made to God from this gathering, then the angel of the prophetic spirit, who abides with him, fills that man and he, filled with the Holy Spirit, addresses the group as the Lord wishes. In this way, then, the Spirit of God shall be manifest. This is the power of the divine Spirit of the Lord.

"Now listen concerning the earthly and empty spirit, which is powerless and foolish. First, the man who seems to have a spirit exalts himself, and is ambitious for a position of importance = *prôtokathedrian*. He is impudent and brazen and talkative and provided with comforts and many other seductions. He takes payment for his prophecy, and if he is not paid he will not prophesy. Now can a divine Spirit receive money and prophesy? It is impossible for a prophet of God to act this way, but the spirit of these prophets is earthly. Further, this sort of spirit never approaches an assembly of righteous men: it avoids them, and seeks out those who are of doubtful or empty mind, and prophesies to them in private and deceives them, speaking whatever nonsense will gratify their desires, for they are as empty as is this sort of spirit... When he does come into an assembly of the righteous who have a divine Spirit, and intercession is made from this gathering, the man is emptied, and the earthly spirit flees from him in fear; he is struck dumb and falls to pieces, unable to utter a word ... Therefore test, by his life and his deeds, the man who says that he is moved by the Spirit." (*Shepherd of Hermas*)[108]

---

[107] Ibid. 11:3–12.

[108] *Hm*, 11:7–16. Sensitivity about the financing of divinely sent individuals goes back a long way. Paul purposely did without support from several communities, perhaps with this in mind: 1 Cor 9:1–4; 2 Cor 12:10; 11:7–8; Phil 4:10–18. Gerd Theissen sees Paul under accusation by Corinthian charismatics: his refusal to depend on community finances is, to them, disobedience to the Lord's command to live as mendicants. *The Social Setting of Pauline Christianity*, ed. and trans. John H. Schütz (Philadelphia: Fortress, 1982), 26–67. Eusebius also records an early condemnation of venal prophets, *H.E.* 5,18,4ff.

When prophets are remembered, it is as a mixed blessing. Looking backward with this perspective, one might note something otherwise not so striking. Paul is identified by Acts as a prophet from his neophyte days, and it must have been publicly known. Yet when he unfurls his various charismatic titles – apostle, teacher, tongue-speaker – never once does he lay claim to the title of prophet.[109] Also, although his nomination by the band of prophets in Antioch might have given him the claim that his apostleship was a divine charism, not a mere church office, he never alludes to his prophetic sponsorship, ignoring it until his later claim to have been commissioned by the Lord personally. Apart from only two brief allusions elsewhere in the proto-pauline literature, everything he has to say on prophecy – and it is mostly cautionary – is in his letters to that most antagonized church, the community at Corinth.[110]

TEACHERS

Before attempting to interpret all this, let us review the fortunes of teachers in the same documents. Teachers, like apostles and prophets, were not officers of the church. They were not appointed or initiated by the community, for their gift came directly from the Lord. They were accredited, but not designated.

In the New Testament, teachers tend to be third in the rosters of the divinely endowed (though it is unclear to what extent the listings were intended to be in a strict order of rank).[111] Their task is fairly specific. They are to make the primary exposition of the Christian message, explaining the scriptures, describing the most basic lineaments of an appropriate, believing response.[112] The teacher's audience is the uninitiated; and so to teach is to be a founder.[113] It is an exalted and influential gift, one that deserves high honor and one that will require a rigorous accounting.[114]

But, as with prophecy, the New Testament has its hesitations about charismatic teachers. There are deceitful spirits and there are demonic teachers who do their bidding. Some people will follow them because, *au fond*, those teachers are catering to their fancies.[115]

---

[109] The claim to apostleship is, of course, in all but one of his letters; teacher, at least in the pastoral epistles, 1 Ti 2:7; 2 Ti 1:11; tongue-speaker, 1 Cor 14:18–19.
[110] 1 Th 5:20; Ro 12:6.   [111] 1 Cor 12:28; Ro 12:7; Eph 4:11; see also Ac 13:1.
[112] 1 Ti 4:13; 2 Ti 3:16; Hb 5:12.   [113] Ro 2:20; 1 Ti 2:7.
[114] 1 Ti 5:17; Js 3:1.   [115] Eph 4:14; 1 Ti 4:1; 2 Ti 4:3.

Some of the movement to restore Jewish observances is an example, according to Paul, of teaching that is untrustworthy.[116] The pastorals begin to specify "sound," "good" and "devout" teaching. And how, when every teacher is carrying a divine license, does one tell who is sound and who deceitful? By what the teachers *do*.[117]

These same premonitory themes are only amplified in the later literature. Teaching is a high responsibility: it is what Jesus and Peter and Polycarp were doing.[118] It is too high a gift for the author of *Barnabas* to claim.[119] It is a companion-charism with that of apostles.[120] But the prince of this world is sponsoring his own teaching which is evil and yet appealing to hypocrites.[121] The true teacher, like the true prophet, is deserving of honor and of a living, and the true teacher could be counted upon not to rend the community into factions, just as you could expect a true teacher to live in conformity with his or her own teaching.[122]

Paul's annoyed treatment of ebullient glossalalia might sound as if those ululating, hardly-tongue-tied Christians were a serious disruption in the assemblies. They were perhaps the least troublesome of all the charismatics. Since earliest days in Jerusalem the communities had understood that certain of their members were occupied by the divine Spirit in ways that could invest their work with Jesus' own power. Those apostles and prophets and teachers left in their wake stories of impassioned evangelizing that had brought whole new communities of believers into being; uncanny discernment that read the hidden character of human hearts; wise and convincing teaching that guided communities in their most troubled first ventures of conversion. These people were like amulets or talismans: they could speak with the authority and the conviction – even the first-person syntax – of the Lord himself. One would naturally hesitate to make major decisions in the councils of the various communities without consulting these charismatics or, more appropriately, without consulting the Lord's wishes through them.

It was only with time that it began to go wrong. God seemed to speak in diverse ways and sundry manners through his chosen, and as a result his communities began to be divided by the pull of competing charisms. When pulses began to return to normal after a wave of

[116] Col 2:22.   [117] 1 Ti 1:10; 2 Ti 4:3; Tit 1:9; 2:1; 1 Ti 5:17; 6:3; 4:16; Tit 2:7.
[118] *IMg*, 9:2–3; *MPol*, 12:2; 16:2; 17:3; Papias, 3:15; *Dg*, 9:6.   [119] *B*, 1:8; 4:9.
[120] *Hv*, 3:5:1; *Hs*, 9:16:5; 9:25:2; *Dg*, 11:1.   [121] *IEph*, 16:2; 17:1; *Hs*, 9:19:2.
[122] *D*, 13:2; 15:1–2; *Hv*, 3:5:1; Ignatius says pithily: *kalon to didaskein, ean ho legōn poiêi, IEph*, 15:1.

conversions, there were serious policy matters to be thrashed out: questions for which precedents could be interpreted in quite differing directions. From their Jewish origins the Christian assemblies had inherited a robust tolerance for debate and they knew reasonably well how to massage a quarrel into a consensus. What complicated that tradition now was the presence of these new charismatics: all accountable to no one but the Lord, and all claiming to be possessed by God's own Spirit.

Understandably, it was community leaders who encountered the problem most keenly. Paul had been the first to confront it, and this he did largely by invoking his own credentials and condemning those who read the divine signs differently. But in the average community the presence of truly gifted apostles, prophets and teachers would attenuate or obscure the need for and development of effective officers and discursive, responsible policy discussion. And the presence of charismatics in whom the Spirit was somehow garrulous, askew or even spurious could, in the presence of a credulous community, make a dedicated officer despair. Simon Magus was surely not the only new Christian who fancied getting up the Spirit for personal advantage. There were communities everywhere who were willing to support charismatic panhandlers and mendicants.

The *Didache* and the *Shepherd of Hermas* set forth what the churches finally resorted to as a containment policy. There was no wish to deny that the Spirit did confer those special gifts, and so communities had to honor the charismatics and listen to their utterances without contradiction: "Let the prophets offer thanks as much as they please."[123] But whenever an apostle or prophet or teacher did one of two things – used the privilege of status for private benefit, or acted so as to threaten rather than ratify the slowly congealing orthodoxy that was emerging – they were to be discredited as charlatans.[124] The formulation of that orthodoxy, in both creed and discipline, was the task that was crucial to the survival of the network of Jesus-worshipers around the Mediterranean, and was eventually being taken in hand by some of the more adroit community officers whose stewardship it was to govern the assemblies, and who set about that governing with a decreasingly timid resolve. Their policy was what brought the sun to set on a period marked in a unique way by

[123] *D*, 10:7.
[124] False apostles: 2 Cor 11:13; Rv 2:2. False prophets: 1 J 4:1; *D*, 11:5–10. False teachers: 2 Pt 2:1; *Pol*, 7:2.

itinerant *pourparleurs* of the Spirit. It would have to be admitted that life down on the assembly was not going to be as effervescent as it had been.

THE COMMUNITY CHIEF

Among Christian communities the title *archisynagôgos* is not used.[125] Like the word *synagôgê* itself, this is part of the synagogal vocabulary which the new group disliked using, even if the institutional protocols might be remarkably continuous with the realities of the past.

Few references are made in the earliest Christian literature to individuals who preside over local communities. Instead, authority is most often attributed to the elders as a group.

James appears to preside over the Jerusalem community. He is remembered as having been accorded an Easter vision of the risen Jesus. It is he whom both Peter and Paul report to at critical junctures. He is in several scenes depicted in the midst of the elders, and on the most decisive occasion it is he who brings a strenuous debate to cloture by saying simply: " I rule, then ..." He is given no title other than "brother of the Lord." Even the letter that was later published in his name only calls him a *doulos* = slave of God and of the Lord Jesus Christ.[126]

3 John has harsh words for someone who may be another early community chief whom we know by name:

I have written a note for the members of the church, but Diotrephes, who enjoys being in charge of it, refuses to accept us. So if I come, I shall tell everyone how he has behaved, and about the wicked accusations he has

[125] There is some evidence to the contrary. Epiphanius, a fourth-century bishop of Constantia in Cyprus, in his somewhat ramshackle account of earlier church developments, reports that a certain Joseph, appointed by Judah the (Jewish) Patriarch as a traveling fund-collector = apostle, found in his study of the Christian documents that they were provided with *archisynagôgoi* and priests and *presbyteroi* and *hazzanitoi*. He later records of the Ebionite Christians: "They have *presbyteroi* = elders and *archisynagôgoi* = community chiefs. They call their assembly = *ekklêsian* a *synagôgê*, not a church = *ekklêsian*." *Panarion Haer.* 30:11, 18, ed. and trans. Karl Holl, *Epiphanius (Ancoratus und Panarion)*, Die Griechischen Christlichen Schriftsteller der drei ersten Jahrhunderte 25 (Leipzig: Hinrichs, 1915), 346, 357. The resemblance of function and perhaps in some places of nomenclature has led Götz to entertain some historical continuity between *archisynagôgos* and *episkopos*: Karl Gerold Götz, *Petrus also Gründer und Oberhaupt der Kirche und Schauer von Gesichten nach den altchristlichen Berichten und Legenden*, Untersuchungen zum Neuen Testament 13 (Leipzig, Hinrichs, 1927), 49–54.

[126] 1 Cor 15:7; Ac 12:17; 21:18; 15:13, 19; Gal 1:19; Js 1:1. If Acts 15:22 is meant as all-inclusive, then James must be included as one of the elders. The hegemony of James and then Simeon as chiefs of the Jerusalem church is suggestive of similar family continuities among synagogue chiefs. Even two generations later Jesus' kinsmen were receiving special deference, *H.E.* 3,20,6.

been circulating against us. As if that were not enough, he not only refuses to welcome our brothers, but prevents from doing so other people who would have liked to, and expels them from the church.[127]

Clement is known to have been the community chief of Christians in Rome. In his letter he makes no reference to himself as chief, yet clearly he writes with authority in the name of that church. His comparison with the levitical priesthood, presided over by the single high priest, may reflect a familiarity with a Christian pattern of one chief presiding over two colleges: of elders and of deacons.

The Letters to the Seven Churches in Revelation 2-3 (three of which were later to receive one of Ignatius of Antioch's letters), each addressed to "the angel of the church" there, seem to be messages to a single person responsible for each community. The existence of a presiding office is one strongly plausible implication, but not yet the existence of a commonly accepted title for that office. That would fit well with Clement, written about the same time, which also gives evidence of such an untitled position.

Ignatius – with whom we must shortly deal at length – mentions by name Onesimus of Ephesus, Damas of Magnesia, Polybius of Tralles and Polycarp of Smyrna, all four of whom he portrays as community chiefs and entitles *episkopos*.[128] Ignatius also refers to himself as the *episkopos* of Syria,[129] and he presents himself as *poimên* = shepherd.[130] Yet Polycarp in his own letter neither calls himself *episkopos* nor refers to anyone of that title in Philippi; he has guidance only for the elders there.[131]

Save for these eight men (plus the unnamed "angels" of Revelation) – James, Diotrephes, Clement, Ignatius, Onesimus, Damas, Polybius and Polycarp – there is no unambiguous reference to a presiding chief in any Christian assembly up to the middle of the second century. There are later reports, in Irenaeus, Eusebius and others, of community chiefs during this period, but we must consider that they may be looking back with an understanding, theology and vocabulary which are of a later period and a later discipline.[132]

---

[127] 3 J 9-10.
[128] *IEph*, 1:3; *IMg*, 2,3; *ITr*, 12:2; *IPol*, address. Those from Magnesia and Tralles he refers to as *ho episkopos*; the other two are designated without the definite article.
[129] *IRo*, 2:2.
[130] *IRo*, 9:1-3. He also writes that now "*monos autên [Syrian] Iêsous Christos episkopêsei.*" Ibid. v. 1.   [131] *Pol*, 6:1.
[132] This is, of course, an extremely cautious and conservative position. Irenaeus had direct contact with the churches of Asia and Rome in the mid-second century, and Eusebius seems to have had available the writings of Hegesippus, another mid-second-century witness.

Ignatius, writing in the latter middle years (*c.* 110) of the literary period now under study, is original in asserting a specific church order throughout the cities of Asia and Syria. Each community has a single overseer = *episkopos* and a bench of elders = *presbyteroi*. The overseer presides over and is distinct from the elders, and sits as master of the household of the entire community.[133]

In the face of these data, one could reasonably conjecture that the communities had gone through an early period of revolutionary populism, with no single presiding officer in the local assembly. On this view Ignatius, with the vehemence of his personality and the credibility of his martyrdom, would have held up a pattern which, in the divisive and acrimonious days of the troubled second century, eventually imposed itself as the universal church order. That order, with its single, authoritative overseer, has been called the monarchical episcopate.

Several considerations must be included in any viable theory of the matter. First, in a network of communities which were typically of Jewish origin, and which retained prominent Jewish dominance for a long while (for example, Clement is apparently the Jewish-Christian leader of the Roman church which was heavily Jewish into the second century),[134] it is extremely improbable that those Christians who in so many ways had organized themselves after the viable and familiar order of the hellenistic Jewish synagogue would have or could have dispensed with the linchpin of the operation, the community chief. Elders always, without known exception, provided themselves with an executive officer who presided over the community and over them. That this officer, now that the single traditional title, *archisynagôgos*, was inexpedient, might have for some years gone under one or another of the corporate leadership titles – without early uniformity from city to city – is not nearly as improbable as that there had been no such officer at all.

Secondly, the episcopate Ignatius portrays is not as monarchical as some have seen it to be. Throughout his letters he calls on the people to obey, not only the *episkopos*, but also the *presbyteroi*.[135] The elders are to be in harmony with him; they are to honor him; they are to sustain him; but never does Ignatius say that they lie under his

---

[133] *IEph*, 2:2; 20:2; *IMg*, 2, 6, 13; *ITr*, 3:1; 13:1; *IPhld*, address, 4; *ISm*, 12:2; *IPol*, 6:1; *IEph*, 6:1.

[134] Esler concludes that Jews comprised a significant membership in the community addressed by Luke around 85–95 AD: *Community and Gospel in Luke-Acts*, 30–45.

[135] *IMg*, 6; *ITr*, 12:2; 13:1; *ISm*, 8:1. So also Polycarp: *Pol*, 5:3.

command (by contrast with the *diakonoi*, who are to obey the *episkopos*).[136]

Third, one must notice exactly how it is that Ignatius vouches for the overseer's authority. Oversight is a divine work: the Father and Jesus are overseers of the Christian assemblies. Overseers, then, preside in a way comparable to God's rule. To conform to the judgment of God, one must then conform to the judgment of the overseer. Less theoretically, Ignatius repeatedly insists that God can be worshipped effectively only in an assembly under an overseer's presidency. Rump sessions at odds with him have no communion with the Lord.[137]

Ignatius in 110 is making essentially the same case for the authority of elders and chief that Clement had made earlier for elders without differentiating their president. It is an argument from legitimacy. Neither one defends the authorities because they have always taken the correct side in controversies. Neither one claims that the authorities are possessed by the Holy Spirit or that they utter divine oracles. What they say is that unity is God's will for the churches, and that solidarity with officers is to be the instrument of that unity. Their precise charism is to steer the entire community upon a single course.[138] Clement and Ignatius harp upon a strong – one might almost say strident – theme: the authority of *episkopoi* and *presbyteroi*. Consistently they argue, not from the divine charism of those officers, nor from their apostolic appointment (though that point is made[139]), nor from their orthodoxy in the face of any heresy like Montanism or Gnosticism, but only from the divinely intended function of these offices: to discipline all Christians into a single community.

From all of this it appears clear who were the targets of the polemic of Clement and Ignatius. It can only have been the charismatic apostles, prophets and teachers. Whatever their contributions to the local assemblies, in time they had demonstrated one serious liability. They were a strong solvent for church unity. Their voices came forth in a forthright, self-assured tone, but they did not always sing in

---

[136] *IEph*, 4:1–2; 20:3; *ITr*, 12:2; e.g., *IMg*, 2.
[137] *IPol*, address; *IRo*, 9:1; *IEph*, 3:2; 4:1; *IPhld*, 3; *ISm*, 9:1; *IEph*, 5:1–3; *IMg*, 4; *ITr*, 7; *IPhld*, 4:7; *ISm*, 8.   [138] Cf. *1 Cl*, 37.
[139] Ibid. 42, 45. Ignatius frequently mentions the apostles in connection with ecclesiastical obedience, but never as the legitimate predecessors of the overseers. Instead, he argues that as Jesus is one with the Father, so by being at one with the overseers (and elders) Christians will be at one with both the Lord and the apostles: *IEph*, 11:2; *IMg*, 6:1; 7:1; 13:1–2; *ITr*, 2:2; 3:1; 7:1; 12:2. Whereas Ignatius roots the legitimacy of the office in its divine ordination, Clement leans more upon its apostolic foundation, *1 Cl*, 44.

harmony. They were virtuosi, not choristers. Disagreement, even strident disagreement, was no stranger to the early Christian churches. But a dissenter with a license to utter God's undiscussable Word presented a threat to communal belief and to the magisterial capacities of the officers that was uniquely daunting. We cannot know whether these charismatics openly defied the elders and chiefs, or whether they were used by others who had political ambitions or envy. But they enjoyed, from the foundation era, such a *cachet* of divine authority that it was inevitable they would be a stress upon those whose role it was to formulate community policy.

The *Didache* and the *Shepherd* did not attack these people head-on. They proposed the one judgment that these men and women beyond all human judgment still had to undergo: the judgment of moral scrutiny. The approach of Clement and Ignatius is also oblique, but they also propose a policy that would limit the immunities of the charismatics. The obvious claim for the superiority of apostles, prophets and teachers was that they were possessed and gifted by the Holy Spirit, whereas the overseers and elders were merely officers of the communities. Officers were elected, but charismatics were divinely called. The reply, from Rome and from Antioch, was not to deny that the authority of the charismatics was divine, but to insist that the calling and duty of the officers was also divine. And since its repeatedly asserted purpose was the governance and unity of the flock, this was set forth as a distinct responsibility: so distinct that even prophetic oracles could not intrude upon it without raising questions about their own source.

Ignatius' usage, then, was to favor one of the titles for elders and apply it exclusively to the presiding elder. *Episkopos* was attractive because it conveyed what needed accenting: authority. The Jews had done this with *hypéretês* and the Christians had done it with *ekklêsia*. Ignatius' new nomenclature would not become normative during this period (it is not yet followed by *Barnabas*, the *Didache*, Polycarp or the *Shepherd*), but we shall see it universally received in later years.

Let us reconstruct the situation of a community chief during the first century of Christian experience. First, he always acted under the shadow of either the founder or the second generation of apostolic deputies. Every major act of his could be sent up on appeal to those absent but very correspondent figures. Second, his presbytery was composed, not of a laissez-faire establishment whose acquiescence was all he needed to secure for his own policy initiatives, but of eager, generously active community workers among whom there may have been persons as qualified to preside as himself. Third, his community included prophets and teachers whose summonses may not always have rallied folk to the same causes he and his colleagues thought wisest – if indeed the charismatics were agreed among themselves. Fourth, as we shall see later, he was always answerable to decisions made in churches of superior authority.

With so many checks on his own initiative and judgment, the president of an early Christian community was hardly going to rise to eminence. A few men of extraordinary character in situations of resonating importance, like James and Clement and Ignatius and Polycarp, did make their marks. Most presiding elders would have been satisfied just to hold all those centrifugal (at least from their perspective) energies in some workable stability. It was a post more for the astute than for the impresario.

Ignatius may have influenced the new nomenclature, but it was not his letters alone which shifted the levers of power. As years went by, great changes were occurring. The founders and their deputies all vanished from the scene. The superior churches had to yield much initiative and judgment to local churches as these latter gained seniority and experience. The local communities finally grew to a size that required fragmentation into several assemblies, and spawned outlying communities in the countryside. The elders were assigned to preside over these constituent churches, and although they continued to form a college of policy-makers for the city-centered collectivity, their executive duties more and more drew them away from center stage which was left to their president. And in time the office of elder did, as we have seen, attract some less motivated incumbents. The charismatics were finally brought down to human scale by the *Didache* and the *Shepherd* and, perhaps, by their own fractious record, viewed by communities that wearied of division. Every one of those changes would reduce the leverage of competing authority. Every reduction enabled – indeed, invited and compelled – the local president to assume a larger say-so in the affairs of the local community. The transformed office, with its wider sweep of initiative, would now elicit the services of Christians of sturdier churchcraft, some of whom would affect the larger *ekklêsia* beyond the perimeter of their own cities.

In their efforts to justify this shift of authority, men like Clement and Ignatius, following Paul's cue and that of Luke, laid down a theology which would in its effects run far beyond the bounds of the issue before their eyes. They were arguing that, if one must recognize the Spirit of Jesus at work in certain individuals whom God has raised up in his abrupt way, one must equally well acknowledge the Spirit of Jesus living in the community and invested in its officers. Henceforth one could no longer speak of elders or others as "merely appointed by the church," for the Spirit was at work in that appointing.

What we perceive, then, is not the creation of a new office but the political transformation of a primeval one. The community chief, emergently entitled *episkopos*, rises to more effective power because the communities could not have survived beyond their heady, helter-skelter adolescence without a coherent discipline. We must remember that it was the need of the churches, and the turn of events, rather than the pedigree or charism of the office, which provoked the change. The new overseers were made by the church, rather than the other way around.

If, in the earliest generations of the church, few presiding officers attained prominence as would some of their successors in the next era, why would one determine (as the consensus has done) that it was the former situation that was to be paradigmatic for the church of later days? A comprehensive view of the evidence suggests, not that there were no presiding officers in that first age, but that they were simply not the ones who counted most prominently or won remembrance. The record also shows that in the even more stressful age that followed, there were numerous bishops who did make the difference. And so we read little about the first bishops, and more about those who came later.

The program of the community

What can we learn of the program maintained by these Christian communities?

As we have seen, there was a variety of activities which would bring the group into assembly. There were weekly gatherings – on Sunday, in purposeful contrast with the sabbath – at which the synagogue service of readings and exhortation and debate was combined with the traditional home rite of bread-breaking and cup-sharing.[140]

[140] Ac 20:7ff; *IMg*, 9; *D*, 14.

Assemblies for prayer, praise and prophecy seem to have been held separately.[141] Despite their chary attitudes towards the old Jewish liturgical calendar, the new believers were beginning to gather to commemorate a few feasts of their own. And for some time they appear to have dined together in an act of social leveling and community solidarity that was not identified with the breaking of bread, which latter was coming to be called the *eucharistia* = thanksgiving. This was one more example of a generic word appropriated as a technical title.

They also assembled at times to discuss community policy. These meetings appear to have been more occasional. Several writers urge their disciple-communities to hold them more frequently: in the hope, perhaps, of bringing them through a season of dissent. These provided the occasion when new and authoritative correspondence was read out.[142] As those letters aged and lost their controversial immediacy, they become more appropriate for inclusion in the corpus of edifying documents re-heard at the eucharist. This may also have been the occasion for communities to choose and commission their representatives. Officers were to be selected (the process is not described) and then presented first to the prophets, who gave oracles over them, then to the elders, who laid their hands on their heads. Apostles were adopted or acknowledged and sent forth to spread the faith in new towns and villages, and seem to have been sponsored in the same way. It was a normal obligation for local assemblies to send out missionaries to aid in the founding of new churches.[143] Embassies were also chosen and accredited in full assembly: to negotiate with other communities, to represent them at celebrations, to convey financial support.[144]

Although Christians could have recourse to civil judges, and although they did not enjoy the Jewish privilege of adjudicating virtually all criminal and civil cases before their own tribunals, the communities quickly provided their own judiciary. It would be difficult to overestimate the cultural trauma these people underwent, having lost a code of behavior in Judaism that had addressed itself to the full span of life's activities, yet being guided more by it as a

---

[141] Col 2:16; Ro 14:3–6; *MPol*, 18, 21.
[142] Ac 14:27; 15; 21:22 and variant; Js 1:27; *IPol*, 4:2; *B*, 4:10; 1 Th 5:27; Col 4:16; Hb 6:10; *Pol*, 13; *Hv*, 2:4:3.   [143] Mt 10:1ff; Lk 9:1ff; Ac 13:2, 3; *IRo*, 3:1.
[144] 1 Cor 16:3–4; 2 Cor 8:16–24; 9:3–5; Acts 15:1–2, 25–30; Phil 4:18; *IPhld*, 10:1–2; *ISm*, 11:2; *IPol*, 7:2; 8:1.

selectively exploited tradition than by any other source. Suits for injury and equity could that way be resolved between Christians, and in the light of the awkwardly developing code of behavior they were elaborating.

> Is one of you with a complaint against another so brazen as to seek judgement from sinners and not from God's holy people? Do you not realize that the holy people of God are to be the judges of the world? And if the world is to be judged by you, are you not competent for petty cases? Do you not realize that we shall be the judges of angels? – then quite certainly over matters of this life. But when you have matters of this life to be judged, you bring them before those who are of no account in the Church! I say this to make you ashamed of yourselves. Can it really be that it is impossible to find in the community one sensible person capable of deciding questions between brothers, and that this is why brother goes to law against brother, and that before unbelievers? No, it is a fault in you, by itself, that one of you should go to law against a brother at all; why do you not prefer to suffer injustice, why not prefer to be defrauded? And here you are, doing the injustice and the defrauding, and to your own brothers.[145]

For purposes of discipline the assemblies also could bring members to judgment. Paul's instruction was that one might first be admonished privately, but persistence in a flagrant offense could bring a sentence of expulsion, a decision which might involve a hearing in full assembly.[146]

Several differences emerge when one contrasts this judicial usage with that of the synagogue. There is no mention of scourging or imprisonment in the Christian documents, for they were more intentional communities than their Jewish counterparts, the ethnic *politeumata* or Jewish municipalities. A voluntary society cannot really punish: it can either admonish or exclude. Thus even the fiercest passages which rule an offender anathema from the community's social life are justified as medicinal rather than punitive: "Have nothing to do with him, so that he will feel ashamed of himself; though you are not to treat him as an enemy, but to correct him as a brother..." "so that on the Day of the Lord his spirit may be saved."[147]

There was a large enough community program to require a significant outlay of money. First, and most traditionally, they accepted the responsibility to support widows, orphans and other

---

[145] 1 Cor 6:1–8; see also *B*, 20:2.
[146] Gal 6:1; 2 Th 3:14–15; 1 Cor 5:1–13; 16:22; 2 Cor 2:6–10; 2 J 10.
[147] 2 Th 3:14–15; 1 Cor 5:5.

indigents who were deprived of relatives and the ability to make their own living. This might include food and lodging.[148]

Further, a community was expected to offer lodging and board for wayfarers. *Philoxenia* = hospitality to travelers is often mentioned as a duty of the assembly or its officers.[149]

We cannot say surely which officers or charismatics were stipendiary, but there is evidence that communities were expected to support apostles.[150] Prophets and teachers had a similar claim, perhaps through tithing.[151] The continual caution that overseers, elders and servants need be disinterested in money may simply mean that they superintended the community funds and thus could skim off some for themselves, or that there was some form of stipend assigned to them, or both.[152] It might even mean that the position had begun to be a profession, and that one lived off its salary. There is a suggestive passage in the pastoral epistles to the effect that elders are entitled to a special allotment.[153]

The constantly strained relations between the fretful mother church in Judaea and the increasingly gentile communities which Paul had founded were regularly assuaged by subsidies sent to Jerusalem. A series of droughts and famines in Judaea made this largesse necessary, but it was also politically helpful. How the funds traveled across borders in violation of imperial restrictions (the Jewish temple tax was granted a rare and explicit exemption) is not clear.[154]

We find no mention of schools. The Christians differed in one relevant respect from the Jews. They seem to have decided quite early to adopt Greek as their common tongue. Palestinian and Syrian communities may have used the Hebrew scriptures, and conversed and worshipped in their semitic vernaculars, but this had little viability in the newer foundations of mixed membership. Intercourse between the churches had to be in Greek, and it was the Greek version and canon of the scriptures which the Christians received: another point of divergence which led them eventually to a wider canon than that which rabbinical Judaism was appropriating. There was thus little need for or interest in Hebrew tutelage in schools. It

---

[148] Ro 12:13; 1 Ti 5:3–16; Js 1:27; Hb 13:16; Ac 4:35; 6:1; *ISm*, 6:2; *IPol*, 4:1; *Pol*, 6:1; *B*, 20:2; *Hv*, 2:4:3; *Hm*, 2; 8:10; *Hs*, 1:8–10; 5:3:7; 9:26:2; 9:27:2.
[149] Ro 12:13; 3 J 5–8; *1 Cl*, 1:2; *D*, 11–12; *Hs*, 9:27:1–2.
[150] 2 Th 3:7–9; 1 Cor 9:4–14; 2 Cor 11:7–9, 20; 12:13; Phil 4:10–20.   [151] *D*, 11–13.
[152] *D*, 15:1; *Hs*, 9:26:2.   [153] 1 Ti 5:17–22.
[154] Gal 2:10; 1 Cor 16:1–4; 2 Cor 8:1–20; Ro 15:25–29; Ac 11:27–29; 24:17.

may be that the intense scrutiny of the sacred documents by the entire assembly made separate schools redundant. And both the immediacy of the community's ethic and its asceticism would, if anything, have dampened the ordinary intellectual ambitions that in other times would assure the existence of schools. In any case, the *didaskalos* of the synagogue has no sure early Christian counterpart. His title has been assigned to a band of enthusiastic preachers he would not have taken to be up to the same thing at all.

These communities treasured their scrolls and their codices. They pored over the scriptures and copied and circulated the gospels and the other accepted contemporary writings. That each local assembly required a repository of those documents is obvious.[155] Despite their lack of civil status in society, it may be that the archival resources of a community served other purposes as well. One must always remember, however, that these documents were likely to have been stored in private homes; hence it is dubitable that the storer would have welcomed a depository of all his or her fellow believers' precious documents, or that any greater security could be provided than what each family had in its own home.

In the absence of the civil functions that synagogues exercised, the Christian communities followed programs that clustered about two main concerns: highly motivated religious assemblies, and generous support for dependents.

The records are silent about any other social services or amenities: water supply, safety deposit facility, hospice, or common scribe. What goes far to explain this is the fact that, as far as the evidence allows, we know of not one public building maintained by a Christian community during this period. When they assembled, it had to be in someone's home. If books and documents were to be safeguarded, it had to be in someone's home. If public funds accumulated, it had to be in someone's home. If widows and orphans had to be provided for, it had to be out of someone's home.[156] The community was dependent upon the premises of its members, and the pivotal importance of the affluent, and of the generous, is readily apparent.

---

[155] See *IPhld*, 8:2.   [156] *Hs*, 9:27:2.

THE SERVANT

The *hazan* = assistant of temple and synagogue appears several times in the gospel accounts, always under the older Greek equivalent of *hypêretês*.[157] In a move that is by now familiar to us, the Christian communities will provide themselves with comparable functionaries, but they will select an alternative title: *diakonos* = servant.

Before studying the office, let us listen to the resonance of the title. The vocabulary of servitude is lavishly used in the earliest Christian literature. There are a very few references to a literal *doulos* = slave or *diakonos* = servant or *hypêretês* = assistant.[158] But the terms have much wider employment as metaphors.

Every Christian believer is to be a *doulos* and a *diakonos* and a *hypêretês*.[159] Moses was a *doulos* and a *hypêretês*.[160] The Hebrew prophets were *diakonoi*; so were the righteous men and women of those ancient days.[161] Jesus was both *doulos* and *diakonos*.[162] Paul is a *doulos* and a *diakonos* and a *hypêretês*.[163] The apostles and evangelists are servants, and the false apostles are servants of Satan.[164] Timothy, Apollo, Epaphras, Tychicus, Archippos, preachers, and those with any of the charisms are enlisted in this calling for service.[165] Even the civil authorities are God's *diakonoi*.[166]

An interesting synonym in the literature is *leitourgia* = public charge. This is a metaphor applied to Noah, the Hebrew prophets, the priests and the Levites, Jesus, Paul, Epaphras, the Christian prophets and teachers, the elders, and the civil authorities.[167] To the Corinthians Paul writes of the charisms as *diakoniai* = services, but to the Romans he writes of *diakonia* as a specific charism in its own right. Years later, 1 *Peter* would list *diakonia* with a more institutionalized roster of charisms.[168] It should not go unnoticed that in this metaphorical application the vocabulary of service and servitude is most often applied to persons in positions of authority. These are

[157] See above, p. 246.   [158] Phlm 16; J 2:5; Ac 13:5.

[159] Gal 5:13; Rv 1:1, 2 and passim; *Hs*, 1:7, 10; 9:27:2; Mk 9:35; 10:43; J 12:26; *Hb* 6:10; *Hm*, 2:6; 12:3:3; *Hs*, 1:9; 2:7; Lk 1:2; 1 Cor 4:1; *Hm*, 8:10.

[160] Rv 15:3; *1 Cl*, 17:5.   [161] 1 Pt 1:12; *Hs*, 9:15:4.   [162] Phil 2:7; Ro 15:8.

[163] 1 Cor 9:19; 2 Cor 4:5; 6:3–4; Ro 1:1; 1 Cor 3:5; 2 Cor 4:1; 8:19; 11:23; Col 1:7, 23, 25; Ro 11:13; Eph 3:7; 4:11; 1 Ti 1:12; Ac 26:16.

[164] 2 Cor 8:19; Lk 1:2; 2 Cor 11:15.

[165] 2 Ti 2:24; 1 Th 3:2; 2 Ti 4:5; 1 Cor 3:5; Col 1:7; 4:12; Col 4:7; Eph 6:21; Col 4:17; *Hs*, 10:2:4; 10:4:1 (using the Latin equivalent, *ministerium*); 1 Pt 4:10–11.

[166] Ro 13:1–7.

[167] *1 Cl*, 9:4; 1:3; 32:1–2; Hb 5:6; Ro 15:16; Phil 2:27–30; *1 Cl*, 44; *D*, 15:1; Ro 13:6.

[168] 1 Cor 12:4–6; Ro 12:6–8; 1 Pt 4:10–11.

servants who command. Yet the point is that their authority has been given for a purpose: the welfare of the community, not their personal aggrandizement.

Out of this usage – both exalted and ironic – was drawn the title for one officer in the Christian community who never was meant to command: the *diakonos*. We know that from the time they began to separate into their own synagogue communities, the Christians would have needed "deacons," whose traditional responsibility (under whatever title) it was to provide sustenance for dependent widows. We know also that this was not one happy family. The Greek-speaking widows were complaining that the Aramaic-speaking widows were being accorded preferential treatment. This can only mean that the "Hebrews" were the in-group and the "Hellenists" were second-class community members. Obviously all the deacons, like the inner circle represented by the Twelve, were of the former group. So vociferous became the clamor that the authorities adopted an affirmative action program, installed seven Hellenists as supplemental deacons (suggesting that the aggrieved Hellenist Christians were becoming numerous, especially if one sees this as evidence of seven hellenist assemblies in Jerusalem, served by the common welfare program for the whole city), and then beheld the unfolding of their darkest misgivings about these less reliable, less traditional radicals.

The story as Luke tells it specifies their task: they are to offer the *diakonia* of eleemosynary work while the Twelve offer the *diakonia* of preaching and prayer. In fact, at least two of them engage in the apostolic or prophetic charism as rivals, rather than as lieutenants. Stephen loses no time engaging his fellow Greek-speaking Jews in violent debate, and arouses a retaliatory wave of terror which empties the city of most of its Christians. Matters only worsen when Philip, another of the hastily appointed deacons, engages in unauthorized preaching and baptizing which enlists Samaritans and an Ethiopian God-fearer in the unsuspecting church. Philip will end his days, not as a servant, but as a celebrated apostle and evangelist.[169]

In brief, one group of deacons in the first years of the Jerusalem community turned the traditional role of janitor-cum-welfare-agent

[169] Ac 6; 8:4–8, 26–40; 21:8; Papias in *H.E.* 3:19:9. That Stephen and Philip comport themselves as apostles/prophets in this context of Hebrew-Hellenist antagonism need not imply that the Seven were never installed as "servants." The critical flare-up between the two segments of the Jerusalem community quite specifically involved the performance of those who provided for community dependents.

inside out. Instead of acting like officers of the community they acted like charismatics of the Spirit – who, after all, were the most interesting people at the time.

Luke's account of these incidents surrounding the early Greek-speaking deacons is a composite of the two roles. As officers of the community they are chosen by the membership in full assembly because they were men who were qualified and filled with the Spirit. They are chosen, not by prophetic oracle, but by a popular show of hands. After election they are presented to the apostles (the Twelve?), prayers are said over them, and the leaders (and possibly the entire assembly; the text is unclear) lay hands on their heads. This much portrays a typical appointment and inauguration of a community officer.[170]

But then Stephen begins to be described in terms conventional for prophets and apostles. He is filled with divine *charis* = grace and *dynamis* = power and displays signs and wonders.[171] He bursts onto the public stage and becomes a dramatic sign of contradiction in the name of Jesus. After the spectacular adventures of those deacons-become-unauthorized-apostles, that particular spirit is quenched, and the office reappears in more ordinary light.[172]

Deacons continue to administer community subsidy to those on the welfare rolls.[173] They do so under the direction of community elders and of the chief.[174] There is also mention of a formalized role for them at worship, which it would be natural to reconstruct by analogy with what we know of the hazans' tasks in synagogue rites.[175] They can function as scribes or couriers (as Phoebe does for Paul and Burrhus for Ignatius),[176] and are sometimes sent as representatives of a leader or a community,[177] or to serve a leader as his assistant.[178] In this more traditional context they serve under the authority of the *episkopos* or elders.[179]

---

[170] Ac 6:1–6.

[171] Ac 6:8; cf. 2 Cor 12:12; Ac 2:22, 43; 4:30; 5:12; 7:36; 14:3; 15:12.

[172] The two stories of the selection of Matthias as one of the Twelve in Acts 1 and of the hellenist deacons in Acts 6 reveal much resemblance. In both accounts: (1) the qualifications are enumerated by the authorities; (2) the *ochlos/plêthos* approves, and puts = *estêsan* candidates before the Eleven/Twelve to be given the *diakonia*. In Matthias' case the event is made charismatic by leaving the final choice to God through a lottery, but the framework of a community officer's election and inauguration structures the story.

[173] *ITr*, 2:3; *Hs*, 9:26:2.   [174] *1 Cl*, 42:4; *IPol*, 4:1; *Hs*, 9:27:1–2.

[175] *IPhld*, 4:1; *ITr*, 7:2.   [176] Ro 16:1; *IPhld*, 11:2; *ISm*, 12:1.

[177] *IPhil* 10:1–2; 11:1; Ro 16:1; *ISm*, 10:1.

[178] *IEph*, 2:1; *IMg*, 2; *IPhld*, 11:1; *ISm*, 13:1.   [179] *IMg*, 2, 6, 13.

That they exercise substantial influence in the communities is implied by the constant refrain that they must be financially reliable. The pastoral epistles, the *Didache* and Polycarp all describe the requisite qualities for this office.

[D]eacons must be respectable, not double-tongued, moderate in the amount of wine they drink and with no squalid greed for money. They must hold to the mystery of the faith with a clear conscience. They are first to be examined, and admitted to serve as deacons only if there is nothing against them. Similarly, women must be respectable, not gossips, but sober and wholly reliable. Deacons must be husbands of one wife and must be people who manage their children and households well. Those of them who carry out their duties well as deacons will earn a high standing for themselves and an authoritative voice in matters concerning faith in Christ Jesus. (1 Timothy)[180]

Appoint for yourselves elders and deacons worthy of the Lord, men who are meek and not lovers of money, and true and approved; for to you they offer the services of the prophets and teachers. (*Didache*)[181]

[D]eacons should be blameless in the presence of God's righteousness, as deacons of God and not of men; not calumniators, not double-tongued, not lovers of money, temperate in all things, compassionate, diligent, walking according to the truth of the Lord who became a deacon of all. (Polycarp)[182]

A similar point is made by the *Shepherd of Hermas* in its own characteristic way: "'[The believers] that have the spots are deacons that exercised their office criminally, and plundered the livelihood of widows and orphans, and made a profit themselves from the services they had been charged to perform'."[183]

Ignatius is determined to establish the diaconate as a considerate responsibility. Repeatedly and pointedly he addresses deacons as "my fellow slaves," and as "deacons of Jesus Christ," "of God's church", to be respected like Jesus, because appointed by his decree and ratified by the Spirit. They are exemplars of the divine *diakonia*.[184] He is doing for deacons exactly what he did for overseers and elders. To counter the claims and authority of the charismatics who draw theirs from God and overbear the officers who hold only church

---

[180] 1 Ti 3:8–13; cf. 3:1–7.   [181] *D*, 15:1.   [182] *Pol*, 5:2; cf. 6:1.
[183] *Hs*, 9:26:2.
[184] *IEph*, 2:1; *IMg*, 2; *IPhld*, 4:1; *ISm*, 12:2; *IPol*, 6:11; *IMg*, 6; *ITr*, 2:3; 3:1; *IPol*, 5:2; *IPhld*, address; *ISm*, 12:1.

warrants, Ignatius is arguing that church officers – even deacons – are fundamentally invested with a divine enablement, not a merely human one. It may be that the hybrid portrayal of deacons in Acts gave this office the enhanced theological respect its tasks deserved for a readership that recognized divine sponsorship best where it beheld signs and wonders. In any case, though there is no real estate to care for nor as wide a range of tasks to perform as was confided to Jewish *hazanim*, the office has been transformed, as it were, from blue-collar work to a white-collar profession. *Koinônia* = sharing of wherewithal with the less fortunate was a major imperative for these communities, and this important office administered that sharing. It offered more managerial initiative and responsibility, and apparently attracted incumbents of high capacity and initiative.

PRIESTS

The Christian dispensation makes no accommodation for priests. Absolutely no one takes up the hint left in Luke's infancy narratives that Jesus might be descended through his mother from the tribe of Levi (Mary's kinswoman, Elizabeth, is descended from the clan of Aaron and is married to a priest).[185] The only notice ever taken of Jewish priests in the Christian ranks is a brief notice that a large group of them had submitted to the new faith before the events of Stephen's death.[186] There is no evidence that their priestly character did anything but go into dormancy.

The first Christians frequented the temple, we know, to join in prayers, to preach, to meet among themselves and to observe the fulfillment of vows.[187] There is no record of their participation in any sacrifices, nor any denial. Eventually they developed a polemic against the sacrificial tradition in Israel.[188]

In large part, however, the allusions to the Jewish temple, priesthood and sacrifices are positive. Paul and the *Didache* use the priesthood as a precedent for the financial support of religious functionaries, apostles and prophets, through community subsidy.[189] Clement, enjoining on the Corinthians the notion of a divinely established hierarchy and order, points to the echelons of Levites,

---

[185] Lk 2:5, 36. [186] Ac 6:7.
[187] Ac 3:1; 22:17; 5:20, 42; 24:12; 5:12; 2:46; 24:17. [188] *B*, 2; *Dg*, 3:5.
[189] I Cor 9:13; *D*, 13:3.

priests and high priest.[190] Ignatius uses the imperative in Israel of a single legitimate altar to underwrite a single authorized worshipping assembly: that which has the *episkopos* for its president.[191] Jesus is hailed as the ultimate sacrificial victim and altar and high priest: he has offered himself, and stands now before God to present our offerings as well.[192]

The New Testament analogizes many Jewish institutions which in their literal reality were being left behind: sacrifice, kingship, nationhood, race, temple. The title of *hiereus* = levitical priest is not applied to officers of the church, but it is applied to Christ and to the church itself. It is the language of oblation which, when applied to the eucharist especially, will leave open the possibility of a later analogical understanding of ministry as a priestly role.[193]

The Christians are, as a whole, a priestly people.[194] Their faith is a sacrifice; so is the self-discipline of their bodies, and so too are their financial contributions to the widows and orphans or to preachers of the gospel.[195] Paul looks on his missionary work as an act of sacrifice.[196] Ignatius understands his impending death as a desired sacrifice.[197] And it is this same attitude of self-expenditure that every communicant must bring to prayer – the sacrifice of praise, the offering of a broken heart – and to the breaking of bread, wherein every individual yields himself or herself to community: one thanksgiving, one flesh, one cup, one altar, one overseer and presbytery and diaconate.[198]

Nowhere, however, despite the range of freedom early Christians felt to draw on the traditions of the temple, priesthood and sacrifice by way of illustration, precedent and analogy, is there a willingness to accord Jewish priests any community prerogative, or to suggest any real continuity with their present officers and rites. The word

---

[190] *1 Cl*, 40–41. He does not, however, use it as an allegorical model for a three-tiered set of offices.   [191] *IEph*, 5:2; *ITr*, 7:2; *IPhld*, 4.

[192] Eph 5:2; *IMg*, 7:2; Hb passim; *1 Cl*, 36:1; 61:3; 64; *MPol*, 14:3.

[193] This same device of analogizing Israelite institutions and thus accepting them in a non-literal sense was also used in the reception of much (though not all) of the Old Testament law. Jean Colson, *Ministre de Jésus-Christ ou le sacerdoce de l'évangile: Etude sur la condition sacerdotale des ministres chrétiens dans l'église primitive* (Paris: Beauchesne, 1966). This has been the analogy that has guided some modern treatments of office in the New Testament: Heinrich Schlier, "Die neutestamentliche Grundlage des Priesteramtes," in *Der Priesterliche Dienst I: Ursprung und Frühgeschichte*, Quaestiones Disputatae 46, ed. Karl Rahner, S.J., and Schlier (Freiburg: Herder, 1970), 81–114.   [194] 1 Pt 2:5; Rv 1:6; 5:10; 20:6.

[195] Phil 2:17; Ro 12:1; *Hs*, 5:3:8; Phil 4:16–18.   [196] Ro 15:6.

[197] *IRo*, 2:2; 4:2.   [198] Hb 13:10–16; *B*, 2; *D*, 14:1–3; *IPhld*, 4.

hieron = temple never once appears, for instance, in this period after the New Testament. It is not that there are no longer any priests: there are no longer any who are not priests. Priesthood is no longer the identity of a clan or a tribe, but the name of an entire people.

OTHER OFFICERS

Apart from overseers, elders and servants, are there any other community officers known during this period? Only a few fragments of evidence survive.

There are several passages which describe an office of religious instruction that is local, and which possibly devolved upon functionaries other than those we have studied. Paul writes: "People under instruction should always contribute something to the support of the one who is instructing them."[199] The *Shepherd* includes this statement:

When I have finished what I have to say, it shall be published through you to all the elect. So you shall write two small books and send one each to Clement and the Grapte. Clement shall distribute it to the foreign cities: that is his duty. Grapte shall teach the widows and the orphans. And you shall read it to this city along with the elders who rule the assembly.[200]

These two passages give slender support to a conjecture that a minor teaching office had been in place in some early communities. It is possible, though not probable, that the title of *didaskalos* which *Barnabas* disavows may by his time refer to such an office, rather than to a charism.[201]

THE WIDOWS

The predominant role of widows in the earliest documents was as the archetypical beneficiaries of the common purse. Not all widows, of course, qualified. Only those bereft of relatives were supported. Once they were accepted, though, it appears that widows somehow became public personages.

Be considerate to widows – if they really are widowed. If a widow has children or grandchildren, they are to learn first of all to do their duty to their own families and repay their debt to their parents, because this is what

---

[199] Gal 6:6. The reference could well be to an apostle or a teacher, but *katêcheô* in our literature often means to make sense for someone of the basic teaching already received, or to give introductory teaching, hence: "catechumen." Both senses suggest a lower-ranking person doing the teaching. Cf. Ac 18:25; 21:21; Ro 2:18; 1 Cor 14:19.
[200] *Hv*, 2:4:2–3.   [201] *B*, 1:8; 4:9.

pleases God. But a woman who is really widowed and left on her own has set her hope on God and perseveres night and day in petitions and prayer. The one who thinks only of pleasure is already dead while she is still alive: instruct them in this, too, so that their lives may be blameless. Anyone who does not look after his own relations, especially if they are living with him, has rejected the faith and is worse than an unbeliever. (1 Timothy)

Enrolment as a widow is permissible only for a woman at least sixty years old who has had only one husband. She must be a woman known for her good works – whether she has brought up her children, been hospitable to strangers and washed the feet of God's holy people, helped people in hardship or been active in all kinds of good work. Do not accept young widows because if their natural desires distract them from Christ, they want to marry again, and then people condemn them for being unfaithful to their original promise. Besides, they learn how to be idle and go round from house to house; and then, not merely idle, they learn to be gossips and meddlers in other people's affairs and to say what should remain unsaid. I think it is best for young widows to marry again and have children and a household to look after, and not give the enemy any chance to raise a scandal about them; there are already some who have turned aside to follow Satan. If a woman believer has widowed relatives, she should support them and not make the Church bear the expense but enable it to support those who are really widowed. (Titus)[202]

Much of this is an attempt to guarantee the community that its most prominent wards are not profligate. But what are we to make of the requirement that the widows made a promise = *pistis*? To what were they bound to be faithful?

An earlier story which told of Dorcas, a Jaffa widow, describes her as a generous giver in the community. She was at the center of a group of widows, and was known as a capable seamstress.[203] Is it possible that widows, once they had definitively turned their backs on courtship and remarriage, and accepted enlistment in the rolls for community-provided support, were expected to form a cadre of dedicated and exemplary women who, in their turn, found services to render in return?

Polycarp writes as follows:

Our widows must be sober-minded regarding the undertaking = *pistis* of the Lord, making intercession without ceasing for all persons, abstaining from all calumny, evil speaking, false witness, love of money, and every evil deed,

<hr>

[202] 1 Ti 5:2–16; cf. Tit 2:3–5.   [203] Ac 9:36–42.

knowing that they are God's altar, and that all sacrifices are carefully inspected, and nothing escapes him either of their thoughts or intentions or any of the heart's secrets.[204]

There is too little evidence to speculate about a formal fellowship of widows. But the clear set of expectations constituted them as a visibly distinct constituency in the community, with no small prospect of honor and perhaps influence for those who lived up to the high calling.[205]

WOMEN OF PROMINENCE

"Since the God who made the world and everything in it is himself Lord of heaven and earth, he does not make his home in shrines made by human hands." Thus Paul on Mars Hill.[206] The people he represented had no cause to link their God with any sacred or select real estate, because they had none. They met, as we know, in homes of their members. One reads of the houses of Mary, Barnabas' aunt and John Mark's mother, in Jerusalem, where the community was gathered to pray;[207] of Aquila and Prisca in Rome;[208] of Nympha and of Philemon in Colossae;[209] and of Gaius in Corinth:[210] all of whom had assemblies meeting in their homes.

The mother and father of the synagogue do not reappear in the Christian churches. The position of host to a local community, though, was one of special dignity for a community that lacked any other *pied-à-terre*. It was one of the avenues for women, who could hold this position alone or with a spouse, to take a role of effective leadership in the church.

Paul reminisces that the early Christian membership could not boast of culture, clout or pedigree.[211] When people of social standing

---

[204] *Pol*, 4:3. This comes between his admonitions to families and to deacons.

[205] Ignatius' curious salute to "the virgins called widows" may imply that *chēra* is becoming a title for women who now lived a distinctive life apart from that of wives and mothers, *ISm*, 13:1.　　　　　　　　　　　　　[206] Ac 17:24.

[207] Ac 12:12; Col 4:10. That she was not a poor woman is inferrable from her having a servant.

[208] 1 Cor 16:19; Ro 16:3–5; Ac 18:2–4.

[209] Col 4:15; Phlm 1–2. This assumes that Nympha is not in Laodicaea, as the Col text might be construed, and that Apphia and Archippus are Philemon's wife and son, and that Philemon is the antecedent of "in your house." If both are in Colossae, we have our first evidence of more than two distinct congregations in a city, yet the ensemble continuing to function and to be addressed as one *ekklēsia*. The Christians showed no disposition at this time to speak of plural assemblies in a city.　　　　　[210] 1 Cor 1:14; Ro 16:23.

[211] 1 Cor 1:26: *ou polloi sophoi kata sarka, ou polloi dynatoi, ou polloi eugeneis.*

did join, their rank was not ignored. Joseph of Arimathea and Nicodemus of the Sanhedrin, Erastus the city treasurer, Manaen who had been brought up with Herod the tetrarch, Zenas the lawyer, the official of the *kandake* of Ethiopia, Joanna the wife of Herod's steward Chuza, Lydia the dye merchant in Philippi: these were well-remembered names.[212]

It is probable that the Way, which was not without its hazards, held a more compelling appeal for the wives of men of high standing than for the dignitaries themselves, who stood to lose more socially than did the women. Lydia converted her husband, but for several others their spouse served as a social reference but not as a cobeliever.[213]

There are specific statements that converts included a notable number of affluent, upper-class women.[214] Several writers deliver themselves of blunt statements about how deferential the communities have become to wealth.[215] Admonitions about affluence turn typically to particular criticisms of conspicuous feminine expenditure.[216] Social conventions of the time – Jewish and Roman – imposed grave restrictions of inequality upon women, even women of the upper classes. But her family's economic advantages were one thing which a woman could dispose of pretty much at will. Perhaps it is significant that in Corinth the community is bidden to expel a man living in an incestuous relationship, yet nothing is imposed upon his consort. But when the offense involves money, as in the case of Ananias and Sapphira, and that of Valens and his wife, the spouses are both to blame, because it is the one sector of life in which she is a responsible agent.[217] It appears that a significant number of ranking women entered the Christian communities and that they enjoyed there an influence which other women may not have had.

Were there also women to whom the church itself assigned responsibility?

The gospels report that Jesus couched his message in ways specifically meaningful to women, that some of his closest disciples were women, that his travelling retinue was provided for by a team

---

[212] Mk 15:43; J 3; 19:39; Ro 16:23; Ac 13:1; Tit 3:13; Ac 8:26–40; Lk 8:3; Ac 16:14.
[213] The Way was not without risk for women, though. Paul, in his days as poursuivant, made it a point to punish both men and women followers of Jesus, Ac 8:3; 9:2; 22:4.
[214] Ac 17:4 (Thessalonika); 17:12 (Beroea).
[215] See, for instance, 1 Ti 6:17–19; Js 1–2.   [216] 1 Pt 3:1–7; 1 Ti 2:9–15; *Pol*, 4.
[217] 1 Cor 5; Acts 5; *Pol*, 11:1.

of women, and that at his death and resurrection appearances it was these women, in default of most male disciples, who stood fast and first received Easter tidings. This was remarkable for the time and place, and radical within the Jewish conventions of the time.

The rest of the New Testament records a host of women who figured in the young church's efforts: Claudia, Mary, Tryphaena and Tryphosa, Julia (?), Apphia, Evodia and Syntyche of Philippi who Paul says "struggled hard for the gospel with me," Prisca, Paul's "fellow worker" who with her husband completed the training of Apollos. But were any women actually in acknowledged offices?

The evidence is clear that women as well as men held charismatic roles in the community. The four daughters of Philip were prophets.[218] No women are ascribed the title of teacher, but one manuscript tradition presents as "kinfolk and fellow prisoners, outstanding apostles," not Andronicus and Junias (both men), but Andronicus and Julia.[219] In the domain of spiritual gifts, social custom is not in control. Christians were familiar with women judges, women prophetesses and women heroines in Israel. The communities would have been ready to receive women as charismatically endowed, and we have evidence that some were.

For offices conferred by the assemblies, it was a different matter. Let a comparison serve to illustrate how this was. It was a commonplace among the new believers that all were one in Christ. No more Jew and Greek, male and female, slave and free. In Christ, all were now brothers and sisters.[220] Those were the general assurances. But during the century to follow, slaves and masters were assured on high authority that their relationship was not structurally changed: it was infused with a new spirit.[221] Master and slave sup at the Lord's table together and partake of the same mystical gifts. But slaves are warned bluntly that they must not get arrogant. Thus we would be irresponsible to conjecture, on the strength of the early sincere slogans, that Christianity promptly dissolved existing social structures among members, any more than it leveled people economically. Moving to another of those ancient divisions said to be radically transformed in Christ, it would be similarly naïve to

---

[218] Ac 21:8; Papias, 3:9. Jezebel, the prophetess of Thyatira denounced in Rv 2:20, may have been a Nicolaitan, but the charism may still have been hers.   [219] Ro 16:7.

[220] Col 3:11; 1 Cor 12:13; Gal 3:27–28; Ro 10:12.

[221] Col 3:22; Phlm 18–19; Eph 6:5; 1 Ti 6:1; Tit 2:9–10; 1 Pt 2:18; *IPol*, 4:3; *D*, 4:10–12; *B*, 19:7.

stipulate that Christian women were accorded a whole new rank and role in the church – to the extent that the community controlled the formalities. Thus, unlike the charismatic arousals which affected the communities but for a long while eluded their governance, church offices were not open to women.[222]

A possible exception to this may be the office of deacon. The reader need recall 1 Timothy's statement on the qualities requisite for a *diakonos*. Planted within it is this sentence: "Similarly, women must be respectable, not gossips, but sober and wholly reliable."[223] Since family probity is a qualification for all offices, and since the character of one's children is mentioned as a reflection on the candidate, one would best interpret the sentence to stipulate the desirable traits in his wife. Some have read it as a special requirement for female deacons. Absent any example, that would be a strained reading.

Some claim, however, that we have evidence of an actual example. Paul writes in Romans: "I commend to you our sister Phoebe, a *diakonos* of the church at Cenchreae; give her, in the Lord, a welcome worthy of God's holy people and help her with whatever she needs from you – she herself has come to the help of many people, including myself."[224]

Phoebe is called *diakonos*,[225] not *diakonissa*. She is possibly the courier for the document: good deacon's work. Her office would require her to be, as described, a *prostatis* = protectress/helper. This would all fit with her holding the office.

But at the time Paul was writing to the Romans *diakonia* had not yet given rise to a title of office; it was still a generic term designating the generic service that any activist might offer. Even later, when Acts describes the Seven taking up the eleemosynary responsibility for their sector of the community, no title is assigned to them. In Paul's same letter, *diakonia* is mentioned in a list of charisms, grouped with the services of the word, not those of financial welfare.[226] Paul is most plausibly calling her a servant like so many others: Tychicus

---

[222] Although women partook of community meals and could pray and prophesy in public assembly, Paul insists that in the latter circumstance they should attend veiled, 1 Cor 11:2–16. 1 Ti 2:11 requires women to be silent when teaching or instruction are given, for women are not to tell men what to do. These references may reveal that there were some local ventures of female emancipation, but they also reveal that they were prevented from spreading.   [223] 1 Ti 3:11; see above, p. 320.   [224] Ro 16:1–2.
[225] Compare much later epitaphs for women with the title of diakonos: G[eorge] H. R. Horsley, *New Documents Illustrating Early Christianity, 1976* (North Ryde, NSW: Macquarie University, 1981), 79; also *New Documents, 1977* (1982), 109.   [226] Ro 12:7.

and Epaphras and Timothy and the rest. This would perhaps constitute a higher accolade, but it would not yet have become a title of office.[227]

As for female elders or overseers: there are none, not even any female titularies that are officers' wives.[228] The men in the communities were not motivated by the new spirit to call women into community governance. But, again, it would be too formal and artificial to conclude that women counted for little. It is important to observe that officers – including elders and the elders who presided – were for a long period not the most influential shapers of the young church's destiny. In its earliest generations women were prominent; when the salient leadership passed over into the hands of the officers, those avenues of prominence were no longer so open.

A HIERARCHY OF COMMUNITIES

Do the various *ekklêsiai* form a network within the far-flung *ekklêsia* in any fashion resembling the hierarchical system of worldwide Jewry? The answer at first is simple: every church answered to its founder, and they all answered to the apostles of the Lord. At first the authority of the apostles was seen to reside in Jerusalem. The church there spoke with secure *kyriotês* = ruling power: "It has been decided by the Holy Spirit and by ourselves…"[229] To take as one example their decision regarding the amalgamation of the uncircumcised, we see that their writ ran without difficulty up through Syria and Cilicia into Lycaonia.[230]

Individual apostles, absent *force majeure* from Jerusalem, could and did circulate, and by the force of their possession of the Spirit as token of their mission for Christ, hold answerable to them the churches where they had preached. On the strength of that divine charge they were the charismatic energizers and adjudicators for local churches. Paul is always writing, "I command … I order … I charge you …" In time, it was inevitable that other persons with a similar display of the Spirit might move into some of his communities and put matters in a different light. Their credentials seemed identical to his, and he was

---

[227] Thus Roger Gryson, *Le ministère des femmes dans l'église ancienne* (Gembloux: Duculot, 1971), 22–24; André Lemaire, *Les ministères aux origines de l'église* (Paris: Cerf, 1971), 93–96.
[228] They begin, however, to appear with the title of *presbytis* in a few inscriptions: Horsley, *New Documents, 1976*, 79.   [229] Ac 15:28.   [230] Ac 15:1–16:4.

obliged to display his own differently. To the Galatians he presents himself as an agent of the Jerusalem policy: a more consistent one than even Peter (an adroit way of dealing with the issue of choosing between apostles). Secondly, he now claims obedience because he was their founder.[231] To the Corinthians he argues that in exotic spiritual performance he is not to be outdone, but then he falls back upon his stronger point: that he was the first to beget them in Christ, and at great personal sacrifice.[232] The appeal was successful – enough for Paul to delegate governing power to his deputies. Even the pastoral epistles, which are written later to reinforce local officers, build upon the memory of men like Timothy and Titus enjoying a continuing charismatic authority.

But the weakness of the arrangement was already manifest. Founders die, and their deputies' warrants die with them. Those who rule with the force of the Spirit are always open to challenge by a new contender who claims the same Spirit in stronger measure.

In time the functioning authority of the apostles was absorbed by central churches. Already when Paul and Barnabas were called before the authorities in Jerusalem, the apostolic claim of that community was largely an anachronism. Only Peter and John were there, and they might decamp at any time.[233] The stable establishment there was not one of apostles, even though the decrees were issued in the name and authority of the apostles. They were assembly officers: James and the elders. Jerusalem has assumed authority in its own right (so much so that the first pseudonymous letter to be issued in the name of a non-apostle was published as of James: as presiding elder in Jerusalem he had come to do what no apostle claimed: to preside over the mother of all churches).

Jesus Christ was confessed as head of all the church,[234] and any exercise of authority had somehow to exhibit a vital and subservient relationship to the risen Lord. What we witness during the first century of experience is the transfer of that claim from charismatic individuals to institutional communities and their officers. Yet during that transfer the older symbols of legitimation served to authorize the new intendants.

---

[231] Gal 1:11; 2:14; 4:12–20.   [232] 2 Cor 10–12.

[233] Peter alone is present in Paul's narratives of his first visit to Jerusalem (Gal 1:18–20); Luke mentions none (Acts 9:26–30). No apostle is present for Paul's final visit (Acts 21:15ff).

[234] Mt 16:18 (a unique use of *ekklēsia* in the gospels as referring to the later community); Col 1:18–19; Eph 1:22.

Polycarp is hailed as a great bishop who has the qualities of an apostle and a prophet.[235] Rome is acknowledged as the city of both Peter and Paul.[236] The fact is, however, that by the latter part of the period under study, the urban churches were, as far as we know, stratified into a hierarchy which corresponded to their traditional civil ranking, not to the rank or the reputations of their founders or bishops. Ignatius is the "shepherd of Syria" because he is *episkopos* of Antioch, the provincial metropolis.[237] Ephesus is the chief church in Asia, not because it is the only church of apostolic foundation there, but because it is the capital. Rome, which will emerge as the first church after the collapse of the Jerusalem community, "has the presidency in the country of the region of the Romans, being worthy of God, worthy of honor, worthy of felicitation, worthy of praise, worthy of success, worthy in purity, and having the presidency in love ..."[238] Ignatius acclaims Rome this way for the same reason that Clement, only fifteen years before, had written, not in his own name nor with any claim to apostolic authority (what would that mean to Christians in Corinth?), but simply in the name of the assembly in Rome, because Rome was Rome: capital of the empire (or of the world, as they thought) and also the metropolis of all metropolitan churches: the new Jerusalem.

Behind the political fact that both cities were capitals of their respective worlds, there was the mystical fact that Jerusalem was the city of Jesus' death and resurrection (as in Jewish lore it held the graves of Adam and David, and was the site of Isaac's sacrifice), and Rome was the city where Peter and Paul had followed Jesus' witness.

The fact that both Peter and Paul had been martyred in the city gave the Roman see a prestige not possessed by others. Ignatius called Rome the instructress of others in the art of dying for the faith and included in the roll are several early bishops ... It is likely that the chain of martyrs was of more importance in the first two centuries than any appeal to the New Testament. Indeed not until the third century was the Petrine text Matt. 16:18 appealed to as supporting any primacy of Peter.[239]

The relationship of one city-church to another, then, was hierarchical. Just as local officers were given eventual ascendancy over the spiritual adventurers by the argument that God the Father had sent the Son / Jesus had sent the apostles / the apostles had

---

[235] *MPol*, 16:2. [236] *IRo*, 4:3. [237] *IRo*, 9:1. [238] *IRo*, address.
[239] L[eslie] W[illiam] Barnard, *Studies in Church History and Patristics*, Analecta Vlatadon 26 (Saloniki: Patriarchal Institute for Patristic Studies, 1978), 180.

commissioned elders to assume their charge, so also certain churches were authorized to hold others accountable by the argument that they had been given the ascendancy through the apostles.[240] And just as the Qumran "overseer of all the camps"[241] and the Nasi of the rabbinical academy were past and contemporary Jewish instances of a presiding officer acting in the name of the presiding community, so the overseers of Rome and the metropolitan cities could speak on behalf of the authoritative communities they led.

When Polycarp was being paraded before a taunting mob prior to his martyrdom, he was howled at as the "teacher of Asia." Yet Smyrna, his city, was not the capital of Asia; Ephesus was. The cry from the crowd is a reminder that even despite the echelons of office and of hierarchy, the true force of spiritual, personal éclat remains unsubjected to the assignments of station. There was a radical and true power that was not ultimately conferrable at human discretion.

Within each urban center, as the number of communicants exceeded the capacity of a single gathering place, the requirements of weekly or more frequent assembly obliged them to divide into plural house-churches. No matter how many physical assemblies in a single city, the unbroken usage is to designate each one as an *ekklêsia* and also to refer to the collectivity of assemblies as one *ekklêsia*. The plural is used of provinces: "the churches in Galatia ... Asia ... Judaea." The plural is not used of a city. We must infer that within a city the Christians retained a single central governance: one college of elders. If those elders also served as presidents of the satellite assemblies (we have no evidence from this period that they did, but it will emerge as the standard practice in the next period), they nevertheless exercised a corporate *episkopê* over the ensemble. Thus within a city, the various assemblies formed a synodal unit. They were not answerable to a single church, but to a corporate authority with representation from them all.[242]

Let us now, in much more summary fashion, review the evidence. We know that the followers of Jesus referred to themselves for a long while in various ways. Sometimes they were known as devotees of Jesus: "slaves" (Revelation), or "Christ people" (Acts, 1 Peter). Other designations staked a competitive claim to being God's

[240] *1 Cl*, 42:1–5; *IEph*, 3:2.
[241] *Damascus Document, CD* 14:8–11. See above, chapter 7, note 189.
[242] Ernst Dassmann, "Hausgemeinde und Bischofsamt," in *Vivarium: Festschrift für Theodor Klauser*, ed. Dassmann and Klaus Thraede (Münster: Aschendorff, 1984), 82–97.

authentic people (Hebrews, Acts). And emergent from earliest documents is the custom of calling themselves *ekklêsia* = assembly, both as a local and as a translocal church (1 Thessalonians, 1&2 Corinthians, Romans, Philemon, James, 3 John, Clement, Ignatius, Polycarp, Hermas).

Locally they would gather for various community undertakings: to deliberate and adopt common policy (Galatians, Acts, *Barnabas*); to read and discuss the scriptures (this we can only infer) and correspondence with the churches (1 Thessalonians, Colossians, Acts, Polycarp); to pray in common (1 Corinthians, Acts); to break bread (1 Corinthians, Acts, *Didache*, Ignatius, Diognetus); to exhort one another to walk morally before the Lord (1 Corinthians, Acts, 1 Timothy) and to discipline those who defaulted (Galatians, 1&2 Corinthians, 2 Thessalonians, 2 John); to designate and empower officers (Acts, 1 Timothy, Polycarp, Hermas); to arrange for collections for the indigent (1 Corinthians, Hebrews). As we have noted already, this goes far to justifying Acts 2:42 as a summary of early Christian assemblies: "These remained faithful to the teaching of the apostles, to the brotherhood, to the breaking of bread and to the prayers."

We know that the communities provided for their own dependent members (Romans, 1 Timothy, James, Hebrews, Acts, Ignatius, Polycarp, *Barnabas*, Hermas) and that they had ready hospitality for fellow believers who traveled their way (Romans, 3 John, Clement, *Didache*, Hermas).

Though each community resolved its own affairs, there was a network of deferential relationships that bound them together (Acts, Clement, Ignatius).

The communities lay under the leadership and influence of two distinct kinds of personage. The first, known consistently as apostles, prophets, teachers and evangelists, were vouched for by their home communities but accredited by the Lord, either through their direct discipleship under Jesus himself or through prophetic prodigies of deed and word.

The second genus of prominent persons comprised what we may call officers, as contrasted with the charismatics. Their selection and accreditation was by the community.

It seems that both groups shared the general Christian calling to be slaves and public servants, by dint of divine gifts and power. The officers emerge gradually in the evidence as having specific warrants.

Their nomenclature, however, was as fluid as that of the charismatics was stable. From early evidence we learn of persons tasked with presiding, guiding, ruling, shepherding, governing, overseeing (1 Thessalonians, 1 Corinthians, Ephesians, Hebrews, 1 Peter, 3 John, Clement, *Barnabas*). Yet alongside these designations we see emerge three distinct ranks and roles of office, eventually known by proper titles: elders (Philippians, Acts, 1 Peter, 1 Timothy, Clement, Ignatius), overseers (Acts, 3 John, Revelation, Clement, Ignatius, Polycarp) and assistants (Philippians, Acts, Pastorals, *Didache*, Clement, Ignatius, Polycarp, Hermas).

The Christian practice of moving from generic vocabulary to specific nomenclature, precisely in order to differentiate themselves from rival Jewish usage, was itself a practice derived from Judaism. What the evidence displays is that the program and order of Christian communities originate in direct continuity with the synagogue communities of Israel.

There are, of course, features found in synagogues which are not attested in Christian communities. The Christians enjoyed no civil standing before Roman law, and no ethnic solidarity as a source of identity. The evidence of intramural doctrinal dissent and of the official intolerance it provoked points to the fragile unity of a community which was neither legal nor racial, but intentional and doctrinal.

There are other lineaments typical to the synagogue but missing in the Christian church – schools, notables, fathers and mothers, secular and purity amenities, etc. If one recognizes the synagogue pattern, however, not as a uniform model but as a type, then the Christians seem to have had no more variations than Jewish sectarian groups.[243]

The triad of officers, then, which stand forth most distinctly in the Christian churches of the second century AD, are already emergent in the earliest authentic pauline documents of the first century AD, and are in complete accord with the familiar elements of Jewish community order attested from the first century BC to the second century AD. It is important to note that the evidence accumulates

---

[243] Contemporary scholarship is taking strong notice of the diversity and flexibility of the synagogue in late antiquity: in its architecture, prayer program and community order. See, for example, Lee I. Levine, ed., *The Synagogue in Late Antiquity* (Philadelphia: The American Schools of Oriental Research, 1987), especially chapters by Levine, A(lf) T(homas) Kraabel, Eric M. Meyers and Shaye J. D. Cohen. The evidence adduced thus far, however, derives mostly from well after the first century AD, and hence the conclusions may not apply to the earlier period under study here.

with the years, but that it is present, though sparse, in the earliest documents known to us. In the final chapter we shall speculate about why the officers receive so little notice in the earliest texts.

Also, though there was no uniform model of synagogue order during the time we are considering, the features which carry over in the church order are among those most widely witnessed in the Jewish evidence: community program, the three officers and networking. The absent features are less widely to be seen in the Jewish evidence.

The officers, then were no more a *trahison des clercs*, no more an abrupt innovation by Ignatius and his knavish contemporaries, than were the eucharist or the delegitimation of the hieratic priesthood.

THE PATIENT OFFICERS OF THE SPIRIT

Our most extensive account of the developing eucharistic liturgy from this period is in the *Didache*. It concludes with this instruction: "But permit the prophets to offer thanksgiving as much as they please."[244] Much lies within this statement. We may suppose, for instance, that for many years prophets had been speaking their minds as much as they pleased. We may also suppose that the day had finally arrived when in one assembly, one person had finally told a prophet to have done with it and sit down. The act of cloture had gone down badly – hence the injunction here – but it was a precedent that was eventually going to stick. And although the liturgical instructions are addressed to no personages in particular, we may suppose that the unidentified recipients who would enact this instruction on the communities' behalf were the unnamed officers who had for so many silent years presided over the bread-breaking and cup-sharing assemblies and who were only now beginning to assume a style of authority. This one brief sentence may serve as a reminder of what had been going on.

From their beginnings the communities of Christian believers had gathered into the shape already familiar from the Jewish synagogues. It is perhaps inaccurate even to speak of beginnings, for what they did at first was precisely to organize a few synagogue communities to gain shelter and solidarity for their movement. It was only later events and estrangements which retrospectively christened this continuity as a commencement.

---

[244] *D*, 10:7.

These communities had assemblies, elders, presiding elders, deacons, and a full program of worship, common policy-making, social welfare and interurban alliances. They lacked the authorization to govern themselves on behalf of the empire. But in other respects they developed patterns of community organization that were traditional to their Jewish origins and members.

The vitality, initiative, derring-do, heroism and summons to sanctity however were not, in those earliest days, to be found in the officers of the churches. Men and women possessed by the fire of Pentecost, often with no official seats in any local assemblies, dashed about like sparks through the stubble, touching off new blazes as they went. In the presence of those zealous enthusiasts, whose whole industry and imagination were given over to the work of the gospel, the most devout and dutiful elders must have seemed humdrum.

In time the enthusiasts proved better pioneers than farmers. They served best when not crowded in on one another. They were powerful at first burst; less helpful over the long haul. Slowly the effective responsibility for community continuance was assumed by the officers of the churches. It was not a mere political movement or *coup d'église*. The earliest believers could see and feel the Spirit of Jesus in the volunteers, much more than in their own neighbors they had voted into office. What they came to see was that the Spirit also lived in the church through the dutiful service of their officers: quietly, immanently, ordinarily, with gentler signs and wonders. The Lord was not only in the storm and the earthquake and the fire, but also in the gentle whisper of the breeze.

This theological discovery underwrote the political transformation in the church during its first century of existence. The first and immediate crisis, of course, was the unforeseen inrush of gentiles into a communion that had thought Jewish reform was quite an adequate agenda. The longer sequel to that battle is what we have been studying in this chapter. First the community had to discover it had a future; then, how to survive it. The courageous, imaginative, forceful men and women who saw them through phase one were not assigned to phase two.

We know the names of almost no church officers in the first half of this centenary story, and we know the names of almost no charismatic leaders in the second half. When church office was merely managerial, it seems to have attracted few great and memorable incumbents. As the need of the communities imposed the task of creative and assertive leadership on these offices, the responsibility summoned more from those who held the posts, and attracted to them some of the men who had most to give.

One must say "men," because the rise to power came on a general trend of conservatism and consolidation. The contribution of the enthusiasts had been to tease the community along beyond its own supply-lines of wisdom. Their insufficiency was their inability to provide for consensus and continuity. The officers who took the baton from them were short on bravado but longer on clarity about who did what. They had a sense of one's proper echelon and place.[245] One of the favorite images among Clement, Ignatius, Polycarp, *Barnabas*, the *Didache* and the *Shepherd* was that of the household.[246] The full range of Greek words rooted in *oikia* = house was put to heavy use. The glorious vision of the *oikumenê katholikês ekklêsias* = the great household of the worldwide church, which came to Polycarp in prayer – prophetic yet episcopal – before he faced the stadium of hatred, was the charge given by the Spirit to this new generation of overseers and elders.[247] Few of them were of Polycarp's spiritual grandeur.

The early generations saw the Holy Spirit in those who did signs and wonders (though some of them had no prudence). They could not see this same Spirit so visibly in the officers chosen by their communities for sense and wisdom. The later generations, however, were taught to see the character of Jesus in the *gnômê* = judgment of the overseers (even though some of them probably had faint pulses).

What developed at the end of this period was not the creation of a foreign and intrusive structure that abused and smothered the native vitality of the new movement. It was the resurgence of what had been its ancestral form: the community organization of the synagogue. No matter that this era saw a significant shift in authority: that is exactly what had occurred, in a timely and corrective fashion, in the synagogues. It was not so much a change in form as a demonstration of the form's malleability. It is fascinating to note that the farther the church moved from the synagogue, the more it reverted to it.

The fact that officers eventually came in for public criticism implies two things. One: they really did now hold a salient say-so in

---

[245] *1 Cl*, 41:1; *ISm*, 6:1; *Pol*, 11:1.
[246] See Ingrid Kitzberger, *Bau der Gemeinde: Das paulinische Wortfeld* oikodomê/(ep)oiko-domein, Forschung zur Bibel 53 (Würzburg: Echter, 1986) on pauline and deutero-pauline use and development of this vocabulary.　　　　[247] *MPol*, 8:1.

the life of the community. Two: at least they could be directly criticized, which no one had ever quite dared do to the apostles, prophets, teachers, evangelists, healers and tongue-speakers.[248]

These believers were perhaps too reverent of legitimate office to notice that all along God had been giving the church some of the more powerful nudges from men and women who had neither the wonders of the Spirit nor the laying-on of hands. But of such, the records of history always say too little, including the scant leavings of those first Christian Wayfarers.

[248] See 3 J 9–10; *Hv*, 2:2:6; 3:9:7, 10; *Hs*, 8:7:4, 6; 9:26:2.

CHAPTER 9

A conclusion

THE CONTINUITIES BETWEEN SYNAGOGUE AND CHURCH

We have been reassembling the evidence for a plausible continuity in community organization from the hellenistic Jewish synagogue to the early Christian church.

As regards the program and undertakings of the two social units, there are multiple similarities. The *synagôgê* and the *ekklêsia* both typically met in plenary sessions for prayer, to read and expound and discuss the scriptures, to share in ritual meals, to deliberate community policy, to enforce discipline, to choose and inaugurate officers. Both maintained a welfare fund to support widows and orphans and other indigents among their memberships. Both accepted the obligation to provide shelter and hospitality to members of sister communities on their journeys. Both arranged for burial of their dead, and maintained cemeteries.

There are also clear similarities in the structures of community offices. The presiding officer, the college of elders and the assistant appear to carry over from synagogue to church. As in a Jewish context, so in a Christian: the authority to initiate and formulate policy on behalf of the community resides in a group, and that group is served by a presiding officer who appears to be stable in that position. He disposes of the services of one or more assistants whose duties can extend to the limits of the community's program, but he is especially occupied with provisioning those whose welfare depends upon community funds.

Each community exists in a network that comprises all others. There are no lawfully autocephalous communities, except for the mother community in Jerusalem. A local community was bound by adhesions in many directions, through correspondence, embassies, hospitality and disaster relief. There was a hierarchical arrangement

339

upward through town, city and metropolis to Jerusalem, with accountability upward and provident authority downward. And in more serious circumstances this tradition of metropolitan seniority might yield to a synod, where representatives of communities throughout a region would convene to present a common front to some problem. This would reproduce, in a wider context, the exposure of the local elders' policies to the dispositions of the local assembly.

To this extent, church and synagogue were functionally alike: typically, if not uniformly. It is fair to say that the Jews who formed the archetypical churches followed the basic structural lineaments of community organization already familiar to them in the synagogue. This would not be unnatural, since it was synagogues they thought they were forming – at first.

DEPARTURES FROM THE SYNAGOGUE PATTERN

There were, however, differences. Our Christian documents give no evidence of some of the dignitaries who were occasionally reported at the synagogues. There is no senior elder = *gerousiarchês*, nor any equivalent by another title. The levitical priests, who had only vestigial identity in the synagogues, have none in the churches. The inner circle of authority, the notables = *archontes*, have not carried over. Nor are the various minor officers mentioned.

The father and mother of the synagogue do not appear among the Christians. But their possible counterpart may be found in the Christian householders whose means made them patrons and hosts of their communities: without title, but possessed of notable influence.

The Christian communities, on the other hand, have the service of active cadres of volunteers. There were the energetic ranks of apostles, prophets, teachers and evangelists, and beyond them other people ostensibly devoted full-time to the cause, who are informally described as "workers" or "soldiers" or the like, without titles. To the extent that the energy level of the Christian churches may have been a salient differentiator from some of the synagogues they had left behind, much of that zeal bounded forth from people who held no office. And the sociological profile of these activists differed from that of the establishment, since they more prominently included women.

Another category of personage appears in the widows. There are

Jewish antecedents for communities of ascetical and even celibate piety, but it is not clear whether the formation of some Christian widows into sisterhoods of community service was knowingly patterned after them.

Within the church program, since the communities appear to have owned no real estate, assembly and hospitality and meals were provided in members' homes. Thus none of the pertinent concerns for land and fabric burdened the Christians as they were beginning to concern at least some Jewish communities. More importantly, the Christians had no ethnic or civil identity, and the church could not function as a political unit the way synagogues did.

Because the Christians were not members of the church by ethnicity, and their membership was more voluntary than membership in a synagogue, doctrinal rectitude and moral discipline were potentially more divisive than in the live-and-let-live environment of late Second Temple Judaism. Since one became a Christian by professing certain radical beliefs, and since reflection on that creed was turbulent in those first years, one's secure place in the fellowship was more at risk if one became strongly partisan in the in-house controversies.

As we have seen, there may have been no uniform tradition in Jewry that many synagogues in a city should somehow federate. The Christian tradition, however, seems to have followed the rule that no matter how many actual *ekklêsiai* = congregations there were in any locality, the collectivity of believers in any city was called an *ekklêsia* in the singular, not in the plural. All individual congregations were segments of one church. This unity was consolidated when the elders of the city church began to serve as presidents of the various satellite congregations.

Assemblies for initiation rites were relatively new in the Christian order. Converts into Judaism (proselytes) may have been baptized (though we know little about that), but most Jews belonged to the covenant by birth.

There is another disjuncture between the Jewish and the Christian traditions, though a more subtle one. The synagogue tradition was that officers, especially the elders and the community chief, were elected and installed at the hands of the community. Whatever their actual aristocratic status may have been, it was persistently the case that they were formally regarded as the creatures of the community, serving at the popular pleasure. The Christian documents, though indistinct and late, place a marked and insistent importance on the recollection that their officers were chosen and installed by the missionary founders.[1] While this may have been done only after consultation with the residents, and while the later incumbents may have been elected, we find no theological reflection upon such popular support. It is on the other aspect, the notion that a Spirit is passed on, a succession is maintained, a spirit and a grace are there to be tracked back through the missionaries to the apostles to Jesus, that reflection is offered. Since the founders seem to have been charismatic volunteers, the point was not that those they installed received the same status as the founders or those behind them. The local churches were built upon the foundation of the apostles and prophets, but their officers had their own distinct task of holding the local community together as a sturdy and stable edifice.

It may be that apostolic succession has been the rogue notion here. The ministries of disciple and apostle vested in Peter and Paul are like the messianic, royal and prophetic ministries of Jesus: unable to be transmitted to certain designated successors because they are to be inherited by all who live in Christ. One cannot deny that bishops succeed to the charism of Peter and Paul; but it is a gift they share with all of their communicants. Nor were the apostles the first bishops. We have no historical evidence that Paul was bishop anywhere, or that Peter was bishop in Jerusalem (where James sat in that chair) or Antioch (a well established church already, and hardly one to his tastes) or Rome (also well established before he arrived).[2]

---

[1] Subsequent to the New Testament texts cited in the previous chapter, we note that Eusebius, relying on several ancient sources, reports that James was chosen as chief of the Jerusalem church by the apostles (*Historia Ecclesiastica* [hereafter *H. E.*], 2,23,1); Simeon, his successor, by the surviving apostles and disciples of the Lord (3,11–12); their successors down to the time of Hadrian, however, by those who had the power to judge such questions (*pros tón ta toiade epikrinein dunatón*, 4,5,2); Polycarp by eyewitnesses and servants of the Lord (3,36,1); Linus by apostles (5,6,1). John occasionally ordained chiefs/bishops in Asia, and some officers who had already been designated by the Spirit (3,23,6). Robert M. Grant points out that in his account of continuity from apostles to bishops in the sees, Eusebius is affirming the authentic anchorage of the churches through the historical character of the episcopate, not a continuity of apostolic charism: "The First Theme: Apostolic Succession," *Eusebius as Church Historian* (Oxford: Clarendon, 1980), 45–59.

[2] As Irenaeus says, Peter and Paul were the foundation pillars of the Roman church, and they established Linus as its *episkopos*. *Adversus Haereses*, 3,3,2–3. This understanding of Peter and Paul as having a ministry more foundational than that of bishop is obscured by the later notion that they were themselves bishops; see William R. Farmer and Roch Kereszty, O.Cist., *Peter and Paul in the Church of Rome* (New York: Paulist, 1990).

Their status made them too important to be bishops. Yet as founders and pillars of churches (John too was remembered thus) it was natural that by the time of Hegesippus and Irenaeus, when it was the bishops who loomed as the chief charismatic figures in the churches, especially in those sees that led the way, retrospect would clothe the apostles in that role, much as artists tend to imagine ancient figures in contemporary garb.

This might be envisioned in a single scene, when the issue of a gentile–Jewish fellowship in Christ was thrashed out in Jerusalem. Peter and Paul, gifted with the prophetic and apostolic spirit, set forth the policy and rationale that carried the day. James, the community chief surrounded by the elders, presided and pronounced the verdict. Both authorities – the charism of *apostolos* and the order of *episkopos* – seem integral to the welfare of the church in crisis. But in later centuries, when for some time the charismatic figures have receded into the shadows, retrospect imagines Peter as a bishop in order to anchor the Roman presidency in his apostolic authority. It was perhaps too early for Christians to appreciate that the authority of the bishops, particularly those bishops who presided over the mother of all churches (as James had and Peter had not), was no less essential, and claimed deference in its own right. Peter prevailed without needing to preside.

The officers of the local community carried a dual identity. They were creatures of the community (unlike the charismatics, even local ones), but the community itself was also their handiwork (as it was of the charismatics). This was embodied in the twofold manner of their mandate: elected by a show of hands within the community, they also required the laying-on of hands from someone in the charismatic discipleship/descent from the Lord.[3]

---

[3] The Christian usage of installing candidates in office by the laying-on of hands is commonly but erroneously thought to have been derived from the Jewish usage whereby rabbis ordained their pupils to the rabbinate by the same gesture. There is no evidence of this as a rabbinical practice before the destruction of the Second Temple and the creation of the Academy. This was a later period in which relations between Jews and Christians were becoming antagonized, and adoption by one group of the other's practices would have been improbable. It is much more likely to have been an earlier practice of Judaism, possibly prophetic in origin, that appeared in both descendant communities. For the commonly accepted ascription to rabbinical ordination see Edward J. Kilmartin, S.J., "Ministry and Ordination in Early Christianity against a Jewish Background," in *Ordination Rites*, ed. Wiebe Vos and Geoffrey Wainwright (Rotterdam: Liturgical Ecumenical Trust, 1980), 42–69; also Lawrence A. Hoffman, "Jewish Ordination on the Eve of Christianity," ibid. 11–41.

It is not quite the case, then, that the officers were managers answerable to the membership, while the charismatics were preachers answerable to the Lord.[4] Already in the pauline literature the charismatics are bidden remember that their every utterance should be for the strengthening of the community (with the clear implication that it was not always so, and needed correction). The officers, by a complementary movement of insight, were said to hold their community responsibilities by God's grace. The two paradigms were blending with each other.

As we have noted, Christian communities used very little of the technical nomenclature of the synagogue tradition. Both had *presbyteroi* = elders. But that was an institution and a title so ancient and so culturally universal that it could carry no suspicion of Jewish copyright. In general, the churches were so thorough in avoiding mainstream Jewish terminology that one might see an intended break with that past. But we know that contemporaneous sectarian movements, whether they harbored an abiding sense of alienation from the Jewish mainstream like the Essenes, or offered a more intensely pious alternative like the Therapeutae, maintained institutional structures substantially similar to those of the synagogue, yet had their own distinctive nomenclature for offices. So a similarity of structure with a distinctive nomenclature was familiar within alternative Jewish communities. It is thus more of a junction than a break with the past.

Christians characteristically adopted nomenclature that was known within Judaism, but was not the current or preferred title. Thus they settled on *ekklêsia*, a substitute word for *synagôgê*, and *diakonos* rather than *hypêretês*, and *episkopos* rather than *archisynagôgos*. This implies, not that their structures were dissimilar, but that despite structural resemblances they thought their officers functioned in a new way. The eucharist absorbed the scriptural service from the synagogue and the sabbath supper from the family; the Lord's day preempted the sabbath; the freedom of God's children transfigured

---

[4] André Lemaire rejects the opposition, classically stated by Harnack, between spiritual charismatics and bureaucratic officers, and offers an extensive bibliography of criticisms of the Harnack thesis, *Les ministères aux origines de l'église* (Paris: Cerf, 1971), 191–192. In contrast with the view that the medium of salvation is possession of the Spirit by individuals, Joseph Brosch reads the texts to say that the gifts of the Spirit are given primarily to the church, which empowers its officers to bestow those gifts to the members. Charismata without church order would be a menace, as would offices without the Spirit. *Charismen und Ämter in der Urkirche* (Bonn: Peter Hanstein, 1951), 144–182.

the Torah. Yet the very innovations were cast in the forms of the past. Paul's rhetoric to the Galatians does not mean the new community has no moral imperatives nor moral code. Indeed, they had a code that differed in few respects from the Law they had known as Jews. The Christians were adamant that something New was afoot, but in many respects they were more innovative in their nomenclature than in their usages and offices. And this itself was a sectarian tradition they had learned as Jews.[5]

Another verbal custom they retained from the old religion was that of converting generic, descriptive terms into official nomenclature. Acts, the pastoral epistles and *Clement* use the word *episkopoi* = overseers interchangeably and descriptively to refer to *presbyteroi* = elders. These men are corporately charged with *episkopê* = oversight. In the second century this synonym becomes the title *par excellence* of the elder (previously untitled, unless at first he was an *archisynagôgos*) who presides over this process of *episkopê*. Later, possession of this title probably helps that officer, the bishop, claim *episkopê* as his unique prerogative.

As things fell out, the new movement eventually chose to call itself *hê ekklêsia* = the assembly. But Acts recollects an early day when there were many synonyms, like *hê hodos* = the way. It would seem that in such an early period of flux, terms would be descriptive. Only when *ekklêsia* had become a title, no longer a description, did it harden, so to speak, from "assembly" into "church." *Leitourgia* = public charge or service, referred to the generous dedication and accomplishments of all activist Christians; later it was restricted to officers, and still later to official worship. *Diakonia* = service belonged at first to every Christian, and ended up as a title for what the assistant did. The same thing would happen later when *minister* = servant hardened into minister = clergyman-in-command. *Presbyteros* had long since hardened from "older man" into "elder" of any age.

Charisma originally meant a benefaction of any kind, understood by Christians to be a gift of God. Then it was applied to the distinctive gifts that Christians enjoyed. It might mean the entire new dispensation, or its outcropping in each individual. It might mean

---

[5] A most remarkable contribution to our understanding of the development of Christian vocabulary and nomenclature has been written by Heinrich Bruders, S.J., *Die Verfassung der Kirche, von der ersten Jahrzehnten der apostolischen Wirksamkeit an bis zum Jahre 175 n. Christus* (Mainz: von Kirchheim, 1904). Much of what follows is indebted to his work.

346 *A conclusion*

dedicated celibacy or marriage, patient suffering or the gift of healing, enthusiastic display or official duty. All were gifts that built up the body of Christ. Our modern usage, referring it to enthusiastic phenomena, is narrower than that of the primitive church, which for so long a time used it so generically that it could not be used to differentiate dutiful public service from exuberant and ecstatic phenomena. Christians then were not unaware of what we mean by the difference between office and charism, but their vocabulary took some time before it offered specifically meant words to express that distinction.

Eucharistein, originally "to give thanks," came to denote their worship gatherings, and then the elements of bread and wine. *Cheirotonein*, "to vote by show of hands," became "to consecrate in office."[6] As the words become specifically Christian in usage, their original literal sense fades and they become technical terms with a uniquely Christian reference. Ignatius uses words that are only partially converted. When he says, "Honor the *diakonoi* as Jesus Christ," that term already means "deacons," specific officers in the church.[7] Elsewhere he can use the same term with its generic overtones to make the point that deacons are servants.[8]

In the earliest period, when the church was in its expansive days of new foundations, there was little concern for community organization. Paul's itinerant assistants are most often referred to by name (we know eighteen of them by name) and never by title. Later they are differentiated by descriptive terms, relating them either to the apostles (co-worker, fellow slave, brother, etc.) or to the ordinary Christians who honored them as forerunners in faith (first-fruits, veterans, rulers, etc.) or by function (teachers, overseers, assistants, etc.). As the need for inner coherence required communities to organize their own affairs more specifically, personal names begin to disappear in favor of titles, and plural words applied to groups give way to singular titles given to individuals.

The very manner in which Christian communities minted their own verbal tender shows how regularly they were overstriking Jewish coinage with their own design and denomination. The offices of the synagogue were the models and antecedents for the offices of the

---

[6] See ibid. 11–15.
[7] Ignatius of Antioch, *Letter to the Trallians*, 3:1. (Hereafter his letters to the Ephesians, Magnesians, Trallians, Philadelphians, Smyrnaeans and Polycarp are identified as *IEph, IMg, ITr, IPhld, ISm, IPol*).   [8] See *IMg*, 2:6.

church, though with a distinctive animation that reshaped their functions – as indeed the various offices typically seemed to have distinctive developments of function within the different sectarian Jewish communities.

The early documentation has left evidence of some very decisive shifts of power within the Christian communities. The officers eventually displaced the charismatics as the decisive spiritual authorities in the local communities. The *episkopoi* came into a more decisive role above and not merely within the presbyteries. The privilege of Jerusalem as the chief among all metropolitan churches decamped to (Antioch, possibly, and then to) Rome. All three changes were of great importance. Some see them as deleterious for Christianity, perhaps drastic enough to have broken faith with their foundational bond with the Lord. Without needing – for purposes of this study – to take a stand on whether those transfers of prerogative and influence were sinister or beneficial, one can recall that similar shifts of power had already been typical of the synagogue's development. The elders had assumed leadership from the assembly, and the notables then emerged at the expense of the elders, and there were times when sovereigns enfeebled them both. The role of chief and mother to all synagogues transferred from Jerusalem to Yavne and beyond. Another continuity threaded through both *synagôgê* and *ekklêsia* is the fact that actual authority could shift and shuttle, accumulate or haemorrhage, while offices and formalities remained intact. These very devices whereby the first Christian generations differentiated themselves from their Jewish antecedents were themselves inherited from their Jewish tradition.

Within the consensus we have been questioning here, it has been conventional to portray episcopal and presbyteral roles as mutually exclusive. Thus one recent spokesman has written:

I maintain that for about a century and a half the church's ministry was basically presbyteral ... Where there was no monepiscopus, matters of discipline would naturally have been the responsibility of the presbyters as a corporate body ... The concept of the *episkopos* as the sole ordainer [a development he identifies with the era of Hippolytus: early third century] carries with it the implication that he, and not the presbyterate, is the sustainer of the apostolic succession. The presbyters derive their ministerial authority from him.[9]

---

[9] Eric G. Jay, "From Presbyter-Bishops to Bishops and Presbyters," *The Second Century*, 1 (1981), 162, 142, 159.

But as Olof Linton had pointed out, in a structured community a strong leader (or leadership cadre) may well empower the members, instead of enfeebling them. Not nearly enough is known about the actual consistorial style of second-century presbyteries and how they interacted with the new presidential style for us to be able to verify that those *episkopoi* turned their benches of elders into thralls.

It has been unfortunate but unavoidable that, because the shifts of leverage came due to stress and contention, they appear to us to involve a gain in power for the officers at the expense of the charismatics, or an advance for the *episkopoi* and a retreat for the *presbyteroi*. That the shifts have been studied by Protestants and Catholics conscious of their own contentions has handicapped critical perspective.

It may help to notice that the officers were construed as the patrons and facilitators of communities that were vigorous rather than torpid. A presbytery with a canny and dedicated chief was probably better empowered than one with a weaker colleague in the chair. Community members who were inspired to warn and confront and nerve the church would make more common cause with officers as both protectors and protégés. Each of the different *leitourgiai* was enabled to coalesce with the others, not doomed inevitably to compete with them. Yet some incumbents did reach for power and ego, as is shown in the ancient records and in some who argue from them today.

A RESOLUTION OF THE LONG DEBATE

We have been reviewing a repetitive and perfervid debate. It has long been held that certain offices were established by apostolic authority, and that the apostles in doing this were acting as plenipotentiaries of the Lord. Those offices – deacon, presbyter, bishop (and patriarch or pope) – therefore invested their incumbents with a permanent authority and grace that empowered them to rule the churches by divine right. That, bluntly put, has been the "Catholic" position.

The "Protestant" critique, which has become fairly consensual among scholars, reads the first-century documents to show the apostles, prophets and other inspired but uncategorized activists as those to whom the early churches deferred. Their rightful successors were seen to be raised up, not by ecclesiastical designation, but by an infusion of that same Spirit. Yet even those leaders would not claim obedience from fellow believers, for the normative polity of the New Testament church was either a form of congregational democracy (so says one variant of this position) or an unstructured, individualist assembly without any established polity, rank or authority. The untraditional appearance of ordered authoritarian offices has its warrant, not from Jesus or the apostles, but from men like Clement and Ignatius, in defiance of the authentic egalitarianism they squelched.

Both of these interpretations read the evidence for a possible legitimation of their respective later models of church. As a result, either side discounts some crucial evidence. The "Catholic" theory projects backward a scenario of dominating clergy who are simply not to be found in the first documents. The "Protestant" theory has had to shrug off the exhibits in evidence – few but unequivocal – that they are unhappy to accept as precedents. For instance, they discount the *episkopoi* and *diakonoi* greeted by Paul in the address of his letter to the Philippians; Paul's call for deference to those put in charge of the church when they give admonitions;[10] the primacy of the Jerusalem church presided over by James, a non-apostle, with a bench of elders; and the assertion by *Clement* to Corinthians who still remembered their earliest days as church, that in their memory apostles had provided their churches with governing officers whose successors were to be chosen by due process (giving credibility to similar texts in Acts).

When one sets aside the preoccupations of precedent that are stimulated by seeing the earliest churches in continuity with what was to follow, and considers instead the plausible continuities those churches display with what had gone beforehand, the evidence rises up to argue that the churches bore the shape of the synagogue, albeit within a movement of vigorous independence and innovation.

As the second century approaches its meridian, references accumulate to a set of offices in the churches. This and the sparse record of these offices in prior documents seems to justify a twofold conclusion: *that these officers existed in the earlier generations as a carry-over of the traditional order, but that they were not the seat of the aboriginal church's vitality.*

---

[10] 1 Th 5:12–13.

A conclusion

One is obliged to infer that in the infancy and first youth of the Christian fellowship, neither the elders nor their chairman nor the deacons *led* the communities. They were "not where the action was." Men and women known as apostles and prophets; men and women who carried no titles but whose activist zeal was accredited by the same divine fire: these were the ones to whom believers most notably deferred. The people who bore most powerfully in their persons the force of divine conviction and transformative impetus were people who, without community screening or authorization, did God's work. They spoke with authority. But that does not mean that they presided. By the same token, Hillel might hold highest authority in the Sanhedrin no matter who the High Priest was, and any prime minister holds more authority than the speaker of the house.

There was another category of men (and it appears that they were only men) who were chosen by the community to authorize policy and to preside and to serve. They were not ungifted persons, but their giftedness was viewed with an eye towards a somewhat different and quite specific set of tasks.

These officers were, with a few exceptions like James and Stephen and Philip, functionaries whose ink on the pages of history faded quickly. To preside was apparently not so crucial while the community was being borne on the expansive waves of conversion, experiment and exhortation within what they then regarded as a reform, not a revolt. It was later, when a sense had solidified that they were now on their own, and when leaders who were gifted with charismatic forcefulness led the community into bitter and self-destructive contention, that the tasks of presidency and *oikonomia* = household management became pivotal, and consequently attracted more impressive incumbents who understandably received more enduring recollection.

The consensus has conjectured that in the early years presidency was in the hands of the charismatics. It requires saying that there is not a single text which describes an apostle or a prophet or a teacher presiding within an established Christian community, or filling the roles which were characteristic of the overseers, elders or assistants. There are texts which tell communities how to govern their activities, without any reference to officers; but that silence is ambiguous, and does not justify the conclusion that there can have been no elders. If officers existed normally, their role would have been normal enough not to need specific mention. There are other texts which describe the prophets and apostles as prominent in worship; but to be prominent is not to be in the first seat(s). Let a modest comparison serve here. Somewhere in Calcutta today there is a parish priest whose name no reader of this book will ever hear, who will make no remembered mark on the story of the church here or there. In his parish a frail Albanian woman in a sari is a worshiping member. From our point of view it is she who counts for most there; but Mother Teresa would surely say that it is he who presides. That we never hear of him does not mean he does not exist. But that he does exist does not mean that he is the leader and she the follower. She may lead though he presides.

There is, by universal admission, a relative (though not complete) silence about community offices in the first century. If one merely relates those years to what follows, it might be reckless to fill in that silence. But if one relates those documents backward to what was so long customary for the people being described, then the lacunae are no longer such a puzzle. In the second century a fledged church order stands forth, with little explicitly described Christian precedent. When we notice, however, that it reproduces, in a multiplicity of forms and usages and inward movements, the durable, ancestral lineaments of the Jewish synagogue, it is less natural to claim those offices as a deviant innovation of the second century AD than to recognize them as a re-emergence from the first centuries BC and AD.

The evidence is more respectfully treated if we conclude that the synagogue was the point of reference for the church. We must also see that the daughter was moving with a mind of her own, in a developmental adventure that took her in new directions. (So also, as Jacob Neusner reminds us, was Jewry, which underwent parallel and contemporaneous transition into rabbinical Judaism.) The old forms were malleable to new inspiration and function, as they had been previously. One would also conclude, not that the offices of the second century were absent from the earliest churches, but that in the later period they were being exercised in a much more aggressive manner for which the provocations are well known.

THE CHURCH IN CONTINUITY WITH THE SYNAGOGUE

The claim, then, which this inquiry must make is a frugal one: that Jesus seems not to have bequeathed to or inspired in his faithful retinue a new and distinctive community organization. Instead, he so inspired his disciples that office was a relatively marginal reality: the energies that drove communities forward in his name and memory were more felt in the currents, sails and oars than at the helm.

We know as well that he offered no formula for a reconstructed economy, no prescribed set of relationships for a revolutionized family household, no "signature" civil polity for Christians, no ethical system all their own. What he did do was commit to those who listened well some uncontainable imperatives that would burst the seams of all previous arrangements. The economy of the Roman empire could not satisfy anyone who truly believed it was more satisfying to give than to get. A man and a woman pledged to one another equally beyond recourse to divorce, and bound to treat children, servants and slaves as brothers and sisters, would have to wreak havoc with all the household traditions known at that time. The political order of the empire was ill prepared for subjects of a defiantly higher allegiance who would not give their worship to any human ruler. And the logical consistency of any conventional morality was given vertigo by the doctrine that justice was too meager a value on which to fix one's heart. The new faith was not creative of new systems. It was subversive of the old ones, however, and repeatedly subversive of all systems that were to succeed them. In the end, it seemed to matter less what social order one began with than how radically one was enabled both to transform and to transcend it.

It is quite the same with church order. Jesus instigated no characteristic new organization or anarchy among those who shared faith in him. They proceeded from where they found themselves. And they found themselves in the synagogue. The synagogue became the church, not by dint of a new social format, but in virtue of new convictions within its members. It developed and adapted and consolidated and searched for its own authenticity. We claim here only that to study that energetic development we must know that it proceeded from the organization of the synagogue. And it *did proceed*.

R EFLECTIONS FROM PAST TO PRESENT

One is reluctant, at the end of a historical research project, to suggest how its findings might be applied in the present. That caution is especially appropriate to the subject at hand, for so many historical reconstructions, both scholarly and derivative, have portrayed the church order of the first hundred years in a light most favorable to whatever ecclesiastical arrangement seemed soundest to their authors. Therefore our lessons to be drawn will be more cautionary than constructive.

If our reconstruction of the church order of Christianity's first hundred years is substantially accurate, then the lesson to be drawn is that polity itself is not all that determinative in the church. During the latter first century there were officers in place, but they were not possessed of notable authority. Then in the second century they rose to great importance. In the first phase they were managers, but not leaders. In the second, their leadership guided the church through some of its most strenuous trials. Thus it would be difficult to argue, from what we can know of that cycle of experience, either that the traditional officers are always crucial or that they are always misbegotten. When they were nondescript little gray fellows, they did not manage to suffocate those who carried the greater inspiration. On the other hand, we have no history to persuade us that an unstructured society is likely to have survived the period when stout officers were so needed, or that a church without officers is all that likely to welcome dazzling charismata when they do appear. One need not have much polity to have mean-minded politics.

Church officers went on to adopt many styles. They have been profound theologians, heroic opponents to totalitarian oppressors, prophetic voices against pathological cultures, indomitable pro-tectors of refugee or immigrant congregations, and transfigured preachers. They have also been martinets, suborned servants of the wealthy, spineless cowards, heretics, and men ignorant enough to have been incapable of heresy. It is not clear that a church without public officers would be spared all these afflictions or provided with all these services. Exactly the same might be said of a church with public officers.

A further point. Some of the most ardent partisans of the consensus take sharp offense at Clement and Ignatius for their early advocacy and exercise of ruling offices among Christians. Clement demanded that the Corinthians restore their deposed elders to their rank as overseers, and offer them honor, reverence and submission.[11] Ignatius very specifically enjoined deference to the three orders of officers.[12]

The grounds for their appeals for obedience were not, however, that the officers were teaching sound doctrine while those who challenged them were unorthodox, or were bound to be unorthodox whenever they were in opposition to the officers. Nor were Clement and Ignatius arguing that the *episkopoi, presbyteroi* and *diakonoi* were *ex officio* more godly. There were indeed later writers who would contend that accession to ordained office would assure the right teaching and/or the right living of the incumbents. But that was not what Clement and Ignatius were arguing. Clement made little comment on the moral excellence of the elders, save that they had led blameless and modest lives.[13] But he did make a scorchingly explicit moral inventory of the rebels. They had acted, he said, out of jealousy for power and factious rivalry, and these had already been disastrous forces in the short memory of the Christian community.[14] Ignatius, who had some accolades for the service records of various *episkopoi*, never even considers public dissatisfaction with their characters or accomplishments or teaching as a plausible motive for resistance, which he identifies instead with pride and factiousness.[15] The reason he gives for deference to the officers is not that they were bound to lead the community invariably in the right direction, but that the community could not be at peace with the Lord if it did not manage to be at peace within itself. Unity was his point. The bishop was to be the gathering point but not necessarily the source of unity and truth. All disagreements were to be dealt with by orderly deliberation within the community. An obvious corollary of that policy would be that worthy leaders must always leave their doctrine and comportment and policies open to orderly challenge precisely in order to protect the unity of the church. And that was exactly what the synagogue tradition had been: policy would be framed by the elders but exposed to comment by the assembly, comment that would ordinarily have been discreet and respectful – but perhaps not always. What honest believers should do if the officers were leading

[11] *Letter to the Corinthians* of Clement of Rome (hereafter *1 Cl*), 1:3; 21:6; 57:1; 63:1.
[12] *IEph*, 6:1; *IMg*, 3:2; 7:1; *ITr*, 2; 3:1; *IPhld*, 7:1; *ISm*, 8; 9; *IPol*, 4:1; 6:1.
[13] *1 Cl*, 44.   [14] *1 Cl*, 14:1; 51:1.   [15] *IEph*, 5:3; *IPhld*, 7:2; 8:2.

the community astray and using their authority to smother orderly debate is a question which neither Clement nor Ignatius addressed.

It is, in any case, a distortion to pluck up Clement's and Ignatius' appeals for deference to elders and overseers as if this were a moral imperative that stood alone. One must read these texts in parallel with the extensive passages in the pastoral epistles which urged that offices had to be filled by persons worthy of deference. For every text that called for respect for the authority of the rulers there was a complementary text that bade the communities select as their rulers men of respectable authority. Obviously failure in the latter duty could only obstruct fulfillment of the former.

We see in Clement and Ignatius and the pastorals no teaching that office itself conferred the requisite *charisma* = divine enablement. What they did both say and imply was that the most honorable gifts had to be recruited in candidates for offices so crucial to the common welfare. The notion that ordination confers the equipage of office was a later teaching by later ecclesiastics. Partisans of the consensus will find much fault with that notion, but they must not visit their grievance upon those gentlemen from Rome and Antioch.

Another point of consideration responds to the determination of women to claim access to the presbyterate and the episcopate and (at least by consistency of argument) the papacy, by seeking evidence that women were officers in the earliest church. The first weakness of this line of argument is that the historical record cannot, without tendentious treatment, yield such evidence. A second weakness is that the claim is sometimes, though not always, made because official rank is what certain persons strongly want. This claim needs scrutiny lest it be a reappearance of the zest for power which so troubled Clement and Ignatius when they saw it at work. It may also lend some legitimation to the conventional and harmful process whereby many men are being ordained for no other discernible reason than that it is what they strongly want. It would seem much sounder to argue, not that women deserve to be ordained, but that there are women whose official service the church deserves.

But the question raised by this historical study is somewhat different. Why base an argument for the ordination of women on the theory that women were officers in the very first generation of Christian experience, when that appears to have been the period in which the officers were not very decisive initiative-takers in the church's welfare? It would be more apt to note from the historical record, not that the first Christians had the inspiration and nerve to elect and install women as elders, overseers or assistants, but that the Spirit went well beyond the imagination of that generation by inspiring women as apostles, prophets and teachers to whom the communities deferred. And in any more integrated era it should be those charismatically gifted persons, regardless of gender or irrelevant classifications, who would best be elected, trained and ordained to office.

A fourth and last observation may be offered with an eye cocked on the contemporary churches. Now that nearly four (or six) centuries have ensued since the reformations during and after the Middle Ages, one can be struck by the resilience of the community organization of the early church.

Outrage at official misbehavior persuaded many Christians that there should be no persons in authority. Strangulation by Rome convinced many that there could be no worldwide network under ecumenical presidency. Political exploitation closer to home led others to sever bonds of operative unity even with other congregations in their region or nation. The conviction that absurdities had been coercively imposed as obligatory for orthodox belief discouraged large numbers of Christians from even considering any doctrine as official if it had been elaborated after the era of the New Testament.

But over the course of their own experiences those same communions have recently been in a more reconstructionist mood. Congregational polity has been spinning networks of fellowship, policy and service. Presbyteral bodies have grown various organs for higher service and coordination and presidency and oversight. Denominations that broke into segments over conflicts of doctrine or discipline are, through patient consultation and deliberation, forging commonly accepted formulae that raise sound doctrine back to honor. Churches that rejected metropolitan authority in favor of synodal authority are asking officers to preside over more active and hence more coordinated communities, while other churches that rejected both metropolitan and synodal authority are also investigating the advantages of structures whose models are to be found in that age when the dust of Galilee had so recently been tracked into Egypt and Greece and the Mediterranean isles. In brief, as the offensive and destructive abuses of office are believed now to be neither necessary nor inevitable (perhaps because, if not accorded absolute clout, the officers are not so likely to be corrupted absolutely) the inveterate ability of those offices to serve the needs of a unified church is once more credible.

It is as if once more, what Paul and Clement and Ignatius and the *Didache* and their contemporaries taught was a restored hope: that

episkopê = presidency could be *diakonia* = service; and *hêgemonia* = governance could be a *leitourgia* = public service; if *pneumatikoi* = inspired people were chosen as the *presbyteroi* = elders.

It is an ancient discovery.[16]

---

[16] Eusebius was not far from this integrated view (which already appears in the authentic pauline letters) when he characterizes the task of the *episkopos* as shepherding (*H. E.* 3,4,10; 3,37,1; 4,11,6; 4,24,1); preaching and teaching God's word (3,34,1); being an elder (3,33,8); a successor of the apostles (4,4,1; 5,22,1; 5,28,7 and passim); ruling (1,1,1; 3,20,6; 3,21,1 and passim); superintending (3,15,1; 4,22,2; 5,23,4); *diakonia* (2,17,23); *oikonomia* (4,4,4); *prostasia* (4,4,1; 4,5,5); *leitourgia* (throughout). Following Irenaeus, he links the succession with the tradition (5,16,7).

Index auctorum

358

Eck, John, 20
Ehrhardt, A., 133
Ehtécham, Morteza, 263
Epiphanius of Constantia, 49, 278, 306
Erasmus, Desiderius, 38
Esler, Philip Francis, 282, 291, 309

Farmer, William R., 342
Farrer, Austin Marsden, 123, 124, 125
Ferrua, A., 245
Finkelstein, Louis, 203, 247
Fletcher, Joseph, 38
Flew, Robert Newton, 122
Fox, George, 52–55, 57, 136
Frey, Jean-Baptiste, 126, 203, 204, 205, 219, 226, 230, 235, 236, 238, 240, 241, 242, 246, 248, 252, 254, 257, 266
Friedländer, Moriz, 204
Friedrich, Gerhard, 154
Fueter, Eduard, 51

Gager, John, 137, 158–160
Gaul (Lyons and Vienne), Martyrs of, 70
Gavin, Frank Stanton Burns, 191
Georgi, Dieter, 221
Gewiess, Joseph, 149–150, 186
Gifford, George, 44
Glamis, Lord Chancellor, 32
Golb, Norman, 267
Goodenough, Erwin R., 265
Goppelt, Leonhard, 154–155
Gore, Charles, 1, 121, 125, 133
Götz, Karl Gerold, 110–111, 137, 306
Grant, Robert M., xiv, 342
Greenwood, John, 44
Grosseteste, Robert, 38
Gryson, Roger, 329
Guignebert, Charles, 203, 219, 230, 235, 237, 241
Gunkel, Hermann, 117
Gutmann, Joseph, 227

Hanson, Richard P. C., 283
Harnack, Adolf von, xii, 1, 82–87, 88, 89, 90, 92, 93, 94, 104, 110, 112, 115, 116, 118, 125, 132, 136, 138, 140, 143, 146, 154, 161, 344
Harrison, Robert, 38, 41–42, 136
Hatch, Edwin, 1, 76–81, 83, 84, 88, 115, 116, 132, 136
Hebert, Arthur Gabriel, 132
Hegesippus, 69, 308
Hengel, Martin, 197, 203, 225
Herodotus, 263
Hippolytus of Rome, 125, 129
Hoffman, Lawrence A., 343
Holl, Karl, 1, 107–110, 137, 140, 306
Holmberg, Bengt, 160–163, 165
Holtzmann, Heinrich Julius, 102–104, 137
Homer, 264
Hooker, Morna D., 184
Horsley, George H. R., 227, 239, 242, 328, 329
Hort, Fenton John Anthony, 1, 132

Irenaeus of Lyons, 64, 67, 69, 70, 74, 75, 80, 103, 127, 146, 273, 276, 342
Iserloh, Erwin, 19, 21

James, William, 117
Jay, Eric G., 347
Jedin, Hubert, 19
Jenkins, Daniel Thomas, 131
Jerome, St., 38
Jervell, Jacob, 192
Josaitis, Norman F., 82
Juster, Jean, 219, 221, 223, 224, 226, 236, 237, 248, 250, 252, 257
Justin Martyr, 75
Juvenal, 225

Kantzenbach, Friedrich Wilhelm, 45
Käsemann, Ernst, 163
Kasper, Walter, 174
Katz, Steven, 279
Kereszty, Roch, 342
Kertelge, Karl, 168
Kilmartin, Edward J., 343
Kirk, Kenneth, 122
Kitzberger, Ingrid, 337
Knox, John, 29
Kraabel, Alf Thomas, xiv, 184, 208, 217, 226, 334
Kraemer, Ross S., 245
Krauss, Samuel, 219, 245
Küng, Hans, 137, 167, 168–171

La Piana, Giorgio, 219
Lampe, Geoffrey W. H., 133, 260
Latimer, Hugh, 38
Lemaire, André, 329, 344
Leon, Harry J., 205, 219, 236, 237, 238, 240, 241, 249, 252, 258
Leube, Hans, 45
Levine, Lee I., 225, 334
Lieberman, Saul, 208, 221
Lietzmann, Hans, xii, 1, 104–105, 235, 236
Lifschitz, Baruch, 237, 238, 242, 254, 257, 258

Index locorum

Thanksgiving Hymns (1QH)

4:25	268

War Scroll (1QM)

3:15	269
5:1	269
7:9–9:9	255

Scroll of the Rule (1QS)

1:16–2:18	255
2:19–20	255
5	268
5:2–3	255, 268
5:9	255
6:1	268
6:3–5	255
6:8ff	255, 268
6:14–16	268, 269
6:20	268, 269
8:1–4	255, 268
8:19	268
8:26	268
9:2	268
9:5–7	256

Rule Annexe A (1QSa)

1:1	268
1:2	255
1:15ff	255
1:20	268
1:23ff	255, 269
2:14ff	255, 269

Rule Annexe B (1QSb)

4:24	268
5:20	269

Early Christian Writings

Didache (D)

4:10ff	327
4:14	285
7	285, 286
9	285, 286
10	285, 286
10:7	306, 335
11–13	315
11:3ff	289, 301, 306
13:3ff	301, 322
14	285, 286, 313
14:1ff	323
15:1ff	294, 295, 297, 301, 315, 318, 320

1 Clement [*Letter to the Corinthians*] (*1 Cl*)

address	277
1:2	315
1:3	297, 318, 353
5:2	289, 292
9:4	318
12:8	301
14:1	354
17:1	301
17:5	317
21:6	353
32:1ff	318
37	310
40–41	322
41:1	337
42	66, 292, 293, 294, 297, 320, 332
43:1	294, 301
44	297, 298, 310, 318, 354
44:3	294
51:1	287, 354
54:2	278, 294, 298
57:1	287, 298, 353
60	299
61	297
63:1	353

2 Clement [*Pseudo-Clement*] (*2 Cl*)

11:2	301
17:3	285

Ignatius of Antioch

Ephesians (*IEph*)

address	277
1:3	278, 308
2:1	320, 321
2:2	293, 308
3:2	287, 309, 332
4:1ff	293, 309
5	285, 286, 298, 309, 322, 354
6:1	308, 353
11:2	310
13:1	285
15:1	304
16:2	304
17:1	304
20:2ff	293, 308, 309

Magnesians (*IMg*)

address	277
2	293, 309, 320, 321